A Legacy of Learning

SUNY Series, The Philosophy of Education

Philip L. Smith, Editor

A Legacy of Learning

A History
of Western Education

Edward J. Power

State University of New York Press

Published by
State University of New York Press, Albany

© 1991 State University of New York

All rights reserved

Printed in the United States of America

For information, address State University of New York
Press, State University Plaza, Albany, N.Y., 12246

Production by Diane Ganeles
Marketing by Bernadette LaManna

Library of Congress Cataloging-in-Publication Data

Power, Edward J.
    A legacy of learning : a history of Western education / Edward J. Power.
        p. cm.—(SUNY Series, the philosophy of education)
    Includes bibliographical references and index.
    ISBN 0-7914-0610-5 (alk. paper).—ISBN 0-7914-0611-3
(pbk.: alk. paper)
        1. Education—History. 2. Education—Europe—History.
    3. Education—United States—History. I. Title. II. Series: SUNY
    series in philosophy of education.
    LA11.P65   1991
    370'.9181'2—dc20   90-37218
                                                                                CIP

10 9 8 7 6 5 4 3 2 1

To
Harry W. "Chipper" Wilcox IV

Contents

Preface

A Legacy of Learning is a history of Western education. Without assuming a commission to be comprehensive, an undertaking too ambitious for one volume, its aim is to concentrate on the principal periods in the history of European and American education and to find in them lessons for assessing the critical and often controversial issues of contemporary education. If Cicero was right in declaring that persons who are ignorant of history will remain forever children, it is hardly prudent for educators and an intelligent, responsible public to ignore their educational heritage. Not much about education, about students, teachers, and curricula, was discovered only yesterday. It may be asking too much to expect history to resolve the educational issues facing contemporary society, but history can be of considerable help in illuminating them. There are stinging complaints that today's Americans are either indifferent to history or are historically illiterate and that this condition will sentence them to repeat their ancestors' mistakes.

Because there was, and is, a cultural and educational bond between America and Europe, and because so much of eighteenth- and early nineteenth-century American education was hardly more than a transposition of European pedagogical purpose and practice, the assumption that our historical appetite can be satisfied by paying attention only to American educational antecedents is a kind of arrogance unbecoming to educated persons and especially to those who aspire to the profession of education as teachers or administrators. No argument could be convincing that American educational history should be discounted, but no argument is persuasive that alleges as inconsequential a knowledge of our distant educational past.

The themes driving the thirteen chapters are both philosophical and pedagogical, for, despite the significance of teachers, students, curricula, and methods, a story of education that begins with ancient Greece and ends in twentieth-century America must represent a good deal more than what occurred behind schoolhouse doors. The overriding theme in every chapter, however, and one with a special contemporary meaning, is what was taught. In the last analysis, throughout its long history the educational enterprise has had to grapple with a seminal question: What knowledge has a worth that recommends it for a place not only in the school's curriculum but, as well, in the repertoire of decently educated persons? That this question remains today without a definitive answer is hardly subject to dispute. Neither a historical perspective nor history's lessons can be expected to supply the answer, but the former can guide us away from fallow ground and the latter are almost certain to be rewarding if we succeed in discovering and mastering them.

The book's design, in essaying to cover the whole of Western education from the ancient Greeks forward, allots eight chapters to the story of European education. Yet, since the book is directed toward an American audience with an entirely understandable desire to have a full portrait of American educational development, five chapters are employed to relate American educational accomplishment. A preoccupation with American educational history is entirely justified even while taking the position that indifference to a historical account of what happened in the long centuries before there was an America is not.

The book's first two chapters are concerned with Greek, especially Athenian, educational practice and philosophy. Chapter one is a description of genuine classical education; chapter two illustrates the invention of educational philosophy and its principal promoters, Plato and Isocrates. But had the classical period not been followed by the Hellenistic age, had it not been for hundreds of thousands of persons who wanted to be like their classical ancestors, the genius of the classical age might have suffered a premature death and we could not have been counted among its beneficiaries. As it was, making culture their religion, Hellenists idealized their classical predecessors and undertook to imitate them. Most cultural monuments are either fragile and perishable or are unamenable to imitation; literature is a prominent exception. Recognizing literature's ability to transmit cultural ideals, Hellenists appropriated it for school use. For the first time in education's long history, the school was defined as a literary agency. This story is told in chapter three.

Halfway through the long Hellenistic period, our historical compass shifts to Rome. Rome played an enormously important part as a mediator between Hellenistic culture and educational perspective, on one hand, and Christian value and educational commitment, on the other. All the while, of course, Romans had educational priorities of their own. How Rome accomplished a mission of mediation and, at the same time, remained true to her own tradition is the burden of chapter four. Yet Rome's accomplishments could not ensure her survival. On the cultural and educational front, Roman vigor was followed by Christian altruism, but it was an altruism that repudiated huge parts of the classical cultural and educational paradigm because it was infused with a pagan assessment of life and value. If Christians were to restore the edifice of European education, left now in shambles with the collapse of Rome, and redress the darkness brought on by anarchy and ignorance, they would not only have to impose on education a Christian perspective, but they would also have to produce a scholastic syllabus capable of restoring intellectual and moral rigor to learning. This was work for a cadre of Christian scholars who took as their commission the reconstitution of the curriculum along lines consistent with the tradition of the seven liberal arts. Chapter five illustrates their false starts, failures, and accomplishments.

When what is characterized as the period of Christian education ended, most of the educational and cultural monuments of the past had been recovered, and some were understood and studied in the schools. Standing on the threshold of the medieval period, we sense an attitude among scholars that further excavation of the Greek and Latin literary inheritance was not likely to produce good results. What was needed instead was an application of the knowledge now in their possession to the practical problems of life. But before knowledge could be applied, it had to be organized. Medieval educators spent the greater part of their scholastic energy imposing an order on knowledge, and when their work was finished, they had hammered out what we now recognize as the great professional specialties: law, medicine, and theology. To master these specialties, however, students needed a preliminary, or basic, education in the seven arts. Without a mastery of the arts, any invasion of the specialties would have met with defeat. The arts, along with law, medicine, and theology, became the standard academic fare for the medieval universities, those great schools whose heritage lives still in contemporary colleges and universities. The principal features of medieval education are related in chapter six.

Chapters seven and eight report on the influence of humanism (that dramatic intellectual and cultural movement conventionally characterized as the Renaissance), the impact of religious ferment on European schools and scholars, and the accomplishments of education now, at long last, put in the custody of national states. Despite frequent failure on the level of school practice, humanists succeeded in teaching later generations of teachers and students that the principal purpose of all education is the development of character. In concert with this purpose, they illustrated how the curriculum of genuine secondary schools should be organized. While humanists asked education to pay heed to character development, religious reformers, usually with humanistic predisposition, defined educational purpose in a way that ensured denominational rectitude and regularity. Education was turned into a handmaiden to religion. But in an age when national states were catapulted to prominence and when political leaders began to perceive how education could be conscripted to serve national goals, educational control was stripped from religious leaders and grasped by the strong hands of politicians. In their custody, education was made to heel to civic objectives.

When we turn from Europe to America and try to follow the story of education, we see, amid all the ferment surrounding European education (a ferment involving humanism, religion, and nationalism), a new epistemology coming over the horizon eager to challenge the conventional assumption that all knowledge worth having is lodged somewhere in literature and the educational process is principally a matter of literary excavation. Rejecting this assumption, a new breed of epistemologists boldly asserted that, while some knowledge is unquestionably in the books and may be acquired by reading, knowledge of most worth surrounds us in the physical world. The new, comprehensive textbook is physical reality, and the new method for acquiring dependable, worthwhile knowledge is empiricism. At almost the same time, however, Rousseau pronounced an audacious proposition that challenged the implicit positivism in Enlightenment philosophy and empiricism. Nature, he declared with reckless confidence, is the only teacher in whom we should put trust. As the first stanchions of American education were set, the equilibrium of the educational world was shaken with the appearance of modern science and naturalistic philosophy. But before centering attention upon the transit of education from Europe to America and subsequent American educational development, a survey is made of nineteenth- and twentieth-century European education.

Never immune to the intellectual movements in Europe, American colonists were nevertheless sanguine about the lessons they had learned about life's priorities. They knew the kind of culture they wanted to promote and were fairly certain about the kind of educational programs needed in order to ensure its realization. Chapter nine tells the story of educational transplantation and it illustrates the level of schooling—the college—wherein our ancestors put their confidence. To be paralyzed by tradition and to stick with transplanted models and institutions after the colonies had obtained their independence would have undermined the prospect for the new nation's success. Education for citizenship, for a citizenship based on the principle that public policy is shaped by public opinion, became an American creed, and a recording of this principle's maturation *vis-à-vis* educational policy and practice is made in chapter ten.

Once the principle was secure in the public mind that education is essential to effective government, the road to popular education was opened. In those 'universities' of the common man, the common schools, in secondary schools and colleges, in the development of educational philosophy, and finally in the professional education of teachers, the educational hope of a nation was realized. The robust work of dedicated educational leaders and the provision of a solid foundation for education for citizenship are related in chapter eleven.

Chapters twelve and thirteen introduce us to more familiar precincts. Americans were unable or unwilling to stand on the record of educational progress. Schools for the preparation of citizens were good— of that there was never any doubt; but were they good enough? Should more be expected from education? Did it have a part to play in social reconstruction and in securing for all citizens the promise implicit in genuine democratic institutions? These vexing questions needed the illumination that only the philosophy of education could supply. Intelligent, sensitive scholars turned to the philosophy of education with renewed vigor and were rewarded when educators and the public alike paid attention to what they had to say. The litany of philosophical systems and the philosophers who shaped them is long, but it is worth reciting. On the fringe of educational philosophy, although always close enough to be influential, was progressive education. As a movement more than a philosophy, progressive education took the vanguard for social and educational reform.

By the time progressive education had run its course, and as American education entered the second half of the twentieth century, new issues (or old ones in disguise) began to preoccupy the attention of educators and the public alike. Equality of educational opportunity, affirmative action, state educational authority, religion in education, and the cost, character, and quality of American schools began to occupy center stage. With chapter thirteen the story is over, and we have seen more than twenty-five centuries of educational experience put on display. Yet, at the end of this long story, we may not have a definitive answer to the vexing inquiry which has always plagued scholars, teachers, students, indeed, all persons who aspire to educational decency: What knowledge is of most worth?

History without interpretation is nothing more than chronology, and, while chronology should not be dismissed as inconsequential, it does not infuse historical data with meaning. And meaning must be what history is about. Even so, extracting meaning from a historical datum often leads to dispute. Historians disagree on the meaning of historical evidence, and it is this very disagreement that makes historical presentation—the writing of history—a permanent industry. If facts could speak for themselves, the work of interpretation would be pointless, but facts without organization and interpretation lead nowhere. So if there is an answer to the question Why another history of education?, it must be found in selection, organization, and interpretation of the historical evidence. These are the elements keeping history fresh, and they add up to the best justification for not stopping the writing of history with the last book to come from the printing press.

But freshness, while important, might not be enough to keep educational historians at their writing desks. Teachers, schools, and students must always be central figures in any history of education, but even the most careful accounting of their work leaves a flawed balance sheet. Education is driven by perspective, and its unavoidable preambles are lodged in philosophy. This history's approach countenances philosophy's penetrating influence in shaping the course education took from the time it was organized by the Athenians in classical Greece until it was faced with perplexing issues in the last years of the twentieth century. By no means a history of educational philosophy, this book's approach is an account of educational progress that neither ignores educational philosophy nor neglects its dynamic force in shaping the educational enterprise. It seeks to protect educational history from neglect by showing that contemporary education is connected to the past by a chain of unbroken links rather than a rope of sand.

Finally, I want to acknowledge the encouragement and advice of two colleagues, Professor Pierre D. Lambert and Professor Charles F. Donovan, S. J., and the good work of the editors of SUNY Press, Priscilla Ross and Diane Ganeles.

Chapter 1

Life and Learning
in Classical Greece

Socrates' (469–399 B.C.) rejoinder to Protagoras' (481–411 B.C.) assertion that the Sophists were teaching virtue ("I never thought that human ingenuity could make men good.")[1] is an illustration of dialectic: from the time of Homer (ca. 800 B.C.) the Greeks had commissioned education to inculcate moral virtue.

The Homeric Ideal

Dating the settlement of Greece by outsiders, or certitude about where they came from, is veiled in mystery. Upon their arrival, the outsiders met a hostile native population. But the invaders, versatile, courageous and strong, and more advanced in the way of conquest than the people being subdued were skilled in defense, made the land their home.

Allowing time for adjustment to new surroundings, these immigrant tribes capitalized the assets of a friendly physical environment. The benevolence of the land can help to explain their later achievement, for human progress and geography are related, but it is hard to believe that climate and terrain can account for the genius of the Greeks. It was evident first in Homer's poetry. Existing in oral tradition, this artistic recounting of great deeds, heroic action, a compact between men and deities, and ideals of altruism and cooperation toward desirable social ends was intended to amuse a comfortable Greek aristocracy. Their abundant leisure was made entertaining by myth turned into art in the *Iliad* and the *Odyssey*.

Ancient feudalism opened avenues only for those who could afford to travel them, so archaic Greece should not be burdened with any premature disposition to democracy or by attributing to it ideals of equity and justice. This disposition and those ideals were illustrated best in philoso-

1

phers' books. Men who must toil to make a living have few interludes for amusement and intellectual refinement, but these architects of Western civilization exploited the assets of their economic life and used the leisure they afforded to aim toward supremely human goals. Their motivation, however, despite our curiosity about it, is shrouded in mystery, but it was strong enough to turn them away from myth and superstition toward civility, reason, erudition, and eloquence. Their accomplishment was a literature abundant in artistic intention. Commanding though it is, motive alone is incapable of reconstructing social life or reaping the full power of the human spirit, so native precocity and motive needed help from social regularity and order.

The Origin of City-States. In early days, Greece was always close to anarchy, and neither person nor property was secure and safe. Later, tribal chiefs imposed a precarious stability on small groups, but anarchy was hard to suppress. With the appearance of monarchy, Greek kings were able to secure a more orderly society; but, being susceptible to frailty, incapacity, and misconduct, the kings' power waned and their authority over the nobles (at best always fragile) atrophied. Except in Sparta, where a limited form of monarchy lingered on, monarchy was abolished, and political power was grasped by the noble families.

The sharp separation of the nobles from lesser people is a fact to recognize. The noble class was the nerve and sinew of the state. Birth was the best test of excellence, and the rule of the nobles was a true aristocracy: government by the most talented. When these aristocracies became oppressive, they were amended or superseded by constitutions and codes of law. The rise of the Greek republics—the city-states—introduced a new historical epoch, one idealized in centuries of European political science as an innovation of immense significance. For the first time, care, ingenuity, and reason shaped and stabilized the machinery of government. Greek city-states, especially Athens, represented a model of government where law became evident, and tradition and custom that heretofore had guided social and political activity were transformed into a legal code.

The Influence of Myth. Reason was applied to government, but another side to the Greek character seems paradoxical: As the cultural ship sailed the mainstream of life, it often altered course to follow tributaries of myth, and sometimes these tributaries were deep enough to blur a route leading more directly to a port of true intellectual culture. Without legend, tale, myth, and historical fantasy, Greek life would have lacked charm and verve; but charm and verve (for all their worth in social settings), when nourished by irrational belief, were bound to be incompatible with right opinion and truth. The traditional investment the Greek legacy made in myth prompted Plato (429– or 427–347 B.C.), later, to take his famous stand on censorship,[2] and it is easy to miss his point. Almost as much fancy as fact formed the intellectual diet of the young. And this was a paradox: How could reason stand on an irrational foundation? With might and main the Greeks tried to make this unlikely formula work.

It all started with their perception of history. Reconstruction of legend was important, and ideas about the past affected their judgment about the present. They allowed legend to influence diplomatic accord and to adjudicate territorial claim. To some extent, day-to-day decision was based on supposed conquest or the fictional opinion of ancient heroes of divine birth. Spared the extreme of self-delusion, they all the same took myth seriously.

A little more may illustrate the point: Before the maturity of authentic history (that is, before it was turned into an art for recording the past),[3] noble families tried to find their origin in a god. Failing this, they tried to trace their pedigree to heroic ancestors, to Heracles, for example, or to a warrior who had fought at Troy. Later, with a refinement of historical sense, although interest in family genealogy seldom relaxed, they tried to discover the relationships of the various branches of the Greek race. And then they solved the problem with a wonderful skill of invention. Artfully and persuasively, but hardly ever factually, they made all the Greek branches derivative of Hēllen, an eponymous ancestor who, tradition said, lived in Thessaly.[4]

The Victory of Reason. The medal, though, has another side where the Greeks, while refusing to expurgate myth from tradition, were amenable to downgrading it. Although myth always had some influence on culture, it turned out to be an unsatisfactory substitute for what the trained reason could produce. Standing alone, incoherent myth could have been a divisive cultural force, but submitted to the arbitrament of reason, without itself being a product of reason, it could be made reasonable. And this was the bridge the intellect crossed before the Greek mind embraced myth. Putting confidence in the power of reason, Greeks redressed an earlier tyranny of mysticism and rescued themselves and their beneficiaries from the swamp of superstition. Rejecting the god of Luck they invested in the power and worth of reason; acknowledged virtue, although hard to win, as superior to strength; and, through their most influential poets, philosophers, scientists, and artists, elected to find human ideals by cultivating intellectual talent.

Athenian Educational Ideals

This combination of mind and motive was illustrated in Athens, the city-state where Greek genius was afforded its best chance to thrive. Yet conditions for its development did not appear suddenly. They evolved from centuries of cultivation and reached maturity around the middle of the fifth century B.C. Schools accompanied this evolutionary process but, according to the code of ancient life, schools were commissioned to instruct more than to educate and to teach what could be taught without assuming responsibility for the preparation of persons for life in society.[5]

To fulfill this expectation, amendment to archaic and heroic way was essential. If Athenians were to have an ideal state, habits of civic virtue (citizenship) were imperative, and this conviction was ratified in political reality. It was easy to persuade aristocratic Athenian youth that nothing took precedence over the duties of a citizen. Unyielding patriotism was at once the greatest virtue and education's most authentic objective. A condition for the achievement of this grand and reasonable social ideal was the cultivation of reason and an embracing of intellectual virtue.

Acknowledging reason as man's supreme talent, Athenians could not then insulate myth from reason's searching scrutiny. In consequence, some of Homer and Hesiod (ca. 700 B.C.), those great poets whose names are inextricably linked with the Heroic Age, needed reinterpretation, and some was jettisoned. Homeric epic put human destiny in fate's hand. Hesiod, in *Works and Days*, venerated heroic myth and, speaking mainly to common folk, asserted (for example, in *Theogony*) that the muses taught truth as well as beautiful fiction. Intelligent Athenians were now ready to assume responsibility for their destiny. Despite a sentimental attachment to a glorious past faithfully reflected in Homer, uncritically accepting Homeric tradition was only substituting the tyranny of tradition for the tyranny of superstition. Still, it was impossible to expurgate Homer from Greek culture, for so much of his epic formed a common, unbroken thread woven into the fabric of Greek life. Athenians, therefore, chose the tactic of paying Homer allegiance, quoting him with approval, but ascribing to his work ethical and metaphysical doctrines of their own invention.

Homer: Educator of the Greeks. Although never a schoolmaster, Homer's reputation as the 'educator' of Greece was earned in Athens. His epics were read, recited, and memorized after schools were organized, probably sometime in the seventh century B.C., but outside the schoolhouse they were the core of an oral tradition that gave succeeding generations an ideal vision of life.[6] This informal design for education worked almost flawlessly, so long as Athenian life remained relatively simple.

Aristocrats held the reins of social and political life, and stability was preserved because citizens had common cultural backgrounds and values. They knew what the heroes had done and how they would react to contemporary life.

Still, however high Homer's ideals and however appealing his art, his poetry was not a moral philosophy in disguise. It neither told the Greeks how to live nor authorized the gods to dictate a course of right action. If any moral lessons were buried in the *Iliad* and the *Odyssey*, extraordinary effort was required to excavate them. Although Homer was neither a moral philosopher nor a textbook writer of ethics, the tradition he perpetuated, qualifying him as the 'educator' of Greece, was a tradition of Greek pride and greatness: Athenian citizens, primed for glory, heroism, and success, were always eager to do the great deed.[7]

The Education of a Citizen–Soldier. Recalling that only children of Athenian citizens could aspire to this inheritance, the simple and unsystematic educational plan was effective. Learning and life, moreover, were closely linked, and the objectives of both were clear and easy to recognize: an Athenian boy was expected to become a citizen, a soldier, and a credit to the class from which he sprang. But those skills so essential to the person who must work for a living were neglected—being servile, they were inappropriate, almost demeaning, for the young aristocrat— and literary ability lacked any clear utility. A fully accredited citizen, judged by the standard of, say, the sixth century B.C., was probably illiterate; he could count, but elementary calculation was a mystery.

From the time of Homer to the middle of the sixth century B.C., an Athenian citizen's primary occupation was military. In the allegiance paid to military objective Athens and Sparta were similar, although Sparta gained her end by regimentation, whereas Athenians were motivated by an urge to duty and a dedication to ideals vividly portrayed in Homer.[8] Athens thrived on her tradition of honor, valor, and praiseworthy conduct, and the influence of this tradition was virile enough to obviate the prescriptiveness of Spartan rule. It cast the mold for Athenian life so long as Athens conducted her affairs according to archaic plan and limited citizenship to an aristocracy.

Education gradually drifted away from military objectives because of a change in military tactics. The soldier in the chivalric age—versatile and resourceful as a horseman and fighter, self-reliant and courageous as he waged his private wars—became an anachronism with the advent of a heavy infantry.[9] Although effective on the battlefield, an infantry battalion was formed by men who substituted routine for romance, the hard discipline of the corps for personal courage and flair, and technical qualification for the wide repertoire of an Athenian knight. No wonder Athenian youth wanted to know why being an infantryman was recommended as a worthy novitiate to civic duty. An old order was passing; a new one was on the distant horizon; but the appurtenances of war were not alone in stimulating change.

Aristocratic Education. The agrarian, rustic economy of Athens had something besides being pleasant and gratifying to recommend it, but now new economic rules were introduced. Persons of means and position searched for economic opportunity, and Athens, rather than standing still in its agrarian tracks, became an important commercial center in the ancient world. Henceforth the perquisites that rank and position had provided were put in jeopardy, and the possibility of preserving them by fleeing to the redoubt of ancient ideal and skill lacked promise. In the wake of this new economic era, a number of democratic tendencies were fused to the most durable of aristocratic traditions, and as Athens changed, her social institutions changed too. The educational program thought for centuries to be adequate was subjected to revision and amendment.

Aristocrats took their entitlement seriously and refused to surrender either power or influence. Ready to fight foreign and domestic foe alike in order to preserve their inheritance, their weapons were both military and intellectual. So, despite appearances, the conventional preoccupation with military excellence persisted. Whatever else a citizen might become, he was first a soldier; as a cavalryman or an infantryman, strength, stamina, courage, skill in the use of weapons, and dedication and devotion to the state's ideals were essential. Technical skill and strength could be developed, courage and devotion could be inculcated, but these excellences could suffer from neglect.

The Sporting Tradition. Maintaining military efficiency at a high peak was a political necessity. And while military and educational issues were clearly related to politics, both were logically subordinate to politics. This may explain why educational theory was always wedded to political philosophy in Greek literature. In any case, keeping citizens ready to meet the requirement of military foray at home and abroad was always more than mere theory. Ready and waiting to do its duty, sport occupied an essential place in Athenian life. The Olympian games attest to sport's notoriety, but in giving these games too much attention, sport's place in everyday life can be missed. It was used to hone military skill, so its first justification was practical. Besides, being fun, it gave the citizen a chance to fill his many leisure hours.[10]

Flirtation with sport could be testimony to frivolity, but the record would impeach it. Sport was attacked and abused by some eccentrics, but it was neither rejected nor discounted by the average Athenian. Even when its military worth became hard to certify, appeals to bodily excellence and beauty, to its consumption of leisure time, and to the sheer fun of it were persuasive and, in the end, convincing. Besides, clever men whose only fault was common birth had time and again succeeded in accumulating considerable wealth. Now they engaged in athletic competition, so sport, once reserved for an elite, became a popular pastime. Direct participation was best, of course, but sport could be enjoyed vicariously: to the dismay and disgust of Athenian blue-bloods, professional athletes soon appeared on the scene.[11]

This pleasant, comfortable society suited the taste of Athenian aristocrats, but it began to show signs of wear. The old gymnasia—the exclusive sporting clubs for citizens—restricted their membership, but new gymnasia opened their doors to anyone who could afford them. When this happened, sport lost its exclusive character, so the old-line aristocrat— the man who opposed change on principle—looked for an alternative, for the elite had no intention of abandoning sport. They wanted something to identify them as elite, so they turned to intellectual cultivation. Attending to things of the mind would not put the state's welfare in jeopardy, because military tactics no longer depended upon the selfless service and sacrifice of individual soldiers. But how could rich merchants and artisans of common origin afford to pursue learning for its own sake? If the luxury of liberal learning were open to them—as perhaps it was—their practical minds and economic instincts refused to countenance it.

Organization of Athenian Schools

Athenians who stood in Homer's cultural shadow were seldom ignorant and illiterate, but they neglected mental development. Now, however, with the aristocracy's status threatened, they became impatient with rusticity. Naturally precocious, versatile, and energetic, they blazed a new trail through an intellectual wilderness full of mystery and superstition. As they did, the significance of schools for instructing succeeding generations became apparent.[12]

Before schools were properly organized (the date of their origin cannot be set), this new attitude toward education recommended that families engage tutors for their children. Such arrangements, however, while not exactly subversive of social solidarity, clearly do nothing to promote it, so without abandoning their affection for individual tuition, Athenians recommended the opening of schools for the children of freemen. Greek dramatic writers Aristophanes[13] (448–385 B.C.) and Euripides[14] (480–406 B.C.), for example, dealt with current social themes, and their objections to the new education, as well as those of conservative aristocrats, were recited in the theater.[15] In the face of these objections, however, schools prospered, and boys left home, usually accompanied by a pedagogue, to obtain instruction in them.[16]

Uncertainty surrounds the nature of early Athenian schools. Before the fifth century B.C., they changed too often to leave a clear historical picture. Undoubtedly, they taught what society said was important and beneficial. Lacking any urgent need for literary and commercial skill, the curriculum was physical and musical with oral literature added for good measure. Freed from responsibility for anything but instruction, schools left the more important objective of educating citizens to the home and the community. School instruction was a humble auxiliary.

But this changed. With the end of the Persian Wars (ca. 479 B.C.) Athenians were ready for another leap forward. Change was still maligned by critics who were often Athens' best and most articulate artists. Their objection to change was not simple nostalgia: In *The Clouds*, where Aristophanes takes social and educational innovators to task, he condemns a weakening of society's fabric by an abandonment of conventional education and the introduction of untested instructional practice.[17] Old-time schools heeded music and sport and did their best to harmonize them. New schools emphasized literature and gave some attention to music, but their promotion of mental formation threatened the status of physical development. Despite vigorous thrust and artistic appeal, the critics expressed a minority opinion that lacked the vigor to impede educational change. Citizens thought only about their own education, and toward the close of the fourth century B.C., the population of Athens was about twenty-one thousand citizens, ten thousand resident aliens, and 120,000 slaves.

Educational Support and Control. For a long time, Athens allowed families almost total freedom in the care and education of children. There is no sign in Athens, as there was in Sparta, of an exigent state watchfully waiting to intrude on a child's life and direct the course of his training and education. Still, it would be wrong to assume that Athens had neither the will nor the means to keep a public eye on youth.

Evidence is ample to show an absence of state support for schooling, except for five public gymnasia—the Academy, Lyceum, Kynosarges, Diogeneion, and Ptolemeion—built and maintained by the city.[18] These, along with private gymnasia, account for what historians are tempted to call Athenian secondary education. But tradition and, perhaps, law made families responsible for their children's education. So apart from allowing teachers and their students to use gymnasia, theaters, and temples as places for instruction, public resources were not used. Add to this the custom of city educational support for sons whose fathers had been killed in battle, and the exceptions to the general principle that in Athens educational support was entirely private have been named.

Support is one side of the educational pendant; control is the other. Here Athens tried to steer a careful course between control and voluntarism. Surely Athenians had substantial theoretical justification for state educational control, and it would be hard to believe that a state so dependent upon the character, ability, and devotion of its citizens could have been indifferent to it; yet Athenian tradition consistently recommended restraint. Following tradition to the letter, Athens never went beyond a general supervision of some of the appurtenances to learning.

The laws of Solon, we are told, prescribed the length of a school day, restricted visits to schools (under pain of capital punishment) to those who had business there, set rules for athletic competition, and published decrees relative to the age of teachers.[19] In addition, an ancient, supposedly inflexible, custom told fathers to educate their sons if they expected support from them in their old age. Although Athens possessed authority over education, it was rarely and discriminatingly used.

The field of state educational control lay fallow because tradition was a competent substitute for law in preserving educational orthodoxy. During the two centuries before the Persian Wars, a plan for schooling was ratified in practice. It remained as an ideal and, infrequently amended, was durable enough to last. This was the conventional Greek education so much admired and so ineffectively imitated by pedagogic practitioners in the centuries following; and it was the plan Plato adopted with only minor revisions as a foundation to the educational utopia he described in the *Republic*.

Conventional Athenian Schools

Athenians knew that schooling is only a small part of education, so the prescription tradition wrote for the care of children before they were sent to the schoolmasters should be read. It was limited to boys. If girls had a place in regular schooling, historians are silent about it. Women who made history's record must always be judged extraordinary, but any tilling of their talent took place outside the circle of conventional schooling.[20] Plato left the schoolhouse door ajar for women, but this was no confirmation of common practice, and, in any case, Plato's confreres refused to take him seriously.[21]

The Pedagogue. Boys were cared for at home in ways intended to form their character. They were taught stories filled with moral lessons, and strict supervision was given to their choice of companions. In addition, home's example was expected to instill good manners and habits. At age seven, a boy was assigned a pedagogue who was a companion, guide, philosopher, and friend. Seldom citizens, these pedagogues, often educated foreigners held in bondage as prizes of war, had credentials of dependability and soundness of character recommending them for the important duty as masters of manners and morals. Wealthy families had a pedagogue for every boy, but even poor families managed to have at least one.[22]

Not schoolmasters, and absolved from teaching letters, although they sometimes heard recitations, pedagogues were constant companions. They kept boys honest and upright and saw to it that no harm befell them. Walking respectfully to the rear and carrying reading material, musical instruments, writing tablets, or slates, they accompanied boys to school, remained nearby while the boys were taught, and returned home with them. Pedagogues were responsible for boys' conduct: they watched manners, saw that the left hand was used for bread and the right hand, for other food; ensured that boys were silent before elders, dressed correctly, walked straight, and sat erect. They were, moreover, allowed to chastise their charges, but were restricted by a rule enjoining them to punish in a way befitting freeborn youth.[23]

A complete school plan takes time to develop, so one must be careful about declaring when any school level, or any part of a school level—for Athenian elementary education in its final form had three schools: primary, palaestra, and music—made its first appearance. The priorities of ancient life discouraged the quick founding of primary schools, and it is possible that they appeared last.[24] Discounting the basic tools of literacy has a strange sound to a contemporary ear, but no great value was put on literary accomplishment which could have been obtained easily without the help of schools.

The Primary School. The first Athenian primary schools seem to have appeared in the late sixth century B.C. Reading and writing stood alone in the syllabus; counting was added later. Versatile and able masters might have taught drawing and painting also, although Aristotle's (384–322 B.C.) recommendation for drawing and painting implies their neglect in the schools rather than their cultivation.[25]

The primary schoolmaster was an academic entrepreneur. If his reputation was good, the class was large and the fees were high. In all cases, the quality and character of a school depended solely on the master's ability. This should warn us to be careful of generalization about the standard and nature of instruction in Athenian primary schools. Yet common features stand out. Primary teaching was unattractive to citizens, so most primary masters were aliens or freed slaves who had enough literary ability to instruct boys in the rudiments. The minimum qualification for a primary master must have been reading ability, for the story that anyone who could read could teach has been repeated too often to lack the ring of truth. And if these masters lacked literary ornament, they appear also to have been morally deficient. Athenian parents, noting this, supplied pedagogues for their sons to insulate them from moral contagion.

A boy's trip to school, accompanied by a pedagogue, ended in a vacant shop, an unused corner of a public building or park, or, if the master were successful, in a schoolhouse with two rooms: one for instruction and the other a vestibule for pedagogues. With primitive instructional materials and crude pedagogic technique, masters began their teaching with the alphabet. Letters were first taught by sound only, followed by practice in combining consonants and vowels, and then the pronunciation of words. Thereafter, students saw the letters and traced them on wax tablets. Next came sentences taught, without the help of formal grammar, by a rule of thumb guide to correct speech distilled from common usage.

This simple approach represents something less than a bold assault on the citadel of literary accomplishment, but books were rare, and their scarcity discounted the worth of reading. Public placards, commercial notices, and documents could be read and understood after such instruction. Yet oral tradition was still virile and, among citizens, universal. Boys harvested this tradition by memorizing passages from Homer, Hesiod, Simonides and the gnomic poets recited to them by their teachers. When the reading course was over, after about three years or whenever the skill was mastered, accomplishment was humble. All the same, the literary legacy remained alive in strong and cultivated memories.

Reading, Writing, and Counting. Masters usually taught reading one day and writing the next. Instruction in writing, as in reading, was routine. Students practiced on wax-coated wooden tablets that had a central panel bordered by a flat, raised edge designed to protect the wax coating. Boys used the pointed end of a stylus to make marks on the wax and the flat end to erase their mistakes. Toward the end of the classical period, ink and reed pens were invented, and, almost at once, the wax tablet and stylus disappeared.

Writing began with boys tracing letters outlined by the teacher,[26] and they traced until they could make letters with help from parallel lines ruled by the teacher. Letters were written in horizontal and vertical lines falling beneath one another, without stops or accents and without spaces between words. Later, teachers dictated simple words and then whole passages. Practice, incessant practice, conspired to make perfect various elaborations of speed and legibility.

Writing instruction must have occupied about half of a boy's time. Instruction stopped with mastery, but mastery of what? Three writing styles were customary in Athens, although hardly any freeborn youth mastered all of them: the formal hand of separate capital letters, the cursive hand, and the short hand. Formal and cursive script were almost certainly taught in primary schools, but the short hand, more appropriate for clerks and scribes, was seldom part of the literary repertoire of a citizen.

This primary school instruction has much in common with contemporary pedagogy, but where today's schooling includes arithmetic, Athenian boys learned only to count. This, though, was harder than it sounds: using their fingers and hands and putting them in different positions, they learned an elaborate sign language enabling them to indicate numbers from one to a million.[27] Counting occupied a place in the school because arithmetic was too complex. Greek letters were used to signify number and lacked the flexibility the arabic notation affords for calculation. What the Greeks called "arithmetic," we call "number theory," and in the ancient order of study was a science, a discipline few schoolboys wanted to sample.

Physical Education. Wanting to be true to their cultural heritage, Athenians enlisted literary masters to transmit it. But wanting to be true to themselves, they sought physical dexterity, grace, and harmony. In earlier years, physical education had been left to chance—at least to personal preference—but with the advent of the fifth century B.C., regular provision was made for it in a special school, the palaestra. Either following the primary school and preceding the music school or operating in concert with them, the palaestra limited its course to physical conditioning, dancing, and games.

This simple school conducted by a paidotribe, a private teacher, needed only an open space or a playground where boys could exercise and play.[28] Yet the simplicity of the school course disguises the status of its teacher. Paidotribes were engaged in work acknowledged by custom to be important, so their compensation was better than their counterparts in primary schools. Besides, teaching in the palaestra was a steppingstone: paidotribes with a good reputation could be promoted to the gymnasium as athletic trainers, and from there, with luck and skill, become osteopathic physicians. Seldom citizens, paidotribes were almost never slaves and, all things considered, were likely the ornaments in a corps of ancient elementary teachers.

The Music School. After about three years in the primary school, boys were promoted to the music school,[29] where at first the only subjects were vocal and instrumental music. Social progress, however, recommended the addition of literature, so fully staffed music schools had teachers of music (*citharists*) and letters (*grammatists*). Understaffed music schools got along with one teacher who gave instruction in the oboe, lyre, and song and added just enough literature to supply students with lyrics for their songs. Better students were supposed to compose their own lyrics. Reverence for tradition and myth was so great that whether songs were composed or borrowed, they recapitulated Athens' glorious history.

The curriculum of the music school was more sensitive to fluctuation in educational mood and need than the palaestra and primary school, so, before long, literature's role was changed from being a handmaiden to music: it was given the status of a staple. Throughout most of the classical period, music schools gave about equal attention to music and literature, and this arrangement seems to have paid dividends. Singing and playing an instrument were social ornaments; the citizen who could do neither was scorned. Similar social pressure popularized poetry, and poetic reservoirs from Homer, Hesiod, Solon, Alcam, Tyrtaeus, Pindar, Aeschylus, and Euripides were stored in the memory. Aesop's fables were popular scholastic literature, too.

Contemporary commentators seldom found fault with music schools; there is, moreover, the vague implication that music-school teachers were accorded more respect and received larger emoluments than teachers in the primary schools. Yet even music teachers were suspected of being engaged in neither a trade nor a profession and, additionally, of lacking any special qualification. This suspicion had a basis in fact, but whatever its currency, the reputation of music schools was left largely unsullied. Even Plato's reservation about them was redressed when mathematics were added to their curricula.

Benevolent disposition, however, was unable to insulate the music school from the shocks of sophistry and the pretensions of ancient science. Before the classical age was over, Athenian confidence in music schools waned, and oratory, trumpeted by the Sophists as the ideal education for citizens, began its persistent aggression on music and literature. But still in its infancy, oratory was too weak to overrun the music school and, in any case, heralds for oratory were by no means sure that their ornamental discipline should be studied in an elementary school. Oratory's assault on music, however, left the school uncertain about its purpose and undermined its resolve, although both were restored in the post-classical age when music, wedded to acoustics, became a science. The music school's course, conventionally lasting five years, was over when students were around the age of fifteen.[30]

Athenian Secondary Education. Students today leave elementary schools and go to high schools, but Athenian boys went to gymnasia. The most ancient of these places—the Academy, the Lyceum, and the Kynosarges—began as sporting clubs for aristocrats, and so they remained, but they were also places where boys trained for citizenship.

The gymnasium's curriculum—if "curriculum" is the right word— consisted of physical training and sport. Entering the gymnasium, boys closed their schoolbooks, although private reading might continue, and left their musical instruments at home to pursue a traditional regimen intended to produce nobility and grace. Continuity between the palaestra and the gymnasium is apparent, so it is safe to call the latter an advanced course in sport. Athletic events with clear links to military excellence were promoted: running, jumping, wrestling, and throwing the discus and javelin. Horsemanship and swimming might have been included, too, although evidence about them is slender. Precise in purpose and well-organized, this was civic education.

Tempted to look for something in the gymnasium indicating an investment in literary culture, we look in vain. Before the fourth century B.C. was over, however, sport's prominence declined sharply, but for most of the classical age, what (for want of a better phrase) is called "secondary education" was only sport. But sport attracted a vast and various clientele, and old gymnasia became so crowded that new ones—some public, but most private—had to be built. Now it was possible for places like the Academy, the Lyceum, and the Kynosarges to remain exclusive, for Athenian boys could attend the newer, more democratic places like the Diogeneion and Ptolemeion.

Athenian boys were not required to go to any school, but social pressure and tradition were worthy substitutes for compulsory attendance laws. Still, obstacles sometimes stood in the way of school attendance. First, despite the public face of Athenian gymnasia, physical training and coaching incurred some expense, and students had to bear it. Those who could not forfeited their chance for citizenship unless, having lost their fathers in battle, they qualified for public aid or their athletic prowess was promising enough to recommend them for scholarships gymnasiarchs were authorized to grant. An unpaid public official, a gymnasiarch was the gymnasium's headmaster who directed a staff of about ten paidotribes (trainers) and ten gymnasts (coaches).

Gymnasiarchs were always respected citizens;[31] trainers and coaches may have been citizens, too, although history lacks assurance on this point. In any case, trainers and coaches were well paid and, because their work was prized, had the status of important persons.

The cost of gymnastic training was substantial and sometimes turned out to be an obstacle, but another obstacle was more ominous. According to Aristotle's eye-witness account of the rite of citizenship, a test of parentage could be made when a boy was ready to enter the gymnasium.[32] Affirmation of parentage, or an oath that a boy's parents were Athenians, was an admission requirement, and if this affirmation were uncontested, a boy simply entered the gymnasium. If the oath were contested, however, parentage had to be proved. If proof was made the matter was settled; if it was not made the boy was sold as a slave. A challenge to parentage could be ignored if, at the same time, gymnastic training and the prospect of citizenship were abandoned. Following this course of action, a boy was allowed to live in Athens as a noncitizen freeman. Considering the erratic nature of Athenian judicial practice, prudence might have dictated that a challenge to parentage go unanswered.

The Gymnasium. The gymnasium, an enclosed stadium with a large playground (called a "palaestra") about twice the size of an American football field, might interest us. A track circled the playground and, in turn, was circled by stands for spectators. Rooms under the stands were used for rest, exercise, and conversation. These athletic clubs also had facilities for bathing, massaging, dusting, eating, swimming, and praying. Gardens and groves invited leisurely walks. Servants and attendants, provided with living accommodations on the premises, were abundant. The gymnasium, then, a huge multipurpose athletic plant of about 360,000 square feet,[33] offered prospective citizens a three-year gymnastic course. When young men completed the course, they were about eighteen or nineteen years old.

Ephebic Training. Aristotle's account of ephebic training, a description based on direct knowledge (although not personal participation, since Aristotle was not an Athenian citizen),[34] is crisp and clear. Aristotle is a credible witness and the program he described was current when he was in Athens, but ephebic training was susceptible to evolution and change. Aristotle's version must be read with this proviso in mind.

An *ephebos* started with a training that was subordinated, naturally enough, to the requirements of current military tactics; as tactics changed, training was amended. According to Aristotle's account, military training lasted a year and was followed by the ephebic oath and then two years of active military service. Despite the ceremony of the oath and a presumption that therewith the last hurdle to citizenship had been leaped, ephebi owed Athens flawless soldierly performance during the period of active duty. Surviving this interlude in the profession of arms without blemish to honor, courage, and martial skill, they were certified as citizens.[35] War was the best test of a man's motive and merit, but without war the regimen and discipline of a soldier's life were severe enough to separate the worthy from the unworthy. All in all, Athens was satisfied with her educational program.

But even satisfactory systems are subject to variation: before Aristotle, ephebi followed a three-year program, including basic training and active duty, before taking the ephebic oath. The oath-taking ceremony was, then, an award of citizenship. After Aristotle, the oath was administered prior to a three-year period of training and duty, so young men in the ephebic program were already citizens.

Decades after Aristotle, the ephebic program was altered so sharply that he would not have recognized it. But this happened after Athens had suffered military decline and had lost political supremacy in Greece. The attention given to physical excellence and military skill, characteristic of better days, was shifted to literary formation and intellectual development, but without any direct intention to subvert sport. Athenian temper and character dictated the preservation of the sporting tradition, but priorities changed and ephebic training changed with them. Ephebi collected books, read them in the *ephebium*, and argued about the novelties they contained. Ideas honed the intellect and conspired to make young men forget the battlefield and remember the courts, the arena (the place where public affairs were transacted), the schools, and the libraries. When Athens went to war after cultural and political change had taken its toll, she depended upon mercenaries and noncitizen conscripts. The vigor and nobility of civic education for duty belonged to the past, but only a few citizens seemed to realize what had been lost.

Life and Education in Sparta

If all the city-states had imitated Athens, life in ancient Greece would have been more pleasant. As it was, only some states thought Athens a good model; others, noticing Sparta's strength and stability, were tempted to follow in her footsteps, but this was not easy to do, for in no ancient land was education given more solicitous attention.

Preoccupied with war and conquest, Spartans, the master class, dominated their city-state and tried to cast their spell over all of Greece. For a while, their formula of regimentation and social paralysis worked, but in the end, as Aristotle said, when other states became accomplished at warfare, Sparta's dominance evaporated.[36] For a long time, however, the Spartans, who came to Greece as invaders, maintained mastery over two subject classes: *perioeci* (freeborn persons whose ancestry antedated the Dorian conquest (ca. 1104 B.C.)) and *helots* (slaves or serfs permanently bound to the land). Spartan education was commissioned to preserve this social system, so it was always severely practical and absolutely unamendable.[37]

Now and then engaging in the dangerous enterprise of conspiracy, Sparta's subordinate classes incited insurrection to shed their yoke of servitude, but the citizens were too vigilant to be caught off guard and too skillful as warriors to be overthrown. Personal, intellectual, and moral autonomy capitulated to an exigent state, and boys and girls alike were nurtured for state service. Citizenship implied subservience, and severe penalty—death, ostracism, or at least disgrace—was the guerdon for persons failing in patriotic duty and dedication to the fatherland. In this armed camp, personal thought, interest, and aspiration were subordinate to the state's good. Neither an enemy nor an innovation penetrated the city's borders.

Education for Patriotism. Dispensed from economic care (because slaves tilled the soil to support them) and without distraction from trade or profession, citizens sacrificed all their time and talent to the state. Patriotism and obedience, although in different measure, were exacted from men and women. Women lacked equal status with men, although they enjoyed more freedom than Athenian women, but were respected nevertheless for the contribution they made in bearing strong, healthy children. Spared military training and the ordeal of combat, their moral strength and resolute patriotism sustained their soldier husbands and sons and urged them to the battlefield with the admonition to return home with their shields or on them.

Education for Women. Spartan girls played and exercised (probably with boys) until they were about eleven, under the supervision of mothers and nurses. Ignoring reading and writing, their tutelage overlooked domestic art and household chores as well, for slaves were plentiful for handling all menial tasks. Even Xenophon (430–355 B.C.), whose admiration for Spartan education was unconcealed, could not brighten this bleak picture of the education of Spartan women.[38]

Education for Men. Boys, too, were excused from literary instruction to follow a regimen aimed directly at military excellence. Sparta needed warriors, not scholars, to ensure her survival, and their training was too important to be left to personal discretion or chance. To this end, boys went through a rigid educational program leading to both citizenship and military proficiency.

Whether Spartans were literate and knew Homer, music, art, and literature is a topic on which authorities disagree.[39] The truth may be missed in harsh judgment, yet convincing evidence of intellectual discipline is lacking. Boys spent years in physical and military training; if now and then they read books or used writing tablets, they kept secret such excursions into literacy. Tradition, however, attributes mental keenness and laconic speech to Lacedaemonians; their diplomats and generals are represented in various accounts as impressive men whose skill, wit, and knowledge made them formidable adversaries at the council table and on the battlefield. But music, art, and literature were poor ammunition for war and must have found few patrons or, some say, thought weakening of moral vigor and martial spirit, were outlawed. Culturally chilly, suspicious of the novel and complex, Spartans ostracized diplomats (and members of their families) who returned from a foreign assignment with unhidden literary or rhetorical skill. Plain language used sparingly was good enough.

Total literary aridity might have been repudiated by an oral transmission of law, sketchy recitations of Homer, and tales about heroes, genealogies, and military encounters. In spite of general neglect of literary skill, boys were well instructed in the social and ethical code that made an indelible imprint on Spartan life. This code, it is said, along with a legacy of law and proper learning, was bequeathed by Lycurgus and preserved in *Eunomia*, but Lycurgus may have been a legendary character. Whatever the truth on Lycurgus, his law, once settled in oral tradition, withstood repeal, had the same permanence as the city-state itself, and contained the prescription for civic education.[40]

Training for Citizenship. Ancient educational practice operated on the assumption that age seven was the right time for instruction to begin. Without debate or doubt Spartans listened to the voice of custom. But before training started, some preliminaries had to be settled. Soon after birth, a male infant was bathed in wine—a ceremony of endurance—and inspected by a state council. Healthy, sturdy boys were restored to their parents' households; weak children, judged unfit, were sentenced to exposure. Left helpless and hungry on Mount Taügetos or elsewhere in the city-state, they died unless rescued by helots or perioeci who could raise them as their own.

From age seven (when systematic training for citizenship began) to eleven, boys, though wards of the state, were allowed to live at home. Thereafter, and until death, they were on active or inactive military duty. Primary training, under the direction of old soldiers assigned to instruct and govern the boys, consisted mainly of games for physical conditioning. The details of the early stages of training need not delay us, but as boys matured, their lives and training became harder. Leaving home for good at age eleven, they spent the next six or seven years in basic military training. Sorted into packs or classes of about sixty boys each, called either *ilai* or *agelai*, these battalions roamed the countryside as foragers and apprentice warriors to steal food or whatever they wanted (although law forbade stealing from citizens), to exercise, and to practice their craft of ambush and homicide.[41]

With basic training over at seventeen or eighteen, young men became ephebi. Leaving their pack schools behind and taking the oath of allegiance to the state, they joined a warrior band under the captaincy of a young chief. These private squadrons fought among themselves to sharpen their skill at arms, to test their courage and endurance, and to illustrate their devotion to Spartan values. This critical test lasted about three years. Men who passed it were promoted to the regular army; those who shirked their duty or lacked courage were drummed from the ranks and the portals to citizenship were closed to them.

Survivors could look forward to an apprenticeship of another ten years. By this time, young men were eager for warfare, and Sparta seldom disappointed them. If they lived through this decade of probation, they were enrolled as Spartan citizens. Their lives, though, were largely unchanged: they would always be soldiers, but custom recommended marriage.[42]

Paralyzed by tradition, nothing in Sparta was allowed to redirect this expenditure of human energy from a fanatical allegiance to the state, not, at least, until Sparta's military supremacy vanished—due probably to a depletion of citizen ranks, for Sparta enlisted only citizens in her army— and her superiority in Greece disappeared.

Educational Change in Athens

The face of Athenian society changed after the Persian Wars. Athenians prized the values of their ancestors but interpreted them to meet different social and economic conditions. The state was paid allegiance but with a different coin, and the ideal of citizenship was unconsciously deflated even while it was eloquently affirmed. Besides, the rolls of citizenship were opened to persons who, according to traditional standard, were unqualified. Wealth, moreover, was more easily obtained by clever and enterprising men, and the dedication heretofore reserved for the common good was now spent for personal advantage and financial gain.

Secure politically and comfortable economically, Athens became less vigilant about enforcing qualifications for citizenship. Out of necessity she had created a navy by enlisting merchant mariners to meet and, temporarily, to defeat the Persians. This rupture of ancient custom—allowing noncitizens to bear arms in the city's defense—resulted in the sailors petitioning for citizenship. Their petition, authenticated by a logic hard to refute, was granted. They and all free men were enfranchised almost overnight, and Athens had a new citizen class, one hardly ready for full civic duty. Their civic deficiency needed redressing quickly, for state policy was framed by all citizens. Issues of justice and equity were debated and voted in the assembly, and citizens were expected to understand them.

Traditionally, civic education had taken a long time, so it is easy to see why a dependable substitute was hard to find. Athenian schoolmasters could have amended school practice to meet this novel situation, but, mesmerized by intuition about scholastic propriety and arrogant advice from conservative aristocrats, they blocked innovation at the schoolhouse door. At worst they were negligent, at best, blind, about the problem of educating the new citizens. When traditional schoolmasters refused to budge, others not petrified by convention saw and did what needed to be done. They were the Sophists.

The Sophists. Over the centuries the Sophists have been both praised and blamed: now, we think, they deserve some of each. Putting Athenian pedagogy in convulsion, they tried, without much help from old-fashioned agencies of moral education—the theater, the assembly, the gymnasium, and the aristocratic home—to teach good citizenship effectively and quickly. So Socrates' question to Protagoras ("Can men be taught to be good?") was a central issue in Athenian life and not just a dramatic device for introducing the dialogue.[43] The new citizens wanted educational decency, but old avenues leading to it were blocked by the intractability of the schools. To suppose that mature men would pursue a course of instruction designed for schoolboys was sheer folly.

Scholastic Innovation. History's lesson that necessity is the mother of invention was recalled again, and Sophists practiced invention, even while Socrates, Plato, Isocrates, and Xenophon excoriated them, by shortening the school course as a temporary measure to accommodate adults and by centering instruction on literature and rhetoric. For the first (but not the last) time, these studies were called upon to teach virtue. Rejecting customary school practice, the Sophists appeared to discount tradition when oratory was idealized as their educational goal and, never diffident about accepting free publicity, they rose to pedagogic distinction by promoting the assumption that eloquence, at least enough to win an argument, is only another name for civic virtue. The curriculum's foundation was shaken by this turbulence, yet traditional schools tried to ignore sophistic assault and pretend that nothing had changed.

Pretense, however, could not conceal the fact that scholastic focus was shifting to literature. Despite protest from stationary teachers— Plato, Isocrates, Aristotle, and others who had heavy investments in schools—the Sophists' business was good. Once whetted, intellectual appetites were hard to satisfy; moreover, schooling had a novel justification: it could accelerate the process of social assimilation, ensure political autonomy, and prepare citizens to exploit political freedom.

Sophistic Critics. This seemed harmless enough to the Sophists; besides, it meant money in their pockets. But stationary teachers were less sanguine about the worth of an educational program that jettisoned so much of traditional culture. Calling the new education dangerous and superficial, they said it confused skill in debate with moral and political wisdom, abbreviated schooling so much that moral and intellectual formation was impossible, and glossed over the fact that genuine talent is an essential condition for the attainment of moral wisdom.[44]

Conventional opinion, along with testimony from ancient days, tends to portray the Sophists as ignorant, evil, pretentious, greedy men who swarmed to Athens, in the years between 450 and 350 B.C., to deceive the people about the nature of ethical knowledge and political wisdom. Indictments, however, are returned only by their enemies, of whom Plato is the most outspoken.

Probably never so shallow and opportunistic as their critics averred, or so pedagogically insightful and loyal to sound learning as their publicity alleged, the Sophists should not be discarded as inconsequential footnotes in the history of education. Neither in speculative nor political philosophy were their accomplishments impressive; so much is readily stipulated; but as teachers they cleared away scholastic underbrush and accelerated educational progress. Besides, being in the vanguard of a secondary education that was intellectual and literary, they tempted Athenian boys away from the playgrounds and coaxed them into schoolrooms.

Sophistic Instructional Practice. Although most popular in Athens, Sophists wandered throughout Greece always ready to peddle their scholastic wares. They attracted attention because they contracted to teach their students how to be successful and, in order to reap profit, recruited large classes with whom the novel technique of simultaneous (class) instruction was used. The law of supply and demand set their fees and this led to the allegation that they made learning a mere commodity. Pedagogic propaganda, it was said, exaggerated their talent in order to keep their classes large and their fees high. Finally, although the Sophists were always solitary teachers, they advanced an arrogant, common doctrine that in one year they could accomplish as much as conventional schools did in twenty.

Their excellence, they boasted, rested on their ability to recognize relevant knowledge and skill and teach them. This trumpeting of relevance recommended them to the new Athenian citizens who, needing adult education, placed a special premium on scholastic brevity, and it posed an attractive alternative for aristocratic boys who were looking for scholastic excitement. Whatever sophistry's worth as a measure of sound learning, it ruptured tradition, broke the fraternal relationship between masters and pupils, and inflated eloquence to the rank of civic virtue. This was enough to earn the enmity of Athenian teachers whose schools were waiting for students while Sophists, travelling the highways and byways, recruited them.

Sophistry is something of a mystery, for the Sophists left accounts neither of their school practices nor educational theories. Some Sophists were efficient, dedicated teachers who gave students their money's worth; others, we are led to believe, wanted only to harvest fame and fortune and cared nothing about the influence of their instruction. Dependable witnesses tell of their preference for large classes; they tell, too, that Sophists charged fees for teaching, but this was a common, generally accepted practice in Athens. What was uncommon was the execution of a prepaid contract with students. Besides being unconventional, such commercial techniques were judged to be unworthy of scholastic art and were condemned.[45] Yet these complaints were ignored by students thirsty for the kind of knowledge the Sophists purveyed.

Had sophistry not threatened the traditional culture and the status of stationary teachers, it would have been small change in history, but because sophistic teaching was fairly popular, although seldom embraced by hordes of students, it assaulted orthodox educational belief in asserting that men can be taught to be good, that knowing what ought to be done leads necessarily to doing it, and that knowledge is virtue. The Sophists' proud boast that virtue can be taught sounded arrogant to Plato, but it irritated cultured Athenians as well, for it violated their principles of character and morality. Additionally, evidence of shoddiness, superficiality and fraud surfaced in sophistry: on various occasions, but especially in Plato's dialogues, Sophists are represented as men concealing their ignorance in an abundance of words and refusing to acknowledge the possibility of objective truth.

The Better Argument. Plato was quick to agree that few people were capable of grasping truth, although he added that a regimen of hard study could lead many people to right opinion. The Sophists, however, taking a leaf from the skeptic's handbook, repudiated truth and right opinion: this left only opinion that was advanced and sustained by the better argument.

If one opinion is as good as another, either force or persuasion becomes the determiner of action, the final arbiter of what is to be done. Sophists, being civil men, disdained force; so these molders of Athenian temperament and character, these makers of citizens, trapped by the rule of exclusion, had to make the art of persuasion their pedagogic preoccupation. The triumph of rhetoric over reason, of skill in debate over truth, illustrates the genius of their teaching.

The appearance of truth, the Sophists knew and others learned, is often better than truth itself. In consequence, sophistic teaching paid special heed to methods of instruction that would promote effective and eloquent oratory. The best of the Sophists should be remembered for their contribution to formal rhetoric, but run-of-the-mill Sophists, teaching fast because their students were eager, settled for one speech. Students composed a broad and general speech leaving blank spaces for an ingenious and inspiring speaker to fill to suit a particular occasion. They practiced the speech, along with a stock of appropriate variations to its theme, until it was safely stored in the memory. With this done, the course was over and, some Sophists said, their students had learned civic virtue.

The Sophists' Contribution to Education. The side to sophistry just described revived the charge of academic fraud,[46] but the indictment was dismissed because the Athenian public liked a quick course that promised success. Besides, sometimes sophistic teaching lived up to its billing, and some students turned out to be real ornaments to it. In the end, then, harsh criticism of sophistry went largely unheeded, although venting such criticism proved to be a popular pastime among philosophers. Critics of sophistry had a point even when their aversion to it was lodged in a fear of men who know too much, in a prejudice aristocrats have against persons who must work for pay, in the envy of those unable to afford sophistic teaching, and in the disadvantage some suffered when they competed with the debaters sophistic teaching produced.

As they went about their scholastic business, the Sophists were not burdened or hindered much by harsh criticism. To their credit they recognized genuine educational need while their counterparts stood mute and, over the span of a century, changed the face of Athenian education. Yet everything was not praiseworthy: Evidence is lacking, for example, to support the bold boast that they promoted educational democracy or, although popular teachers, that they marched in the vanguard of popular education. Anyone who could pay was taught, but Sophists' interest in elementary education was abandoned early and, moreover, they were silent about equality of educational opportunity. Most of their students were young aristocrats who aspired to a quick, if crude, route to cultural and political advancement. Sophists geared their instruction for social leadership, success, and fame; they felt no compunction about abandoning common men who needed a basic civic education.[47]

Prodicus, Antiphon, Thrasymachus, and other Sophists whose names time has obliterated taught the eager youth of Athens by staying generally within the broad boundaries marked out by Protagoras, Gorgias, and Hippias. If these Sophists did nothing more than foment controversy to stimulate the growth of educational thought among their successors, their contribution, although largely negative, was eminently worthwhile.

Chapter 2

The Genesis
of Educational Philosophy

Pride in eloquence antedated the classical age, but as the city-state and democratic sentiment matured, oratory's worth was inflated. A citizen who spoke well could command attention and influence public policy. In Athens, more than elsewhere in Greece, citizens were jealous of their rights and eagerly engaged in litigation to ensure them. Yet, approaching the bar of justice was a solitary affair: persons represented themselves without help from attorneys or advocates.

Eloquence, although prized, could not win a case. One side to public speaking is delivery and here, teachers say, practice makes perfect; but they notice, too, such personal qualities as platform manner and voice control. The other, equally important, side—because empty eloquence cannot long be hidden—is content. It was common for litigants who lacked confidence in their ability to compose a speech to hire writers and memorize their compositions. This tactic could work in trials where the dispute was narrow, but was almost worthless for illuminating and analyzing genuine public questions. Capable citizens composed speeches full of meaning and delivered them persuasively. Sometimes, though, controversy was urgent, and speakers, unable to craft orations at leisure, had to employ judicial, deliberative, or demonstrative oratory extemporaneously. Requirements for speech were lodged in the nature of public life, but conventional education had, up to now, left oratory largely uncultivated.[1]

By the fifth century B.C., oratory was a novelty with enough luster to challenge the traditional melding of civic education with military training. Besides, old-fashioned schoolmasters were in the habit of leaving ethical issues untouched, not because they lacked import, but because life in society handled them. However, life in the classical age changed enough to make men worry about the efficacy of its moral influence, so, to be safe, they reassessed the school's compact with virtue and commissioned teachers to instruct their students in the duties of public men. For the first time, civic virtue's fate and the state's good were entrusted to teachers.

With this heavy burden, the more talented and responsible Athenian schoolmasters searched for a guide to their work. They pondered educational philosophy and tried to apply it in their schools. With the boldness characteristic of genius, they set a course for the future, but tempered their enthusiasm for novelty by leaving elementary schooling alone to spend their energy on reshaping higher learning.

At this point, educational philosophy made a bid for attention, but the most eloquent and intelligent educational philosophers—Plato, Isocrates, and Aristotle—were at pains to subordinate educational to general philosophy, almost making it a footnote in their books on politics and ethics. Reading these books today, we are awed by their lucidity, wisdom, and genius, but we suspect that they might not have been written at all had their authors been less hostile to sophistry. Praiseworthy as it was, their educational thought was not honed only on a disinterested devotion to knowledge.

Socrates (469–399 B.C.)

The history of educational thought, although barren of direct Socratic testimony, is nevertheless generous in appraising Socrates' contribution. He disclaimed both the title of teacher and the possession of knowledge. Yet he was sentenced to death for his teaching: "Socrates is guilty of crime in refusing to recognize the gods acknowledged by the state, and importing strange deities of his own; he is further guilty of corrupting the young."[2]

Although disciples proved the indictment spurious, Socrates' enemies used it to destroy him. The case, his defenders say, rested on an incredible assumption. Socrates admitted to searching for knowledge in company with others, but he denied being a teacher. Besides, Athens' tolerance of teachers whose reputations for moral and intellectual integrity were soiled undermines the merit of the court's allegation. A picture of Athenians, moreover, fretful and anxious about their children's religious belief and solicitous about interdicting atheism, is too distorted to be taken seriously. Atheism was a popular belief for which almost everyone in Athens could have been indicted. Being vindictive rather than just, the court convicted Socrates to be rid of him.[3]

Socrates made enemies by being a gadfly. He stirred up the people, cultivated unpopular sentiments, and befriended revolutionary causes at a time when Athens was tired of political and intellectual friction. Constant interrogation put conventional opinion in jeopardy, and incessant questioning irritated and embarrassed men who pretended to have the truth. Socrates, moreover, justified the aristocracy's right to political control and poked fun at democracy. Plato and Xenophon say he understood his predicament but refused to acknowledge the right of his accusers to limit the range of his thought.[4] Refusing to answer the indictment and foregoing a chance to speak in his own defense, Socrates' doom was sealed.

Yet Socrates seems an unlikely hero. Born to poor parents and educated for citizenship in the conventional way, he followed the trade of his sculptor father. For a time he was a soldier and earned a reputation for courage in battle, but upon returning to civilian life he pursued his trade with indifferent success. Then, suddenly, he became addicted to the search for wisdom.

Despite Socrates' protests to the contrary, friends and colleagues called him a teacher, and some said he was a Sophist. If they were right, his sophistry was extraordinary: he neither recruited students, made contracts, charged fees, rented lecture halls, nor advertised or promised success. In company with the Sophists, however, Socrates tried to educate social and political leaders, although he rejected sophistic teaching formulas, and undertook to elevate knowledge of civic virtue to a level consistent with the ideals of Athenian culture.

Socrates' Philosophy. An evaluation of Socrates' philosophy must be tentative, for its recording is imprecise. Plato and Xenophon, both friends and admirers, recount the measure of his thought and the detail of his life. In Plato's dialogues, Socrates' erudition is paraded, but are we listening to Socrates or to Plato? Clearly the dialogues are not stenographic reproductions. Plato was not an amanuensis, but a literary artist who might have used Socrates to articulate his own philosophical convictions. Working our way through myth and legend, the bases of Socrates' philosophy can be discerned. He riveted attention on human nature and action and on rational psychology and ethics. All have profound meaning for educational philosophy. Method, however, idealized in his pedagogic repertoire, was his most durable educational bequest.

Socrates wanted to know what human acts have worth and what have none, so moral philosophy captured his attention. Justice, temperance, courage, gratitude, and friendship are easy words to pronounce, and one is tempted to assume their meaning. But Socrates rejected assumption. Never wearying of discussing moral virtue or of probing for its meaning, he and his companions asked questions about everything. Questioning themselves and others, they disturbed the tranquil and convenient convictions of their countrymen, but at the same time they opened new frontiers for thought.

The Socratic Method. This technique of inquiry, of asking questions and never finding the answers satisfactory, of finding fault with conventional opinion, adds up to the Socratic method. And this dialectical method was consistent with Socrates' conception of knowledge. If we understand him, knowledge is intuitive and, belonging to persons as an original endowment, does not depend upon or issue from experience. With this theory of knowledge, Socrates could dispense with instruction—transmitting facts, opinions, and information—to concentrate on mental cultivation and therefrom to make people aware of what is buried in the recesses of their spirit. Socrates said he was a midwife, a cooperative artist, ready to help persons discover truth. Granting the validity of his theory, what better than dialectical method could pave the road to knowledge?

This method, entirely faithful to Socrates' philosophy of knowledge, and a charter for intellectual autonomy, encouraged students to inquiry. So Plato features Socrates as more a student than a teacher; his questions are profound and when there are answers, they are tentative. Room is always left for more. This is not mere pedagogic technique, for Socrates is candid in admitting to ignorance. In any case, dialectic is illustrated as an investigation, a way of searching for knowledge without any assurance whatever of attaining it, and not, as its imitators pretend, a trustworthy guide for teaching boys and girls what they do not know.

Liberal Education and Teaching Virtue. Although Socrates used method as an indispensable aid to the discovery of knowledge, he refused to pursue knowledge for its own sake. His testimony for liberal learning was weak, but it would have impeached the doctrine of utility, too. Illustrating this elusive point, Socrates endorsed geometry because it had practical application, praised astronomy when used to forecast seasons, and approved arithmetic—he meant computation—for keeping business accounts. Yet his enthusiasm for practical knowledge was blunted by a promotion of knowledge of self, of insight into personal motive, and of prudence for knowing what to do and doing it.

How, Socrates asked, could persons be virtuous unless they knew virtue's meaning? Could justice have various meanings? Could it, for example, mean one thing to him and another to Protagoras? All of this troubled Socrates, but he refused to despair of discovering an ethical truth to form a bedrock for social discipline and decency. His thesis has the ring of moral orthodoxy, for there is a tendency to believe that right action, doing what ought to be done, is braced by accurate knowledge. But

Socrates, if Plato's rendering is accurate, went a step further: dependable knowledge unerringly leads to right action. In the history of philosophy, the "Socratic fallacy" is this merging of knowledge and virtue.

Plato (429 or 427–347 B.C.)

Plato was Socrates' friend and constant companion, so his account of Socrates' philosophy is worth heeding, but Plato' credentials were ornamental, too: he cut a wide, distinctive swath through philosophy's history. Elements of truth are lodged in the assertion that all speculative and educational philosophy have their origin with him.

Plato grew up in Athens and, though the record of his early life is incomplete, followed the social and educational convention befitting a wealthy, aristocratic, precocious boy. His perquisites included wealth to travel and leisure to study, to think, and to associate with Athenian poets, dramatists, sophists, and philosophers. But Socrates influenced him most.

For a dozen or so years, Socrates was Plato's teacher, and Plato implies that he took part, if only as an attentive listener, in every important conversation (or debate) that Socrates had during this long interlude. But the fraternal relationship was rudely ruptured when Socrates was indicted, found guilty, and sentenced to death. Recognized as Socrates' disciple and one who shared his distrust for democracy, Plato's freedom and life were in jeopardy so long as he remained in Athens. Faced with a threatened indictment, Plato left Athens for twenty years. Using these years for travel and study, he associated with the best ancient scholars and, without much success, served as an adviser to princes and monarchs. Urgent necessity drove Plato from Athens, but in memorializing Socrates, he turned out to be something more than Socrates' philosophical disciple. Plato's genius raised philosophy to a level of extraordinary prominence from which it seldom slipped, and he embellished his philosophical writing with poetic eloquence. In days to come, persons without any appetite for philosophy read his books because he wrote well.

Plato's Academy. Returning to Athens when fear of sedition abated, Plato, now about fifty years old, opened the Academy, locating it on the outskirts of the city near the ancient gymnasium with the same name. And to smother old doubt about his patriotism, the Academy was incorporated as a religious fraternity, although Plato's intention was to conduct a school to educate political leaders.[5] They needed the foundation the Academy could supply before venturing into moral, political, and intellectual philosophy.[6] Plato, ever solicitous about their education, preferred informal discussion to direct teaching and seldom lectured. He tried to give eager and intelligent students—the cream of the Athenian crop— some intimation of mankind's universal moral problem by asking search- ing questions and leading them through the discipline of critical thinking. Beyond this, knowledge of his pedagogic technique is vague, although, had he wanted to use it, the dialogues demonstrate his mastery of the dialectical method. The school's informality is striking. With social grace and cordiality, students and teachers met for instruction at dinner, and wine, temperately consumed, added to the zest and good humor of instruction.[7]

Politics and Education. The Academy was an ornament to learning and Plato was a skillful and successful teacher; yet had he been able to court his first love, he would have been a politician rather than a school- master and philosopher. In Plato's political philosophy, education has an integral status.[8] The *Republic* and the *Laws* illustrate the pattern of Plato's political thought and express his social idealism. States and so- cieties, however, are human inventions, and their character depends upon the citizens directing them. Realizing this, it was impossible for Plato to neglect the education of citizens who were the state's living substance. Plato's attention to educational principle and practice must not be inter- preted as needless preoccupation or miscalculation: Plato's philosophy of education is the bedrock whereupon the excellence of states is built.

Yet Plato's appraisal of education followed the mainstream of ancient social thought, demonstrated most clearly in Athens and Sparta, so there is nothing prophetic about his praise of good citizenship and civic virtue. Nevertheless, Plato added novel interpretation to orthodox educational opinion and meant it to be implemented in his ideal state. Adhering strictly to traditional opinion crippled the Sophists' political philosophy, and following, some think, in their footsteps, Isocrates' otherwise cogent briefs sound anachronistic; but in Plato's hands, orthodoxy was a depen- dable rudder for safely sailing the ship of state through heretofore un- charted waters. Athenian opinion idealized civic duty and demanded mili- tary training and service for and from citizens, but Plato took a wider view of civic duty and allowed citizens to discharge it through public service.[9]

Good citizenship, honed chiefly on intellectual accomplishment, sharpened enough could become political wisdom. Still, leadership needed credentials whose roots ran through the schools to more fertile soil below: in Plato's Academy, only carefully selected students from solid aristocratic homes were admitted. The same care in opening the school- house door to boys whose background recommended them for political leadership is evident in Plato's educational philosophy. This clear preference for an elite makes Plato and the Sophists strange bedfellows, for they, too, were committed to teaching an elite for social leadership. Ascribing to Plato sentiments promoting equality of educational opportunity puts us, at once, on the wrong track.

The coin, however, has a side that should not be hidden. Plato's educational experience persuaded him that ability belonged to aristocrats, and all ancient thought confirmed this conclusion. Yet a discriminate reading of the *Republic* reveals that, although Plato rejected popular education, he wanted all of the state's inhabitants to have some training, for states need citizens with diverse accomplishment. Yet he refused to abandon the belief that leaders were to be found among a natural elite.[10]

Plato erased the caricature of a talented, lazy aristocracy, educated too much for its own good, but he condemned frivolity and may also have diminished the worth of liberal learning. Constancy in seeking the highest virtue was incompatible with a life of unproductive leisure: he refused to applaud knowledge for its own sake. At the same time, however, he withheld approval from merely practical or useful knowledge.

Put another way, Plato's commitment was to an always possible but seldom realized universal truth. "Man is the measure of all things" was interpreted by clever Sophists to mean "what appears to be true, is true." This put Plato and the Sophists at loggerheads, and it marked out the terrain whereupon philosophers uncompromisingly debated the conflicting assertions of idealism and pragmatism. Sophistic pragmatism idealized result; but Plato, while unready to discount result, prescribed a critical intellectual process for winnowing the false and superficial from right opinion and truth. Plato's allegiance to a fixed, eternal truth had important consequences for the school's curriculum. In a long and ornamental history, education has wrestled with the question, What should be taught?

State Educational Control. If, in anxious moments when political stability was threatened, Athenians paid tribute to a theory of state educational control, they, at other times, exhibited enough cultural self-confidence to restrain its practical application. Athens trusted to luck when she appealed to citizens to act habitually for the public good, and generally, her trust was rewarded. Although subscribing to the admonition that citizens should subordinate the personal to the common good, Plato demurred from leaving the formation of civic disposition to chance. The *Republic* and the *Laws* illustrate his embrace of state educational control.

Plato's democratic sentiment is tentative and fleeting, but the principle is evident that the highest political good, not to be confused with a state's welfare, depends upon public unity. And public unity or social solidarity is cultivated by practicing unremitting allegiance to the state. Unwisely cultivated, public unity can generate totalitarianism and state worship, which Plato abhorred; yet the state, he declared, is an essential instrument for elevating human life to the highest level. A strong and diligent state ensures order and regularity, and both were essential conditions for the realization of human talent. Climbing a ladder to culture, decency, and civility, men and women need the confident assurance of law and authority; upon reaching the pinnacle of cultural perfection, law could be forgotten, because men and women would be ruled by ideals of truth and virtue.

Sparta's model was too clear to miss, and Plato imitated it; but where Sparta repressed men and women and made citizens civic automatons, the *Republic* promises a nicely coordinated political system prompting free and liberal citizens to excavate truth and virtue and thus realize their inherent human gifts. Once Plato's purpose is understood, his apparent capitulation to a doctrine of law and order is easier to tolerate. At its best, Plato concludes, education renders law and the authority of the state redundant.

Book II of the *Republic* reveals Plato's theory of educational control, and the *Laws* repeats it. A fifty-year interlude separating the composition of the *Republic* and the *Laws* did nothing to change Plato's mind. In the *Laws*, he introduces the "minister of education" and asserts "that of all the great offices of state this is the greatest; for the first shoot of any plant, if it makes a good start, has the greatest effect in helping it to obtain its mature natural excellence; and this is not only true of plants, but of animals wild and tame, and also of man." Then comes the frequently quoted pronouncement: "Man, as we say, is a tame and civilized animal; nevertheless, he requires proper instruction and a fortunate nature, and then of all animals he becomes the most divine and most civilized; but if he be insufficiently or ill educated he is the most savage of earthly creatures."[11] The minister of education was authorized to manage the schools, to issue regulations on disciplining children, to organize the curriculum, to prescribe methods of instruction, to define compulsory school age, and to make all necessary decisions.

Education for Women. In the ancient world, women lacked opportunity for intellectual refinement because, it was supposed, they were naturally and irreparably inferior to men. From time to time, this harsh appraisal was mitigated by giving girls domestic training and instruction in polite accomplishment, manners, and morals. Various accounts tell of exceptional women talented in poetry, music, or philosophy, but they were rare and, in any case, seldom benefited from schooling. With help from admiring parents, suitors, or husbands, and more often than not in stealth, they travelled solitary avenues to learning; their literary assets, whatever praise they deserve from their successors, were assessed by a curious public to be eccentric rather than pleasing.

This dark cloud of discrimination was cast over ancient Greece, too. In Sparta, women's contribution to the state, although noted and exploited, was assumed to be exclusively maternal. That Sparta was this liberal is probably praiseworthy, but it would be rash, and wrong, to suppose that the Spartans were progressive enough to contemplate equality of the sexes in education or anything else.

Sparta was a poor place for women, but Athens was worse. Athenian girls were offered training for domestic duty and for supervising their servants and slaves, but this was all. No side of ancient life escaped Plato's sharp eye: entirely familiar with the status of women, he knew that neither Sparta nor Athens was out of step with social convention. Yet he jettisoned convention that obstructed the political ideal: social and political unity were essential conditions for the public good, so some attention to the education of women for state service was imperative. A state aspiring to perfection could ill afford to ignore half its human resource. Still, praise for Plato should be restrained: despite prophetic anticipation, fundamental altruism was lacking, and it is closer to the truth to interpret Plato's bold recommendation as being generated in practical necessity rather than generous liberalism.

In the end, though, motive is less important than proposal: In Plato's progressive plan, the doors of schoolhouses were open to girls. His theory emancipated women, and, had it been adopted, their course of instruction would have been the same as for men.[12] In elementary and secondary schools, the sexes were to have been educated separately, but advanced schools were coeducational, because intelligence and enterprise, Plato averred, made gender irrelevant.

Plato's Recommendations for Elementary Education. The Academy's policy of admitting only the best students had its genesis in Plato's inflexible commitment to the preparation of political leaders. As a secondary school, and in some respects a junior college, the Academy counted on elementary schools to supply students with the tools of learning—reading, writing, and counting—as essential foundations to subsequent achievement. Lacking them, students could hardly expect to reap much profit from superior instruction in even the best of higher schools. Admitting this, and recalling, too, Plato's reason for founding the Academy in the first place, an overhaul of Athenian education would have been consistent with his educational idealism. But Plato stopped short. Clearly, he knew the worth of habits of discipline and thought learned early; for the most part, however, he found Athenian elementary education satisfactory.[13]

Still, some repair was necessary. Traditionally boys went to the primary school at about age seven. Plato worried about lost years and wondered if schooling should not begin earlier (say, at age three), thus using these years to develop favorable attitudes toward learning and to inculcate a genuine affection for excellence. Besides, play, toys, games, and various amusements could be employed to lay a foundation for later schooling. Progressive though he was, Plato had no illusion that learning is always fun or that excellence is possible without discipline, and he never supposed that schools were able to generate a basic good will toward learning: "The most important point about education is right training in the nursery."[14]

Rewording the dogmatic assumption that schooling begins at age seven, Plato nevertheless kept seven as the entering age for primary schools. And their curricula were amended by changing counting to calculation, for calculation, Plato said, strengthened the faculty of reason and was an essential prerequisite to dialectic. Old assertions that mathematics were too abstruse for schoolboys were rejected: Reason alone, Plato declared, is sufficient for a mastery of mathematics, and everyone, in some measure, possesses reason.[15]

Physical education, too, was hauled in for scrutiny. The efficacy of physical training, health, and gymnastics for making citizens went uncontested, but an overemphasis on sport could harden and dehumanize men's souls. Respected tradition recommended gymnastics for the body and music for the soul, and tradition was supposed to preserve their proper balance. In this frantic period, however, when some men, preoccupied with music, became soft and cowardly and others, caught up in the idealization of sport, pursued gymnastics to the exclusion of all else, music and gymnastics were out of balance.

Wrestling and dancing were the main culprits. Superiority in either never troubled Plato, because he was eager to praise excellence; but the spirit and environment of their practice conspired to destroy, rather than build, character. Wrestlers should strive for perfection, but an excessive zeal for defeating opponents led, Plato said, to brutality. Similarly, grace, harmony, and beauty of movement in dance were good and noble, but when dancers revelled in applause and praise they became base and professional. Plato's loyalty to sport could not conceal his disgust for professional athletes; and while he believed that human beings were naturally competitive, he wanted them to understand the difference between virtue and victory and nobility and notoriety.

The Music School. Plato knew the difference between reality and utopia, so the *Republic*'s plan was not designed for Athens. Yet an Athenian audience's conversance with education allowed him to move swiftly over elementary teaching to higher study. Redesigned along the lines already described, Athenian elementary schools seemed to be good enough to prepare boys for the college of utopia. But then Plato had second thoughts. Giving about equal attention to music and literature, did music schools build a foundation strong enough to bear the weight of later study for political leadership? Doubting that they did, Plato began again to reshape their academic character. Vocal and instrumental music had high priority in ancient life, and Plato is almost certainly sincere when he attributes heavenly birth to good music and credits it with shaping character. With this credential, music belonged in every curriculum, where its integrity would be insulated from innovation by sound instruction and, if necessary, by law.

Censoring Literature. Despite its worth, music needs help from literature. Homer's was best, but other poets—Simonides, Hesiod, Euripides, and Aristophanes—were prominent as well, and Plato made room for their stories in the curriculum. Literature's language bound men to common purpose by recounting heroic deed and recapitulating ideals that could inspire excellence. Yet literature has another side: poetic license permitted writers to dress up myth, indulge fiction, and to make error ornamental and truth base. With truth as an ideal and right opinion as a practical possibility, Plato restricted literature's freedom in the schools. The poets' fiction, which Plato called "lie," should not be allowed to compete with truth. Censorship has an ugly and unprogressive sound, but Plato might have been right. If character is molded largely by experience, can he be criticized for trying to control experience by suppressing a literature that misrepresents reality? Literature, however, was too important to education to be banned, so Plato declared that teachers should expurgate, select, and salvage parts of it for use in school.[16]

Unquestionably Plato endorsed censorship, but what was he protecting? Throughout most of education's long history, scrupulous persons have picked their way through the classics, excising anything that appeared offensive to morality and decency. Christian teachers, in years to come, condemned and excavated lewd and lascivious episodes in a treasury of classical literature. Their justification rested on moral grounds. But when Plato censored poetry, he was silent about morals and concentrated instead on myth that offended truth and, in consequence, contaminated the intellect.[17]

With music and literature tamed for school use, genuine mathematics were added to the curriculum.[18] With them in place, secondary education had the academic character that, without much success, the Sophists had tried to supply. Plato, we recall, included calculation in the primary-school course, and now number theory, geometry, and arithmetic are put in the music school. With them the program of secondary education was complete, and this program had enough durability to serve as a model for the nine-year secondary schools of the sixteenth century. When Plato reorganized the music school curriculum, he proposed that music, literature, and mathematics be studied intensively in successive three-year periods. These subjects, although proper to all parts of instruction, needed, Plato said, a time reserved for concentration.[19]

Plato on Sport. Ever faithful to tradition, Plato had affection for gymnastic training and sport. But besides affection, with their excesses stripped away, both were necessary to his school program. Acting partly on his own preference and partly on the place sport had in Greek life, a two- or three-year period when students left their books behind was reserved for the gymnasium.[20] Without distraction, physical education concentrated on the training of strong and dexterous bodies that were essential to the state's welfare. Besides, the gymnastic course was a test: it had a special gift for sorting men and women according to their capacities for the rigor of advanced study and leadership.[21]

Higher Education: Plato's Long Course. With a solid foundation in literature, music, and mathematics coupled with training in gymnastics and sport, the stage was set for higher study, for rigorous intellectual exercise designed to appeal to men and women whose talent was evident. Plato has Socrates say that higher learning should begin when gymnastics are over, and he is careful to add: gymnastic "training is useless for any other purpose; for sleep and exercise are unpropitious to learning; and the trial of whom is first in gymnastic exercise is one of the most important tests to which our youth are subjected."[22]

Students who survived, and now about twenty years old, should begin ten years of scientific study. Arithmetic, geometry, music, and astronomy were staples in the scientific course, and were studied to reveal "the natural relationship of them to one another and to true being."[23] After mining the secrets of science, students who passed this test of talent moved on to a five-year assessment of their meaning. Without teachers (for instruction on so advanced a level was impossible), they crossed the boundary line separating the known from the unknown and undertook, employing dialectical technique, to map the unbroken frontier of wisdom. If the promise of this dialectical enterprise were realized, its contribution to human welfare could be immense, but with landmarks absent or obscure, dialecticians could become mired in error without ever adverting to their danger. Plato, nevertheless, thought the promise of reward worth the risk.

Fortified by knowledge and standing on the threshold of wisdom, these scholars, whose ranks were thinned by constant tests of talent, should have been ready for positions as state leaders, but Plato's standard was high. He wanted more. Although about thirty-five and having spent the past twenty-eight years in study, these persons needed practical experience for welding theory to practice. For the next fifteen years, still preparing for political leadership, they were exposed as interns to the froth and foam of political reality. Now, after this long interlude spent with practical affairs of state, they were ready "when their turn comes, toiling also at politics and ruling for the public good, not as though they were performing some heroic action, but simply as a matter of duty" to occupy the political role for which these long and intensive years of study had prepared them.[24]

Plato's Influence. Plato's political and educational utopia achieved reality only on the pages of his books. Although philosophers and educators the world over have heeded Plato's wisdom without always following it, his educational program was never adopted anywhere.

As a school for exceptional students—the tale persists that women were there, too—the Academy has won universal praise. Aristotle, for example, found its intellectual climate invigorating enough to stay for twenty years. Its purpose, we know, was to educate political leaders. Yet evidence is lacking that Plato ever intended it to be a working model for his utopian educational program.

It would be a mistake to overstate Plato's influence and extravagant to declare that he monopolized educational philosophy, but on one point his advice was penetrating and permanent: The bedrock of education is truth, and truth is obtained only as a consequence of dedicated and determined effort. This allegiance to truth recommended a curricular emphasis on those studies capable of disciplining the mind and preparing it to accept truth. Whenever and wherever Plato was followed, the curricular core—those studies that were hospitable meeting places for good minds and from which even less talented youth were not excused—was composed of courses with an undisguised commitment to the cultivation of intellectual discipline through an expenditure of zealous effort. Flying the banner of discipline, Plato's educational doctrine was justified and promoted by educators who found this assertion persuasive: without discipline, any degree of excellence is impossible.

Isocrates (436–338 B.C.)

Called either a philosopher or a Sophist, Isocrates had to wrestle with a question of scholarly identity throughout his life. By his own testimony he was neither, although in a long, impressive career he aspired to both. Dominated by an urge to succeed, he wanted acclaim from the people of Athens as well. In various ways during a long and active life, he won attention and fame, and as a patriot tried to assure Athens' political stability by spreading her influence to all of Greece. Preoccupied with political policy, his career as a schoolmaster awaited the realization that education could shape Athens' political destiny, so he opened a school that resembled Plato's Academy and commissioned it to prepare political leaders.

Finding Isocrates' educational philosophy in dozens of essays and short books is a trying exercise, because he tried to tack his position to catch the wind of popular opinion. Although sophistry had aspects worth imitating, he found its skepticism repugnant and its ethical nihilism abhorrent. Everything Plato did had the mark of excellence, but being a carbon copy of Plato was unacceptable. Isocrates wanted to make a name for himself.

Life and Career. Born five years before the Great Peloponnesian War (431–421 and 414–404 B.C.), Isocrates had direct experience with the economic and social distortions of war. When his father was wealthy, Isocrates could afford the best teachers in Athens. Gorgias, the famous Sophist from Leontini, instructed him in oratory and, according to Plato, Socrates thought well of his talent for philosophy if "only some divine impulse" would lead him.[25] If life's circumstances had been different, Socrates might have been proved right, but now Isocrates was poor—his father was bankrupt—and unable to afford a career in philosophy. Required to work for a living, the prospect of making philosophy pay, if Socrates were a typical example, was dim, so, turning his back on philosophy and forsaking a chance to become a seeker after wisdom, Isocrates began practicing the profession of words and wrote orations for defendants in Athenian courts. During a twenty-year interlude as a writer of law-court speeches, Isocrates came to recognize the practical worth of eloquence and kindled an affection for rhetoric.

Tiring of writing speeches for others, disdaining an occupation isolating him from the public, Isocrates abandoned his legal briefs and, at about age forty-two, opened a school. His school attracted attention and prospered, and he became Plato's competitor. He essayed to promote a philosophy of education to attract students to his school rather than to the Academy or the schools of the Sophists.

Educational Theory. It was hard for Isocrates to be inventive, for Plato had preempted almost every theoretical stance opposing sophistry, and the Sophists themselves, always ingenious in practical matters, occupied the ground of pedagogic technique. So Isocrates' excursion into educational philosophy lacks the mark of originality, and scholars have been slow to recognize him as an educational philosopher. Yet leaping to the conclusion that, because his philosophy was neither comprehensive nor original, his influence on Western educational thought and practice was slight is misleading, and to endorse it blinds us to his contribution to education. Despite the range of Plato's and the Sophists' educational philosophy, Isocrates was left some room for maneuver.

Plato's, Isocrates', and the Sophists' ultimate educational objective was the same: all together they urged upon schools and teachers the state's imperative need for good citizens. In the last analysis, education's principal function is to generate civic virtue, and Plato said this could occur only when knowledge precedes action; the Sophists, however, dispensing with knowledge, were ready to rest their case on what a better argument could justify. They doubted that searching after truth would be rewarding, for knowledge (if any existed) was too elusive to be grasped. Isocrates tried to find a middle ground between these two positions and erect an educational plan upon it.

He began by calling the long years of study recommended by Plato a waste of time.[26] Truth, defined as a sufficiency of knowledge, could not escape persons of average intelligence, so a three- or four-year school course filled with general information ratified by common sense rather than by intensive research should be satisfactory for guiding prospective citizens. An ethical disposition to be always responsible and good was, in any event, better than knowledge about what ought to be done. But could this ethical disposition be taught? The Sophists said it could, but when this bold assertion caught them in a thicket of confusion, they embraced skepticism. Plato, doubting that virtue could be taught, was confident that knowledge of virtue could contribute to ethical conduct: How can persons choose what is best unless they know what is good?

Theory of Virtue. Debating the relationship between knowledge and virtue, Isocrates declared confidently, is futile, because moral virtue, or what is called "sound and decent character," is innate. Boys who come to school without virtue leave the same way, and nothing that teachers do matters. But naturally virtuous boys might become effective citizens and superior political leaders if learning cultivates their virtue, and it in turn, by influencing the conduct of others, will ensure the state's welfare. Taking Isocrates at his word, teachers forgot about investing time and attention in moral formation and concentrated on giving students enough dependable information to function effectively in society.[27]

Knowledge was essential to success, and Isocrates paid it reverence, but knowledge was incapable of affecting a person's natural disposition toward good or evil. Yet, in emancipating teachers from responsibility for moral formation, Isocrates refused to authorize moral neutrality: well-schooled but evil men are dangerous; unschooled they lack the eloquence to disrupt and mislead society.[28] In Isocrates' version of pedagogical integrity, teachers were commissioned to admit virtuous youth to their classrooms and instruct them in social and political effectiveness, and they were told to expel boys whose moral disposition was blighted.[29]

Political Leadership. Despite Isocrates' aspiration to be a neutral arbiter affecting politics with judicious and eloquent analyses, his latent fear of democracy led him to take sides. As part of a loyal, aristocratic opposition, he, like Socrates, worried about the political consequences of decisions made by citizens unprepared for, perhaps incapable of, self-government. Trying to stem the democratic tide could be both futile and dangerous—it had put Socrates in deep trouble—but Isocrates was clever enough to escape jeopardy and, at the same time, articulate a responsible political analysis publicly.[30]

Unable to make a commitment to philosophy and thus fulfill Socrates' prophecy, yet finding the turmoil of an active political life distasteful, Isocrates ended up as a moralist and a political pundit. Wanting to be effective in shaping the state's destiny, he turned, one way, to political journalism and, another, to education. As a journalist he tried to preserve decent, traditional political priorities; and to promote education's contribution to politics, he grafted eloquence to the school's syllabus and charged it to make political prudence, or common sense political morality, appealing and effective. No one, not even the Sophists, matched Isocrates' determination to teach students to use written and oral language clearly and persuasively.[31]

Isocrates illustrates the validity of the maxim that one who refuses to engage in political life forsakes the chance to influence it. He only analyzed Athenian politics, but in education, by opening a school and expounding on pedagogy, he made indelible marks on theory and practice. His work as a schoolmaster is worth a closer look.

Isocrates the Schoolmaster. Being a teacher in Athens was one thing: the city had plenty of primary masters, citharists, paidotribes and gymnasts; to erect a school good and ornamental enough to compete with the Academy and the Sophists was something else. Understanding the effectiveness of words and appreciating the worth of advertising, Isocrates published a short book, *Against the Sophists,* to outline the general regimen of his new school and to parade the weaknesses he alleged to the schools of his competitors. *Against the Sophists* is a less forthcoming prospectus than we might like, but it has the distinction of being the first school or college catalogue.

Against the Sophists, coupled with the amazing durability of Isocrates' school and the often redundant *Antidosis*—a book preoccupied
with justifying Isocrates' career—gives a fairly complete view of the most
famous school of antiquity. Conventional elementary education satisfied
the exigent Plato, and Isocrates appears to be satisfied too. When boys
left the music school and gymnasium, Isocrates' school was ready for
them, gave them a three- or four-year course similar to a contemporary
American high school, and launched them into civic life.[32]

Convinced that sophistry was a fad, Isocrates declared its practice
vulgar and its philosophy of education puerile. The usual sophistic course
was too short to transmit knowledge effectively, and the one speech its
students learned could never qualify as a substitute for genuine instruction in oratory. In addition, nothing was done to impress upon students
their obligation to practice responsible oratory. For the Sophists, Isocrates said (and he was striking the center of the target), making the
better argument, regardless of the consequences attendant on winning a
debate, was all that counted. Plato, though, stood on firmer philosophical
and pedagogical ground; so Isocrates tried to demonstrate that his academic theory and practice were superior to Plato's.

Practical Knowledge. Plato had a virtual monopoly over philosophy,
although philosophy was seldom, if ever, a staple in the Academy's curriculum, and Athenians were infatuated with a science of reason that promised to teach them about truth and justice; so Isocrates challenged Plato
on this point. Claiming for himself the title of a genuine philosopher,[33]
Isocrates dismissed Plato's philosophy as a bundle of pretension. Rather
than being a dreamer finding satisfaction in chasing unattainable intellectual and moral virtue, Isocrates declared a commitment to a body of
practical knowledge essential to the management of domestic and civic
affairs. Only knowledge contributing to responsible oratory and giving
practical direction to conduct was worthy of being called "philosophy."
This philosophy (what Plato called "prudence") could, Isocrates averred,
be taught quickly and effectively, although never effortlessly, to schoolboys. Marking time, as in Plato's long course, before tackling the hard
business of translating principle into policy and practice and transporting
philosophy from the schoolroom to real life was repudiated.

Scholars disagree in appraising Isocrates' definition of philosophy, of
his converting it from a speculative enterprise to an art of living, but this
much is certain: his students became eloquent citizens and effective political leaders. They were the best advertisement for a school where care with
educational technique more than philosophical investigation made it the
envy of the ancient world.[34]

Pedagogic Technique: Care and Imitation. Taking a leaf from the paidotribes' book on physical training, Isocrates adopted two techniques for use in literary and oratorical instruction: care and imitation.[35] Care was interpreted to mean that only a few students could be taught. Zealously adhering to this principle, Isocrates always limited his school's enrollment to about ten students a year.[36] Books and other material for instruction were scarce and expensive, so students were taught individually. Yet Isocrates used a class method of instruction for recitation and oratorical practice. And here we begin to see slight differences in emphasis between Plato's and Isocrates' pedagogy. In the Academy, teaching was mainly informal, occurring in casual, at least unconventional, scholastic settings (such as the dining room) where the art of discourse and the friction of mind on mind were practiced. Exercise and practice, and pedagogy capable of encouraging mental refinement, were used by Isocrates, too, but frivolity was suppressed, and banquet halls never became classrooms.

Important as care was, imitation had precedence. Instruction began with a curriculum of grammar, composition, essay writing, elocution, history, jurisprudence, citizenship, religion, ethics, philosophy, political science, geography, and strategy. Mathematics and science, studies Plato prized, are absent, but Isocrates wanted his students to master conventional information and not waste time testing the authenticity of knowledge at every turn of the scholastic road. Having equal standing with knowledge to equip students to write speeches full of meaning was facility in the use of language. Regardless of the number of subjects in the curriculum or the intensity of their study, the school's main purpose was to teach rhetoric for which rules and models were essential.

Rules, Models, and Practice. The rules and models in Isocrates' repertoire were not always original, but he was inventive in converting them into instructional technique. Isocrates' first models—Homer and lesser known Greek poets—were sometimes inappropriate for illustrating political oratory, so substitutes had to be found. The substitutes were usually of Isocrates' own creation, and in preparing them he showed considerable psychological insight by enlisting student help. With his direction and guidance, students revised and polished their compositions, learned by demonstration and doing, and in the end produced permanent models for scholastic oratory.

With rules and models in their possession, students moved on to drill. Under the solicitous direction of their teacher, and as a class rather than individually, they repeated their lessons. The aim was mastery. Nothing on the level of necessary knowledge escaped unrelenting, repeated attention. Polished oratory was the great goal, but Isocrates was wise enough to know that a speech without solid, dependable content could not be convincing.[37]

After students mastered their lessons, Isocrates introduced them to formal rhetoric. They wrote speeches and delivered them to the class; thereafter, the orations were criticized and corrected publicly by students and Isocrates himself. The details of rhetorical instruction would be burdensome here, but this much is clear: Isocrates paralleled his teaching with the techniques commonly used by paidotribes, stressed diagnostic procedure in the preparation and delivery of speeches, allowed ample time for practice, revision, and application, and aimed at fluency. On his record of having produced the finest orators of ancient Greece Isocrates' reputation as the most famous schoolmaster of antiquity rests.

Isocrates' Influence. The history of philosophy, filled with thousands of references to Plato, pays scant heed to Isocrates. For the most part, history is right, for Isocrates, despite his own opinion, lacked genuine philosophical credentials; but his contribution to educational practice was impressive and educational historians who neglect him miss the architect of literary humanism. Plato, we remember, made mathematics and science the foundations of learning. Calling these studies the common meeting place for good minds, he gave them prominence in his school program, but his example was only infrequently followed. Isocrates, however, taking a different view of human excellence, made literature the curricular core and called upon literature and language to cultivate expression as the supreme human ability.

The excellence of his school made this decision all the more persuasive, and throughout Western education's history, the practical advice of Isocrates was adopted by teachers and educational philosophers. Besides, Isocrates' commitment to the culture of Greece led him to define education's principal function as cultural transmission, and cultural transmission has no alternative but to depend upon skill in the use of words.[38] Life's most fundamental experience reposed in the classics, Isocrates thought, and could be reaped only with rhetorical skill. Persons conversant with the ageless wisdom of the classics, privy to its ideas and ideals, and capable of clever, elegant expression were, Isocrates declared, soundly educated. And because they were fluent, they could be a positive influence on the whole of society.

Whether coincidence, accident, or conviction led Isocrates' pedagogic successors to adopt literary humanism and make it their academic creed, Isocrates blazed a trail for them to follow. His definition of schools as literary agencies committed to eloquence went almost unchallenged well into the nineteenth century. Perpetuated by the classical tradition, a refinement of the human abilities of thought and expression was the final outcome of literary humanism. Throughout education's history, this schoolmaster of antiquity had a profound and permanent influence upon the curriculum and purpose of secondary schools.

Aristotle (384–322 B.C.)

Born in the Macedonian town of Stageira, the son of a court physician, educated for twenty years—from age seventeen to thirty-seven—in Plato's Academy, Aristotle was not an Athenian citizen. Aliens were excluded from political debate in Athens, where education was a branch of politics, so he had to be careful about educational pronouncement. Search is vain for his appraisal of Athenian scholastic practice. Unprotected by convention, Sophists were fair game, and Aristotle's hostility to them was expressed without making Athenian education an issue.[39] In the absence of a book on educational philosophy,[40] one must go to Aristotle's school, where one is illustrated, and to books on politics and ethics where the subject is introduced.

The Lyceum. Five years after leaving the Academy, Aristotle became tutor to Alexander the Great (356–323 B.C.). After seven years with Alexander, Aristotle returned to Athens and opened a school. Two stories circulate with respect to the relationship between the Lyceum and the Academy: one makes the Lyceum an extension of the Academy, a satellite whose principal purpose was to complement Plato's famous school; the other asserts complete independence for the Lyceum, without leading strings to the Academy, and with an educational approach different from Plato's.[41]

Now forty-nine, with a reputation for scholarship, Aristotle was ready to test a novel educational philosophy: scientific empiricism. He discarded the dialectical method because it allowed personal disposition and emotion to interfere with the educational process and impede the pursuit of truth. Scientific empiricism sent students to the study of persons and institutions, and it sent them, too, to the natural world, where they could classify and compile data. With minds filled with information, they could employ deductive reasoning to arrive at dependable conclusions.

We know less about the day-to-day activity of the Lyceum than we do of the Academy or Isocrates' school. Yet some things are fairly clear. Aristotle prized writing as an instrument of learning, so students spent long hours at their writing desks. But this alone could hardly make the school's pedagogy unique, for Plato's and Isocrates' students wrote too.

Still, there was a difference: composition in Aristotle's school was scientific prose, possibly a new genre, with a style paring away both the poetic prose of the Academy and the rhythmic elocution of Isocrates' school. With versatile pens, Plato's students expressed rational truth clearly, prudently, persuasively, and artistically. Isocrates' students, dispensed from pursuing truth, were preoccupied with eloquence. But Aristotle's students were expected to report the data of experience and to codify and classify them without rhetorical embellishment.[42]

Lyceum students did more than write descriptive essays. Most of their time was spent in direct classroom instruction. Plato's students debated and discussed everything, but the Lyceum was unfriendly to dialectic. Its instruction concentrated upon communicating information and, jealous of time for learning, reserved few moments for arguing about what had been learned. Lectures were the Lyceum's principal teaching method, and teachers armed with charts, pictures, and diagrams illustrated and amplified their content. Inspired by intuition, an Academy student might leap forward to change places with the teacher, but in the Lyceum conventional instructional decorum was heeded, and students knew, and kept, their place. Aristotle, moreover, was a public teacher. In addition to school lectures, he gave public lectures open to anyone who wanted to attend.

Emphases in Aristotle's scholastic approach that reveal the Lyceum's distinctive character are scientific empiricism and indifference to the dialectic method. But these emphases could not obscure the similarities between the Academy and the Lyceum. Both were communities of scholars, although, because the students tended to stay longer, the Academy community was more closely knit than the Lyceum's, whose clientele was varied. Neither school followed the sophistic practice of contracting with students, and neither charged tuition, although gifts were accepted, and probably encouraged, from satisfied students. Yet money for tuition was no barrier to attendance at either school. Being wealthy, neither Plato nor Aristotle needed income from teaching. Still, there is the amusing story of two students who, working for a miller after school, earned money to support themselves through the Lyceum. Working students, however, are unheard of in the Academy.

Finally, neither school prescribed philosophical orthodoxy, good evidence that, as secondary schools, they essayed to offer basic education rather than promote philosophical positions. This liberal policy was evident in the Academy where Aristotle, who sometimes differed from Plato on substantial philosophical issues, was treated with civility and respect and never suffered from any infringement of academic freedom. Both schools abandoned the convention of catering to the sons of wealthy and prominent citizens, but considering the social habits of Athenians, neither was a genuinely democratic institution.

Political Philosophy and Education. In books seven and eight of the *Politics*, Aristotle inquired into education's proper function and whether it should be public or private. "All art and education," he declared, "aim at filling up nature's deficiencies."[43] Intellectual, moral, and physical capacity is the foundation whereupon all education rests, but this natural endowment can be improved by carefully formed habits. "We learn some things by habit and some by instruction," so any learning unaccounted for by habit belongs to the province of instruction.[44]

Depending upon habit and instruction, education leads persons to happiness; all its resources should be used to this end. To immunize persons from vulgarization as schooling equips them to seek for happiness, an essential safeguard is introduced. Neither students nor teachers, depending solely upon personal experience, have the wisdom for choosing what is best. Help is needed and it comes, if it comes at all, from the state, for the state is the ultimate reservoir of social, political, and educational wisdom. It must define desirable political and social objectives and supervise the molding of youthful disposition toward their attainment by controlling both schools and teachers.[45] And educational officers, acting as state agents, must be guided by reason and prudence.

Public Education. This design for public education, Aristotle admitted, might be imperfect, but it is better than abandoning education to the whim or personal opinion of students, parents, and schoolmasters. His justification for this bold position was vigorous: First, the stability of society depends upon the cultivated intelligence and moral sensitivity of its citizens, and as a political society, the state has the right to sustain itself; second, all political societies have a supreme objective to serve the common good, and this can be done only with a system of education capable of disposing everyone to work habitually for the good of all; third, state educational control can provide for uniform educational opportunity and a common social outlook; and finally, a common acceptance of moral and social value is cultivated by sound learning, and according to Aristotle, state-controlled education offers the best chance to ensure sound learning.

Having found education's principal bases in natural endowment and state control, Aristotle moved on to consider other issues. He had something to say about the curriculum, although—probably out of a sense of political insecurity—innovation was seldom promoted. Almost without amendment, he endorsed conventional Athenian schools. Gymnastics, the Greeks maintained, help build strong bodies and good moral habits, so

Aristotle acknowledging that education's primary function is to form character pays them special heed. Music, too, including the literary monuments of Greece, was ratified. None of this could put Aristotle or his school in jeopardy.

Yet Aristotle's urge to escape any charge of political subversion does not explain his reluctance to blaze a new curricular trail. It is explained, rather, in the genuine conviction that on schooling's lower levels the transmission of information is less important than the shaping of character. Relatively little stock was put in the stories of the classical authors, and it hardly troubled him when a boy stumbled over long passages from Homer or Hesiod, but he was vitally concerned about the kind of virtue this scholastic experience inculcated.

He refused to endorse the sophistic boast that knowledge is virtue, and he doubted, moreover, that direct ethical instruction had much influence on the formation of character, so he delegated schools to maintain a social environment to ennoble students' souls. Finally, in commissioning schools with liberal rather than practical objectives, he called upon them to be solicitous of the soul's genuine vocation to virtue rather than to bodily appetite, and directed them to teach necessary things without vulgarizing their students.

Quick to admit that moral virtue—good character—comes from habit and instruction rather than from nature, because persons are born morally neutral, Aristotle recommended that teaching invest attention in the techniques associated with imitation and emulation in order to make the grand ideas of heroes, generals, and orators become the personal possession of students. Yet, even adopting the thesis that imitation could help shape character, Aristotle stopped short of saying that virtue can be taught the same way that knowledge of things can be communicated. In the end, wedding educational and speculative philosophy, Aristotle was responsible for the scholarly tradition that education is a rational enterprise, whose policies and practices are necessarily the outcome of reason.

Aristotle's Influence. Aristotle's reputation in the history of educational thought rests upon his work as a scientist, philosopher, and teacher, but his stature in intellectual history has little to do with his philosophy of education or his profession as a schoolmaster. Aristotle was, nevertheless, the principal model for a cadre of scholars who habitually subordinated educational to speculative philosophy. His educational philosophy appears mainly as commentary, a long footnote or a short paragraph, in books on politics, ethics, and metaphysics. So one finds Aristotle's philosophy of education in rational principle that started with metaphysics (the nature of human beings and the universe), added politics and ethics, and ended up with rational psychology. Reason and knowl-

edge, he concluded, are the architects for designing an educational process whose moral and intellectual standard inspires all persons to seek for
happiness as the ultimate human objective.

Reading Aristotle to learn about educational organization (except for
the state's role) and the purpose and content of schools and colleges shall
almost surely be disappointing. He stayed with philosophical principles
and neglected their translation to practice, so the treasure in his educational thought is found in rational principle. But this was work too hard to
be appealing to his successors. Apart from Plutarch (A.D. 45–125) (whose
The Education of Children[46] imitated Aristotle), some anonymous Syrian
scholars, a few erudite Hellenistic educational theorists, and the wisest
schoolmen of the Middle Ages, few educational philosophers followed in
his footsteps. Despite monumental accomplishments in philosophy and
science, Aristotle's shadow over education was never as long as Plato's and
Isocrates'.

Chapter 3

The Hellenistic Age:
Education for Cultural Transmission

Greek city-states were preoccupied with territorial expansion, and ancient history attests to their colonization and exploitation of the Mediterranean world. Motives for expansion, doubtless, were mixed, but economic acquisitiveness was primary. Colonial revenue helped to keep taxes low, stimulated economic activity, and allowed the merchant and commercial classes to thrive. Colonial policy was geared for promoting the domestic welfare rather than for planting culture and civilization in foreign soil.

Until about 350 B.C., and over the protest of Isocrates, who counseled manifest destiny,[1] Greek city-states were satisfied with colonial policy. Their most eloquent patriots—say, Demosthenes (385?–322 B.C.)—declaimed against exporting culture to barbarians[2] and justified their objection by arguing that Greek culture was either too precious to be shared or that its assets were too low to stand the drain of export. Jealous of their culture, they guarded it as a national treasure.

This policy of cultural conservation might have gone unamended had it not been for a social metamorphosis that came in the wake of Philip of Macedon's (382–336 B.C.) conquests and the policies of military expansion and world dominion adopted by his son, Alexander the Great. When Philip was assassinated in 336 B.C., Greece had been brought to heel; but earlier, Philip's attention had drifted from affairs of state. Divorcing his first wife, he married a second who, if her station had been lower, would have been kept as a concubine. Amid these princely diversions, some Greek city-states risked secession and formed the Thessalian Federation.[3] Thus affairs stood when Philip died.

Upon ascending the throne, Alexander the Great undertook to restore his father's domain. He suppressed insurrection in Greece so swiftly and effortlessly that hardly a Greek hand was raised to stall him. Marvelling at his military prowess, and now repentant, the Greeks, with a little urging, elected Alexander their supreme general. With Greece secure, he hungered for greater conquest and, with an ambition to become the emperor of the world, sent his army to overrun vast areas of Asia and northern Africa where it conquered a native population thought to be of little intelligence and courage, fit only for slavery.

No stranger to Greek culture (after all, Aristotle was his teacher), it was perhaps natural for Alexander to suppose it superior, well worth transplanting in conquered lands for tranquilizing barbarian people. Eventually, though, culture could do better work: fastening itself to life in these conquered lands, its genius could spread. For all his military zeal, Alexander was too brilliant to miss the civilizing and humanizing influence of the culture to which he himself had converted.

Alexander's preconception about the native ability of the Egyptians, Cappadocians, Mesopotamians, Babylonians, Indians, and others in Asia and Africa was wrong. Their armies were weak but their intellectual and social tradition was strong. Following a benign, sensible policy, Alexander redressed his earlier misconception about his new subjects and allowed them to follow the ways of their ancestors. Even so, Greek immigrants, some of whom had marched with Alexander's legions, infected these annexed people with cultural convictions similar to their own. Eventually the Greek spirit of inquiry, of culture, and of life came to dominate the countries which once had formed part of Alexander's Empire. This Hellenization occurred when Greek settlers, first, and then non-Greeks embraced Greek cultural ideals and undertook to convert the Alexandrian world to a cultural legacy that had reached its epitome in classical Greece.[4]

The Spirit of Hellenism

The Hellenistic age began with Alexander's conquests and ended in the second century A.D. when, although some fusion of Greek and Roman culture was permanent, Roman schools were organized to perpetuate the Latin heritage. With Roman dominion over most of Alexander's old empire, the cultural force of Hellenism was diluted.

Before Rome mustered enough self-confidence to chart her own educational course, Hellenism had been solidly welded to Roman life. So, although appearing to march alone, Roman education kept step with an invisible but influential Hellenism. At this point especially, the significance of Rome in the history of Western education is striking: had it not been for Rome's nurturing, the classical Greek inheritance might have died a premature death.[5]

A popular ledger, sometimes kept by educational historians, credits Rome equally with Greece for the classical inheritance, but a more precise record makes Greece the principal benefactor and Rome a precocious beneficiary. Long before Virgil's (70–19 B.C.) *Aeneid* inaugurated a genuine Latin literature, Romans were infatuated with the Greek legacy. For the most part, however, this infatuation came from a cultural association with Hellenistic rather than classical Greece. Secondhand, this legacy had been transplanted from Athens, and elsewhere in Greece, to Asia Minor and northern Africa where it was zealously husbanded.

Over the centuries, residents of the Hellenistic world made pilgrimages to Athens, expecting to renew allegiance to a cultural past; to their dismay, they found the classical legacy dormant. Unpracticed in life, its treasure had to be rescued from literary sources. Hellenists learned then what their successors mastered by arduous effort: to discover and understand the values of earlier societies, the best guide is literature. So Hellenists committed to restoring Greek culture opened the books to mine from them the classical standard of human excellence. This was slow work and few Hellenistic scholars were equipped for it. Their lack of skill, though, may have been a blessing in disguise, for they were not yet ready to follow the subtleties and apprehend the full meaning of the books they undertook to explicate.[6]

Committed to imitating their ancestors, Hellenists idealized life in the classical age. Culture became their faith, and they began by living in a past portrayed in the classics where fiction, not dependable history, dramatized human vision, virtue, and wisdom. If the classics were reservoirs of culture, literary skill was essential for reading and understanding them. Little wonder that education was thought to be important, although as it prospered in Hellenistic cities and towns, it became clear that schools would have to be different from those of the classical age.

Schools and school programs were designed to accommodate cultural objectives, and some features of classical education were preserved. One was education's aristocratic character, but this feature, although a natural consequence of Athenian life, seldom involved schools. Other, better ways, classical educators thought, could graft time-tested values to young minds, so they restricted schools to the humble task of teaching reading, writing, and counting. This confidence in the efficacy of informal social education had been rewarded both in archaic Greece and classical Athens, but the Hellenistic world lacked a living classical culture capable of infusing social education with meaning and spirit. If traditional ideals were to be communicated, something better than oral tradition and the social transactions of city life were needed.

Education for Cultural Transmission. While paying allegiance to education's aristocratic character, Hellenists, nevertheless, changed its form. Instead of cultural communication being left to chance, it became a formal objective, and schools concentrated attention upon literary accomplishment. Making cultural transmission education's primary goal, and commissioning the schools as literary agencies, may have been Hellenism's most important scholastic contribution to the West. At the same time, interest in educational philosophy was renewed.

Important as these contributions were, they did not occur suddenly. It took time for the casual features of classical education to atrophy. Sport, for example, had a prominent place in classical life; excellence in it was a mark of an educated citizen. Some philosophers had worried about the excesses of sport and condemned professionalism, yet sport's claim on education was strong throughout the classical period and an educational commonplace in early Hellenistic centuries. Time, however, took its toll and, although sport remained as part of everyday life and gymnasiums were maintained in every Hellenistic city, sport declined in the schools. A literature filled with ideals Hellenists resolved to honor, and one equipped to revitalize the spirit of Greek antiquity, took its place.

Rejecting little from the classical inheritance, Hellenism synthesized and symbolized more than it generated and created. It stood at a cultural crossroad to embrace, integrate, and perpetuate the classical tradition. In this respect, for the future of education, it might have been more important than classical education.

Important as Hellenism was to education's future, its contemporary significance should not be discounted. Alexander created an empire and gave it absolute authority over subordinate jurisdictions, although authority was sometimes delegated to cities and towns. The autonomy of the ancient city-state had no counterpart in Hellenistic cities, for they lacked the moral and political authority to control their inhabitants. With a supreme central government, nothing in these Hellenistic municipalities reminded their residents of the allegiance Athenians paid to their city.

The moral and political weakness of Hellenistic cities impeded a revival of Greek patriotism, but it had the effect of keeping alive the classical inheritance reposing in the books. If city life could have kindled patriotism, it would have superseded the literary legacy, but without any semblance of autonomy, the cities' political culture was unequal to the task. At this point the importance of literary education becomes clearer; it, almost alone, could supply the moral bases for individual and social discipline. Despite its cultural worth, the first duty of Hellenistic education was practical.

Culture, however, could not be neglected, so as the decades passed, and as Hellenists became more familiar with an Athenian humanism illustrated most ornamentally in the golden age of Pericles (d. 429 B.C.), they expected education to do more than set the foundations for discipline.

They wanted it to assume responsibility for shaping the personality of the people, but this goal was always too great for schools to achieve, despite its appeal. Educators talked about the educational consequences of social life and pretended that classical society had been reborn. Their pretense overburdened the schools and led to a conflict between scholastic expectation and realization, one that renewed interest in educational philosophy.

Hellenistic Educational Philosophy

Political discipline in the empire curtailed the participation of citizens in civic affairs. An Athenian citizen had pride in political activity, but in a regime where authority was vested in and executed by an absolute monarch, an exercise of political initiative was foreclosed. Even military duty, once the exclusive right of citizens, was reserved for mercenaries. And political oratory, a rhetorical genre that had matured in democratic Athens for hammering out affairs of state, was proscribed by an exigent government that refused to countenance debate about public policy.

Men of wit and intelligence were deprived of opportunity for useful political thought and action. Their talent would lie fallow unless it were employed in connection with education, the one topic whereupon, for some inexplicable reason, state policy was indifferent. The Hellenistic state missed the political significance of education and, moreover, refused to heed Plato's and Aristotle's cogent argument making educational control one of the state's principal responsibilities.[7] Its indifference to education made the field of educational philosophy a safe territory over which fertile minds could roam.

It took clever scholars only a short time to discover that education's objective of cultural transmission needed their attention. The implication was evident: Schools had to become literary institutions. Without dispute, scholars turned to answering this question: How should school programs be designed to ensure cultural transmission?

Educational Philosophy: An Independent Discipline. Urged on by this question, educational philosophy carved out for itself a prominent and independent place as a new academic discipline. Prominence came easily in an age eager to invest capital and confidence in education. Independence came harder. Plato, Isocrates, and Aristotle had speculated about preparing virtuous citizens and had subordinated educational philosophy to politics and ethics. Now, however, as almost the sole intellectual field left for men of talent and industry to cultivate, educational philosophy seceded from politics and ethics and began to stand on its own.

Despite its independence, this new educational philosophy almost always suffered from comparison with the work of Plato, Isocrates, and

Aristotle. And no Socrates was around to prick minds and trouble consciences. All the same, it was sturdy enough to call attention to education and the need for principle to govern scholastic practice.

The intense industry of educational philosophers can be illustrated by a few examples.[8] Aristippus (ca. 435–350 B.C.), who belongs to the early part of the period, and Clearchus of Soli (third century B.C.) wrote books entitled *On Education* which recited the literary skill students needed in order to read and understand the classics.[9] Theophrastus (ca. 370–286 B.C.), Aristotle's successor as headmaster of the Lyceum, wrote *Of the Education of Kings* and *A Polemical Discussion of the Theory of Eristic Argument.*[10] In the first of these books, he evidences an eagerness to endorse absolute monarchy and recommends a superior education for kings; the second book exhibits a technical discussion on rhetoric. The classics' authors had employed rhetoric, so Hellenistic students needed to know it in order to understand them. Aristoxenus[11] (third century B.C.) produced the *Rules of Pedagogy*, and Cleanthes (ca. 331–232 B.C.) wrote five books: *Of Education, Of Usage, Of Dialectic, Of Moods or Tropes,* and *Of Predicates.* Although the worth of books by too busy writers is sometimes distrusted, Cleanthes' were good enough for Quintilian (A.D. 35–97), the great Roman educator, to quote from them in *The Education of an Orator.*[12] Zeno (ca. 333–261 B.C.) was preoccupied with Stoic philosophy, but he found time to write *Of Greek Education* and *A Handbook of Rhetoric.*[13] In *Concerning Pedagogues*, Cleomenes (second century B.C.) reminded his readers that pedagogues were moral masters whose services were still important.[14]

Separation of Learning from Life. This scholarly industry, probably regularly duplicated by others whose work has perished, is evidence of a healthy interest in education. Nothing before could match it in abundance. This was a good omen, but in its eagerness to justify the primacy of cultural transmission, educational philosophy allowed school learning to be severed from life. This severance might have been implicit in cultural doctrine, yet on the level of educational practice, it meant that schools could be indifferent to natural learning situations in everyday life. The assumption was clear: ideals and values paraded in classical literature superseded anything students might meet in daily life, and this commitment to literature as a superior school objective protected those humble curricular auxiliaries essential to a competent understanding of literature. Skill in reading was essential for maintaining cultural links with the past, but skill alone could not ensure an understanding of classical literature whose vocabulary, style, and category were both novel and difficult for Hellenistic students. As aids to understanding literature, grammar and rhetoric were endorsed as essential school studies.

The Integrity of the School. Although Hellenistic education can be indicted for basking in the literary culture of the classical age, educational philosophy managed to guarantee the place of the school in education. Besides, it justified the professional intellectual's vocation to learning and scholarship. Without learning and scholarship to disclose them, the meaning and significance of the classics would have remained hidden for a long time, possibly forever. Because of the special value Hellenists attributed to the Greek legacy, scholars capable of probing its meaning were elevated to positions of prestige and wealth. Cultured minds were prizes worth having, and schools could help produce them.

State Control of Education. Educational philosophy achieved scholastic independence, but the accomplishments of the great Greek philosophers could not be ignored. Some ancient theorists idealized the state's role in education, but while stopping short of this, neither Plato nor Aristotle counseled state indifference to education. Hellenistic educators tried to follow suit, although on this point they turned out to be poor imitators. So, throughout the greater part of the Hellenistic period, the state was aloof from schools and education, and this aloofness persisted until Rome discovered how both could help the state. Nevertheless, the Roman state's activity in education was only a faint copy of Plato's recommendation. Its grasp of state educational control was half-hearted and incomplete.

Hellenistic educational philosophy was better at imitation than at innovation, yet it showed signs of boldness with respect to the education of women. Plato might have inspired it, but in any case, girls and boys began to attend the usual literary schools, and girls were permitted, although probably not encouraged, to play in the palaestra and exercise in the gymnasium.

Schools in the Hellenistic Age

Scholastic organization in this era is shrouded in some mystery. School objectives were clear, but, because cities were free agents in education, generalization about school structure is hazardous. Schools lacked good classical models to imitate, so cities, eager to exercise their educational independence, allowed imagination to roam in designing schools.

Despite the appearance of scholastic divergence from city to city, some features common to pedagogical practice and curricular content emerge. Although the tendency to prize diversity and variety went undiminished, no city took its educational autonomy so seriously as to countenance indifference to the schools' obligation to transmit the cultural legacy. This feature was universal and, in the end, had a more penetrating influence than differences in school organization from city to city, titles of educational officers from one place to another, or civic relationship between schools and municipalities.[15]

Sport Disappears from Schools. Every city of any size seems to have had gymnasia, but their character varied enormously. Some, imitating their classical ancestors, followed a syllabus of sport. Others, as sporting clubs for adults, encouraged exercise and sport, but their main purpose was social. Still others, taking a page from the Sophists' book of pedagogic priority, introduced lectures on rhetoric, conducted dialectical encounters, and promoted literary studies.

Recalling the attention classical education paid physical conditioning and development, and the Hellenists' determination to imitate their Greek ancestors, the deterioration of physical education in the schools is surprising. This scholastic side to the sporting picture, though, is unrepresentative of sport's place in life and the allegiance Hellenists paid it. Physical education and sport were used in Athens to induct youth into a life of leisure and culture; and anything perpetuating the ideals and values of the past was fervently embraced by Hellenists, so sport had an enthusiastic reception in a broad, although unacademic, educational program. Without exception, Hellenistic cities and towns had sporting facilities, where young and old, men and women, boys and girls, played their games and mastered a variety of athletic skills. Unquestionably the sporting tradition was both prized and praised.

Perceptive educational philosophers justified sport, and tradition recommended physical education. Yet the usual schools declared sport inconsistent with literary objective. Apart from *ephebia* and gymnasia, Hellenistic schools refused to conduct or supervise athletic training and contests. Still, sport was essential, and every Hellenist counted the social grace and physical benefit from it to be consistent with educational decency.

Throughout life, Hellenists patronized sporting clubs, and when skill and condition matched enthusiasm, they competed in athletic contests. Imitating the disposition of their Greek forebears, they sought competition and savored the honor of athletic superiority. If this were not enough, they played and exercised for the sheer fun of it. Hellenistic towns resembled vast playgrounds whereupon an extensive and various clientele satisfied its appetite for sport. Coaches and trainers were ready to instruct anyone, and their students paid them directly.

Although preference for sport varied, running, jumping, wrestling, boxing, and throwing the discus and javelin were the beneficiaries of special attention. Both children and adults engaged and sought excellence in these activities. The missing sport is swimming, a skill most ancient people thought important and one that most of them possessed. Yet neither in the classical gymnasium nor in Hellenistic physical education does it appear prominently and, sometimes, not at all.

The Elementary School

With the exception of schools kept by extraordinary masters, the order of school studies was haphazard. Educational philosophers, especially those who speculated about learning, had recommended a solid foundation of fundamental skill and basic knowledge whereupon higher learning could stand. But most teachers engaged in introducing children to the first elements of letters were poorly equipped to ponder the complexities of pedagogic technique. They taught what they knew, hoped to produce good results, and maintained a decent respect for their work.

Such scholastic definition (or its lack) suited the classical age, although Plato and Isocrates, for example, had recommended sturdier and better planned elementary studies, and Aristotle had deployed a logical order of study imperative to superior learning.[16] Despite mild protest, only infrequently heeded, revision of elementary studies waited until general educational objectives were altered, but alteration was slow to come despite the commitment Hellenistic education made to cultural transmission. When it did, schools became full-fledged literary agencies and designed their courses of study to ensure instruction in subjects essential to a continuation of the classical heritage.

This was a lot to ask of elementary schools. If schoolmasters found solace in being literary teachers only, it must have been because anything other than literary learning was now none of their business. All ancient educational philosophers talked boldly about holistic education, and Hellenists were almost dogmatic about it.[17] Yet elementary teachers were dispensed from any responsibility to social, moral, and physical education.[18] Later analysts of Hellenistic school practice were sure this was a mistake,[19] but it had the effect of leaving elementary schools with precise and limited responsibilities. Although physical education was important, it was removed from the schools; and moral education, traditionally the responsibility of nurses, pedagogues, and families, was too important to be left to teachers. In the end, only literary elementary education was left for schools.

But this limited commission for elementary schools represents the final stage of their evolution. For a long time, elementary schools were burdened (some masters thought overburdened) with teaching drawing, instrumental and vocal music, and dancing.[20] These subjects, all rem-

nants of ancient practice, were hard to dismiss, and some Hellenists insisted upon keeping them, in the interest of cultural adequacy.

Drawing and Dancing. Drawing had close friends. Large cities had
dozens of drawing masters. Yet drawing's claim on a primarily literary
curriculum was tenuous, so its decline in schools was inevitable. Drawing
and drafting, although clearly related to art, had trouble illustrating the
past. Visual art is perishable and, with little art to transmit, drawing was
regarded as mere technique. Dancing, an art also, suffered the same
cultural disadvantage as drawing. With social and religious meaning
stripped away, it was fit only for professional performers.

Music. The case of music was different. Esteemed in Athens and
elsewhere in Greece, music had credentials of social significance and a
close relationship with literature. Without the printed word, music was
the principal means for keeping the oral tradition alive. No Athenian
citizen was truly accomplished or a credit to his station in life without
musical ability, and this ancient attitude lingered on to affect Hellenism.
Yet, even at its best, music could hardly match literature's cultural contribution; moreover, it was in the repertoire of professional entertainers,
who infected it with their reputation for immorality and indecency. In
time music might have overcome this guilt by association, but time was
lacking. Music changed. As a social skill it was respected and practiced by
anyone wanting to be Greek-like, but invention made it a study of
acoustics—an investigation and analysis of rhythm and interval—rather
than a social skill. By the end of the Hellenistic period, music's scholastic
standing was scientific, and the attention it had commanded atrophied
almost to the point of extinction.[21]

Stripping physical education, drawing, dancing, and music from elementary study left reading, writing, and counting to be taught by masters
without much pedagogic skill or imagination. Day by day instruction went
on, usually without interruption, but appeals (if any were made) to accommodating it to the nature of learning, the interest of students, or the
true art of teaching went unheeded.

Reading, Writing, and Counting. Reading began with the alphabet.[22]
Students learned their letters by sight, then went on to syllables, to words,
and, finally, to whole sentences. When strange, difficult words or literary
allusion appeared, teachers offered assistance. Sometimes, though, anticipating these difficulties, they explained the story in a general way and
handled special problems of vocabulary and syntax. After these preliminaries, students read and re-read stories until they were memorized.[23]
Thus, reading began with an elemental textual criticism that centered on
handling any difficulties the students encountered and ended with a comparison of the teacher's and the students' copy of the text. This *prelectio*,

if not an invention of elementary school teachers, was a technique they honed so skillfully that it attracted the attention of teachers for centuries. Writing followed the same rule of thumb method. Letters were traced, first on wax tablets and later on paper.[24] Counting, still a complicated and detailed sign language, completed an elementary school syllabus whose content and approach imitated classical school method.[25]

Teachers. Such elementary schools were found everywhere, but almost always as private enterprises conducted by masters of varying qualification. These masters, on a low rung of the vocational ladder, seldom commanded better pay or more respect than day laborers. Under these circumstances, they could not afford school buildings, so classes were taught in their homes (if they had them), in groves, on playgrounds, in vacant rooms of public buildings, or any suitable place. Materials for instruction, infrequently adverted to in the sources at our disposal, must have been meager.[26]

Despite the arid atmosphere of elementary schools, students were eager to learn, because Hellenism's devotion to culture made learning an attractive prize. If, however, a few refused to keep step with the march toward culture, teachers had the authority to beat them. In the absence of other motives, fear was depended upon and teachers punished lack of effort and poor achievement with enthusiasm and zeal.[27]

The Secondary School

When Hellenistic elementary school students could read, write, and count, they were ready to take another step up the educational ladder. But secondary education needed a good deal of organization and definition before it was sturdy enough to support the cultural goals so much admired by Hellenists.

The classical gymnasium could afford indifference to literary study, because after having been introduced to literature in the music school, citizens received solid and satisfying cultural nourishment in the theater. Allegations of cultural illiteracy in the classical age are false, although no classical school made a commitment to cultural transmission. From time to time, the Sophists, practicing innovation, encouraged boys to forego the gymnasium and come to them for instruction in literature and rhetoric. So historians who find the seed of literary secondary education in sophistry might be right, but classical models of literary teaching and experiments with post-elementary education were too indistinct for imitation by Hellenists. Secondary schools turned out to be places where ingenuity had plenty of range.

Once recognizing the need to establish genuine secondary schools, Hellenists proceeded to do so, but deciding what should be taught turned out to be a problem. Literature's claim on the curriculum went un-challenged, but which authors should be read and studied, and how much grammar and rhetoric, both essential for interpretation, should be taught?[28] Grammar—an analysis of Greek's linguistic structure—was in its infancy when Protagoras and other Sophists elaborated a code of correct speech. It came to maturity about two centuries after the classical age was over in a little book, *On Grammar*, by Dionysius Thrax (b. 166 B.C.). Despite its tardy codification, grammar was indispensable to any understanding of classical authors, for classical Greek, no longer a living language, had to be studied to be mastered. Rhetoric's case was the same. Classical authors had employed rhetoric as a natural ally to expression, so its codification was mainly a matter of reconstructing the style of classical texts, although a few novelties to technique and rule had been invented by Gorgias and Isocrates. Everything pertaining to grammar and rhetoric needed the attention of good scholarship before being introduced to the curriculum.

But there was more. Plato, we recall, promoted science and mathe-matics, and his sponsorship gave them classical credentials. So without much enthusiasm, but to maintain cultural integrity, Hellenists embraced them, too, although without any illusion about their equality with gram-mar, rhetoric, and literature.

The Study of Literature. Following a cultural doctrine whose prem-ises we know, Hellenistic schoolmasters put literature at the top of the curricular list. But the whole of classical literature would have overbur-dened instruction, so selection was imperative. The *Iliad* and *Odyssey* must have been read—even memorized—by every student, for Homer was the giant and his influence in perpetuating the ideals and traditions of ancient Greece was monumental, but he was not alone. Euripides, Men-ander, and Demosthenes were authors whom no educated person left unread.[29] To this fixed repertoire lyric and tragic poets, dramatists, and others were added, and it would be surprising if Hesiod were not read in hundreds of schools. With so rich a literary heritage, schoolmasters could fill a curriculum without fear of criticism that something essential was being neglected.

What could have been, but seldom was, criticized was the way these illustrious authors were studied. Perhaps teachers themselves lacked the skill to find the treasure in them. They neglected literary taste and ig-nored appreciation while concentrating on a kind of literary analysis.[30] Students were to look for unusual words and expressions and to search through their books for the elements of style. Almost always too busy searching for literary detail, their teachers' fetish, they missed the story. Some textual analysis, along with attention to strange words and archaic expression, was probably justified as a preliminary to reading, but with the exception of the best schools, literary instruction halted with it.

The Study of Grammar. Oral tradition had conveyed classical ideals without help from grammar. But time and geography took their toll, and ancient assumptions about the use and meaning of language lost validity. To most people of the Hellenistic world, the Greek language was a foreign medium.

Although a few scholars, some of them Sophists, had speculated about the nature and structure of language, a prescriptive code of correct Greek usage waited until Dionysius Thrax published a sixteen-page book, *On Grammar.* Used almost at once in secondary schools, and considered authoritative, it defined grammar as a practical knowledge of the use of language by writers of prose and poetry. Dealing, in turn, with accent, letters, syllables, and the eight parts of speech, the book concluded with a treatment of the declension of nouns and the conjugation of verbs.[31]

Grammar is an essential auxiliary to the study of literature: a language must be known if it is to be read and understood. What stands out, however, is the scientific and abstract way grammar was taught in Hellenistic secondary schools; its mastery became an end in itself, and students spent more time reconstructing the Greek language than in using grammar as a guide to reading and writing. With few exceptions, grammar became an arid exercise that in both rule and composition regularly missed the chance to introduce coherence between life and schooling.[32]

As a matter of general scholastic practice, schools of rhetoric were responsible for teaching the art of oral and written composition, so secondary-school teachers were discouraged from teaching composition in a way that would intrude upon the work of higher schools.[33] In rare instances, though, an enthusiastic grammar master violated convention and taught students to compose and deliver a speech. What was more common and passed muster as secondary-school composition—but was really a pedestrian exercise in written expression—began with teachers telling a short story, probably as long as a page, and students recorded it word for word. More imaginative teachers authorized students to reproduce the story in their own words. But even when students were ambitious and wrote on topics assigned by the teacher, they were discouraged from employing either artistry or ingenuity. As a genuine art, composition belonged to higher education, and most secondary masters were comfortable with this deferral of scholastic responsibility.

The Study of Science. Although the scientific curriculum in Hellenistic secondary schools was fairly broad (including geometry, arithmetic, music, and astronomy), it fought a losing battle in competition with grammar and literature. Despite a commendable record of scientific accomplishment in the classical age, science remained on the fringe of classical culture. It could explain the operations of nature, but it said little about life. Besides, science in the classics was difficult to excavate and hard to understand. It required an investment of time, effort, and intelligence that never paid the cultural dividend of literature, so most students avoided it.

Still, science was studied by some secondary-school students. Euclid (ca. 300 B.C.) had justified geometry as a liberal study, called attention to its capacity for disciplining the mind, and played down its utility.[34] Hellenists, however, stressed its utility, and with good reason. Arithmetic, as number theory rather than computational skill, was almost useless in daily life, so geometry was pressed into service to handle all those problems related to quantity.[35]

The case of music was more complicated. Outside the school, music was prized as a social amenity. In the schoolhouse, though, despite excellent classical credentials, music became a branch of mathematics. Hellenists were captivated by the intricacies of sound and, although music as an acoustical study never achieved any degree of popularity, converted music from a social accomplishment to a scientific study.

Astronomy, the most popular of the four ancient sciences, had something in common with geometry. It could be approached in different ways. Students read Ptolemy's (d. A.D. 168) *Almagestes* and studied astronomy with confidence that such knowledge was good in itself. Further justification was unnecessary but could have been mustered. With a knowledge of astronomy, seasons could be predicted and charted, and dependable calendars could be constructed. Besides, astronomy was astrology's first cousin. Persons at this time, eager to draw back the veil of the future, flocked to astrologers to have horoscopes cast. Although astronomy and astrology were never confused as school subjects—the latter was always kept out of the school—this fondness for astrology helped sustain astronomy's scholastic popularity.

In the last analysis, though, the scientific curriculum could not break literature's and grammar's grip on secondary education. Difficult and specialized, science was a study for a few unusual persons who wanted to be expert. The vast majority, infected with the cultural doctrine of Hellenism, rationalized their indifference to scientific study by characterizing it as scholastically barren and emotionally unbearable.

Higher Education

Higher schools of rhetoric and philosophy flourished almost everywhere, although the most ornamental were located in Alexandria, Pergamon, Delphi, Rhodes, Beirut, Antioch, Constantinople, and Athens.

While their devotion to liberal learning was genuine, in concentrating on certain parts of the cultural legacy and neglecting everything else, they came precariously close to making their preoccupation an end in itself. Other kinds of higher education, if rhetoric and philosophy are counted cultural and liberal, toyed with professionalism, and this undermined their popularity. Technical education—medicine, engineering, architecture, and, perhaps, law—had good recommendations, even in an age habitually underestimating the worth of technique, so an account of Hellenistic higher education should go beyond rhetoric and philosophy.

Ephebic Institutes. Ephebic institutes were scattered throughout the empire. Some did their best to preserve a curriculum of physical and military training inherited from ancient days, but most, trying to keep pace with change, introduced literary study. Yet they lacked status as genuine schools and seldom advanced culture. The teaching, in the hands of Sophists or wandering masters, was sporadic and incoherent. More academic circuit-riders than scholars, these teachers appeared, gave a prepared lecture, and then moved on. As heralds for a point of view, their stay was too brief to develop a regular course of study or to enlist a dependable cadre of students. The regular disciplines of the higher learning were medical, scientific, rhetorical, and philosophical, and all were pursued separately in training programs and schools.

Medical Education. Societies able to support the care of health and relief from pain do so. The rapid rise of medical schooling during this era is unsurprising.[36] What is surprising was the tendency to downgrade medical education because it lacked cultural appurtenances and, at the same time, cultivate it because of the good it could do. In any case, medical schools admitted students after secondary school, and in a quick academic program—likely only a year or so—taught conventional medical theory. After this brief encounter with the books, students gave full attention to clinical practice.

Customarily, an aspiring physician apprenticed himself to a practicing doctor and accompanied him on his rounds, as an observer and nurse, until he was ready to practice medicine alone. Neither law nor convention prescribed the term of an apprenticeship, so some physicians began their practice after six months. Others, perhaps more sensitive to the mystery of medical art, stayed longer. Galen (A.D. 130–200?), for example, the ancient world's most eminent medical authority, continued his apprenticeship for eleven years.[37]

The Museum. The scientific higher learning, because it paid attention to literature, grammar, and rhetoric, enjoyed a station slightly higher than medicine. Yet scientific institutes, where energetic scholars pushed back the boundaries of knowledge, were research institutes rather than schools. Hellenists called them *musea* (museums).[38]

Scholars in museums enjoyed academic freedom to investigate the whole of human knowledge, so museums were more than laboratories. The only impediment to a scholar's quest for knowledge was in the support museums had from philanthropy and, sometimes, from public subsidy. But too little is known about the generosity, or its lack, of these sources for keeping the pace of a museum's scholarship fast and its results superior.[39] Museum scholars, eager to publish their discoveries before their colleagues and an educated public, used public lectures, and in this respect museums resembled schools. Publishing scholars communicated knowledge to anyone willing to listen, but museums never organized regular courses of instruction or recruited students.

Ephebia, medical schools, and museums played an important role in higher learning, but, whatever their worth, they were subordinate to the kingpins of academic significance: schools of rhetoric and philosophy.

The School of Rhetoric. A majority of secondary-school graduates who continued their education attended schools of rhetoric. Philosophical academies were, of course, open to them, but rhetoric was more captivating. Along with their classical ancestors (although for different reasons), these students demonstrated an interest in oratory, but their interest is hard to justify. They were untroubled by the fact that oratory had become an art without political significance. Although its public voice was muted because citizens were excused from shaping public policy, rhetoric was praised (as if the ancient city-state were intact) and studied with care and assiduity. Amending its rich past, rhetoric's perspective was altered from deliberative, demonstrative, and judicial oratory—all having abundant political meaning—to a new, politically antiseptic oratory meant to be read: the literary oration. This emphasis proved to be a boon to composition, because written speeches could be preserved and analyzed, whereas spoken oratory's appeal, sometimes fleeting, was only to the ear. Even so, composition always took second place to platform delivery as the true ornament of rhetorical skill.

Rhetoric was a long course of four or five years for students devoting full-time study to it, and perhaps twenty years for those who pursued it along with their regular work in a kind of adult education. Fairly clear signs imply that physicians, engineers, and merchants, believing they had missed something of substantial value, studied rhetoric into old age. Student motive aside, rhetoric deployed a three-part syllabus: information, style, and delivery.[40]

The content of a speech intended to be read was especially important because it could be studied and analyzed, so students had to know the classics thoroughly in order to cull from them appropriate phrases, names, and allusions. This instruction was the principal business of the grammarian in the secondary school. If teachers of rhetoric had confidence in the accomplishment of previous study, they exposed their students to a refresher course in literature and then concentrated on rhetorical technique. But when confidence in lower schools was lacking, the course in literature was repeated.

When the informational side to rhetoric was accounted for in literature, and assuming that preliminary instruction in rhetoric had already been handled, teachers introduced style and delivery. Apparently ranking first in importance, style was cultivated by using superior classical models. Aspiring orators were encouraged to imitate the style of classical orations, and teaching devices to facilitate imitation were introduced.[41] Delivery applied more to platform speaking than to composing, and to perfect it students had to practice an arsenal of rules which, over the decades, became fuller and fuller.[42] Conscientious teachers left nothing out, so students drilled and practiced every rhetorical device and detail, including the law of gesture (*chironomy*).[43] When the course was finished, students were expected to be accomplished speakers and writers who thought, spoke, wrote, and acted like their classical ancestors. Achieving this, they belonged to a cultural elite.

The School of Philosophy. Although its classical credentials matched rhetoric's, philosophy could not match rhetoric's popularity. But teachers of philosophy were untroubled, because large classes, they said, broke the fraternal bond between teachers and students. Besides, convinced that knowledge and wisdom were too precious to be distributed indiscriminantly, they asserted that only the best minds should be privy to philosophy's secrets. Although these secrets were hard to discover, and only gifted students were encouraged to enroll in philosophical schools, one suspects that this was a self-serving declaration. Philosophy competed with rhetoric for the good students, but rhetoric was not easy either, and must sometimes have matched philosophy both in abstruseness and aridity. Firmer historical ground for philosophy's inferior station can be found in its indifference to a Hellenistic cultural ideal automatically subordinating the content of thought to the power of expression. This indifference kept classes in philosophy small.

In an intellectual world where literature and rhetoric were the true cultural ornaments, it must have taken courage and zeal for students to forsake the academic mainstream and sail a tributary. And philosophy was a tributary. When students declared for philosophy, they were faced, first, with making a decision about which of the four branches of philosophy to follow: Platonism, Aristotelianism, Epicureanism, or Stoicism. After an introductory course covering every branch, sometimes taken several times in different schools, they made a choice.

With headquarters in Athens, these schools of philosophical thought were represented by various academic institutions in the Hellenistic world. But in addition to the four prominent and official philosophical systems, there were others. Eclecticism was promoted by wandering scholars who, selecting philosophical doctrine to suit themselves, never worried about inner consistency or systematic exposition; and Cynicism was spread by eccentrics who refused to become part of society. More hermits than teachers, and abandoning the conventions of decency, they dressed as they pleased, refused to wash and cut their hair. Whatever their accomplishment as philosophers, their intransigent personal and social unorthodoxy concealed it.

In schools dealing with the four systematic philosophies, the regular curriculum began after students made their commitment, something like a religious conversion, to the philosophical doctrine taught in that school.[44] Then serious study commenced with a course in the history of philosophy that today is handled in the first chapters of standard books. Next came the respective doctrines of the school. Depending upon affinity, the books of Plato, Aristotle, Epicurus, or Zeno were studied with such attention to detail as to account for every philosophical loose end. Instruction was overburdened with erudition, but some teachers tried to relate principle to practice, the rule of reason to the problems of life, and to accommodate philosophical wisdom to the burning issues of the day. Philosophy teaching seldom achieved such excellence, but it was Hellenistic higher education at its best when it did.

The philosophical classics taught in all schools elaborated elements of logic, ethics, and physics, but, imitating ancient preference, intensive scholarship was reserved for ethics. With ethics, as with other parts of philosophy, philosophers were preoccupied with principle rather than fact: they wanted to understand the moral code and too frequently were indifferent to its practical application. This preoccupation was deceptive and unrewarding, for sometime in its early history philosophy lost its way. Philosophers began a long battle among themselves over who possessed wisdom, and they began to prize polemical skill over philosophical principle. When the acrimony of debate engulfed rhetoric, rhetoric's credentials were challenged by philosophers who, taking a page from Plato's book, declared rhetoric to be nothing more than knack, unfit for serious study.[45] Rhetors responded in kind to question the worth of philosophy, where everything was always an open, unanswered question. In the end, these two branches of the higher learning, each asserting superiority, were swamped by hostility, debate, and academic artificiality. When the Hellenistic age ended, neither philosophy nor rhetoric was on speaking terms and neither was in a position to illuminate the fundamental issues of life.

Chapter 4

Consolidating Educational Tradition in Rome

For a long time, Romans were satisfied to remain on the Italian peninsula where outside influence seldom disrupted social and cultural convention. But as Rome became energetic and ambitious, she sensed threat from foreign states and undertook to extend her policy and power to the whole world.[1] Success in military conquest and political control put her in contact and, to some extent, in competition with Greek and Hellenistic culture. Roman cultural tradition was threatened, and history's verdict that captive Greece conquered master Rome is almost certainly correct. Before this happened, however, Rome enjoyed cultural independence and, in the education of youth, ignored the developments going on around her to follow a plan that was entirely her own.

Education in Early Rome

From about 800 to 275 B.C., Rome was politically and socially rustic. For the most part a rural people, Romans tilled the soil, herded their cattle, took up arms to defend their property when they had to, and lived their lives in a manner consistent with the primitive nature of their surroundings and needs. The few aristocrats among them, grateful to fate for good fortune, were content with the old, solid, traditional social values, and, save for their greater wealth and position, were little different from the peasants from whose ranks they had sprung. This autonomous culture was ratified because it was Roman in evolution and taste, and most men and women neither knew nor cared about cultural and intellectual change occurring elsewhere. In time, of course, they became enamored of Greek and Hellenistic cultural monuments and tried to appropriate them, but for now they were eager to restrict allegiance to a tradition where literary skill played a minor role.

Education in the Family. Roman educational philosophy was concerned with maintaining conventional standard in connection with the physical care and the moral behavior of children; this, in fact, is what early Romans meant by "education." And while they might not have been careless about such things as reading, writing, and literary culture, they were indifferent to provision for their realization. With a preoccupation that may fairly be called nonliterary, the reins of educational control and responsibility were held in the strong hands of the family. Should a Roman family have wanted a child steeped in erudition, it might have secured the services of a tutor, but for education—which could have included erudition—the family was prepared to depend upon its own, not inconsequential, resources.[2] Although this might sound redundant, the Roman definition of education during this early period meant physical care, sound upbringing, and the inculcation of virtue. Erudition, something different from education, meant the cultivation of literary skill and culture.[3]

Little children needed a mother's care, guidance, and love. And from her, or from a kinswoman, they learned reading, writing, drawing, painting, the elements of citizenship, and the foundation for moral value. Daughters as well as sons were taught, and were instructed in spinning, weaving, and sewing, although candor requires the admission that the picture of a Roman girl's education is too faint to reproduce with certainty. It is fairly clear, however, that when Roman girls were instructed, their mothers, or their mother's helpers, were the teachers, for other instructional provision was seldom made. From this point on, we hear principally about the instruction boys had from their fathers, but sources agree that a mother's influence extended well beyond the early years of childhood.[4]

When a boy was old enough, he accompanied his father, and this arrangement put almost total trust in the pedagogic technique of learning by doing. Sons worked with their fathers to learn vocational or professional skill as well as something about social and political responsibility and how to become Roman citizens.[5] This practical syllabus, shaped by the duties and responsibilities of daily life, featured the principal virtues in the Roman moral code. Constancy, courage, piety, prudence, and devotion to duty were foremost among the virtues, and fathers, knowing what was expected, obtained the desired results without help from pedagogic skill. They possessed authority over education and discipline, for tradition and law were on their side. Yet the severity implied was seldom exercised, and then only in extreme cases. In the literature, we find almost as many complaints about indulgent as we do about harsh fathers. In any case, censors alone had the right to interfere with the exercise of paternal discipline, and their interference seldom amounted to anything more than a public declaration condemning either excessive leniency or severity.[6]

In these early years, Romans were indifferent to schools. The family was an ideal. It took children to its bosom, cared for them during their early years, and was solicitous of their welfare thereafter.[7] The family, in turn, expected allegiance and reverence from its members. It was a social unit with a history, a position, and an abundance of corporate pride. Family members were honor-bound to maintain the position and reputation of the family; from early years, children learned this unforgettable lesson: as an essential fabric in society, the family was owed unstinting allegiance.

Education for Public Life. Although throughout the early centuries Roman education was severely practical, mental training was given some attention along with all those other accomplishments considered essential to a person engaged in an active public life. This was a side to education that the family could not always manage by itself, either because fathers were too busy, too long away from home on military expedition or public business, lacking in ability, deceased, or (and this condition is often overlooked) the family had too many sons. Yet boys from citizen families anticipated an active involvement in civic or military affairs, and their families, according to Roman convention, were expected to equip them for it. Family instruction, built on a solid moral foundation, was a starting point, but only a starting point. Something more was needed, but despite the urgency of preparing boys for public life, neither schools nor schoolmasters were mustered into service.

A knowledge of Roman law was important for public men. Later, after Roman law had matured, an extensive code was promulgated and its mastery demanded careful scholarship, but for now, law existed mainly in oral tradition and could be learned informally. Law, summarized in the Twelve Tables and commentary on them, expressed a code for governing public and private life, and fathers who were able explained it to their sons. In the best circumstance—say, for Cato the Elder's son—legal training was comprehensive and thorough; but Marcus Cato was an exceptional father with a knowledge of law, and having married late, his age freed him from public duty to attend to the education of his son. Even so, Cato Licinianus disappointed his father. More often, having followed their fathers or grandfathers through the labyrinth of Roman law, young men, not lawyers in any modern sense, were equipped for a place in the legislative assembly and were ready to manage public and private affairs.

A young man's education was always a father's responsibility, one that could be delegated but not abandoned. Many Roman fathers were unable, for one or another reason, to superintend this part of a son's education, so they looked for help. At age sixteen, a Roman boy's *toga* was replaced by a *toga virilis*, symbolizing his maturity. Besides, as a citizen eligible for military service, he was ready to cross the threshold to public life. This step, however, was probably too great for most sixteen-year-old boys to manage without more seasoning. The first period of seasoning usually took a year, although in exceptional cases (such as Cicero's), it lasted for eight.

A friend or relative of position, sagacity, and experience was asked to take a young man under his wing and teach him about public life and private business.[8] Next came military service.[9] Already a citizen, a young Roman, often accompanied by a kinsman, entered the ranks as a common soldier, and after one year could become an officer. Now, developing further virtues of steadfastness, discipline, courage, and obedience, he learned to lead men in battle. After two years of military service, he was ready for a career as a public man. But if too young for politics, he either extended his military tour or went home. A good record as a Roman officer was always an excellent recommendation for a place in the public and private arena.

Later Roman Education

By 275 B.C., Greek culture had been exported to many parts of the Mediterranean world, and in Italy, Greek-speaking settlements were extant. Besides, by then Rome was an active, energetic, and inquisitive city eager to expand her horizon. The civilization of Greece, never entirely unknown, began to solicit attention; moreover, as Rome's sphere of political authority was extended by military conquest, her citizens met Hellenistic civilization and the classical heritage. Traveling as soldiers, diplomats, and commercial emissaries, they felt socially rustic and culturally inferior. To suppress feelings of inferiority, they tried to insulate themselves from alien cultural influence and cling to their own tradition, but cultural influence is insidious: they were Hellenized.

Greek Influence. As early as the third century B.C., trying to block cultural invasion, Rome had laws prohibiting the teaching of Greek language and literature. Greek captives of war were sometimes employed as teachers, so when Roman legislators became excited about cultural melding, such teachers were compelled to abandon teaching or were driven from the city. But laws to halt teachers of Greek were infrequent, temporary, and, for the most part, not meant to apply to elementary instruction. Greeks who could teach rhetoric were the ones to be feared, because after hearing a Greek orator, Romans were sure the difference between truth and error had been blurred. Yet this campaign against Greek and Hellenistic literary culture failed. In the end, although with a troubled conscience, Rome tentatively and selectively embraced the language, literature, and philosophy of the lands she had conquered.

Rome wanted to select those parts of literature, philosophy, law, and science that were consistent with her own values and graft them to Latin culture. But success along these lines was incomplete: the Greek classics were stronger and more vigorous than any extant Latin literature. Besides, when Greater Greece surrendered to Rome at Tarentum in 272 B.C., and when Rome became a bilingual empire with the annexation of Greece and Hellenistic provinces in northern Africa and Asia Minor, it became almost imperative for Roman citizens to know the language and customs of the people they governed. Although some resistance to Greek language and literature was bound to persist, it was never strong enough to halt the forward march of cultural assimilation. In the end, as Rome's military and political power became greater, her effort to adopt the hallmarks of Hellenistic culture was intensified. The chance for old Roman education to survive was small.

Greek influence had a modest beginning when people from Italian towns, where Greek was spoken, were brought into Roman homes. While Roman families never gave these people full instructional authority, wealthy and prominent Romans wanted their children to have the comprehensive education for which the Greek educational tradition was famous. Against this background, a more ambitious practice of introducing teachers of Greek began to unfold.

Greek slaves were brought to Rome and utilized as teachers, as was Andronicus, a "half-Greek" from Tarentum, captured in battle by Livius Salinator. After a period of servitude, when he was used as a tutor, Andronicus was freed and, for the next sixty-five years, made a good living as a teacher, a translator, and a literary artist. But Livius was only one among many who taught the boys and girls of wealthy families something of the Greek literary legacy.[10]

Once convinced of the worth of Greek literature and language, and now conceding that the Greek legacy was superior to anything in Latin, Romans flocked to Greek teachers. Eager to have instruction in Greek, Romans sometimes assigned unqualified slaves to teach, for intelligent, educated slaves with teaching skill brought high prices.[11] Greeks were encouraged to emigrate and become teachers in Rome.

Elementary Education

Reading, writing, counting, and measuring were taught at home when parents had the time and ability, but later, and when parents could not afford tutors, children were sent to the *ludus*, an elementary school, where the *litterator* was schoolmaster. Instruction in Greek was given only in the home by tutors. The *ludus* was a Latin school and so it remained, although eventually a dual system of elementary schools—one Latin, the other Greek—was established.[12]

Whether schools taught Latin or Greek, their teachers' responsibilities were limited to literary instruction. Moral education, something too important to neglect, and traditionally the prerogative of mothers and fathers, was sometimes delegated to pedagogues, especially in families with home-born slaves or *verna*. These slaves, reared with the natural children of the home, were usually well cared for and treated affectionately. When they were able, they cared for the "infant masters" and, in general, assumed the role of guardians. Being in close and constant association with natural children, they too benefited from home and school instruction.

The nurses about whom Quintilian wrote would have received their education in such family situations,[13] for evidence is convincing that either girls or boys could have been guardians for natural children. Home-slaves, all slaves for that matter, were more valuable when literate, so a prudent Roman, careful to enhance the value of his property, would likely have wanted instruction for them. Good and loyal service sometimes led home-slaves to freedom, and when they turned to teaching, elementary schools became common in Rome.

Pedagogues. In this setting the adoption of the pedagogue is less a surprise. Although pedagogues were supposed to supervise manners and morals,[14] Roman families would not have relinquished their primary educational role to them. Yet, either as home-slaves, servants, or trusted freemen, pedagogues in Rome are commonly reported as having been moral masters, and eventually they might have been given such responsibility. But Rome was not Greece and the conditions that recommended pedagogues in Greece did not exist in Rome. Now and then, a Roman primary teacher had a bad reputation and was accused of contaminating the morals of students, but once discovered he was put out of business. It was more likely that Roman children going to and from school, exercising on the playground, or just being home, needed protection, care, and attention that parents could not supply. They found pedagogues useful. But sometimes pedagogues' duties included preparing food for the children or tasting it to see that it was not poisoned. In addition, pedagogues in Rome, following the Greek model, were to supervise manners and enforce a moral code. They were authorized to correct and punish boys and girls under their care.

Schools and Teachers. Following the traditional beginning-school-age to the letter, boys and girls who went to school went at age seven. Schooling for boys is unsurprising, but for girls, although hard to explain, it may illustrate a Roman attitude capable of acknowledging the worth of feminine talent. Elementary-school instruction lasted about five years, and the children became fairly proficient in reading, writing, counting, weighing, and measuring, although both instructional material and pedagogic technique were crude and underdeveloped. Books, maps, writing material, and other teaching aids were the same as in Greek and Hellenistic schools, and schools themselves were kept in porches, booths, corners of public buildings and playgrounds. No effort was made to locate them away from the traffic and distraction of commerce. As a matter of fact, most elementary-school teachers thought it good business to conduct their classes in public view and thus to recruit more students.

A strict silence about the qualifications of elementary schoolmasters makes us suspect that, although elementary instruction was considered important, the assumption was common that anyone could be a teacher. This assumption allowed all manner of persons to take up teaching, but few were Roman citizens.[15]

Most primary masters were in business for themselves, so the reward of success and the penalty of failure might have been the best safeguard against incompetence. But if little attention was given to teachers' qualifications, much was paid to their zeal in enforcing discipline. Disciplinary codes were severe, and students were certain to regret lapses in deportment or lack of scholastic diligence: no time was wasted debating the dictum "Spare the rod and spoil the scholar." This was conventional practice and few primary masters were in any position to tamper with it. Besides, a school with a reputation for severity made it more difficult for parents to withhold payment of fees by alleging that their children had not been well-instructed because of flawed discipline.

But this sounds worse than it was. Conventional school practice followed a Greek model, one supported by a wealth of experience in handling the fundamentals of elementary education. When elementary education was over Roman children were reasonably well prepared for life.

Without becoming swamped in detail, we should take a closer look at the work of the schools. Instruction began with the letters of the alphabet and moved to syllables, words, sentences, and, finally, short continuous passages. Recitation, of which there was plenty, was done in unison, and the louder the better. Cicero refers in a not altogether laudatory tone to the "obligatory chant" in the primary school, and St. Augustine, later, writes about his own "hateful sing-song" experience in schools that followed Roman practice.[16] And this practice put confidence in the learner's ear, although Quintilian, and perhaps others, recommended a visual presentation of letters as well.

When letters were heard and seen often enough, students were directed to identify them by calling out their names, of tracing them, first with the helping hand of the teacher and then, in some schools, with special teaching aids that allowed a student to follow an impression of the letter made on a wooden tablet. Some schoolmasters perceived the natural relationship between play and learning, so they encouraged their students to make or purchase letters carved from ivory or wood and play with them. When all of this was accomplished, boys and girls were told to write the letters in their own hand. Teachers watched and corrected, although the remains of school assignments indicate that some teachers were not especially careful in correcting student work.

Syllables came next in instruction where consonants were combined with vowels: seven vowels in Greek and five in Latin. When these sounds were mastered, words of one syllable were introduced. Now teachers could follow a list of their own or use words from the school-exercise books of the day. Both oral and written repetition fixed these words to a student's vocabulary, and when they were ready for a stronger diet, more complex words (for example, the names of rivers, gods, places, and persons) were presented. In bilingual schools, Latin and Greek words were shown side by side.

Reading. By now sturdy students were ready to read sentences, but this could be cumbersome and difficult, for words were not separated in the text, so a reader, without spaces between words, would have to recognize word endings. Punctuation was equally complex. The marks now taken for granted were not used, so readers would have to figure out meaning to supply suitable, although by no means standard, marks of punctuation. Even when skill in reading was mastered, it was rare for anyone to read a passage at first sight. Material to be read had to be prepared.

When students could read, they read short selections, and since the Romans were interested in steeping children in morality, these selections were usually filled with maxims taken from the best Greek and Latin poets and dramatists. Repeated often enough, these fragments of wisdom became permanent possessions. But this was not the end of primary education; it was not even the end of the literary part of it. Schoolmasters wanted their students to be able to write, so they spent time dictating passages. When these passages were written, they were recited until learned by heart.

Grammar. Although the level of instruction in grammar in the primary school is something of an open question, it would seem that this instruction needed some help from the rules of grammar. How much is hard to say. First-year students were in the same schoolroom with fifth-year students, and most teachers found it hard to organize lessons for them. Anticipating by centuries the monitorial plan of instruction, older, more advanced students were enlisted to hear the lessons of younger ones after they themselves had been taught the lesson by the teacher. This takes us about as far as we need to go with literary primary education, but along with it, students were taught arithmetic.

Arithmetic. Rome owed a considerable debt to Greece for a knowledge of arithmetic, but in primary-school instruction, the Greeks were content to teach counting, whereas the Romans wanted calculation. Still, they followed the Greek practice of starting instruction in arithmetic with counting, so boys and girls in Roman primary schools used their fingers or pebbles to indicate quantity. Knowing how to count has obvious practical advantages for day-to-day life, but counting had a relationship to oratory. Quintilian reminds readers that orators have often to indicate number and that their speech will be more effective if they are able to illustrate number in "finger language."[17] But children in the primary school were a long way from using arithmetic in public address.

They had to master addition and multiplication, to which were later added. respectively, subtraction and division. Teachers supplied the information and students repeated it in the conventional schoolhouse chant. The next step was to recognize and write the symbols (V, X, L, C, D, M, and I) in Latin, and in Greek the twenty-four letters of the alphabet (with a horizontal bar above the letter to indicate that it was being used as a number) plus three additional signs. Fractions and the decimal system were part of the syllabus, too, so students were required to attend carefully to their lessons if they were to succeed.

When primary school was out, students had reading, writing, and arithmetic in their scholastic repertoire; besides, they were reasonably well equipped to cross the doorstep to life in society or, if their condition recommended, to matriculate in schools kept by grammarians.

Secondary Education

Before about 150 B.C., according to the reports of educated Greeks who visited there, Rome lacked any system of schools. Whether this changed much over the centuries or, in fact, whether Rome ever had an official school system, is a hard question to answer. Some schools were now and then supported by the state, some ornamental scholars were appointed to public professorships, and teachers were frequently dispensed from paying taxes and bearing arms. But these subventions and dispensations, for all their luster, do not bespeak a system of schools.

The point to be illustrated, though, is how educational opportunity was extended in a society that put a high value on preparing persons to become responsible and competent public men. We have seen the part played by the family in providing for the early education and training of children, and have observed the introduction of guardians, pedagogues, and tutors to do things that families could not do. Against this background, provision for advanced or (for want of a better phrase) secondary education was made.

Family tutors, who liked to distinguish themselves from pedagogues, were capable of giving instruction beyond the rudiments. Most began their career as slaves and served their families for a long time, but for many, loyal service was rewarded with freedom. As free men, they could engage in home teaching or extend their horizon and increase their income by opening schools and recruiting students. Those who chose the latter were the founders of Roman secondary education, and they called themselves grammarians.

Grammarians and Grammar. Nothing in traditional Roman education blazed a trail for secondary schools, so when grammarians looked for a model to follow, they turned to Greece. Their search was fairly easy. Most of the first grammarians were slaves captured from Hellenized towns in Italy or Africa or imported from Greece. They were educated men or they would not have been employed as tutors: they knew grammar and were familiar with teaching it. So despite the appearance of being indigenous, grammar schools were steeped in the prescription of Greek education, and historical instinct tempts us to believe that this was a permanent condition.

Their curriculum, borrowed from the Greeks, had three parts: the structure of language and rules for correct speech, mythology, and literature. These three parts became staples in Roman grammar schools, even Quintilian adverts to them,[18] but they were not given equal attention. Grammar and literature were counted as superior and, in time, scant heed was paid mythology.

But grammar—the rule, structure, and correctness of language—and literature are not the same. It would have been extraordinary, even in the best Greek schools, to find one teacher excelling in both, so despite a teaching theory recommending a balance between the two, it was common for one or the other to be given almost exclusive attention. In larger schools, with several teachers, specialization was possible. Some teachers concentrated on the technical aspects of grammar, while others taught literature. Literature was taught by expounding texts, by illustrating and explaining them in detail, and texts were in verse. Poetry was a preoccupation: convention recommended it and teachers of rhetoric prescribed it.

Despite grammar's acknowledged worth, neither its schools nor its teachers were given the attention they deserved. School buildings were rare when educational support depended upon the income of private teachers who, in turn, depended upon tuition from students.[19] Only the most prosperous and resourceful grammar masters had their own scholastic edifice; others rented rooms in public or private buildings. In either case, they showed good sense in locating their schools off beaten paths to spare students from distraction. And they were usually ingenious enough to supply academic decor, although those who decorated and ornamented their classrooms were probably thinking as much of their own comfort and prestige as the welfare of their students. Putting up a good front gave the impression of success and was a clever ploy for attracting students.

To polish an image of success, masters dressed fashionably in colorful, ornamental cloaks. Ostentatious ensemble made them feel important and enabled them to lord it over their elementary counterparts. Their income, though, with a few notable exceptions, was hardly more than that of an ordinary tradesman—although about four times greater than that of a primary master—and to make matters worse, the lack of prestige attached to their work always kept them in the social underclass. The more ambitious and ingenious among them looked for ways to improve their positions, and one way, they discovered, was to secure social and political connections.[20]

This lack of respect for secondary masters and their work is surprising. Romans might have had a basis for believing that anyone could teach reading, writing, and arithmetic, but grammarians possessed knowledge of literature and grammar, subjects learned only by serious study. The inconsistency of Roman parents sending children to school, eager to introduce them to sound learning, while refusing to value the teacher's work is an anomaly, and the only explanation for it is that these teachers, usually of humble origin, did not belong to the citizen class.

Roman secondary-school teachers had a problem in asserting their worth, but all the same they were pioneers. Before Greek slaves made Latin translations of the Greek classics, Roman secondary education, without a literature for its curriculum, did not exist. But Latin translations were not good enough for ambitious Romans who wanted to master the Greek classics in the original. Still, whether the literature in the secondary-school curriculum was in Latin or Greek, it was Greek in origin and outlook. When Roman grammar schools matured, and could afford to do so, they secured specialists to teach Greek and Latin literature.[21]

Latin Grammar. Greek literature commanded the attention of teachers and students, but to profit from its study, an investment of attention was not enough. Knowledge of linguistic structure and rule was essential for understanding literature, so grammar followed literature into the schools. Grammar's tardy appearance was a natural consequence of its evolution. Homer anticipated Dionysius Thrax by seven centuries, but Homer was understood because his idiom was part of a living tradition. That tradition, however, had atrophied in parts of the classical world where the Greek language was a foreign medium without social or cultural affinity. So Thrax's grammar was studied as closely in Virgil's and Horace's time as it had been in Hellenistic schools. In Rome, though, it was studied in Varro's (116–27 B.C.) translation of Thrax's *Grammar*, his own large volume *On the Latin Language*, and later in Palaemon's standard textbook.[22] Hellenists, naturally enough, used Thrax's *Grammar* in Greek, but Varro's translation allowed grammar to remain Greek, without any fundamental transition to the Latin idiom. This anomaly is further evidence of a Roman willingness to idealize Greek culture and imitate it with a spirit that was reflected in the grammatical work of Donatus (fourth century A.D.), Servius (fl. A.D. 200), and Priscian (fl. A.D. 500), who followed Dionysius' well-blazed trail. The first genuine Latin grammar, by Remmius Palaemon, redressed this exceptional dependence on Greek, but Romans had to wait until the first century A.D. for it.

Grammar's explicit Greek heritage troubled some Roman students, but what was worse, it did not meet Latin's requirements: some Greek grammatical rule had no application to Latin. All the same, following a determination to leave nothing out, Latin grammarians filled their syllabus with the full corpus of grammatical knowledge, and grammar began a long march through western schools with two strikes against it. While satisfying to pedants, it annoyed students who had to analyze their vernacular according to an alien linguistic code. Had grammar been given free rein, the history of secondary education might have been different, but grammar was checked and literature assumed precedence in the schools when genuine Latin authors made their appearance. This Latin literature—represented most ornamentally by Virgil—swept at once into the schools to satisfy literary appetites, but haste ruptured tradition: living authors had not before been studied in the schools.

Latin Literature. Because Romans were eager and impatient for Latin literature, they read the best along with the mediocre authors, and this led to a temporary unevenness in the school's literary syllabus. Shortly, the giants of Roman literature—Virgil, Terence, Sallust, and Cicero—were accepted as immovable authors for secondary schools, but before this occurred, the convention was observed to restrict the literary syllabus to the poets. Teaching poetry, countless authoritative commentators assured grammarians, was their principal occupation. It would have been hard, however, for grammarians to be thorough while ignoring prose writers entirely, for in order to illustrate some rules of linguistic structure, prose models were required. In any case, they paid heed to prose only when they had to.

Instructional Technique. The predominance of literature in the schools recommended two standard pedagogical techniques: *prelectio* (prelection) and *ennaratio* (exposition). *Prelectio* was probably essential for reading the Greek classics, but it was useful for Latin authors as well. Before students began to read a classic, teachers gave them its gist, explained unusual grammatical constructions, defined strange words, and more often than not read an entire passage aloud. If students had questions about the text, now was the time to ask them.[23] When students were able to read a passage, teachers employed the technique of *ennaratio* to help them find its meaning. *Ennaratio* was elementary interpretation of a text and in this respect was an essential part of reading. But the more ambitious grammarians undertook a word by word excursus that sometimes turned out to be more an obstacle than an aid to interpretation and understanding. The theory, though, appears to have been sound. In explaining a text, it was possible to introduce an abundance of information and to expand the reading lesson beyond what the text contained to a course in liberal or general education. Used prudently, *ennaratio* and *prelectio* promoted learning, but when teachers made them an excuse for parading knowledge and indulging in pedantry, their worth diminished.[24] A strange phrase, a new word, prompted some teachers to exhibit their reservoir of erudition, but as often as not, these exhibitions turned out to be dull or shallow. Yet, on occasion, they could illustrate an excellence of scholarship from which students profited. But there was another technique that, now and then, found its way into the teacher's repertoire: *historia.* Using this technique, masters gave their students the background to a story. Sometimes such information could be considered essential to understanding the story, and when teachers did not introduce unnecessary detail, *historia* was given the endorsement of such experts as Quintilian. Yet Quintilian is careful to say that teachers should not use *historia* as an occasion for parading their knowledge.

Composition. It would have been strange indeed had teachers of grammar neglected composition entirely, and the record indicates that they did not, despite the prescription so long promoted that composition was a part of rhetoric and therefore belonged in the custody of schools of rhetoric. In the first place, many of the grammar teachers, either conducting schools or acting as independent tutors, could not have offered a marketable course of instruction had they ignored composition. In the second place, even in fairly large schools, it would have been poor pedagogy for teachers to have concentrated only on grammar. They had students who were ready for instruction in rhetoric. Almost naturally, then, despite convention to the contrary, grammarians became involved in teaching composition. What they taught might be considered elementary, or a preparation to the composition that would have been required in a full course of rhetoric, but it freed teachers of higher education to go into the details of rhetoric without spending time on the preliminaries of composition.

Almost enough has been said about the study of literature in secondary education. Poetry did not enjoy exclusivity, but it was primary. Poetry, it was assumed, was easier to understand than prose and more suitable to the age and ability of grammar-school students. Besides, its rhythm and cadence recommended it as a training exercise for future orators. In addition, since Romans were vitally concerned with moral formation, poetry could more easily and directly convey memorable moral lessons and maxims. Learned by heart, they could inspire the will and whet the imagination. The grammar school was an academy with the duty to lay a foundation for oratory, and poetry, it was thought, was more than equal to this task.

We should take a closer look at composition. Its affinity to rhetoric is natural. Yet rhetoric is a complicated study whose ancient code literally bristled with technicality and rule. It was simply too complex for secondary schools, and no evidence suggests that Roman schoolmasters tried to put rhetoric in them. Conceding that rhetoric was a specialized study requiring ability and concentration for mastery, secondary-school students knew they needed skill in written and oral expression. Any curriculum that neglected composition entirely would have been judged deficient. Still, grammarians who were competent to teach grammar and literature usually lacked command of the essentials of rhetoric, so in many places students divided their time between grammarians and rhetors. If "dividing their time" is too strong, it can at least be said that during the last part of the grammar course they studied composition in the school of rhetoric. But where they studied was less important than what they were expected to learn.[25]

Types of Composition. Secondary-school composition was supposed to be a fairly easy, and always preliminary, study of prose writing. And the types of composition are easy to identify, although one cannot be certain of the order of their study. In any case, grammar schools had some commission to give their students practice with fables, sayings, maxims, and narratives. Oratory was more than this, however, so any detailed and intensive investigation of fables, sayings, maxims, and narratives was left for teachers of rhetoric.

A fable contains a moral; a saying is a statement of principle attributed to a person; a maxim is a principle that, without attribution, has achieved universal acceptance; and a narrative is a story. Teachers told or dictated fables, sayings, and maxims and then directed students to reproduce them in their own words along with a brief comment on their significance.

Compositions of more than one page would have been extraordinary. Students then read their compositions or memorized and recited them to the class. In this way, both the teacher and the students had a chance to correct or amend them. Narratives were a little more demanding. The writer was expected to tell a story, very likely on a topic assigned by the teacher. Narration, of course, is the heart of oratory, so no one would expect that instruction in it ended in the grammar school. Still, by introducing narration to grammar schools, teachers were assuring their students of some command of descriptive prose.

Quintilian reports that instruction in grammar-school composition varied a great deal.[26] Instruction sometimes began by giving students a sketch of what was expected, by offering hints on presentation, and by indicating a proper order of treatment. Other times, prefatory instruction was neglected, only the slightest guidance was given, and after the compositions were finished, they were analyzed for faults and omissions. Teachers dissected them word for word and sometimes illustrated corrections with versions of their own. The best teachers allowed students some range and encouraged them to capitalize on their ability. It is here especially that Quintilian applies the pedagogical principle of having teachers adapt their pace to the student's.[27]

Quality of Secondary Education. Roman secondary education, despite undebatable accomplishment, began—and, to a considerable extent, ended—by living in the past, so after reaching the pinnacle of Latin literary accomplishment, schoolmasters and humanists became conservative and spent a good deal of time defending the principle that the genius of the Latin classics could be imitated but never surpassed. Literary scholarship and the science of grammar were approached with assumptions similar to those that had dominated Hellenistic studies. Now and then, Roman scholars tested innovation, but uncomfortable with novelty or afraid of it, they returned to well-travelled roads of educational convention. Convention, it turned out, was the trademark of Roman secondary education. Despite this, however, and in the hands of good secondary-school teachers, the grammar course was the most valuable, and likely the most durable, part of Roman education.

Higher Education

Rhetoric. After completing grammar studies, Roman students climbed the educational ladder to the school of rhetoric, where they expected to learn the art and science of public address. Rhetoric's scholastic arsenal was filled with rules, methods, and customs, all solidly entrenched in the rhetorical tradition, that had to be learned exactly. Along with mastering rhetorical rule (which might have taken three years), students composed speeches covering the full array of oratorical expression. At the same time, they were steeped in examples of good rhetoric, for the principle of imitation was never forgotten.

Combining theory and practice—for neither could be neglected in a good school—students proceeded through the course until they were able to prepare and deliver orations. They were expected to be proficient in judicial, deliberative, and literary oratory, although judicial was by far the most important. Orations were delivered to fellow students, who, along with the teacher, were expected to analyze and criticize them. This was intended to be practice for genuine oratory, but in the best schools, this regimen might not have been counted good enough. Most of these orations dealt with topics rescued from the past and were broad enough to allow for an application of every rule and theory.

The real world of litigation and deliberation, however, although in need of effective oratory, had to contend with problems that had few counterparts in the themes students practiced. Many teachers shied away from real problems because they were unfamiliar with them, and these are the teachers Quintilian scolds. Quintilian could afford to be critical: he became a teacher after a long and distinguished public career and had an experience with practical oratory that few of his colleagues could match. Only in the best schools, under the direction of the best teachers, could students hone their oratorical skill on the burning issues of the day.[28]

Teachers of Rhetoric. Whether teachers of rhetoric had experience in the courts or approached their subject academically, they presided over the kingpin of Latin higher education. These rhetors, all independent teachers and the most illustrious of Latin schoolmasters, had reputations for excellence. The greater their success as teachers, the larger their income (estimated to have been at least five times that of a primary teacher); the more successful among them built elaborate school buildings. If they could afford fine garments, they decorated them with the symbols of their profession and, like the costumes of actors, wore them in their classrooms. Prominent rhetors were rewarded with appointment to government office, and a few were given the title of public teachers with entitlement to a salary from the state.[29] But state professorships, so frequently mentioned in secondary sources as being regular and nearly ubiquitous, were, in fact, extraordinary.

Medicine, Law, and Philosophy. After studying rhetoric for five years, and now about twenty years old, young men either entered public life or continued study in schools of law, medicine, or philosophy. Students electing medical study found the calendar turned back to the Greeks. The sight of apprentices following practicing physicians as they made their rounds is familiar. Students watched and learned. Sampling medical theory, they read Galen (A.D. 130–200). But theory was kept to a minimum; practical bedside experience counted more. Philosophy, too, attracted some students, although always fewer than medicine, for philosophy, preoccupied with mysteries of the universe and problems remote from life, seemed unprofitable and impractical to the Latin mind.

Rhetoric, with law its only serious competitor, was supreme. This was strange, because rhetoric's origin was Greek, whereas law could claim to be of Roman invention. Origin aside, prospective lawyers began their study with grammar and rhetoric, study easy to justify because every jurist was expected to interpret the texts and speak well. In addition, an ability to cite legal authority, to be aware of precedent in analogy and tradition, and to administer the law with justice, goodness, and order were essential. Legal scholars began to write systematic expositions on elements of Roman law (Gaius' *Institutes* is an example), commentaries on the statutes, and books on legal procedure. These books catapulted to classical status, for in addition to being the first formal works on law, they were recognized also as being authoritative, and the teaching of law was organized around them. Teachers and legal writers, making full use of their knowledge of the literary classics, devoted themselves to illuminating and interpreting the law books. Working at first as solitary scholars, they soon perceived the advantage of pooling their talent and knowledge in law schools. In some respects, although allowing for inevitable temporal distinctions, these early legal academies anticipated the faculties of law in medieval and modern universities and contemporary colleges of law.[30]

Roman Educational Theorists

When Roman educators conceded that everything in Greek educational philosophy was subject to doubt and, moreover, that too much in the Greek scholastic paradigm lacked the trustworthy ring of practicality, they became excited about an educational philosophy of their own. As schooling became more important in Rome, and burdened as it was with the monumental responsibility of amalgamating Latin and Greek culture, Roman writers grappled with various sides to educational philosophy. Yet the standard of educational excellence in and out of Rome for the next fifteen hundred years was set not by the writers who, whatever their brilliance, occasionally took education for their topic, but by the giants of Roman educational thought and practice: Cicero and Quintilian. Perceptive educators were right when, in later years, they admitted that like pygmies they were standing on their shoulders.

Marcus Tullius Cicero (106–43 B.C.)

Few authors were better equipped than Cicero to outline a scholastic regimen to prepare students for public life. Not a schoolmaster, and without any professional axe to grind, Cicero could nevertheless shape an educational ideal and speak as an educated man about education's method and purpose.

Cicero could be indicted for incompleteness—his only concern was with the education of citizens—but his silence on some points should not blind us to his worthwhile pronouncements on educational decency. This son of a Roman knight, whose family roots were not deep in Rome's history, capitalized on every opportunity his social station afforded. After a conventional education in the lower schools and graduation from a school of rhetoric, he apprenticed with a public man, a sign of allegiance to a practice by then archaic or strikingly uncommon.[31] By the age of twenty-five, he was a pleader in the courts, extraordinary for one so young.[32] Illness led him to abandon pleading, and during a two-year recuperation, Cicero studied philosophy in Athens and Rhodes. Upon returning to Rome, he resumed pleading and, at the same time, began to climb the ladder of political preferment.

Politics in Rome had both perquisites and pitfalls, and despite his rapid rise to prominence in a profession unsuited to the faint of heart, Cicero was immune from neither. Exiled for political reasons about 55 B.C., he devoted his time to reflection and writing. After exile, it was hard to regain the public's confidence, so Cicero looked for a way to restore his political reputation.

The Orator. A book on education seemed to fit the bill. Always worthy of a citizen's attention, education was neither politically controversial nor personally dangerous. Besides, years earlier Cicero had written *De Inventione*, a book on education that he characterized as "schoolboy notes,"[33] so a new book offered a chance for a mature exposition. Moreover, Cicero's son, ten years old when *De Oratore* was published, and a nephew, a year older, could benefit from a carefully reasoned guide to schooling. *De Oratore*, though written with mixed motives, gained and maintained the stature of an educational classic.

This great book, really an essay on oratory, exhibits preoccupation with the teaching of rhetoric. It sets high goals for oratorical education and, going beyond the schooling of a public speaker, is a manifesto on the formation of a noble and cultured human being. Cicero's program of study takes conventional elementary schooling for granted to concentrate on the bountiful field of the liberal arts.

Cicero's expectation for secondary education might have been unrealistic, or he might have been ingenuous, but his personal standards were high and his educational proposals were likely based largely on his own scholastic experience. He refused to apologize for the rigor and breadth of the orator's course of study. Instead, he fortified his position: "No man can be an orator possessed of every praiseworthy accomplishment unless he knows everything important and all the liberal arts."[34] Poetry and history were given special emphasis, as were law and philosophy, for public men would be deficient without them. Finally, Cicero is at pains, after endorsing the substance of speech—for oratory without rich meaning is puerile—to pay heed to form. The ancient dictum, sometimes attributed to Socrates, that "All men are sufficiently eloquent in that which they understand" is scorned. Cicero means to have polished expression cultivated as a separate accomplishment.

Higher Education. When secondary education was over, students were ready for advanced instruction in rhetoric, philosophy, history, and law. But instruction was coupled with practical experience. Cicero praised learning by doing, but only up to a point. A classroom is not a courtroom, yet it is the one place where techniques for effective oratory can be learned. And writing was promoted as a dependable route to oratorical excellence. Cicero praised writing as a "teacher" of oratory: Should orators be called upon to speak extemporaneously, they will be able to recall what was written, and their speech will be the better for it.[35] Finally, ever a child of tradition, Cicero recommends imitation of oratory's best models as the surest route to excellence,[36] and deliberative, demonstrative, and judicial oratory were restored to their former place of significance.

Polished oratory, however, is only part of Cicero's educational code; equally important is forming the orator with civility, culture, and philosophy. Thought and speech are distinct abilities, so, according to Cicero, education must unify them. He appears to renew an ancient debate over the reciprocal status of philosophy and rhetoric both in school study and practical life. Plato's scientific humanism and Isocrates' literary humanism implied an inevitable incompatibility between thought and expression, but Plato and Isocrates may have refused compromise because of vested interest—each had his own academic citadel to protect—rather than principle. Without any school to husband, Cicero called for an accommodation between philosophy and oratory.

Yet even Cicero's exceptional eloquence could not close the breach between philosophy and oratory. So without much abatement, old hostility continued to plague education. Had Cicero been heeded, the good of education could have been served. Call the philosopher, he wrote, one "who instructs us fully in things and words, an orator," and an orator, one who "represents wisdom united with eloquence, a philosopher."[37] Then he adds: "No man has ever become a great orator unless he has combined a training in rhetoric with all other branches of knowledge,"[38] and "No one can hope to be an orator in the true sense of the word unless he has acquired knowledge of all the sciences and all the great problems of life."[39]

Coupling a detailed and intensive study of literature, rhetoric, histo-

ry ("To be ignorant of what happened before you were born, is to live the
life of a child forever. For what is a man's life, unless woven into the life of
our ancestors by the memory of past deeds?"),[40] law, and philosophy with
the experience of life will produce, Cicero wrote, "the cultured orator.
Grant me that such a man is also a philosopher, and the controversy is at
an end."[41]

    Cicero's Influence. Cicero's analysis of education was both practical
and philosophical, but it was not especially technical. He never intended
to write instructions for schoolmasters, although something in his exposition could have been useful to them. His intention, rather, was to set a
sound and prudent course for the education of Roman citizens. His readers, however, were tempted to interpret his advice as an ideal that, while
it might be aimed for, could never be achieved. In this context, it was easy
to strip away what was more difficult or demanding, so in the end, any
assessment of Cicero's influence on Roman education from the middle of
the first century B.C. to the end of the fifth century A.D. must take this
into account.

Marcus Fabius Quintilianus (A.D. 35–97)

    When ancient educators paid so much attention to oratory, some-
thing more than training in public speaking was at stake. In *The Education of an Orator*—sometimes ranked as education's greatest book—
Quintilian declares that education should produce "a good man skilled in
speaking."[42] This definition, interpreted in a context of Roman educational priority, was a guide to the formation of versatile and responsible
citizens.

    Quintilian examined every side of Roman education; though not a
Roman, his influence was exceptional. Alien status can be overstressed:
despite his birth and early education in Spain,[43] later education and life
in Rome made him Roman. After a brief interlude as a pleader in Roman
courts, and about twenty-eight years old, Quintilian went to Spain for
eight years. Upon returning to Rome, he resumed a career as a pleader
and became a private teacher of rhetoric. His success as a teacher was
immediate and noteworthy, so when the emperor Vespasian decided to
create a public professorship for Latin rhetoric in A.D. 76, Quintilian was
an obvious choice. This post, besides being one of honor, with a yearly
salary of 100,000 sesterces, made Quintilian a wealthy man. He kept the
professorship for a dozen years.

    The Education of an Orator. When Quintilian retired from teaching,
friends sought his counsel on the education and upbringing of their children. The record is scant with respect to this request, and it appears that

he was reluctant to comply; but his friends persisted. In any case, Quintilian acquiesced and, according to his own report, began to prepare a short book. Soon recognizing that a summary treatment of so important a subject would not do and, moreover, could blight his reputation, he amended his original intention and spent two years writing *The Education of An Orator*.[44]

Books one and two, dealing with issues fundamental to the care and education of children, have universal appeal, and Quintilian's exposition is pedagogically fresh and philosophically mature. Books three through seven are long, detailed treatments of rhetoric, a subject important to Quintilian but of far less interest today. Books eight through eleven dwell on elocution, memory training, and pronunciation, with an interpolation in book ten to list and annotate the great books. The orator's character has Quintilian's solicitous attention in book twelve, for an intelligent, well-educated immoral person can be dangerous.

Before Quintilian, educational literature had neglected two important periods: the pre- and elementary-school years. This neglect is prudently and expeditiously redressed, and education is characterized as starting with birth and ending with accomplishment in oratory.[45]

The Nurse. Beginning at the beginning, and taking into account Roman practice in connection with child care, Quintilian sets the qualifications for nurses. First and foremost, they must be morally sound, for in infant years the foundation of character is laid, and nurses, children's constant companions, are bound to give direct and indirect moral instruction.[46] In addition, they must use Latin correctly.[47] Readers wondering how nurses were prepared for this responsibility forget that Quintilian was counting on home education. In any case, it was Quintilian's constant conviction that habits learned early are permanent, and he was so solicitous about correct speech that linguistic impropriety was proscribed even for, especially for, children.

When nurses were efficient and successful, primary schoolmasters and pedagogues had their instructional burden eased. Pedagogues were supposed to supervise character formation (although they sometimes imparted literary instruction), so it was important for them to watch over the behavior of children, especially on the playground.[48] This attention to character puts Quintilian in a class by himself. Earlier educators had noticed the efficacy of informal education, especially in morals, but none was so precise in setting a secure theoretical foundation for the inculcation of moral excellence. The perfect orator, Quintilian declares, "should be a good man, and consequently we demand of him not merely the possession of exceptional gifts of speech, but all the excellences of character as well."[49]

Elementary Schools. Primary masters were common in Rome, and no one questioned the worth of their instruction, but such teachers were never praised. Quintilian, too, withholds praise and, though tempted to suspect their qualifications, is careful to acknowledge the importance of their work. Their character should be without flaw: nothing could supersede this. And they should be able to teach Greek, because Quintilian believed that orators needed to know it. In his school plan, the first four years concentrated on instruction in Greek.[50] Besides Greek, boys were to practice handwriting, copy poetry from dictation, learn the rules of spelling, and cultivate their memory.[51] Latin, the vernacular, could be learned in the regular intercourse of life, although in later schooling, Latin grammar was to be studied intensively.[52]

In all education, excellence is the goal to which students should aspire: "Those whose aspirations are highest, will attain to greater heights than those who abandon themselves to premature despair of ever reaching the goal and halt at the very foot of the ascent."[53] Quintilian, moreover, was optimistic in declaring that most boys are quick to reason and ready to learn. Curiosity and willingness to learn are instinctive qualities too often blunted by faulty pedagogy.

Two dogmatic assumptions dominated conventional educational practice and conspired to undermine Quintilian's sensible advice. For almost longer than anyone could remember, schooling had commenced at age seven, and Romans kept in step with tradition. Yet Quintilian was ready to jettison this practice: Schooling, he declared, should begin when students are ready, for "though the knowledge absorbed in the previous years may mean but little, yet the boy will be learning something more advanced during that year in which he would otherwise have been occupied with something more elementary."[54] The second assumption was that public education threatened the morals of youth and undermined confidence in public schools. Quintilian undertook to deflate it and improve the status of public schools by arguing that neither morality nor learning is jeopardized in them.

Individual Differences. Almost every sentence in *The Education of an Orator* stresses education's primary objective to create and encourage mental activity, and throughout the book references are frequent to such phrases as "sharpening intelligence," "native power," and "capacity." Anticipating modern educational theory, Quintilian tried to accommodate the curriculum to the intellectual ability and interest of students; and he recognized individual differences. Doubtless his educational outlook was infected with a fundamental optimism illustrated in the hypothesis that nurture can correct deficiencies in nature. Haste should be made slowly and nothing should be left out. Following this prescription, the faculties of memory, imagination, and sense perception can be strengthened by study even when originally they are weak.[55]

Secondary Schools. Grammar masters should be selected with more than ordinary care, for grammar, although belonging to the "elementary stages of the teaching of literature[,] must not therefore be despised as trivial."[56] These teachers are responsible for starting students down the road to excellence by teaching correct speech and introducing literature. Neither study depends merely upon mechanical skill, so the theory of composition and the art of reading need attention. Finally, the principles of criticism must be learned and applied to reading, writing, music, geometry, and philosophy. In secondary schools, though, philosophy was to serve mainly as an integrating discipline.

Grammar and literature are prominent in secondary schools because both contribute directly to genuine eloquence, but Quintilian wanted to be complete, so music and mathematics were added. The case for music was strong because music could contribute to refined modes of expression, to the development of vocal patterns, to rhythm of gesture, and to grace, harmony, speech, and movement. Besides, music's relationship to literature gave it an informational side that Quintilian was eager to capitalize. Geometry was harder to justify, although orators had a definite need for a command of number.[57] Quintilian abandoned classical teachers' indifference to mathematics as a science and refused to endorse their definition of geometry as a practical discipline. Geometry was a liberal study with an immense capacity for disciplining the mind, and his endorsement was ringing: "no mathematics, no orator."[58] In the end, however, for reasons never entirely clear, Quintilian's curriculum neglected geometry and arithmetic.

Rhetoric. Schools of rhetoric began where grammar schools stopped, but were warned to articulate their studies with those of the lower schools. Quintilian, moreover, deplored the tendency of schoolmasters to repeat what had been taught or to anticipate what would be taught.[59] They were to teach the theory of eloquence and give students enough practice to ensure their effectiveness as public speakers. The objective of higher learning is clearly and simply stated, but this objective depends upon a vast network of rhetorical theory and rule that had to be mastered. We can skip over this network, along with the pedagogical directives accompanying it, although Quintilian used the greater part of nine books to elaborate this thicket of detail.

In addition to a recitation of rule and regulation about rhetoric, Quintilian appended a list of orators and historians to be read.[60] Criteria for selection were easy: only the best authors were on it, and those recognized for transparency of style and lucidity of expression were preferred.

Livy was better than Sallust, but Cicero's books were the standard for excellence.[61]

Boys entered schools of rhetoric in early adolescence and continued their study until they were young men. During this scholastic interlude, in addition to sound instruction in eloquence, they needed teachers whose morals were without flaw and who had, besides, a talent for shaping the character of young men with a bold spirit. As models of self-control, these teachers were expected to have the vigor to govern the behavior of their students. When students were disciplined, Quintilian recommended a melding of severity with moderation,[62] but he never forgot that learning was hard, that it demanded effort, and that cleverness in the use of teaching devices could not substitute for diligence and application in study.

Teachers on every scholastic level played some part in the formation of orators; while Quintilian was eager to acknowledge their importance, he could not resist singling out teachers of rhetoric for special attention. If these men melded eloquence and prudence with skill in teaching, they would almost surely enjoy success. The most obvious indication of prudence and skill was a teacher's ability to meet students on their level of accomplishment.[63] The coin of sound instruction, though, has another side. Standards are always to be set by teachers, never by students, so while it may be important for teachers to adjust their instruction to student need when instruction begins, the level of accomplishment must be raised as instruction proceeds. In everything—manners, morals, and scholastic achievement—teachers are expected to be models for students to emulate.

Memory and Imitation. In this connection, teachers should be demanding but not unreasonable, and this introduces a complex issue which must have been a conundrum for Quintilian: variation in students' abilities. Neither provision for individual differences nor standard of excellence could be executed with confidence unless teachers were somehow equipped to assess the ability of their students. A good memory, Quintilian declared, is the surest sign of ability; next is quickness at imitation.[64]

The Importance of Writing. Cicero had praised writing as a handmaiden to oratory and Quintilian follows suit. Writing, he says, is learned by writing; practice has no substitute. Students should begin with a draft and use it as an outline to be filled, finished, and polished. And an eraser should be used as freely as a pen. Excellence in composition comes from revision: "Write quickly and you will never write well; write well and you will soon write quickly."[65] Still, although practice in writing is imperative, instruction is essential. Students must be taught the importance of revision, what to revise, and the dividend of self-criticism. Without such instruction, they will not, when they leave school and have no one to correct their mistakes, be able to criticize and revise their speeches.

Nature and Nurture. Instruction should accommodate to differences in ability, but both teachers and students must realize that learning is difficult. Knowledge, moreover, has a logical order that cannot be sacrificed to pedagogic expedience. Even so, optimism is justified, for knowledge and discipline can correct deficiency in nature.

The best education takes advantage of every opportunity to form the mind and shape the will and, according to Quintilian, the best chance for success comes during the infant years. During years of early youth, mental work should center on play so learning will be pleasant and favorable attitudes toward it will be fostered. And to ensure a good start up the long avenue to learning, only teachers with superior qualifications should be engaged to teach a variety of subjects simultaneously, a tactic for making schooling congenial to students. At the same time, relaxation, amusement, rest, and play are essential, but even in periods free from study, students must be supervised, for a great deal can be learned about children by observing them at play.

Punishment. Punishment, a traditional corrective recommended for boys who refused to follow the disciplinary regulations of the school, is nowhere proscribed in Quintilian's great book, but beating boys for infraction of rule only disgraces them and does little or nothing to encourage greater effort. Corporal punishment has superior substitutes that include competition, commendation, affection for the teacher, and the interest aroused by the subjects studied.[66] The normal child, Quintilian asserted, is eager and curious;[67] when either eagerness or curiosity is suppressed, teachers are at fault.[68]

Teachers' Duty. Teachers, according to Quintilian, have a duty to their students and should use their skill to instruct them well, but they have a duty to knowledge that must not be neglected. So high goals must not be lowered even when student accomplishment is deficient and disappointing. Yet whatever their zeal for accomplishment, teachers are warned about the evil effect of overteaching and from needlessly intervening between students and their studies. In this respect, discovery is recognized and encouraged as the principal element in learning. Finally, Quintilian makes a statement that will always be considered extraordinary: Teachers who are confident of their talent and skillful in directing the complexities of instruction will arrange to have large classes in public schools.[69]

Leaving Quintilian, we know we have listened to educational advice heeded by our ancestors; we know, too, that his influence on educational practice, while sometimes matched, has never been surpassed.

Rome and the Future of Education

Roman education was affected by Greek and Hellenistic models, so it is hard to credit it with originality. But, while originality is important, it is equally important to recognize, utilize, and preserve ideas. And here is where Rome was precocious. She borrowed educational practice for her own use and, of greater significance to cultural life in Europe, husbanded and kept intact a culture beneficial to future generations. Her legacy with respect to state systems of education, however, was of smaller scale. Cicero's and Quintilian's influence upon Western education was strong, and for centuries the Latin classics dominated the curricula of good schools; but the story that Rome created and maintained an extensive system of state-controlled and -supported schools is mainly hyperbole.[70]

Such schools flourished in Rome during the republican period (ca. 300–100 B.C.) but were found rarely in the provinces. Official policy had the effect of encouraging the opening of schools, but throughout the greater part of Rome's history, neither compulsory education nor a state school system was enforced or erected. Late in the republican period, politicians perceived how schools could serve political purpose, so in the early empire (31 B.C.–A.D. 192), Augustus, for example, banished all foreign teachers from Rome, and Vespasian, although he distrusted philosophers and drove them from the city, appointed Quintilian to the state chair of rhetoric. Several emperors, moreover, built libraries, collected books, subsidized teachers and exempted them from military duty, and made educational grants to outlying cities and towns.[71]

Without ever enlisting in a crusade for state education, Rome nevertheless succeeded in obtaining considerable control over schools and schoolmasters, and in consequence, the schools developed habits of subservience and dependence. This was a bad omen that at the time went undetected, but when Rome decayed and finally collapsed, schools had neither the will, the skill, nor the independence to survive. By the early decades of the sixth century A.D., only remnants of genuine Latin education survived outside the boundaries of the city of Rome.

Chapter 5

Christian Education: Competing Loyalty and Common Value

For four hundred years, at least until the first monastic schools appeared in the fourth century A.D., Christians in Rome depended upon classical Roman schools to instruct their children. Schools infused with a religious spirit and outlook were unknown, and Christian boys and girls attended classical schools where pagan literature dominated the curriculum and where Christians were often employed as teachers.[1] In these early centuries, most Romans, still pagan and insensitive to the conundrum faith and learning posed for Christians, refused to change the character of their schools to accommodate the educational appetite of Christians. Besides, lacking sympathy for people trying to live in the secular world without becoming part of it, Roman political policy erected obstacles to smother the growth of Christianity.[2]

Christian anxiety over a potential erosion of faith in classical schools was entirely justified, and time and again, Christian leaders called attention to the danger lurking behind the schoolhouse door. Even the presence of Christian teachers was of little help, for they were powerless to alter the standard course of instruction or to annotate it to suit a Christian temperament. Christians had to choose between abandoning the schools altogether, turning their backs on learning—as some did—or establishing their own schools where learning could proceed without threatening faith.

Abandoning learning was a poor solution (although intemperate spokesmen sometimes took this hard line), because Roman Christians wanted to be good citizens as well as constant in their faith. Education and culture were essential to a full participation in civic and economic life. After Christianity had survived a precarious first century, it might have engaged in genuine educational novelty. Although it would have been hard, Christian schools could have been erected. Yet this alternative was rejected for what was then considered to be sound religious justification.

A case has been made for a Christian indifference to learning, and the myth has been repeated that the early Church was content to wade in ignorance and illiteracy, oblivious to the complementary relationship between intellectual illumination and moral formation. Despite a fundamental rusticity practiced by thousands of early Christians, crass indifference to learning was not the Church's policy. The educational question was complex, and so were its various answers. One must pay attention to the basic motive inspiring all Christians: eternal salvation. The conventional religious wisdom sounded ominous in predicting the world's imminent end. Persons of faith naturally gave priority to the things of life capable of ensuring eternal reward, and any sensible Christian used the gift of time for moral perfection rather than intellectual finishing. As a mediator between the human and the divine, the Church felt compelled to use its resources to lead communicants to heaven rather than to school.

Years passed without a Judgment Day, and the apprehension tormenting the spirit of early Christians was replaced by optimism. Christians looked forward to a life where temporal goals figured larger, but they remembered their obligation to care for the good of their souls as they searched for ways to use the things of Caesar to pave the road to salvation. Yet either appropriating the classical schools or mounting an educational effort where classical learning could be husbanded alongside deposits of Christian faith in schools of their own never occurred to them. The Church's mission was moral and religious, and the weight of divine authority was behind it. Could the Church afford to amend its mission to pay heed to the classics and spend its moral authority on an ornamental literary education, however useful or attractive ornamentation might be?

Besides, nothing in the educational picture of the ancient world illustrated a melding of a secular and a sacred educational program. Without a scholastic model to follow, and with the profound conviction that excavating classical treasure was not God's work, Christians hesitated to mount and manage their own schools. Still, something could be done to ensure the integrity of faith and preserve it for future generations. They turned their attention to Christian education, an education based on a common core of Christian belief whose perpetuity was imperative to the stability and future of the Church. Christian education, defined as the moral and religious formation of a child, was a family responsibility.

The home, then, was the first Christian school, although its teaching proceeded without help from grammar and literature. Qualified by nature to set the first stanchion of moral and religious habit, the home's instructional charter was certified both by the writings of the Apostle Paul[3] and by the tradition of Roman family life. But had Christians paid closer attention to Jewish tradition, they might have found a model of family education to imitate.

The Christian family enjoyed almost total autonomy in teaching. Instruction was to be orthodox, of course, so Church authorities stood ready to lend assistance, although families took the doctrine they understood and, without any systematic theology to guide them, taught their children the elements of faith. The object of this instruction was the formation of devout Christians, but there was more: children should be ready for the sacrament of baptism. Thereafter the family continued its solicitous attention to the essentials of a Christian life and, in the manner of a Roman family, kept an eye on its members into their mature years.

So long as Christian education was meant for children, the home was the place for instruction in religion to begin and, sometimes, to end. But thousands of adults converted to Christianity. Nothing in their experience substituted for the work of the Christian family, so Christian leaders quickly perceived the need to organize catechumenal schools to prepare converts for the sacrament of baptism.

The First Christian Schools

Reacting to urgent necessity, the Christian community turned attention to religious instruction when the weight of this responsibility became too great for families to bear. Sometime in the first century A.D., the nucleus of religious schools was formed, but in evaluating this invention, there should be no premature attribution of genuine scholastic purpose. Neither the catechumenal school—the first offshoot of this nucleus—nor any of the religious schools that followed were authentic schools. Without any pretense whatever, they centered effort on religious instruction and ignored a literary curriculum. Employing conventional nomenclature, historians are tempted to call these catechumenal, catechetical, and episcopal institutes "schools," but they are imprecise when they do. By the time educational practice reached the Christian era, the standard definition of a school specified a literary curriculum. And these schools, the evidence indicates, lacked such a curriculum. Yet what they did was critical to the vigor and zeal of Christianity and thus to the education of the whole of Europe. Something of their history is worth our attention.

The Catechumenal School. Most popular during the first two centuries of the Christian era, catechumenal schools lasted until the ninth century, when infant baptism became the standard ritual of entrance into the Christian community. Although they enjoyed a long life, their years of prosperity were brief, and after the second century A.D., they existed only on the fringe of religious education.

Catechumenal schools—thus styled because instruction in them was exclusively oral—were kept by steadfast and loyal Christians who, without being schoolmasters earning a living from their work, offered competent instruction in Church history and Christian doctrine and practice. These teachers were usually bishops and priests, because the Church took with the utmost seriousness its mission of spreading the gospel to the unconverted. But the pressure of ecclesiastical and sacerdotal business was sometimes too great for bishops and priests to spend their time teaching, so clerics in minor orders and trusted laymen were recruited. They were guided by a considerable body of literature about what should be taught.

The three- to five-year course of instruction outlined in this literature was neither difficult nor demanding and it never presumed student literacy, although this concession was probably unnecessary since most adult converts were already classically educated. Care was essential in preparing candidates for baptism, so questions and answers were adopted as the approved pedagogic technique. Explanation and interpretation could be either distracting or unorthodox; departure from instructional formula was always discouraged and sometimes strictly prohibited.

Catechetical Schools. Baptized persons crossed the threshold of the Christian community with enough knowledge to seal their affirmation of belief. These elemental precepts satisfied most Christians, but some were anxious and curious. They wanted more. Christianity's first principles were simple and precise, but the deposit of Christian belief was both broad and deep. No one could achieve fluency in doctrine without advanced instruction. Catechetical schools were commissioned to offer it.

Courses of instruction designed to meet the needs of students, most of whom were adults, varied too much to leave an indelible mark on history. Evidently both clerics and laymen were teachers in these schools and, motivated by an intense devotion to faith, volunteered to teach Christian doctrine to anyone willing to learn. Doing God's work, they neither expected nor received compensation. Catechetical schools flourished during the early Christian period only to recede into the background when better means were found to give sound instruction in doctrine.

While one type of catechetical school functioned with a generous but imprecise commission to offer advanced instruction in doctrine to baptized persons, other types had a more precise assignment. After completing their study in classical schools, young men aspiring to holy orders needed a refresher course in Christian doctrine before apprenticing themselves to a bishop for training to the priesthood. Special catechetical schools offered this course. These schools (always fewer in number than regular catechetical schools) had a fairly standard curriculum, because their teachers—always priests or bishops—knew the points of doctrine that needed to be taught. Besides, bishops had a special interest in the formation of priests and were careful to keep their religious instruction both essential and orthodox. We may suppose, therefore, that the curricular variety characteristic in catechetical schools for laymen was absent from schools that remind us now of minor seminaries.[4]

Another type of catechetical school always figures larger in educational history because it was a genuine school, but—and this is the problem—schools of this type might not have been Christian. The most famous among them was in Alexandria, although others, in Rome, Nisibis, Edessa, Antioch, and Caesarea, achieved considerable scholastic notoriety. The Alexandrian school had Clement (ca. 150–215) first and then Origen (ca. 185–254) as illustrious and successful headmasters. The schools representing this type, following the model of Alexandria, filled their curricula with the classics and taught grammar, literature, and rhetoric in traditional ways.[5] But we look in vain for instruction in Christian doctrine and are confident that if they were ever centers for the study of theology, this emphasis was fleeting. Their commitment to secular learning was clear, and their excellence in its communication, legendary. With so much about them beyond doubt, the temptation to inquire into the story of their connection with Christianity is strong. This alleged connection is mainly myth. Still, we wonder about its origin.

Although teachers in these catechetical schools were usually Christians (sometimes deacons or priests, as in Clement's case), they lacked the Church's authorization to teach Christian doctrine, an authorization teachers in the other types of catechetical schools possessed.[6] As independent schoolmasters trying to earn a living and add luster to the reputation of their schools, they might have cultivated the illusion that they were conducting Christian schools. Almost certainly, many among them were Christians with a deep devotion to a faith they labored to encourage and would do nothing to injure.

With this attitude toward Christian belief, teachers often added an elective course in Christian doctrine to the school's regular syllabus of instruction but were careful to teach it only after the school day was over. The arrangement allowed the school to show its classical face, thus encouraging the matriculation of pagans, and it helped to maintain the traditional standard of educational decency. When this formula was adopted, religion did not intrude upon the regular course of instruction.

As an academic afterthought and a concession to Christian students desiring such instruction, courses in Christian doctrine were available. On this precarious basis, these schools won their reputation for being Christian.

Episcopal Schools. Although it took a long time for episcopal schools to become theological centers and seminaries for the intellectual and moral formation of priests, they originated with the apprenticeship arrangement bishops had with young men who aspired to the religious life. Not until the sixth century was academic character imposed on clerical training,[7] so before then, prospective priests, under the direction of their bishops, learned by doing to perform the rituals and conduct the liturgy of the Christian Church.

After young men completed their study in Roman classical schools and took a refresher course in doctrine in catechetical schools, they were ready to enlist as bishops' apprentices. Learning by doing (along with some instruction on the finer points of faith), they spent several years preparing for ordination to the priesthood. Bishops' standards varied and the Church's needs differed from place to place, so any precise description either of the nature or the length of this training would be hazardous.[8]

The Christian Educational Dilemma

Had Christians ignored literary culture and discounted its relevance to their way of life, they could have concentrated on strictly moral and religious objectives and excluded all else. They could have stood firm in their faith without countenancing any compromise between the classics and religion. Or if Christianity had no leading strings to the past, the classical legacy could have been ignored. As it was, Christians could neither deny the relevance of culture nor pretend immunity of their faith to ancient social, political, and cultural values.

With an ardent resentment of it, Christians wanted paganism destroyed, yet they knew instinctively that its destruction would be tantamount to annihilating the civilization they knew, had come to admire, and wanted to preserve. With an undiminished devotion, Christians were eager to practice their religion without abandoning the conventions of Roman life. No wonder dilemma weighed them down.

Besides, they both embraced and spurned classical literature, then the basis for grammar and rhetoric, as a staple subject in the schools. With all its ambiguity, this fluctuating mood can be understood. In addition to being the foundation for educational decency, classical literature was a national heritage whose pagan ideals and values were persuasive

enough to undermine the sturdiest profession of Christian faith. Caught
in a cultural dilemma, Christians matched their affection for literature
with an intense hatred of pagan practice and belief. At one time, they
defended the worth of grammar and rhetoric, studied authors with whom
they disagreed, and protested Julian's decree prohibiting Christian teachers from teaching the classics.[9] At another time, they tried to sterilize the
classics by stripping moral significance from them. Any way they turned,
the path of compromise was hard to find.

Some intemperate Christians—Tertullian (A.D. 160?–230?) is the one
usually cited—eschewed compromise and zealously opposed a cultivation
of reason. But Tertullian has suffered from bad press. When he asked,
"What indeed has Athens to do with Jerusalem?", a lack of enthusiasm for
secular learning is plain, yet as a man of considerable learning (educated
in philosophy, law, and medicine, and able to write in both Greek and
Latin), what he opposed was not philosophy generally, but heresy or the
philosophy generating it. Rather than seeking the abolition of reason,
Tertullian put it to apologetic use. Despite danger in it, philosophy had a
place in the armory of Christian learning. Still, he was eager to put first
things first. In absolving Tertullian from a charge of extremism, one must
nevertheless admit that there were extremists, although their influence
was slight, and moderate Christian spokesmen—say, Tatian, Augustine,
and Jerome—demurred from forging an alliance between Christian doctrine and the classics.[10]

Plans to Resolve the Dilemma. Neither capitulation nor rejection
characterizes Christian educational activity as it followed the pathway of
uneasy compromise. This pathway took children to classical schools for
the conventional course, but always with premonition of danger and
sometimes with protest about the sacrifice of Christian wisdom on the
altar of the pagan gods. Under the circumstances, safeguards to faith
were essential, for even a superior conventional education was too great a
price to pay for abandoning faith, and the best safeguard was solid training in piety in the home. Christian education should be strong to keep
pagan learning from undermining faith. With this safeguard and with
constant reminders that they could be dangerous places, Christian
children attended the classical schools.

Uneasy compromise existed in academic practice, where it must have
been hard to sustain, but on the level of theory, hostility between faith and
classical learning refused to subside and the dilemma remained. Yet hostility was more intense in Latin than in Greek Christendom, although
Eastern Christianity was not immune to echoes of doubt and recrimina-
tion from the West.

Habitually familiar with classical learning, Eastern Christians had

discovered how to keep realms of faith and reason distinct. Eastern scholars studied the classics and followed the speculation in ancient philosophy
with little fear of moral or doctrinal contamination. Without being a
burning issue, the problem of paganism was evident to them. Acknowledging pagan learning, they never meant to embrace the whole of ancient
philosophy or adopt its polytheism. Eastern Christians were able to write
and speak like educated pagans without surrendering to paganism's cultural ideals. Western Christians, however, with a lower threshold of
awareness fueled by the human tendency to fear the unknown, chose to
appeal to faith and, in doing so, were cool to the ornaments of reason.

Christian writers sometimes worried about their inability to use
grammar and rhetoric skillfully and to dress faith in the finest literary
garments. Still, truth was entitled to clear and persuasive elaboration, so
as Christian doctrine matured, its exposition needed a literary refinement
that only competent schooling could supply.

St. Basil's Recommendation. St. Basil (A.D. fourth century) began his
career as a friend of the classics and spent enough time with them to know
them well. Thereafter, posing as a compromiser, he recommended an
accommodation between faith and classical learning, a means for supplying faith with a substantial rational foundation. But his flirtation with
the classics was temporary. One of his books, *On the Reading of the
Profane Authors*, appears upon superficial reading to be a guide to mining the classical treasury without jeopardizing faith, but a closer reading
leads one to suspect that he meant to tell his readers how they could
obtain conventional literary skill without using the classics at all. This
book was intended for clerics, who were told to avoid the classics; but for
laymen, the door to classical study was left ajar: they could read the
classics if they had to.

Clement of Alexandria and Origen. Basil's ambiguous endorsement
for studying the classics was amended by Clement of Alexandria, but
Clement's counsel, despite its progressive sound, had the effect of magni-
fying the confusion in Christian policy concerning the use of the literary
legacy. As an Eastern scholar whose reputation for learning was ratified in
a long association with the Alexandrian catechetical school, Clement was
the first Christian to leave a record wherein the fundamental issues of
educational policy were pondered.[11] He was sanguine about the contribution the classics could make to Christian thought and untroubled by the
dangers to faith that were alleged to be lurking in them. He understood
how an intellectual culture subserving doctrine could consolidate and
strengthen it, and he advanced an audacious argument that championed
learning as one way of achieving human perfection. When known thoroughly and interpreted properly, he said, the classics were harmless, for

their moral doctrines were similar to those of Christianity and were, he implied, drawn from a common source.[12]

Clement's successor at the Alexandrian school, Origen, followed Clement in trying to find a formula for harmonizing sacred and secular learning, but the curtain of hostility was too dense to penetrate. Origen refused to affirm the independent worth of secular knowledge and, instead, chose to regard it as merely a means for probing and understanding Christian doctrine. St. Jerome recounted how students flocked to Origen for instruction in all subjects and, after praising his skill and genius, added that Origen taught his students "in the hope that through the instrumentality of secular literature, he might establish them in the faith of Christ."[13]

Despite Origen's cautious endorsement of the classics, some scholars have praised him for freeing Christians from scholastic narrowness and for promoting a broad and liberal approach to culture. But the temptation to alter their interpretation is strong. Origen was neither an uncompromising enemy nor an unwavering friend of classical learning, although he helped Christian education by rejecting the untenable stand that secular study should be avoided altogether.[14]

St. Ambrose and St. John Chrysostom. In company with Clement and Origen, St. Ambrose (340–397) and St. John Chrysostom (344–407) sensed the weight of the problem of paganism. They, too, tried to resolve it. Speaking from the position of an educated man who had benefited from classical learning, Ambrose refused to participate in the declamation against the classics or to repeat the common argument that intellectual formation was an obstacle to salvation. As a bishop of Milan with an impeccable reputation for orthodoxy, his pronouncements supporting intellectual refinement and a broad utilization of classical learning had the ring of credibility. Yet, while he had the power to open a gateway for liberal culture to pass to the early Middle Ages, Ambrose listened instead to the voice of caution and used his eloquence to demonstrate that intellectual formation was not an impediment to salvation. But rather than demonstrating this principle and applying it to the whole of Christian education, he spoke only about the education of clergymen. More a book on theology than on education, *The Duties of the Clergy* repeats Clement's exemplary theory about the good secular learning can do.

Growing up with them, St. John Chrysostom displayed less fear of the classics than his Western confreres, yet he, too, refused to take them for granted and, moreover, inquired whether Christians could use the classics with impunity.[15] Recalling his own nurture, Chrysostom thought he knew how the classics could be used so their pagan spirit would not cloud the vision of faith.[16] His refusal to proscribe them testifies to his prudence rather than to his enthusiasm for them. Despite its undeniable worth, danger lurked in classical learning.

Our Christian ancestors must have been bewildered by the words of advice that came from their leaders. Did they need a kind of education they should not have? The testimony so far is incomplete, but it tells us that hundreds of Christians were preaching a sermon of caution and confusion. Optimistic one day about finding a way through the thicket of paganism, they despaired the next day about discovering a satisfactory formula for accommodating the classics to Christianity. The witnesses were eloquent and prominent, but they seldom said anything of much use to Christian parents faced with making a critical choice between erudition and salvation. Until St. Jerome (331–420) and St. Augustine (350–430) tackled it, the dilemma was unresolved.

St. Jerome's Formal Study. When Jerome had his books (and he wanted them even when asceticism sent him to mountain caves and desert huts), his exceptional scholarship produced the great Latin version of the Bible, the *Vulgate*, dozens of commentaries on sacred scripture, and *Lives of Great Men.* He was, by any account, a model for Christian students and scholars to emulate. But when he spoke to the Christian community, there was no endorsement of classical learning or any recommendation that schoolmasters depend upon the ancient authors for their course of study. Jerome practiced scholarship with the intention of preserving the integrity of Christian doctrine. The doubts and recriminations that plagued his Christian confreres weighed on him too, and we are left to wonder whether his scholarly example or the report of his famous dream was, in the end, his legacy to Christian learning.

At one time, searching for spiritual solace on a desert retreat, Jerome had a dream that in his recounting of it has achieved enduring fame. Dreaming that he was a victim of fatal illness and "haled before the judgment seat of God," Jerome heard a voice inquiring into the condition of his soul. "I replied that I was a Christian. 'Thou liest,' answered he that sat upon the throne. 'Thou art a Ciceronian, not a Christian; for where thy treasure is, there shall thy heart be also.'"[17] If these were not sentiments of hostility toward classical scholarship, they at least implied that the classics occupied a low rung on the ladder of Christian value and, if used imprudently, could be serious obstacles on the road to eternal salvation. Proof is lacking that Jerome's dream tempered enthusiasm for the classics, but nothing in it coaxed Christians to invest very heavily in them.

Jerome meant to tell Christians that knowledge of the elements of grammar and rhetoric was essential to decent Christian learning, for without it the truth of Christian doctrine could be neither understood nor promulgated. But how should these elements be obtained? Now, for the first time, we meet the doctrine of "formal study."[18] The classics were reservoirs of grammar and rhetoric, and because the doctrine of usage was still intact, students needed to tap these reservoirs to obtain literary skill. But when they did, the germs of paganism could contaminate them. Jerome told generations of schoolboys to read the classics for style, to pick from them the essential rules governing good speaking and writing, and ignore all else. Stripped of their stories, the classics were antiseptic and could be used in Christian schools. For centuries, the record reveals, Christians tried to follow Jerome's advice. Teachers did their best to rivet attention on elements of style and to preoccupy their students with the doctrine of use. But this technique, while perhaps manageable for advanced students, must have been close to impossible for beginners.

St. Augustine: Textbooks and Anthologies. Augustine's entire educational background was classical, but upon embracing the Christian faith, he began to question the worth of pagan learning and, time and again, expressed doubt that it had any legitimate place in Christian life. This expression of doubt put him in the company of a cadre of Christian leaders whose anxiety on this point was evident. Pleading for a policy of caution, they preferred ignorance to infidelity, but Augustine was bolder. Without ever repudiating one word of his criticism of the classics, Augustine was nevertheless prepared to use them selectively, and he ended up recommending an educational program wherein elements of the classical corpus could be used in the cultivation and promotion of faith.[19]

In Confessions, The City of God, On Christian Doctrine, Catechizing the Uninstructed, and The Teacher (De Magistro), Augustine expounded a theory of knowledge broad enough to accommodate the liberal arts, but he was careful to pare away their seductive character, and this sometimes led him to repudiate large parts of classical literature. Prepared himself to use reason, he nevertheless distrusted it and told his Christian companions to guard against its enthronement. He instructed them to be prudent and selective in their reading of ancient authors, and he enjoined them to cast out anything dangerous to faith.[20] They should follow the example of the prince who, after capturing a comely, uncivilized maiden, cut her hair, pared her nails, had her bathed and dressed, gave her time to adjust to new surroundings, and then married her.[21] Augustine wanted the liberal arts to be clean and inoffensive when they entered the school. Critics have sometimes accused him of scrubbing away their substance with the dirt.

Augustine's recommendation had elements of soundness and pedagogic applicability that Jerome's formula lacked, yet it has been interpreted in strikingly different ways. Augustine is accused of abandoning reason and of intimidating scholarship with religious discipline and authority; but he is praised, too, for constructing a lasting intellectual foundation whereupon Christian learning and scholarship can stand. What needs stressing, however, was his separation of the classical literary inheritance into definable parts, keeping some for Christian use and discarding the rest. Teachers, he said, must employ the principle of selection to compile for student use carefully expurgated anthologies of the classics. In this way, the great deficiency of Jerome's plan was avoided: the story was allowed to survive. Textbooks on grammar and rhetoric were to be written, and with them on their desks, schoolboys no longer found it necessary to go to the classics to discover grammatical rule and rhetorical regulation. When models of style missing from anthologies were needed, they should be found, Augustine said, in scripture.[22]

The Collapse of Roman Schools

Long before Jerome and Augustine produced their compromise plans, thousands of Christians had undertaken to resolve the instructional conundrum on their own terms. Church law was lenient with respect to the education of laymen, so Christian children and teachers flocked to Roman schools, but the education of prospective clergymen was a different matter. They were warned to eschew both the Roman schools and classical learning.[23] Christian teachers benefited from a tolerant policy that did nothing more than urge them to abandon the teaching of "secular science" (the classics), if they could. But many Christians earned their living by teaching the classics, so they stayed in the schools and, from all accounts, enjoyed the respect and trust of their pagan colleagues. To earn and maintain their professional status, Christian teachers must have refused to proselytize, otherwise their reception in the Roman schools would not have been cordial.

Still, pagans must sometime have wondered if they were being too tolerant. By A.D. 313, the decree of Milan, promulgated by Constantine (who reigned from A.D. 303 to 337), ended the persecution of Christians and gave them full civil rights. Constantine's generous spirit, moreover, encouraged schooling, and everywhere in the empire, education enjoyed an unexpected resurgence. Nowhere more than in advanced studies, especially in Constantinople, were scholars encouraged and rewarded; but lured by high salaries, privileges, and immunities hard to find elsewhere, teachers flocked to the lower schools as well. In a period of educational prosperity, Christians became teachers in greater number than before. Later, this worried the Emperor Julian, so in A.D. 362, he issued an edict intended to drive them from the schools. The edict required all teachers to obtain permission to teach, but a circular accompanying it declared morality to be their essential qualification, so they were enjoined to take an oath affirming belief in what they taught.[24] Julian stood on solid ground, one could argue, because persons professing what they know to be false are surely immoral. Now Christian teachers were put in a quandary. They could either abjure and swear the oath or withdraw from teaching. Any Christian teacher taking such an oath would have been vulnerable to an indictment for perjury.

Julian's edict was rescinded in 364, but had it remained in force, Christians would likely have created a system of schools of their own, and the educational vacuum of those long centuries following the sixth might never have occurred. As it was, however, a few Christians reacted to the humiliation and intimidation inherent in the edict by undertaking to impose classical style on the scriptures, but they were never influential enough to generate a scholastic movement. Failing to capitalize on what may have been a blessing in disguise (Julian's edict temporarily restricting their academic freedom), Christians missed a chance to alter the course of educational history. This lost chance, coupled with the general deterioration of Roman schools in the early sixth century, set the stage for a dense shroud of darkness that began to threaten learning and education in Europe.

Christians were justified in not establishing a system of schools. Vigorous as it was, classical education was never able to undermine the foundations of faith; and as centuries rolled past, despite the nostalgic yearning of influential Romans, classical values began to decline. With their decline, the stature, zeal, and strength of the Roman state began slowly and steadily to decay. As early as the second century, especially on the outskirts of the empire, Romanism was in jeopardy.

The Anglo-Saxons seized control in Roman Britain in the early fifth century, and an order and tranquility to life guaranteed by an exigent state were replaced by barbarism and violence. Earlier, in 276, Roman dominion in Gaul was challenged when Germanic tribes crossed the Rhine River, so by the fifth century, Gaul was hardly more than an insecure outpost of Roman influence. Exceptions to erosion of Roman power were evident in Africa, where the Roman system lived on to supply a cultural link between the past and the future, and in a few European enclaves.

Until the early sixth century, such great cities as Milan, Ravenna, Pavia, and Rome stood as the last bastions of classical education and culture. The earlier barbarian invasion had halted at the Alps, and Roman citizens revelled in their good luck at having been spared assault from invaders who were regarded as crude, cruel, and ignorant. They should have recognized their danger. They were to be next. About the middle of the sixth century, Lombards came as conquerors, swarmed over Roman cultural monuments and ornaments, and laid waste to everything in their path. After this destructive march, the land was intellectually barren and the schools whose excellence had commanded the admiration of all were hardly more than dim scholastic outlines. So for the second time, Christians entered the field of instruction, but this time their vision was broader and the need of society was greater. The simple religious institutes of earlier days were all but forgotten, and schools with genuine literary objectives began to make an appearance.

The Appearance of Genuine Christian Schools

Monasticism and Monastic Schools. Sometime in the fourth century, monasticism began to flourish in the West, and these spiritual communities needed literary skill if monks were to fulfill their religious duties. The attainment of literary skill did not, of course, demand the establishment of schools, but it did nothing to discourage them. Monks entered monasteries and nuns joined convents to dedicate themselves to a life-long service to the Lord. These religious houses were "schools" for asceticism. Isolated from secular society in monasteries and convents usually tucked away in the country, and without much need for a standard classical education, the religious persons in them were preoccupied with labor and prayer. Labor dispensed them from literary accomplishment, but prayer was another matter. Religious rule obligated monks and nuns to public and private prayer, explicitly required literacy for devotional reading, and usually adverted, as well, to the care and education of children in the monastery and convent.

So much was certainly expected of religious women and men alike, but the record we have gives a fuller and more precise account of monastic than of conventual regimen. It is hazardous to write about typical monastic novices, for they varied greatly in age, ability, and education upon entering the monastery, but many, certainly, were unable to read and write. Even the literate had to be taught the regimen of religious life, and this instruction, moreover, admonished them to abandon unfruitful memories from profane books and replace them with spiritual reflection. The novitiate, then—a period of preparation when religious fervor and dedication were tested—must also have been used to introduce both young and old to the tools of literacy. From the fourth to the sixth century, this instruction was rudimentary and not very well planned. Without a prescribed curriculum, some older monk, using whatever pedagogical skill he possessed, taught reading to a few novices. The mysteries and intricacies of grammar and rhetoric were ignored, and poison water from the well of classical learning was left untouched. Novices too dull to master reading learned by heart the psalms, epistles, and prayers essential to a regular monastic life.[25]

When reading was mastered—and likely writing, too—monks were exhorted, and in some rules required, to read spiritual works or to listen to them in common reading at the evening meal.[26] Personal reading, in any case, was important, and several hours a week were reserved for it in the monastic schedule.[27] The Bible and the rule of the monastery were the most popular readings, but monastic libraries contained other Christian literature that was consulted too. The monasteries, as their rules attest, were no doubt committed to education and culture, but it was a religious education and a religious culture that they promoted rather than a classical education and a profane culture.[28]

We must be careful about following this narrow trail too far; it does not tell the full story. Monasticism, in fact, wore two faces: Eastern and Western. Eastern Christians were used to holy, illiterate monks and appeared to prefer a kind of monasticism where monks fled to the desert and lived in solitude. Whenever Eastern monasticism followed the practice of community life, and when some book learning seemed to be essential to the cultivation of spirituality, the bare bones of literacy were enough.[29] St. Basil's Rule delegated some old monk to teach reading to novices, but according to the Council of Chalcedon in 451, these lessons were prohibited to anyone outside the monastery.[30]

Benedictine Monasticism. Although never accepting scholarship or intellectual refinement as legitimate substitutes for moral perfection, Western monasticism drifted in another direction. Social and educational conditions were different from East to West, and they help to explain Western monasticism's investment in education and Eastern monasticism's studied indifference to a cultivation of learning. This drift had little or nothing to do with the fundamentals of monastic life. In both East and West, monks took vows of chastity, poverty, and obedience, but few received the sacrament of holy orders, so they were absolved from the duties the priesthood imposed and the requirement it had for something more than a mastery of the rudiments.

When Western monasticism cultivated learning, it was without apology, although sometimes with a suspicion that the door to temptation was being left ajar. In any case, few monks ever attained a reputation for scholarship, but monks and nuns alike were expected to study and to be able to teach others. By the time St. Benedict's Rule appeared (ca. 525), this association between asceticism and education was close enough to give reading and study an unassailable place in monastic life and duty. The Benedictine Rule, moreover, called for a monastic school and commissioned it to prepare boys for monastic life.[31] These thoroughly Christian scholastic enterprises abandoned altogether any dependence upon the classics. Humble as they were, monastic schools became the true homes for Christian culture in the dark centuries about to descend on Europe.

Episcopal Schools. In earlier centuries, episcopal schools were the places where bishops trained their priests. And with classical schools in abundance, it was unnecessary for clerical training to pay attention to literary instruction. But classical schools disappeared in the wake of Rome's disintegration: now bishops had to make their own arrangements to offer a kind of education heretofore available in classical schools. Episcopal schools always varied immensely in their embrace of liberal learning and, intended only for candidates for the priesthood, were normally closed to all other prospective students.

In the fourth and fifth centuries, however, because of a general absence of secular schools, the ancient practice of clerical apprenticeship conducted by bishops in episcopal schools could not produce the desired results. Some perceptive bishops in Italy, Gaul, and Spain organized schools and introduced in them the monastic practice of communal residence. In these scholastic communities—which were open to young future clerics on the first level of minor orders—instruction was given in general education and sacred literature.

As these men proceeded toward major orders, they were given spiritual nourishment from communal life and prayer and were trained for the profession of holy orders. When they were ready for major orders— about eighteen—they were expected to choose between a career in the Church and secular life. Those electing to become priests were usually attached permanently to the church where they had been educated and, when ready, were ordained. Wherever such schools flourished, the supply of priests was usually good, for the monastic rule of "stability" authorizing a monk to remain in one monastery for life had an affect outside the monastery. The temporary effect of such an arrangement, however, was to produce an overabundance of priests in cities with cathedrals and a poverty of clergymen elsewhere. The more permanent outcome from these episcopal schools, though, was to institute a carefully organized system for the education of priests.

Parish Schools. During those years when the Christian religion stayed close to urban areas, the episcopal arrangement for sustaining a body of clergymen was satisfactory. But as Christianity spread to the hinterland, episcopal schools neither supplied all the priests the Church needed nor took into account the religious vocations of rural boys who, without schools to attend, were cut off from an avenue to the sacrament of holy orders.

The tales about ignorant priests with too little learning to pronounce Latin have elements of truth, yet the hierarchy perceived the need for educational opportunity in those regions of the country that were off the beaten cultural path. Searching for a solution, they found it by adapting the episcopal arrangement to parishes where the parish priest took promising boys under his wing and instructed them in the elements of decent learning and, in some parishes, continued to teach them until they were ready for ordination to the priesthood.

Although it may be true that most parish schools only started boys on their way to a clerical life, there is a good deal of evidence that parish priests took seriously the injunction of the Second Council of Vaison (529) "to gather some boys round them as lectors, so that they may give Scripture and the whole law of the Lord and so prepare worthy successors to themselves;"[32] and the Council of Toledo (527), called by Riché the birth certificate of the parish school,[33] that had issued a similar canon. This legislation was responsible for the establishment of village or parish schools that never before had been either general in appearance or systematic in operation. In many parishes, moreover, it appears that children who gave no sign of a religious vocation were regularly admitted to these schools. From then on, parish priests, in addition to being pastors of souls, became also teachers of children.

Despite their subsequent ubiquity, parish schools did not suddenly fling open their doors to all the children of the neighborhood, and parish priests were not turned into schoolmasters. These schools were supposed to cater to students who appeared to have a religious vocation. Furthermore, pastors must have varied enormously in their qualification and disposition for teaching.

Scholastic Contribution. Monastic, parish, and episcopal schools were the main source of educational opportunity in the sixth, seventh, and eighth centuries, and the medieval educational system was based on them. Yet these schools existed only in faint outline so long as classical schools survived. When they assumed almost total responsibility for the educational need of Europe, as in time they did, these Church schools clung tenaciously to their original purpose and cultivated carefully their technical objective of producing monks and priests. But as time passed and as classical schools faded into oblivion, they broadened their course of study and liberalized admission policy to admit to their classrooms any member of the Church. Still, even in medieval times, the supposition that learning was mainly an occupation for clergymen was amended with caution and hesitation.

Amending the Tradition of Christian Education

Sometimes disposed to make schools suitable places for the instruction of lay as well as religious persons, Christian educators began by reappraising what must seem to us a threadbare issue. Obscured by time and intimidated by barbarism, the model for classical education was indistinct but, in any case, clear enough for sincere Christians to worry about its pagan elements. Among the many directions Christian educators might have chosen for schools, a revival of classical education was not one. Yet Christian schools familiar to them lacked broad and respectable studies capable of supplying the skill and knowledge indispensable to the vitality of religion and the welfare of society.[34]

Old theories defined the character and pronounced the ultimate purpose of Christian education, and never tired of reminding teachers and students of the danger lurking in the classics. Christian teachers about to step over the threshold of the sixth century had an abundance of advice about what learning should be suppressed; they were remarkably uninformed about the studies that could be cultivated with impunity.

St. Augustine's Program of Study. Augustine's fourth-century book *On Christian Doctrine* had something to say about what parts of profane scholarship could be put to Christian use, but his generally sound advice attracted little attention until the sixth century. Even then, only sections of the book were used to guide the curriculum of Christian schools. The sections used, though, were consistent with a fairly narrow educational perspective: the training of persons for religious scholarship.

What Augustine said about natural science, mathematics, music, dialectic, and rhetoric was repeated by commentators, but his analysis of the worth of history, physical science, and astronomy was ignored. What readers noticed, and almost always quoted, was his analogy comparing classical knowledge to the treasure the Hebrews took from the Egyptians in order to put it to better use. They took what they wanted and ignored the rest.[35] Augustine had written a charter for a fundamentally Christian culture, but his sixth- and seventh-century readers were either unwilling or unable to adopt it.

Boethius and Liberal Art. Boethius' (ca. 480–525) *The Consolation of Philosophy*, although scaled smaller than Augustine's *On Christian Doctrine*, helped to redress ignorance about the curriculum of a Christian school. It is characterized as one of those books that no educated person leaves unread, but at the time, too few were able to understand it, so it was influential only among Boethius' friends. Despite its lack of contemporary influence, it succeeded in integrating huge parts of the classical legacy with a healthy and orthodox Christian faith, and became a principal textbook for later centuries. But despite the praise heaped upon it in the early Middle Ages, *Consolation* dealt with philosophy, and philosophy, a subject about which Christians were both unsure and uninformed, was confused with an occult science condemned alike by Church and state.

By the ninth century, both in casual reference and extensive borrow-ing, *Consolation* was quoted thousands of times, and Boethius' reputation as a saint and a scholar grew by leaps and bounds.[36] Versatile, learned, and apparently orthodox, he could be depended upon to map a course to educational decency. "One must call the roll of practically everyone of account in the Middle Ages," Howard Patch says, "if one is to include those who showed indebtedness to him."[37]

Aptly described as prison literature, *Consolation of Philosophy* illus-trates the excellence of its author's memory, for it was written without help from sources. The title gives some clue to the benefit one might expect from knowledge: convicted of being a magician, an astrologer, and a traitor, and rotting in jail awaiting execution, Boethius found solace in recalling the liberal arts. And for the most part, the liberal arts are what the book is about. They are recited, described, and explained. All the while, Boethius is careful to represent them in a way that no Christian could doubt their orthodoxy or, if this is too strong, their antiseptic character.

The Consolation of Philosophy supplied a comprehensive account of the liberal arts, and for this, Boethius was indebted to a playful and pedantic pagan, Martianus Capella (ca. fifth century).

Capella's Dramatic Account of the Arts. In Carthage, between 410 and 430, most authorities agree, Capella wrote a book whose theme and artistry captivated hundreds of Christians, some of whom mistook him for a Christian. Exhibiting allegory at its best, the book led readers into the nature of the liberal arts. Although its author was pagan, *The Marriage of Philology and Mercury* enjoyed enormous notoriety. The assertion that it is the world's most successful textbook is hyperbole.[38]

Capella recited how the god Mercury, disposed to marry, chose Phi-lology for his bride. At the wedding reception, with Apollo as master of ceremonies, Mercury gave his new wife an elaborate gift: the seven liberal arts. Dressed as maids, each of the arts—grammar, rhetoric, dialectic, arithmetic, geometry, music, and astronomy—stepped forward and de-scribed herself.[39] Capella was having fun, but his book became the popu-lar source of information about the spine to classical culture, the liberal arts.

St. Benedict and Monastic Education. While others were trying to preserve parts of the classical legacy for Christian use, Benedict (ca. 480–546), described by his biographer as being "sagely ignorant and wisely uneducated,"[40] had a part to play. If the architect of Western monasticism was ready to turn his back on all remnants of classical learning while others promoted them, the conflict between the sacred and the profane was being revived. But Christianity's dependence on the written word and the need monastic life had for literacy make one skeptical about monasticism's alleged hostility to learning. The liberal arts were not prominent in Western monasticism, but they were there, and history's sharp arrow points straight to monastic houses as oases for European culture. Yet had secular schools been available to cultivate the kind of learning monasteries were uneasy promoting, Benedict and his followers would have abandoned the liberal arts. This alternative was seldom open to them.

Although by the early sixth century classical schools were all but gone, signs that Benedict and his successors ever contemplated restoring classical education or erecting a complete scholastic ladder in the monasteries are absent. Monastic schools instructed novices, and sometimes others, in reading, but such instruction would have been delegated to other schools had they been available.

So Benedict's contribution to the intellectual and educational development of the West is found in the character of monasticism and the rule he wrote to keep it on a straight and steady religious path. We are struck by monasticism's fundamental altruism: by its dedication to the welfare of monks, of course, but to the good of all Christians as well. This altruism motivated monasteries to open their gates to schools, to culture, and to men of learning.[41] Too precious to be discarded, the monks harvested vast portions of the intellectual inheritance and stored them in their libraries and, to some extent, cultivated them in their schools. But they lacked both experience and dependable models for managing libraries and conducting schools. At this point, and in this connection, we meet Cassiodorus (ca. 480–575), the man who instructed monasticism in the management of the classical legacy, left now, almost by accident, in its custody.

Cassiodorus' Definition of the Seven Liberal Arts. Born into a distinguished family whose record of public service was long and impressive, Flavius Magnus Aurelius Cassiodorus Senator followed in the footsteps of his illustrious forebears. Educated in Rome's classical schools, fluent in grammar and rhetoric, Cassiodorus, paying heed to Quintilian's counsel that public officers should be cultured, stayed on friendly terms with classical literature. As a sincere Christian, he had plenty of practice wrestling with the ancient dilemma hovering around faith and learning.

When Cassiodorus retired from public life, he tried to organize a school—apparently with the encouragement of Pope Agapitus—that could have become a model for teachers who wanted to enlist the liberal arts in the cause of Christian learning.[42] This bold venture failed, but later, about 550, Cassiodorus showed his devotion to religion by founding two monasteries. One, Vivarium, was commissioned to promote the study of Christian doctrine, for which conversance with liberal learning was essential, so Cassiodorus wrote a famous manifesto, *An Introduction to Divine and Human Readings*, to guide its work.

The *Introduction* is preoccupied with religious subjects but, at the same time, is hospitable to the liberal arts. Cassiodorus was a product of an age that wavered about the reputation of the classics to promote good and foment evil. Classical authors could sometimes be tolerated, and Christian spokesmen showed some tendency to justify the liberal arts for students who had an imperative need for them; yet it was always better to be safe than sorry, so a more cautious course of avoidance was usually followed. Practicing the virtue of prudence, the praise of the arts, found here and there in the *Introduction*, while almost certainly genuine, is nevertheless reserved.[43]

Along with Augustine and most Western church fathers, Cassiodorus was convinced that the arts were nothing more than aids to the study of Christian doctrine and that everything in profane science—which included all the liberal arts—was either hidden away in scripture or derived from it. In such a philosophy of knowledge, one making scientific and cultural study either redundant or unnecessary, it is extraordinary to find any recommendation for the study of profane subjects. And nothing in Cassiodorus' *Introduction* explicitly repeals this view. Despite considerable evidence of scholarly interest and habit, he neither encouraged nor forbade a reading of classical literature, although for the monks at Vivarium he prescribed, in addition to bible reading and some study of sacred science, a fairly comprehensive regimen of secular study.

In the preface to part two ("Secular Letters") of *An Introduction to Divine and Human Readings*, Cassiodorus explains his reason for writing the book.[44] Monks had at least a need for modest literary accomplishment, so some program of education was essential. Cassiodorus wanted to show them how study of the liberal arts could be both safe and faithful to the ascetic ideal.[45] Divided into two parts, the book begins with "Divine Letters." Arranged into thirty-three chapters, but hardly more than seventy-five pages in print, this part is an abbreviated compendium of the books monks should study to master doctrine and scripture.

Any study of sacred learning, and especially advanced study, needed to rest on a foundation of liberal culture. Monks should be able to read the books, of course, but they should understand them too.[46] At this point the liberal arts were recruited. Although the investigation of secular knowledge was far from zealous, it was tempered by a liberal and generous spirit. Other authors had been censured for such liberalism, but Cassiodorus' reputation for strict orthodoxy was so good that for centuries his word in the *Introduction* was trusted. Readers expected to find a safe pathway through a labyrinth of secular knowledge and, in this respect, Cassiodorus seldom disappointed them. "Secular Letters" has a preface, seven chapters containing brief descriptions of the seven liberal arts, and a conclusion. It purports to handle the whole of secular knowledge vis-à-vis divine study, but it is only about sixty-eight printed pages.

For his exposition of secular and divine letters, Cassiodorus' debt to earlier pagan and Christian writers was heavy; although he tried to acknowledge and faithfully follow his predecessors, failure was frequent. Despite shortcoming in his recitation of the nature of the liberal arts, this compendium was the source medieval teachers most often consulted. In fairness to Cassiodorus, though, the *Introduction* was intended as a guide to the education of monks in Vivarium and Castellum. It was not supposed to be a textbook.

Speaking an educational language both his contemporaries and men of the Middle Ages understood, Cassiodorus' chief scholastic recommendations were persuasive to teachers who wanted to keep academic priorities straight, so his influence on the education of later generations was clear, precise, and profound. *An Introduction to Divine and Human Readings* proved to be a quick, useful, and dependable bibliographical guide for librarians, schoolmasters, and students. The part dealing with human readings took its place alongside the books of Capella, Boethius, Priscian, and Donatus as one of the important schoolbooks of the Middle Ages. Besides, Cassiodorus' commitment to literary monasticism was clear enough to encourage his own monasteries as well as others to collect all manner of books and manuscripts.[47]

Literary Monasticism. Literary monasticism redefined the monastic obligation of work. In the ordinary monastery of the time, monks worked in the fields and supported the religious house by their labor. Literary monasticism allowed some monks to desert the fields and spend their time in the scriptorium, usually located in the monastic library, where they copied books and manuscripts. In consequence, this redefinition of work turned many monasteries into publishing plants. Henceforth, monastic libraries were depositories for early medieval culture and, in preserving culture, succeeded in doing what no other extant institution was capable of doing.

Cassiodorus' Contribution to Christian Education. Although literary monasticism alone is enough to secure Cassiodorus' place in history,[48] it should be noticed that he wanted to improve, not merely to describe, traditional educational practice, and to find a safe and easy equivalent to classical schools. He offered a reasonable alternative to Quintilian's education for oratory, while, at the same time, acknowledging how times had changed and how education would have to change as well; and in trying to preserve what was worthwhile in Quintilian's prescription, he sought also to reconstruct it as a practical and useful program of education for Christians. Studied eloquence, Quintilian's educational aim, was replaced by a goal that teachers could understand and embrace: Education should prepare persons to solve religious and secular problems and equip them to manage public affairs. In these undertakings, however, the scholar's study replaced the public platform, solitary analysis superseded oratory, and rhetoric, stripped of its ancient magnificence, was deflated. It and all the linguistic disciplines that had dominated classical education were demoted to the status of basic subjects in a syllabus of general education.

Isidore of Seville's Etymologies. Cassiodorus' achievements were praiseworthy and, in many respects, permanent, but he had some help. Isidore (560–636), the bishop of Seville (who, because of his ecclesiastical status, had to be more conservative than Cassiodorus), endorsed ubiquitous dogmatic assertions forbidding Christians to read the lies of the poets; but picking his way through the classical literature, he found elements essential to the education of clerics who were to invest talent in the study of religious culture. The program of study he recommended was remarkably similar to the one in Cassiodorus' *Introduction.*

The arts, he said, were secular and subordinate, but it was better to be a grammarian than a heretic, so they could be used by Christians as tools for more important studies. Isidore's huge thesaurus, the *Etymologies*, purporting to contain all knowledge, became a standard reference book from the seventh through the eleventh century. The section on the liberal arts was used as a textbook when nothing better was available; because dependable literature on the arts was hard to find, this must have been frequent. Although the flaws in Isidore's scholarship have been recognized and reported, he had a reputation for erudition and, with Cassiodorus and others, was one of the architects responsible for rebuilding the edifice of learning in the West.

Gregory the Great: Hostility to Classical Culture. By now, the temptation to believe that Christians had at last found a way to cut through the thicket of scholastic confusion and ignorance is nearly overwhelming. In the century following Cassiodorus' death, Christian literature had grown in volume and dignity, and the schools, which in the last analysis must be given some credit for this revival, were becoming stronger and better attended. Poets, who used classical style with skill, and prose writers, whose preoccupation, while not strictly theological, was at least broadly religious, were producing books that commanded a respectable readership. With the work of Christian authors at their disposal, schoolmasters began to show signs of confidence that this literature was equal to the task of illustrating textbook rules on grammar and rhetoric.

Pope Gregory (540–604) exhibited the same confidence, and this led him to follow in the footsteps of earlier authorities (say, Augustine and Cassiodorus) to find a path between humanism and a total anathematization of antique culture. The old issue of paganism would not disappear, but Gregory, who was intelligent and well educated, took a novel position. Recognizing that language is alive and is affected by its environment, Gregory rejected the practice that allowed ancient rules to dominate contemporary style. It was pointless, he said, to try to write and speak like ancient Greeks and Romans; and this conviction led him directly to the conclusion that for language's conventional use, further contact with pagan literature was useless. But there is no hint anywhere that Gregory meant to condemn, and thus ostracize, everything in classical literature.[49]

Gregory's assessment of classical education was promoted by the plausibility of his argument, but it was promoted, too, by his position. As pope, his views on education had enormous influence, although they never became Church policy. Living and working in Rome, where Latin was the vernacular and where remnants of classical culture remained alive, he missed the significance of paying some heed to Latin's ancient foundation. This neglect is illustrated in the famous letter Gregory sent to Desiderius, the bishop of Vienne. After telling the bishop of reports that had come to him about the bishop conducting grammar classes for young men—work, he wrote, "unfit even for pious laymen"—this warning was added: "The same lips cannot sound the praises of Jupiter and the praises of Christ."[50]

When Gregory used the word *grammar*, he meant classical literature. It should be said, as well, that the report Gregory had on Desiderius told how the bishop had either composed a pagan poem or read one to his students. Church law forbade bishops from teaching and writing poetry, so an interpretation that Gregory's proscription of classical teaching was personal, or that the letter was an outright condemnation of the antique literature, is too harsh. Yet Gregory cannot be represented as a true and constant friend of the classics.

He ignored the fact that Gaul was not Rome, that Latin is not an easy language to learn without a teacher, and that the boys in the bishop's class were prospective priests. They had either to learn Latin from Desiderius or not at all. Rather than reprimanding the bishop, Gregory should have commended him for teaching Latin, with an admonition to keep an interest in classical literature from intruding upon episcopal duty. Gregory's commitment to educational reform is evident. He endorsed the monastic-school model with the proviso that it abandon any assignation with the tradition of secular schools and maintain the precedence of divine over profane wisdom.

It was in this setting, where a practical Christian education received praise and encouragement, and where, at first, Gregory's words sound harsh and uncompromising, that Cassiodorus' *Introduction* and Isidore's *Etymologies* grew to full stature and exerted a penetrating influence. Although Gregory's and Cassiodorus' appraisal of the liberal arts was different, it was, in the end, Gregory's encouragement of educational reform that allowed Cassiodorus' humanism, one where the arts were subservient to divine learning, to thrive in the next two centuries.

Irish Education

A Heritage of Distrust. With the cultural framework disintegrating and the schools falling into disuse, learning was put in jeopardy on the Continent after the early sixth century. The debilitating effect of barbarism and political chaos account for much of Europe's sharp slide toward intellectual, educational, and cultural impoverishment, but the story has another chapter, one written by a cadre of church fathers whose fears were fed by the bold paganism they sensed in the classics.

A quick embrace of the classical educational paradigm might have equipped educators to pull these generations from the swamp of ignorance by giving them the literary means to make another assault on the citadel of learning. As it was, however, despite the compromises proffered by Jerome and Augustine, the main influence of the patristic tradition was opposed to the free study of the classics. All the Fathers, even Jerome and Augustine, were ready to accept some restriction, and a few, such as Gregory, have been interpreted as wanting to have the classics outlawed altogether. So the chance for a revival of learning depending upon tried and tested means clearly evident in the classical tradition was slim.

Yet barely visible to the naked eye, this cloud of hostility toward classical education had a silver lining. Latin, the official language of the Church, was in trouble in many parts of Europe, and the schools were recruited to teach it. In the end, even when timid churchmen said the classics were dangerous to faith, the practical educational need of the Church was imperative, and this led to some measure of ecclesiastical support for classical learning. Practical necessity kept segments of classical education alive, and in consequence, the classical heritage influenced the life and mind of the Middle Ages. But attitudes antagonistic to the study of the classics, although incapable of controlling educational practice, could nevertheless be influential, and their influence led to a canalization of classical study into certain preferred areas. What was apparently outside the ambit of religious perspective was neglected. Following the principle of selection, the cultivation of classical learning in the schools proceeded unevenly.

Education for Religion. Unevenness was characteristic of Irish educational ambition, although because Ireland's cultural tradition owed little or no debt to the classical inheritance, literary curiosity was suppressed less than on the Continent.[51] In the early sixth century, the Irish possessed a fairly rich literature, all of it steeped in Irish paganism, and a systematic legal code.[52] Besides, their own schools had matured outside the Roman Empire and were immunized from the educational infection associated with the fall of Rome. Had it not been for Ireland's conversion to Christianity, there is no telling what educational and cultural course she might have taken. As it was, the Irish embraced the Christian religion with enthusiasm and tenacity, and this led them to reconstruct their educational program to meet the needs of religion.

Standing on the fringe of European civilization and largely unaffected by the Continent's trouble with paganism, Ireland could practice the art of selection in importing the classical legacy by taking what she needed and ignoring what was useless or too difficult. Her range of choice was great but not total: parts of the classical legacy could not be abandoned by faithful Christians. Latin, a language with which the Irish were almost totally unfamiliar and for which they lacked cultural affinity, was such a part. So beginning with the assimilation of Latin, and recognizing that some parts of the classics were essential to a Christian educational syllabus, the Irish turned out to be precocious students. As they studied the classics, they noticed that elements of style—linguistic structure, vocabulary, and the arts of persuasion—could be segregated and mastered without any premonition of danger. Hardly recognizing their accomplishment, the Irish invented a cultural theory in connection with the classical legacy: they took parts of it without ever allowing the ideals, the values, or the stories to influence them. With their view of classical culture limited to what the books contained, they adopted the classics as a way of learning rather than as a way of life.

The educational requirements of religion recommended a reconstruction of the Irish school system, and to supplement the work of bardic schools—schools that antedated Christianization—the monasteries renewed their scholastic effort and conducted schools whose academic vision was broader and more liberal than their continental counterparts.[53]

Irish Elementary and Secondary Schools. Except for programs in theology and biblical study, monastic schools made their principal instructional investment in elementary and secondary education. Their teachers, some of whom were laymen, taught all the children who came, regardless of gender or religious or secular scholastic motive. Students were spurred by their own curiosity and the encouragement of their teachers to follow a safe trail blazed through the classical literature because, by appealing to an inherited educational wisdom, their mentors convinced them that this was the route to educational decency. All the while, of course, they were directed to subordinate secular knowledge to religious objective and to master those branches in the corpus of learning demonstrated to be of most worth. But first they had to know Latin, and this, as it turned out, was a monumental instructional problem.

As a medium for study, the importance of Latin was clear; as a language for religious liturgy, ceremony, and devotion, its worth was incontrovertible. In any case, skill in Latin was essential, but without cultural affinity for it, the Irish found Latin hard to learn; and teachers, burdened by a poverty of pedagogical technique, found it hard to teach. Help from the ancient grammars, all written in the tradition of Dionysius Thrax and Varro, was slight, and we know why: such books were written for students familiar with Latin and, proceeding from the assumption that grammar was not meant to familiarize novices in the use of any tongue, engaged in philosophical speculation about the nature and structure of language.

Before much could be accomplished, Irish educators had to rewrite the old grammars. They picked their way through classical fragments and, in the absence of dictionaries, made up long word lists for their students to memorize.[54] To ensure idiomatic correctness, little readers, primers of sorts, to illustrate how Latin should be used were introduced. Although always doing their best to teach an accurate Latin, teachers' best was sometimes not good enough, for complaint was heard in the schools and churches that the Irish were using "nouns whose declension remained a mystery, [and] verbs to whose conjugations they had no clue."[55] Still, despite the obvious deficiencies in language teaching, the classics were kept in the schools to perpetuate a teaching tradition whose worth was not subject to discount. Shortly, however, the crudities of teaching Latin were redressed in the pedagogic innovations and refinements introduced by Bede and Alcuin.

Capitalizing on these refinements, Irish monastic schools were able to elevate the culture of antiquity, after it had been carefully interpreted to complement Christian thought, to a new level of significance. They became academic preserves for the seven liberal arts: studied unevenly, of course, but always there.[56] Yet while taking into account the Irish monastic school's hospitality to the arts and the relative breadth of its curriculum, its linguistic and religious aims were distinct, precise, and honest. Apart from the school, every monastery in Ireland, paying close heed to Cassiodorus' words of encouragement, had a scriptorium and a library.

Ireland's Contribution of European Education. Ireland cultivated education and preserved an intellectual culture until, toward the end of the eighth century, the Danes invaded the land and, with a fury directed especially at literature and religion, destroyed everything they could not understand. By this time, though, Ireland's work as a transmitter of culture was nearly complete. What she had imported was husbanded for a long time and was then returned to the Continent by Irish monks and scholars. This cultural export was not in itself illustrative of a genuine renaissance, but it was enough to stimulate, although hardly to generate, what has been called the "renaissance of the ninth century."

An Alien Educational Legacy

The accomplishments of the ninth century were essential to a restoration of vigor to European education, and one is wrong to discount them. Yet it is historical hyperbole to attribute to literary monasticism or to the often brilliant contributions of Irish scholars the credentials of genuine humanism and to credit them with having led a genuine renaissance that on all points resembled the great revival of ancient learning in the fourteenth century. What was done to rebuild the castle of education during the long interlude between the sixth and the ninth centuries was motivated by an intense devotion to religion rather than to culture. Unlike their humanistic successors, the scholars of the period were never infatuated with the classics. And their perfectly understandable diffidence made it all the more difficult to accommodate to a classical tributary now slowly but surely making its way into European life from its headwater in Africa. This tributary carried accretions from the Greek heritage that were winnowed first by Hellenism and then by Mohammedanism.

The disciples of Mohammed (569–632) carried their Arabic civilization with them when, in the eighth century, they crossed the Mediterranean to land in Spain and then scaled the Pyrenees to inhabit the towns and cities in other parts of southern Europe. This civilization, for all its excellence, was a mixture of classical paganism, religious mysticism, and philosophical pantheism. As it spread, its threat to Christian value and goal became greater, for unlike the classics, which could be decontaminated by separating style from story and other ingenious literary devices, Arabic music, science, architecture, literature, and philosophy were unsusceptible to such convenient compromises. Christians with keen intellects began to perceive the threat to their faith and their conviction about life's priorities.

Christians lacked the means to halt this cultural invasion and to suppress its influence, but in the long run, this may have been a blessing in disguise. The matchless scholarship of the Greeks and Hellenists—of

Aristotle, Euclid, Ptolemy, and Galen—was husbanded by quick, intelligent Arabs, thus enriching an already rich European reservoir of classical learning. Although the hazard of multiple translation of many classical sources—from Greek to Arabic, then to Castilian, and finally to Latin—cancelled some of the subtlety of their thought, this period of European intellectual history was indebted to Arabic accomplishment and cultural transmission.

Christian philosophers and theologians were frequently overmatched in their contest of wit with the clever Arabs, so they sought to redress their scholarly inferiority. Besides, Arabic natural philosophy was at once both fanciful and mystical and subversive of Christian doctrine. Thus motivated, medieval scholars spent their best resources in the storehouse of learning to erect unassailable theological and philosophical fortresses. All this took a long time and recommended the founding of schools where genuine scholarship could be prosecuted, but in the end, Christian scholarship succeeded in blunting the edge of an ideology that represented a serious threat. Arabic cultural and intellectual influence, although more negative than positive, was nevertheless real.

Sobered by the prospect of erosion of faith and mindful of their obligation to reject what was dangerous in Arabic learning, Christians were astute enough to recognize beneficial sides to the imported scholarship. In this context, the abstractions of natural philosophy—today called "physical science"—and theology had a less ominous sound, for among the books Arabs brought with them were volumes on arithmetic, mathematics in general but especially algebra, and medicine. Arithmetic, taking into account its past and future, should attract our attention: so long held back as an art of computation because it lacked a flexible notation, arithmetic belonged to the higher echelons of schooling and was a study of number theory. Now, with the Arabic notation, arithmetic surmounted one last great obstacle and became a standard subject in Western elementary schools.

In practical art, too, Arabs were skillful enough to add some luster and ease to an otherwise dreary and dull medieval life, but one of their practical achievements stands out because of its service to learning: the manufacture of a kind of paper suitable for the printing press.

Foundation for an Educational Revival

Crossing the doorstep to the ninth century, signs of past progress can be read: Monastic literary and linguistic reservoirs were ready to be tapped; Irish and British courses of study, shaped by a two-century expe-

rience in monastic schools, were available for imitation; and Arabic scholarship was eager to lend a helping hand. Fuel to run the generator of
European education and to relight the lamps of learning was at the disposal of anyone with skill enough to distill it. Now we meet Charles the
Great—Charlemagne—(768–814) and Alcuin (ca. 735–804).

A Model School. Charles the Great, one of those extraordinary men
who occasionally crosses history's stage (and probably illiterate at that),
had the ability to identify the critical problems in the Frankish Empire
and the prudence to solve them. Only his Christian faith was dearer than
the welfare of his kingdom. Both, he was convinced, could benefit from an
elevation of educational standard.

The question has been asked countless times: What led Charles to
become learning's great ally? The answer, though elusive, may be found in
the reconstitution of the Aachen palace school as a model for the empire.
Palace schools existed in Gaul and elsewhere long before Charles became
king, but if young aristocrats who attended them were literate, most likely
they had been instructed at home. Palace schools trained them as military
officers and bureaucrats. Now teachers from monasteries and towns the
country over were to use the Aachen school as a pedagogical oasis whose
fresh, healthy water could be used to irrigate the educational landscape.
To his credit, Charlemagne was perceptive enough to see how much irriga-
tion was needed.

Charles' school needed an exceptional teacher. The story of Europe's
educational drouths and intellectual deserts has been told so often that
had the emperor been unable to find such a teacher, no one should be
surprised. But this story too often ignores those pockets of learning and
scholarship that somehow survived despite tremendous odds. From one of
these pockets, Pisa, Charles enlisted the services of Peter, who, it is
supposed, was the palace school's first headmaster. Although Peter's
scholarship in grammar and literature was both broad and sound, his
tenure at the school was brief. Despite ornamental credentials, he must
have lacked either the skill, not unusual for advanced scholars, or the will
to teach elementary school students. Such students needed the elements of
grammar and the rudiments of Latin, not the classics, literary criticism,
and philosophy, so Peter returned to northern Italy.

After Peter's departure, Charlemagne secured the services of Alcuin,
a master in the monastic school of York, for the palace school. With
Alcuin as his adviser, the emperor in 787 and 802 issued the famous
capitularies, or laws, commending education to the attention of all ecclesiastical and secular officers of the land and enjoining them to open a
school "in each bishopric and monastery."[57] Neither episcopal nor monastic schools were innovations, but what is striking is the provision applying

the laws to every diocese and monastery. Anyone able to teach children was expected to do so, and all children, rich and poor alike, were to be instructed gratuitously: Let teachers "exact no price from the children for their teaching, nor receive anything from them save what the parents may offer voluntarily and from affection."[58] With Charles' policy in place, responsibility for leading an educational crusade was Alcuin's; to some extent, the future of European education was in his hands.

Alcuin the Teacher. In an old but seminal book, Andrew West made an appraisal of Alcuin's educational contribution: He added nothing "to the sum of learning, either by invention or by recovery from what [had] been lost. What he [did was] to reproduce or adapt from earlier authors such parts of their writings as could be appreciated by the age in which he lived."[59] This faint praise is consistent with the common assumption that contributions to education are certified only by erudition and originality. The modesty of Alcuin's scholarship in philosophy and theology is conceded, although he appears to have been an eternal student of literature and scripture. The latter received special attention at York. Yet even modesty of scholarly attainment should not strip from Alcuin the remarkable significance of a rare insight enabling him to discern the fault in educational practice and find ways to remedy it.

More clearly that anyone else of the day, save, perhaps, Charles the Great, Alcuin recognized that the edifice of education needed a solid foundation. An age in the habit of going to the books for all knowledge knew no substitute for reading. After elementary reading lessons were mastered, one could seek for the ornaments of learning. Following this principle to the letter, Alcuin directed elementary schools to emphasize the teaching of a flawless Latin.

Latin's correctness, he averred, although his meaning is obscure, is determined by nature, authority, reason, and usage. Including nature, authority, and reason downgraded the importance of usage, and this downgrading absolved grammarians from making a fetish out of reading the classics for style. Yet Alcuin appeared to be unafraid of ancient writers and never adverted to the old problem of paganism; but this, as some of his critics declare—and we concede—can be taken as evidence of literary insensitivity or poor scholarship. When he assigned priority to the liberal arts, he forgot Cassiodorus' famous argument (if he knew it) that the liberal arts are intruders to be exploited but not loved. Alcuin, instead, welcomed them not merely as useful tools for Christian education but as indispensable instruments for the prosecution of divine learning.

Whenever Alcuin's influence penetrated the schools, the liberal arts—grammar, rhetoric, logic, arithmetic, music, geometry, and astronomy—could hold up their heads without shame and, without being reminded of their pagan heritage, take their place in the curriculum. This somewhat novel respectability for the arts was seldom capitalized in school practice, because educational need was usually at the introductory level of grammar, rhetoric, and logic. Alcuin could afford to be generous in an endorsement of the full complement of the arts, and with classical literature generally, because students following his regimen of study hardly ever got to a point in reading where Christian doctrine collided with the pagan ideas buried in the classics.

Acknowledging the worth of the liberal arts was a great forward leap, and Alcuin is entitled to praise, but this acknowledgment was not the apogee of his educational program. His preoccupation was with language, where it should have been, for any reconstruction of European education depended upon fluency in Latin. Yet Alcuin's confident assumption about Latin is hard to endorse: he preserved the myth that it was invented by God especially for Christian use. It would be hard to make a stronger case for its careful and universal study.

Graded Readers. Recalling the techniques Irish schoolmasters had used for teaching Latin to schoolboys who lacked cultural affinity for it, Alcuin improved and multiplied the graded readers. Latin should be correct, of course, so vocabulary and grammar were introduced in carefully written graded readers where language instruction could be natural. Students read these books to fix the meaning of words, and they learned to use them correctly by paying attention to syntax without resorting to the formality and aridity of grammatical rule. This was the heart of instruction, but understanding the slippery scholastic motives of schoolboys, dry subjects were made interesting by introducing little dramas. The stories in the readers were artfully conceived to relay, as well, a wealth of general knowledge. This combination of good pedagogy and sound scholarship carried students through a complete course of elementary instruction and gave them, in addition to a firm grasp of Latin, an abundance of useful information.

At the end of this long period of cultural unrest, where the integrity of learning and education hovered on the brink of disaster, where conflicting values competed for human allegiance and loyalty, a revival of educational common sense and a restoration of sound foundations to learning are evident. When Alcuin's work was finished, when the worth of his pedagogical techniques was perceived by all manner of schools throughout Europe, educational and cultural reconstruction was resumed with renewed vigor.

Chapter 6

Medieval Education:
Cultural Assimilation and Academic
Order

By the end of the tenth century, the pedagogical achievement sponsored by Alcuin and the broad educational reform inaugurated by Charles the Great and his successors had returned huge dividends to the education and culture of the Continent. This educational revival had its beginning with the Celts in Ireland, moved to Britain, and continued to France and Germany. With each eastern step it increased in efficiency.

The foundation for this revival had been laid centuries earlier, and without safeguards might have been virile enough to seduce curious students to adopt a pagan legacy. But safeguards were introduced. Thirst for education was motivated by Christian and civic pragmatism rather than by humanism. The men who wrestled with Latin grammar and read the classics wanted, first and foremost, a fuller understanding of scripture and patristic literature. Most were monks or men in holy orders, and their investment in study was husbanded by an unshakeable allegiance to faith.

At the same time, and not entirely outside the realm of faith, were the needs of the Church for a cadre of men with the skill to conduct its administrative business. Under any circumstance, an organization as large and complex as the Church needed competent managers, but when civic was added to ecclesiastical necessity, the urgency for educational decency became greater. Without a civil state capable of governing, the Church filled the vacuum to ensure order and dependability for secular life and affairs.

The mainstream of intellectual motive carrying culture and education had a tributary, one that allowed some room for purely humanistic maneuver. So when literate men sought diversion, when they closed the books that helped them solve technical and practical problems, they turned to the classics for pleasure and refinement. Humanism was mingled with pragmatism, and as a subsidiary in the main current of intellectual activity the antique literature was read and studied.[1]

A Period of Cultural Assimilation

Now equipped to make a full assault on so long untapped treasures in cultural mines, and ready to cross the threshold of the eleventh century as well, these curious Christians might have halted their quest for cultural advancement had it not been for two conditions. Besides, by now the urgent practical problems of the previous centuries were temporarily solved. Perplexing theological issues were settled and the technical skill needed to conduct the business of Church and state was available. Although they might have been wrong, scholars of the age were confident that intellectual effort could be spent on cultural refinement.

Conditions for Cultural Progress. The first condition permitting cultural and educational progress was peace. More or less frequently from the eighth to the tenth centuries, the empire that Charlemagne had welded suffered from political disorder and unrest, and in addition, parts of Western Europe were under attack from invaders: the Norsemen, the Moors, and the Magyars. By the eleventh century, however, external threat was eliminated and internal ferment was suppressed. Politically tranquil and with relative military security, Europeans could afford to make an investment in cultural refinement.

The second condition was a lenient policy on a literary inheritance that the principal keepers of Christian conscience in earlier centuries had found repugnant. Perhaps any study now of the classics might have been thought too elementary to pose a threat to faith, but the point is that scholars who wanted to read the classics were neither intimidated by ecclesiastical disapproval nor restrained by Church regulation. This permissive policy kindled an interest in the classics, but such tolerance for their study must come as a surprise because the old dilemmas *vis-à-vis* the classical legacy were not resolved. In the schools, the compromises of Jerome and Augustine were practiced, so it must have been that, throughout the Church, a sense of security on matters of faith was strong enough to tolerate a disinterested approach to study.

The supposition is common, and probably correct, that progress is generated in practical necessity and that naked curiosity plays only a small part in the advancement of learning. One of the few exceptions to this condition and where curiosity marched alone in the vanguard, without any leading strings to urgent calls from society, occurred with the advent of the eleventh century. The tenure of this exception was short, but it was long enough to allow, perhaps even to encourage, an embrace of knowledge for its own sake. This interlude enabled scholars to get their academic bearings and to add to their storehouse of knowledge vast quantities of an ancient legacy that, except in a few unusual enclaves, had been left uncultivated and unharvested. When curiosity was exhausted, reservoirs of knowledge were ready for use, and clever men were not backward in finding practical ways to apply the knowledge suddenly put at their disposal.

No longer motivated only by the simple and praiseworthy desire to know, the curiosity characteristic of previous years was redressed and men began to tread familiar ground where progress was goaded by economic, religious, and political need. The groundwork had been laid for cultural and educational progress by intrepid readers and scholars who in earlier decades had picked their way without discrimination through the classics at their disposal. Their reading included a literature on legal, medical, philosophical, and theological subjects or, at least, one with a relationship to these infant disciplines. It might not have occurred to this generation, but it did to its successors, that once excavated and codified, the knowledge in this literature could be useful. Besides, a utilitarian urge found ample support in a European society whose increasing maturity almost automatically disclosed new practical applications for knowledge. With greater maturity, society began to perceive the value of special branches of knowledge; this perception led to an awkward development of the specialties of law, medicine, philosophy, and theology.

The conditions promoting the development of these specialties varied somewhat, but they could not have existed at all without the improvement in basic education that began with Alcuin. Standing on a solid educational foundation that often accommodated fragments of special knowledge unearthed by curious scholars, and prompted by the needs of the age, the specialties of law, medicine, philosophy, and theology made a great surge forward.[2]

Progress in Law. Rome was proud of her legal code, and Roman jurists had worked diligently and skillfully to erect its ornamental literary monuments. As the centuries wore on, however, they lost their luster from disuse, although their spirt remained to affect European life. In addition to a thin residue of Roman law, a code of feudal and tribal conduct persisted in oral tradition. It was strong enough to influence, and sometimes to infect, one that derived its inspiration and strength from Christian morality. These legal traditions had currency, sometimes distinct and sometimes melded; but alone or together, they had been forged on an anvil by now centuries out of date. It would have been futile to import, or to resurrect, fifth-century Roman law for eleventh-century

Europe, and it would have been pointless, too, to try to adapt tribal or feudal convention to this society.

Christian morality was prized and praised, and there is no reason to suspect the sincerity of anyone who acclaimed it; but religious morality, while theoretically touching every side of life, needed translation. Translating moral value, and at the same time paying allegiance to a complex legal tradition grafted to European society, required a kind of scholarship, a sense and feel for the law, that only serious and competent study could provide.

At this time the spirit of anarchy, while far from dead, was checked mainly by the authority of the Church. Murder, theft, and adultery were condemned, but what penalty should be prescribed? Fortunately, the great reservoirs of Roman legal wisdom were preserved in manuscript editions of the *Institutes*, the *Code*, the *Digest*, and the *Novels*,[3] but their secrets were hard to expose. To find the solution to practical legal problems—or better, to reap the wisdom from these books and apply it to contemporary dispute—required a firm grasp of the techniques and technicalities of Latin grammar and rhetoric. Skill in these disciplines could not by itself be of much help in the settlement of a legal dispute, but it was essential for finding the meaning stored in these great legal documents.

Grammatical and rhetorical skill, a thorough knowledge of the law, and courtroom technique were accomplishments that had to be learned, and for their development law schools were recommended; but a legal curriculum needed definition before such schools could make a genuine contribution. What prerequisite knowledge qualified students to enter these schools to follow a course of study surrounded by so much uncertainty, to follow (to put it another way) a route to a legal career that was still without either philosophical or methodological signposts?[4] This question was answered later in university schools of law, but our main interest here is in the assimilation of legal knowledge from ancient sources.

Progress in Medicine. Which of the specialties had priority in this inquisitive age? It is not easy to know. Medicine, however, must have been high on any eleventh-century list. Yet despite its obvious worth and general need, the development of medicine was tardy compared to law, and eleventh-century sources were less likely to have had the same classical vintage as the sources for other specialties.[5] This indifference to or neglect of the classics was not accidental.

In the first place, physical knowledge, including geography and physiology, was considered to be, at best, incidental. More important, however, the relationship between physical science (botany, biology, and chemistry) and medicine, so obvious now, was evident to eleventh-century scholars, too. And physical science, then called "natural philosophy," carried a weight barely allowing it to float on a Christian sea of learning. Pumped from un-Christian wells, natural philosophy, like contaminated water, could have been used only with the greatest precaution. The history of natural philosophy cannot be rehearsed here, but something should be said.[6]

Neither law nor logic (the latter an indispensable handmaiden to philosophy and theology) was an easy subject to master; only a well-trained mind could profit from the study of ancient authorities. Yet compared to medicine, their disciplinary borders were fixed: law and logic can be codified without much help from other subjects. Medicine, though, whenever it abandoned its mystical and magical tradition, needed help from science, from a natural philosophy whose origin was authentically classical. Medical writers and natural historians, all the way from Aristotle, Pliny (fl. second century) Porphyry (232?–304?), and Macrobius (fl. fourth century), had depended upon it. Their work, however, was repeated, amended, translated, and interpreted by a cadre of Arab scholars who broke ground for Avicenna (980–1037) and Averroës (1126–1198). Avicenna and Averroës turned philosophy into theosophy (a study claiming knowledge of God derived by direct mystical insight) and raised perplexing issues that conspired to undermine faith's foundation. The philosophical and theological range here is complex and sometimes bewildering, but the main point is that the cosmology of these precocious Arab scientists was pantheism, an assessment of the physical universe and God that could not have been countenanced by Christian scholars. Because Arab medicine, which evidenced considerable genius, was wedded to a repugnant natural philosophy, the bulk of its clinical theory was either declared anathema or ignored by European Christians.

A course of outright rejection might have been doctrinally prudent, for had Christians accepted pantheism, they would have had to abandon their faith. But the need for good health, for the treatment of illness, and for relief from pain could not be ignored, especially in a society able to pay for medical care and among the secular and regular clergy who began to give more attention to their health. Unsurprisingly, more doctors were needed and their work was handsomely compensated. Public demand created more and more lucrative openings for practitioners of the medical arts, and clever men were not slow in filling them.[7]

If the flow of medical knowledge from Arab lands were halted (or partially halted, because no stream carrying knowledge can be blocked completely), other tributaries had to be opened. An indigenous herbal medical tradition, full of ancient remedies and fanciful treatments, cluttered the medical corpus, but eleventh-century physicians aspired to a more solid and scientific regimen. Beginning about 1050, medical scholars and natural philosophers renewed their effort to solve the problem. Tentative and uncertain, they turned to sources apparently uncontaminated by Arabic mysticism and, at the same time, especially in centers of southern Italy, imported medical knowledge and technique from the Moslem world.[8] Their work paid dividends along both lines, although it was a return to ancient sources that gave medicine full stature in the Christian world.

Latin sources of ancient vintage were consulted first, and the record gives precedence to Caelius Aurelianus (fl. tenth century). But even a full Latin medical treasury was incomplete and deficient. More by accident than by design, the medical writings of tenth-century Arab physicians and scholars were obtained. The mediator here was Constantine (?–1087), who possessed these works and made them available to his colleagues in Salerno. But this was not all. Because Arab medicine followed the tradition of Hippocrates, Constantine followed him, too. He translated a few of Hippocrates' medical books and some of Galen's commentaries on them. From this point on, medicine gave the appearance of having separated itself from a spurious natural philosophy; in consequence, two sources of medical knowledge, the Greek and the Graeco-Arabic, were at the disposal of the early medieval world.

Progress in Philosophy. Logic, we are surprised to learn, and not metaphysics, epistemology, or ethics, commanded the attention of eleventh-century scholars, and in an extraordinary development of logic, philosophy enjoyed a revival. The Latin intellectual tradition—there is plenty of evidence of this preference in Quintilian—had allowed rhetoric to supersede and dominate logic.[9] In law especially, but sometimes in medicine, it was better to be persuasive than right. Roman advocates had time and again gained a practical advantage by adopting the sophistic deceit that the appearance of truth can serve as well as, or better than, truth itself; and for a long time, physicians had resorted to rhetoric in order to convince patients to submit to treatment. Grafted to an orthodox system of thought, this persistent attitude of downgrading logic and inflating rhetoric survived until almost the tenth century. Even tenth-century theologians saw how a careful use of the rules of logic could lead to unassailable, although conflicting, conclusions on matters of faith. Was it possible that logic's affinity to dialectic—that ancient art perfected by Plato—was so intimate as always to be an undependable ally? Was it prudent to suppose that a pagan Aristotle could supply Christians with rules for correct thinking? Whatever the answer to these questions, the apparition of faith's foundations being supported by rhetoric's unsteady beams was too ominous to contemplate. Sound logic was indispensable.

Intellectual timidity might have kept eleventh-century scholars closer to the safety of convention, but timidity was uncharacteristic of this inquisitive age. Spurred on by curiosity, they ignored counsels of caution and, beginning with the logical works at their disposal (most of which were derivative of Aristotle), studied logic as far as their resources, imagination, and intelligence allowed. This was not as far as Abelard (1079–1142) went later, but it was far enough for them to see that sensible advantage could be gained from an investment in the study of logic.[10]

It would be hard to pretend that logic is cultivated for its own sake. In the eleventh century, it was correctly regarded as a means to cogent thought and a way to organize secular and ecclesiastical enterprise. By this time, a bureaucracy of clerks and minor officials administered the affairs of Church and state. Without any need for ornamental scholarship, such men could derive a practical benefit from an ability to think clearly. Rhetorical skill was unnecessary and, moreover, might have landed them in trouble. But this is only one side, and a minor side at that, to the rising prominence of logic. The other side reflects theology's new popularity.

Progress in Theology. Theology had been cultivated in the Carolingian period, but marred by logical drouth, the harvest was too often undependable. Uncomfortable with speculation that could lead to error, tenth-century scholars kept to safer avenues of liturgical and devotional development. But unresolved theological issues attracted the attention of eleventh-century priests and monks who, better educated than their predecessors, and benefiting, too, from the quieter conditions of the age, were eager to use talent and energy on a close examination of articles of faith. For this they wanted exact and detailed laws of thought.

The classics could not help to resolve genuine theological dispute, but they demonstrated how logic was essential for dealing with deduction and induction, scientific demonstration, the form of argument, and the common fallacies. With renewed vigor, the scholars opened the books (sometimes depending upon incomplete or deficient ones, such as Cassiodorus' quick compendium) to begin a long intellectual march that ended by forever linking Western civilization with the classical culture.

A century later, the sources for exploring the hinterland of logic were better, especially when Aristotle's authentic works on logic were used; but at first the quest was dependent upon translations of Aristotle's two introductory books to *Organon*, the *Categoriae* and *de Interpretatione*, and commentaries on them by Boethius and Victorinus. Other, although not substantially better, information came from Isidore's encyclopedic account of the liberal arts, Capella's playful parade of the arts in *The Marriage of Philology and Mercury*, Cicero's *Topica* and *de Inventione*, and *ad Herennium*. This was a poor crew for a ship being fitted for theological controversy, but it was just good enough to sail into the wind of St. Anselm's (1033–1109) *credo ut intellegam.*

Confident that faith is reasonable, novice logicians and theologians refused to heel to the popularity of Anselm's dictum: *credo ut intellegam* (believe in order to understand, or begin with belief and then aspire to an understanding of belief). They pressed on to cultivate a field that produced a bountiful harvest with the appearance of Abelard's *Sic et Non,* a seminal book wherein the power, worth, and independence of reason were proclaimed.[11] These early scholars were neither notorious nor arrogant: they never anticipated Abelard's bold assertion that logic could reveal truth, or his doctrine of doubt. Their practical objective was to understand the Bible, to reconcile the writings of the church fathers, and to organize canon law. In this ambitious enterprise, they expected to confirm rather than threaten the mystery of faith; despite modest accomplishment, they broke ground for twelfth-century logicians.

Interest in General Literature. Law, medicine, and logic (the latter a handmaiden to philosophy and theology) were practical intellectual and academic pursuits, but the whole of life is unaccounted for in work. Recreation, refinement, and pleasure are practical human needs also. Although much has been left unsaid about the husbanding of knowledge for the development of the great professional specialties, another phase to cultural progress in this age of assimilation should be introduced. Now we meet a literature—today called "fiction"—that had been relegated to the fringe of decent learning: assessed as useless or dangerous, its popularity was depressed. In the eleventh century it enjoyed a resurgence.

As opportunity for education became greater and better, more persons used an increasingly abundant leisure to read the books so often left unopened. Yet any declaration that a casual reading of the purely literary classics became a popular pastime is plain hyperbole. Such reading was reserved, instead, for those with leisure, for coteries of the nobility, the wealthy, and the secular and regular clergy. With time on their hands, anticipating Vergerius' (1370–1444) pert advice, they read for genuine pleasure rather than catching flies.[12] Sometimes something more than the pleasure from reading motivated them to polish their image for erudition. Persons of wit, intelligence, and literary accomplishment were considered ornaments to the noble court, the mansion of a wealthy merchant, and the monastic common room. Personal satisfaction was derived from a reputation for erudition; it could, moreover, offer preferment to ambitious scholars and clerics in civic, ecclesiastical, and business affairs. In the noble court, however, the principal reward for literary ornamentation was found. There, besides being luminous pendants reflecting a charm and grace worth imitating, men of learning could use their superior skill to invent and organize new avenues to pleasure. This, though, was capital too easily exhausted, and it seldom led to a full exploration of classical treasuries. To find the place where literary sources were most zealously excavated, we must go to the monastery.

In religious houses, genuine delight from reading and imitating the classics was accompanied by the enjoyment derived from reflecting on masterpieces. Pious and devout monks read the classics to find illustration of unselfish love, pure devotion, altruism, and sacrifice. Laymen read to renew their interest in such things as the complex, sometimes rewarding, sometimes disappointing relationship between the sexes. All readers probed the classics for clues to human personality and overlooked the sometimes lewd and lascivious tales in them. Some were thus prompted to write about the human condition and to notice its scars.

Cicero was resurrected, too, mainly because he was considered the best author to imitate; but eleventh-century readers, although precocious students of prose style, were philosophically naïve and became infected by a Ciceronian moral philosophy whose precepts complemented hedonism and ran counter to Christian ethics. This fundamental conflict, so often unnoticed, whetted an eleventh-century appetite for a literature idealizing impulsiveness.

By the end of the century, some moralists declared the literary diet of the age unwholesome and warned that it could lead to temptation and sin. The more eloquent among them were heeded, at least enough to arouse old distrust of the classics, and a vigorous attack on them was mounted. By this time, however, an interest in general literature could be retarded but not repealed, and the proscription of reading for pleasure failed. Although it took decades to forge, a compromise of sorts was reached: organize the classics into categories, permitting free use of the uncontaminating and interdicting the rest. But this exercise in restriction often became one of rejection that, considering the awakened literary disposition of the age, was rarely successful.

The Organization of Knowledge

The early twelfth century evidences a recession in the spirit of inquiry that over the past one hundred years had opened so many classical vaults. Despite their enthusiasm for novelty, indefatigable scholars had not exhausted all the treasure in them, but enough had been removed to ensure an acquaintance with antique wisdom. Some of its worth was recognized immediately, and parts were at once put in the school's syllabus, but some rich ore was suspected of being either too recondite for application or too subversive of faith to be used with impunity. Yet the same spirit of inquiry that had inspired scholars to lay bare the classical heritage infected them with a zeal to keep every kernel of knowledge now at their disposal.[13] A policy of rejecting the apparently useless or dangerous was unacceptable.

Curiosity has limits and a spirit of inquiry captivating late eleventh- and early twelfth-century students of ancient lore began to wane. It was superseded by a conviction that with the storehouse so full, further collection of ancient sources was unnecessary, or that the well of classical wisdom had been drained. They turned to organizing the entire corpus of knowledge in their possession into the mosaic of Christian value and life that they understood, cherished, and were determined to preserve.[14]

It would be unrewarding to search the archives for an explicit definition of this mission of organization; likely no twelfth-century scholar stated or understood it in these terms. In retrospect, the intellectual and educational activity of the twelfth and thirteenth centuries is clear, however much it may have been concealed from, or disguised by, the participants. In consequence, the parade of Scholasticism started, moved more quickly and successfully over some terrain than other, but in the end had a range great enough to affect every side of medieval learning.

The problem facing twelfth-century scholars was by no means new: its dimensions had been stated and authenticated time and again by reputable authority. How could the culture of an alien and pagan world be utilized in a society that rejected its fundamental preconceptions? And if utilization were not enough, how could ancient knowledge, seemingly so complete and consistent, be melded with inflexible conviction in Christian theology and devotion? This old problem, wrestled before, was unresolved, and the old dilemma surrounding pagan learning vis-à-vis Christian faith was revived on a grand scale, probably because the antique legacy was better known.

A litany of scholars who spent energy and skill taming logic, grammar, and rhetoric, and domesticating law, medicine, and philosophy, is long; and some names, erased or eroded by time, are missing. Every specialty, though, had principal contributors, and the roll should be called for them.

Abelard's Logic. Brilliant, eccentric, arrogant, romantic, and proud, Pierre Abelard's name fairly leaps to the forefront of philosophy.[15] Historians often call him a theologian and educators say he was a model teacher; both, to some extent, are right, but Abelard's seminal contribution was neither in theology nor pedagogy. It was in logic. Possessed of the best knowledge of logic that the authorities, including Aristotle, could supply, Abelard was preoccupied (even as an unauthorized and unlicensed master) with reconciling differences of opinion on doctrine that infected the writings of the church fathers and remained to puzzle their readers.[16] Abelard was not the first to notice these discrepancies, but his predecessors had skirted such thorny problems. They simply made a decision on the basis of the reputation of the Fathers, and adopted the interpretation of the greatest authority.[17] This technique of criticism usually worked, but what was to be done when authorities of equal standing and reputation were in conflict? With a command of logic, Abelard found a way, one leaving intact the reputation of the greatest authorities and at the same time supporting the citadel of faith. His solution, a novelty then and sometimes today as well, was linguistic analysis. In the best illustration of this logical technique, *Sic et Non*,[18] Abelard demonstrated that logic was necessary for revealing an author's meaning. Sometimes meaning was clear, but sometimes it was clouded, confused, or convoluted. Meaning, nevertheless, was buried somewhere and could be unearthed. When correct meaning was discovered the authorities were shown to be in agreement, although a literal reading of the texts could give the opposite impression.[19]

Abelard's dialectic is another story (one that cannot be told here), but it was revolutionary because it demonstrated how logic could support and construct orthodoxy and demolish heterodoxy. Theology was not logic's lone champion, but in theology, logic secured a solid reputation as an indispensable instrument for finding and asserting truth. With this reputation, its use in all other fields is unsurprising.

Logic's Influence on Grammar. For almost as long as anyone could remember, grammar included the structure of language and literature, and on any disputed point, language was expected to follow the doctrine of use. Compiled centuries before, Dionysius Thrax's little book *On Grammar* was a brave beginning in codifying the structure of language. As the calendar turned, suitable supplements enlarged upon it. But whenever more direction or proof than any of these grammar books supplied was needed, the classics were expected to demonstrate the best authors' use of language. Approached this way, it was inconceivable for any code of correctness to stray far from literature, and in the schools, grammar masters were careful to keep literature in the pedagogic fold. They would have been helpless without it.

This theory of grammar had tradition's support; besides, before the twelfth century, no alternative would have been taken seriously. But now, supremely confident of their ability to plow new fields with the sharp share of logic, clearly better equipped than their predecessors, and more sensitive to contamination from classical sources, twelfth-century grammarians transformed their subject by making its canons dependent upon reason rather than, as was traditional, upon usage. Language (at least, the Latin language) was dogmatically assumed to be logical, so logic could be used to remake, to construct, or to dissect it and, at the same time, could declare any appeal to classical usage redundant.

The credentials of logic had to be firmly established before the relationship between various parts of speech could be illustrated; in any case, dialectical grammar's use was postponed until Donatus' and Priscian's textbooks were mastered.[20] Still, this enthusiasm for a logical grammar undermined the influence of traditional authorities. Scholastic grammar had its genesis when Peter Helias (fl. 1140–1150) introduced dialectic to grammar. Helias' work, while influential enough to affect grammar teaching in the schools, was tentative and experimental. It was followed with greater success and popularity (more than 279 editions) by the *Doctrinale* of Alexander of Villedieu about 1199 and a few years later by the *Grecismus* of Evrard of Bethune.[21]

Logic's Influence on Rhetoric. Cogent and correct expression sometimes fails the test of persuasion. We have seen how rhetoric had dominated logic and, to some extent, grammar. But this is only one side of the story: in order to understand a book, some knowledge of rhetoric is essential. Scholasticism invaded every field of knowledge and influenced every subject in the school's curriculum. Rhetoric was not excepted, although Scholasticism's contribution to rhetoric is hard to find. Rhetoric's two parts, expression and exposition, appear to be of about equal worth, but if they were equals in the twelfth century, they were treated in vastly different ways. One side of rhetoric aims for clear and felicitous expression, and twelfth-century writers used Latin as well as educated Americans use English. If school composition is taken into account, medieval students might have been superior to their American counterparts.

Logic has less range in rhetoric than in grammar, although rhetoric is not immune to techniques of analysis. Our medieval forebears wanted to express their thought with force and accuracy and be understood, so they returned to the ancient books on rhetoric. What they found should have been satisfying, but they could not resist an impulse to be creative. Matthew of Vendôme, in *Ars Versificatoria*, was typical of a class of rhetoricians who undertook to rewrite the old books on rhetoric to suit themselves.[22] These reconstructions paid undue heed to detail and technicality and gave almost no attention to generalization and implementation in writing and speaking.

It is hard to believe that even talented students would have been eloquent after studying these books. But they served a purpose by setting rules for expression in law, philosophy, and theology, and each of these disciplines developed its own technical language and form of approved expression. No one could be successful in these fields without a mastery of the rhetoric developed for them. Some of this was probably warranted in philosophy and theology, where good rhetorical canons were lacking. Yet on the other side of the coin, rhetoric infected the specialties with a technical language that made written and spoken discourse unintelligible to the uninitiated.

Rhetoric's close relationship to the professional disciplines tends to obscure its more general use. By now, correspondence of all kinds was important, and letters were expected to follow the rules invented for them. "Invented" is not too strong, because letter writing was a new rhetorical class. Ancient teachers never supposed that persons able to produce a composition would have to be taught how to write a letter. But times had changed: rules were laid down for the proper style and form of every possible type of correspondence, and letters were expected to illustrate them. Should a letter be flawed by departure from approved form, it would be judged offensive by the person to whom it was addressed.

Because letter writing was considered so important, it became a school subject and some students mastered it. Others, however, lacking confidence and with letters to write, used models. A writer could consult a collection of letters for one that suited his purpose and supply the particulars to make it appropriate. If this were too demanding, the services of *dictatores*, who now began to make a good living writing letters, could be engaged.

Exposition is rhetoric's other part. Its function is to reveal the meaning in written discourse, and the rules governing it are old and clear. They have to do with exposing (revealing) an author's style of expression, including allegory, figures of speech, and the story.[23] Textual exposition, by no means merely an artistic enterprise with an ornamental aim, was serious business. With varying degrees of success, it had been used to find meaning in the Bible, especially in the Old Testament. Unquestionably a holy book containing truth, the Bible was also meant to be edifying. How to make some biblical stories edifying was a rhetorical riddle that could puzzle good scholars.

Zeal for biblical interpretation had not abated, but now rhetoric was expected to reveal in the classics a meaning consistent on all points with incontestable theological conviction. Eleventh-century scholars and their successors, captivated by the luster of classical literature, were curious how it could stir emotion by artistically rehearsing universal and perennial human problems and at the same time be morally offensive or a foe to faith. Enamored of it, they were understandably stubborn about giving it up. Still, voices warned them of temptation to sin from reading these books.

Interpreting the Classics. If there were a solution, twelfth-century rhetoricians were determined to find it by beginning with an assumption that these stories, despite being shocking to the pious, must have some place in a Christian corpus of knowledge. Did these stories have a concealed meaning? A preliminary solution to the old problem of paganism was discovered in the first half of the twelfth century, but its author is unknown. Conrad of Hirschau's book, *Dialogue on Authors*, records the solution in about 1125, but he was not its inventor.[24] In any case, he recites the method for exposing the classics then used in the schools.

Roman grammarians, we remember, had used two pedagogic techniques for literary instruction: *prelectio* and *ennaratio*.[25] *Ennaratio* was interpretation, a clue pursued by twelfth-century rhetoricians. Conrad reports how it was used.[26] After a review of the story, the author's intention was examined. What meaning did he want to convey? All this was fairly conventional. But then two novel techniques were introduced: teachers were to find and elaborate the final cause, and the final cause (unknown to the author) is God's meaning in the story. Teachers completed exposition by illustrating how the final cause complemented human experience and conformed to religious conviction. Handled this way, any story could be edifying, but this method tended to be artificial, unconvincing, and dissatisfying. Something better was needed.

While Conrad's book was still in use and its advice on exposition was followed, Hugh of St. Victor (1096–1141) wrote the *Pursuit of Learning* (*Didascalicon*). Intended as a philosophical discourse on the unity of knowledge, Hugh's book supplied an order and hierarchy to knowledge. Aspiring to be complete, Hugh undertook to define the place of the classics in the citadel of Christian learning. He declared Conrad's formula deficient and proposed a solution that, while barren of novelty, turned out to be efficient. Hugh kept the traditional techniques of exposition—style and story—and added a third, inner meaning. Teachers of the classics instructed their students how to find both an author's style and meaning; but for the purpose of discovering inner meaning—God's meaning— Hugh added allegorical interpretation.[27]

With Hugh's formula in place, allegorical interpretation became a valuable ally in the study of sacred and secular literature. But there is more: For allegorical interpretation to be effective and convincing, every device in dialectical logic had to be used, so Hugh's technique cemented the bond between rhetoric and logic.

Not every schoolboy could master the intricacies of allegorical interpretation (nor could every schoolmaster), but some scholars were equipped to discover inner meaning. They rushed into print with interpretations allowing every classic to find a place in the school's curriculum.

The old conflict between pagan literature and Christian conscience, some optimists declared, was over. They were wrong, but rhetoric had become Scholastic.

The Influence of Rhetoric on Law. Although civil law needed codification, it was largely unaffected by Scholastic effort until the end of the thirteenth century. This tardiness is explained partly by law's comprehensive character, one touching all of life and making the development of a full civil code exceptionally complex. In addition, ecclesiastical necessity riveted attention on canon law, where in many places it substituted for civil law.

In the twelfth century, scholars had returned to the Roman legal tradition to meet the *Code*, the *Digest*, and the *Institutes*. They soon discovered that rhetorical skill was essential for understanding and applying the principles in these books. Roman law had at least to be interpreted to comply with existing social conditions; as often as not, it had to be rewritten, and this required legal scholarship.

The history of legal scholarship is obscure before the appearance of Irnerius.[28] Born during the second half of the eleventh century, Irnerius' reputation complements the rise of Bologna as a center for the study of civil law and the establishment of the university there during the middle years of the twelfth century. This much seems certain: Irnerius was not a genuine pioneer in this complex field, although his work for law's development was both substantial and extensive. Starting with legal documents inherited from Rome, and being a rhetorician, he interpreted them and prepared commentaries. The commentaries were probably oral, for what is known about them comes from marginal, likely lecture, notes made on manuscript editions of the *Code* and the *Institutes*.[29] Although Irnerius concentrated on law's past, his successors, building on the foundation he set, organized and adapted Roman law for contemporary society.

Such work was forwarded by Bulgarus. Irnerius had elucidated principle, but Bulgarus was more ambitious: he analyzed Roman law philosophically. *Ordo Iudiciorum*, written about 1140, was a persuasive appeal and demonstration for a contemporary interpretation of Roman law.[30] Using imaginary cases argued by his students, and keeping a record of proceedings, Bulgarus supplied educators with a case literature illustrating an application of legal principles to litigation.[31] Classroom disputation was good practice, but transcripts from real, not imaginary, cases were better. With such records, teachers could use judges' decisions wherein legal principles were applied to cases at the bar. And these decisions, with proper examination and analysis, were the bases for comprehensive accounts demonstrating how Justinian law could fit the life and time of the Middle Ages. Such a demonstration—likely Scholasticism's final influence on law—was made by Accursius' *Glossa* during the first half of the thirteenth century.[32]

Thereafter, scholars' attention centered on the interpretation and codification of decisions rendered on practical judicial problems. In the end, law had a philosophical coherence and, besides, a full complement of illustrations, all taken from actual cases, to give practice clear signposts to follow. When students graduated from the university's faculty of arts, equipped to unravel the mysteries in grammar, logic, and rhetoric, they could matriculate in a faculty of law ready to study an extensive, demanding, and well-organized discipline.

The Status of Medicine. Medicine's development during the Scholastic age, both earlier and simpler than law's, had a less striking result: a consequence, no doubt, of medicine's preference for theory over experiment. Medical theory, the special forte of Scholastic medicine, had the support of Galen's authority, and Galen, although himself an experimentalist, subscribed to Aristotle's thesis giving the soul precedence as the principle of life. So Galen was idealized as the ultimate authority, and after him, empiricism was unnecessary.

The Rise of Philosophy. Law and medicine were cultivated, but philosophy attracted good scholars, too, and their work illustrates the apex of Scholastic thought.[33] Logic had been philosophy's preoccupation, but theologians, uneasy about Anselm's *credo ut intellegam* and determined to find a way to maintain a sensible distinction between the realms of reason and faith, were quick to perceive its worth. Inspired by faith, all thirteenth-century Christians, not just monastic and university philosophers, were eager to preserve and justify religious conviction by any rational means. More than religious devotion, Christianity was a way of life. The Church, moreover, was an externalization of Christianity, and its authority in society was acknowledged by all to be a fundamental good. If this society were to remain intact, if its values were to be sustained against confusion and disharmony, some institution capable of imposing an order to ensure social decency had to be maintained.

Hundreds of scholars undertook to reconcile philosophical and Christian principles. The bulk of ancient philosophy, already in their possession, had elements that appeared to supply a basis for a synthesis that would satisfy reason and faith. Scholastic philosophy seems to have had its origin between 1230 and 1245 with the appearance of Alexander of Hales' *Summa*. Alexander tried to reconcile the philosophies of Plato and Aristotle with Christian belief, but this ambitious enterprise failed.[34]

The complete synthesis was made by St. Thomas Aquinas (1225–1274). Working from translations of Aristotle prepared by William of Moerbeke, Thomas had the advantage (not enjoyed by his predecessors) of using a genuine Aristotle, and he reconciled Aristotelian philosophy with Christian belief. With Aquinas' synthesis at their disposal, philosophers and theologians could keep reason and revelation distinct and, at the same time, demonstrate the reasonableness of faith.

Organization of Knowledge Outside the Specialties. The specialties always had priority, but given a Scholastic addiction to explain everything, general knowledge was given attention, too. Yet some contemporary school subjects were unknown. No one studied biology, history, political science, economics, geography, or psychology. The knowledge that could form these disciplines was an amorphous mass, and organizing it was a vexing task. A fixation for having everything in the right place on a hierarchy of knowledge spurred scholars on to construct categories.

Something along this line had been tried before by Isidore of Seville, Rabanus Maurus (Hraban Maur, 776–856), and others, but the result was unrewarding. Workers in this literary vineyard had rescued an abundance of information but, being compilers, only planted the seed for a twelfth- and thirteenth-century harvest. In the twelfth century, Thierry of Chartres' large *Heptateuchon*, a medieval catalogue, divided the seven arts into the trivium (subjects concerned with expression) and the quadrivium (subjects containing material for thought) and, in a philosophical declaration, asserted the unity of knowledge. Thierry's declaration was used to good advantage in John of Salisbury's *Metalogicon*.[35]

Before this, however, Hugh of St. Victor adopted Thierry's assumption about knowledge's unity and produced a philosophical analysis that fairly bristled with scholastic distinction and organization. *Didascalicon* contained a formula for textual exposition, but its systemization of knowledge was of greater significance. In a fourfold classification, philosophy meant all knowledge, and Hugh was careful to subordinate each category to the totality of human experience. Theoretical or scientific knowledge (theology, physics, and mathematics) was first; second came practical art; mechanical skill was third; and the arts of expression were fourth. Every kind of knowledge had a place, and in addition to stressing its unity, Hugh assigned worth to knowledge by elaborating an explicit hierarchy.[36]

Good as it was, Hugh's plan was not definitive. There was more to do. From Hugh's *Didascalicon* in the middle of the twelfth century to Vincent of Beauvais' *Speculum Maius* in the middle of the thirteenth, scholars worked at a steady pace to assert, demonstrate, and refine Hugh's proposition that knowledge is one.

Vincent's enterprise was destined for success, and *Speculum Maius* was the final chapter in Scholasticism's crusade to impose philosophical order on knowledge. In three massive volumes Vincent organized all natural knowledge. The first volume contained today's science; the second and third volumes treated the relationship between men and the universe. All knowledge was given a proper place in the plan of Creation, so a reader who finished Vincent's account knew where the various categories of knowledge belonged and knew, too, that this knowledge, ultimately ordained by God, could not conflict with articles of faith.[37] What philosophers and theologians had done to reconcile philosophy and religious dogma Vincent of Beauvais and his predecessors did also by organizing general knowledge and reconciling it with theological doctrine. But where others stopped before giving careful philosophical consideration to the education of women, Vincent, in *De Eruditione Filiorum Nobilium*, without anticipating the educational progress women were to make in the future, introduced the subject as a tributary to educational thought.[38] Closing Vincent's books tempts us to believe that the Scholastic age was over.

Medieval Schools

Not having crossed the threshold of a schoolhouse, we are uncertain about provision for the education of the people in a society where the primary beneficiaries of schooling were clergymen. Always evident, but also always secondary, was a recognition of laymen's educational need for some instruction if they were to hue to the safe, narrow path to eternal salvation. As a corollary, instruction could prepare them for practical life, so it was taken for granted that schools of some kind should be available.

Despite shortcoming in execution, what should be stressed is the Church's acknowledgement of a commission to see to the education of the people. The Church then assumed the role in education that today is filled by the state, so the imperial educational plan of Charlemagne was a temporary interruption in a tradition that recognized the educational authority of the Church. No one, not even civil officers of great medieval cities, challenged this authority. The hierarchy was expected to issue binding directives on the conduct of schools, but this did not mean that a coach carrying educational cargo met a clergyman at every stop.

As early as the tenth century, for example, a decree of the English church directed priests to "have a school for schoolteachers in their houses" and admonished the teachers prepared there to be generous in their instruction of others. The decree, moreover, forbade these teachers to demand payment for their service. They could accept gifts, but not direct compensation.[39] Toward the end of the twelfth century, the Third Council of Lateran (1179) enacted a general church law formalizing century-old practice: Every cathedral was to have a school for ecclesiastical students and for "poor but studious youth"; schoolmasters engaged in the instruction of poor children were to be given an income; free schools for the children of the poor were to be opened in connection with churches and monasteries; and teachers with ecclesiastical income would lose it if they charged students for instruction.[40] The decree of the Third Council, repeated by subsequent councils, was binding upon every diocese. It and succeeding pronouncements reduced a traditional preoccupation with the instruction of clerics and began to recognize the need laymen had to study secular subjects. As this preoccupation was amended, schools of all kinds multiplied.

Stories are recounted how educated men traveled about twelfth-century Europe without seeing schools, but they were either poor observers or blind. From the end of the Carolingian period to the beginning of the fourteenth century, schools were common and students by the thousands attended them. But their quality and character varied enormously.

The schools to be seen on a journey through a distant past, bordered on one side by the advent of the eleventh century and on the other by the last years of the thirteenth, operated under a variety of auspices, catered to vastly different kinds of students, and enforced standards of accomplishment that varied as much among schools of the same level as schools on different levels varied from one another. A comprehensive account of medieval schools is hard to give; yet schools of different levels and types had some common features that help to tell the story.

Private Schools. Private schools, opened and conducted by enterprising persons, depended for their legality, their right to exist in the first place, on a license from a church officer, usually the diocesan chancellor or his delegate. With a license, any master could teach whatever he knew and could take students as high up the educational ladder as his knowledge and their talent allowed. Most private schools began as tutorial arrangements, with a student and a master, and some matured into prominent academies. For the most part, however, private schools gave elementary instruction in reading and writing. If students wanted more and masters were able, elements of grammar and literature were added. The worth of these schools should not be discounted: a fairly high degree of literacy among medieval people was due mainly to their existence, and on those rare occasions when girls received literary instruction, only private schools welcomed them.

Monastic Schools. Historical assurance about private schools notwithstanding, their record is fragmentary. This puts them in a scholastic tributary while monastic schools sail the mainstream of attention. At the outset, of course, monastic schools were reserved for *interns*, boys or men aspiring to the religious life, and so long as this restriction was observed, they made only a slight impression on general education. But Charlemagne's capitularies clearly and explicitly demanded more from the monasteries than they were in the habit of delivering.[41] It would be unfair to allege monastic indifference to the education of children living near the religious house, for some monastic schools admitted secular students, but the capitularies told them to broaden their scholastic perspective. Taking small steps at first, but larger ones as time passed, monastic schools came close to being the public schools of the medieval world.

Some active and ambitious monastic schools offered a comprehensive curriculum that started with primary instruction in reading and writing and ended with a complete arts course. Others, somewhat more selective in choosing an academic ground, offered, in addition to a curriculum in secondary education, advanced study in law and medicine. Most, however, had neither the desire nor the ability to conduct anything more than elementary instruction. But whatever level of instruction monastic schools maintained, by the eleventh century, their original and exclusive commitment to the preparation of religious novices had been shed, and they enlisted in the parade of genuine schools.

Joining the parade without sacrificing religious perspective, they taught the traditional arts course, recognizing the wisdom of Alcuin's advice that the arts were stepping-stones to divine learning, without being enamored of it. In any case, what, if anything, was lost in this lukewarm embrace of a secular curriculum was balanced by the happy circumstance of their having a regular and relatively permanent cadre of teachers. Monks were attached to a monastery and rarely left; if they were teachers as well, they stayed in the classroom for a lifetime. Scant records that may contain elements of truth report that monastic schools sometimes employed lay teachers, but too much should not be made of this.

The concentration of scholastic effort was on elementary and secondary teaching, so a word should be added about the place the arts occupied in secondary curricula. For the most part, the curiosity so common to eleventh-century scholars enabling them to reach into the crevices of knowledge, and the determination of their twelfth-century counterparts to apply this new-found wisdom in and out of schools, was either ignored or played down in monastic schools. Monks could be as inquisitive as anyone, and many exhibited extraordinary scholarship, but their schools remained reservoirs for the tested, the traditional, and the true.

When the curriculum adopted the trivium and the quadrivium, the latter paid the penalty to inattention. Arithmetic, geometry, music, and astronomy were cultivated for their practical value; all else about them was ignored. Grammar (always first), rhetoric, and logic were the subjects to be mastered.

Latin grammar had the reputation of being a product of reason, and Alcuin and others had hinted at its being a divine language. With this reputation, monastic grammarians might have embraced the novel theory that grammar was a dialectical exercise. Instead, they invested confidence in the authorities—Donatus and Priscian—who promoted the doctrine of use. When prompted by ambition and wanting more, monastic grammarians turned to even older authorities, such as Capella, Boethius, and Cassiodorus.

By the twelfth century, however, their resistance of logical grammar had crumbled, so as late comers rather than drivers, they jumped on its bandwagon. Even so, grammar could not be divorced from literature. The Greek classics were ignored, but Latin classical authors, especially Virgil, were carefully selected along with some Christian writers. If monastic schools had liberal scholastic sentiments, the literary syllabus seldom illustrated them.

All the arguments for logic's worth were heeded in monastic schools, so logic was studied as a guide to correct thought. This had the effect of turning logic into an arsenal of rules. The dialectic so prized by Plato, and used later for Abelard's bold assault on the citadel of traditional scholarship, was too hazardous to embrace. Logic, therefore, was constructed of formulas to immunize students from contagion; with them in their possession, their knowledge and faith were safe. But Abelard's contribution to logic (always abetted by the enthusiasm of his disciples) was too substantial to be halted in a world where the guerdon from learning was so great. Monastic schools capitulated. Halfway through the twelfth century, no one would have known that monastic schools once regarded linguistic analysis with fear and trepidation.

Rhetoric, probably last in import in monastic schools, deserved higher status. Discounting the platform oratory extolled in the old books on rhetoric, monastic rhetoricians aimed their teaching at a practical prose style. They were interested in effective communication, especially for ecclesiastic and civic business letters, and their teaching reflected this. Study of rhetoric in monastic schools discouraged students from living in the past.

Monastic schools were hidden away in the country where they could afford the luxury (if luxury it was) of finding eddies in the mainstream of academic life. A blessing in disguise, no doubt, parish, collegiate, and cathedral schools sailed the turbulent water of active life.

Parish Schools. Medieval parish schools could be called "village schools," because they were similar to contemporary public elementary schools. Besides, the justification accompanying their origin was no longer asserted; as a result, the elementary course in Latin characteristic of their early history was replaced with a vernacular curriculum. Parish priests, who in former times had taught a few boys, now deferred to convention and appointed teachers, although direction of the schools remained in their hands. Parish schools, in any case, were in the country; in municipalities where tutors and elementary schools were available, they were little more than a flicker on the scholastic horizon.

Cathedral and Collegiate Schools. In towns and cities with either cathedral or collegiate churches and where elementary schools were in abundance, higher type academies were established. They were cathedral and collegiate schools, although the distinction between them was nominal, not academic. A cathedral school represented the educational effort of a college of canons—priests assigned to a cathedral church—and a collegiate school was conducted in conjunction with a church large enough to have a college of canons, too.

Canons were priests who lived according to canon law and organized themselves into guilds or colleges. The character of a cathedral or collegiate school was unaffected by the relationship it had to a church. Priests, canons, or masters obtained licenses to teach and offered courses of instruction under the general supervision of the chancellor of the diocese in cathedral schools and a *scholasticus* (a headmaster elected by his confreres) in collegiate schools.

Their original commission, unsurprisingly, centered on the preparation of priests, and for a long time, despite the appearance now and then of a student lacking a vocation to holy orders, this commission was heeded. But now, in the early years of the twelfth century, with curiosity about the wisdom of the past urging them on, and with all kinds of opportunity for clever and educated men to profit from learning, students literally flocked to the schools so convenient in the cities. If they had to demonstrate a disposition to the priesthood by taking minor orders, they did so, but more likely a majority of students simply masked their secular motivation in order to gain admission to the school. When masters either failed to penetrate this camouflage or were not scrupulous about whom they taught, admission was easy.

Students' motives and masters' temptations to cultivate their academic interest tended to make these schools places for specialists. Theology, canon law, and ecclesiastical administration were well represented in the curriculum, but were neither alone nor most eagerly studied. The day for specialization was dawning, and logic, with its multiple practical and theoretical applications, was craved to quench academic thirst. Masters served huge goblets of Aristotle, and students, draining them dry, were

better versed in Aristotelian logic than any previous generation of scholars. Captivated by law, they mined every treasure in the *Digest* or, in
medicine, learned their lessons from Hippocrates and Galen. When scholastic interest whetted a classical appetite, as it did at such famous academies as Orleans and Chartres, students flocked to the schools specializing
in classical study.

The fame of cathedral and collegiate schools for a specialty was due
to chance: they had a master with a reputation for brilliance in that
specialty. For most schools specialization was ephemeral; it came with a
master and left with his departure or death. Another master of repute
might come to invest in his specialty, but interest in the specialty usually
subsided upon his departure. There were exceptions: some schools set
their academic sights on excellence in a specialty and remained constant
in their commitment. Specialization, though, was by no means universal
or essential in the cathedral and collegiate schools that formed a substantial part of the foundation for the universities making their appearance in
the middle of the twelfth century.

Municipal Schools. Municipal, court, guild, and chantry schools
must be etched into the portrait. In large towns and great cities, the need
for education could not be satisfied without help from schools opened and
maintained by municipalities. Sons of merchants, wanting to follow paternal footsteps, needed elementary instruction plus some additional study
in grammar, rhetoric, and logic; sons of tradesmen and artisans were
expected to be literate. Both elementary and secondary municipal
schools, the record suggests, flourished in large number throughout the
medieval world. Sometimes they were progressive enough to admit girls,
but whatever direction they took on curriculum and admission, their
commission to operate came from the Church.

This matter of delegation could be a source of friction between town
officers and Church authorities. No one had the temerity to dispute the
Church's educational voice, yet town officers were irritated when clergymen licensed to teach refused to conduct elementary-school classes, thinking such work beneath them, and then demanded positions in secondary
schools despite lack of qualification. If this were not enough to cause
trouble, civil officials were offended by an exercise of ecclesiastical authority over the schools when the money to maintain them was furnished
by the town. For the most part, however, these irritations never erupted
into serious battles between town and Church, nor did they intimidate the
educational worth of these schools.

Most municipalities were satisfied when they had secondary schools,
but some towns were ambitious, and others wanted to be notorious. They
aspired to specialization in academies able to compete with cathedral and

collegiate schools. When they succeeded in establishing them and attracting famous masters, they, along with cathedral and collegiate schools, accelerated the growth of universities.

Guild Schools. Although a considerable amount of educational opportunity was at their disposal, medieval men and women were not satisfied. Guild schools, with literacy as an instruction goal, were added for the children and apprentices of masters. Masters supported them because law and tradition imposed an obligation of educating and training apprentices.[42] The teachers were usually guild chaplains. It should be stressed, however, that these were not vocational schools and they aspired to nothing more than basic elementary instruction.[43]

Court Schools. Sons and daughters of noblemen wanted, and needed, a training in manners and courtesy befitting their station in life, and some wanted, besides, practical instruction for handling affairs of property. Manor lords arranged for masters to conduct schools whose quality depended upon the masters' ability. Penurious lords did as little as possible (sometimes nothing at all), but those who sought acclaim and allegiance from their subordinates recruited talented masters with an ability to take students through a full course of instruction in the arts. Court schools, some scholars allege,[44] were the civil counterparts of cathedral and collegiate schools, and while this is probably exaggeration, it is fair to credit court schools with raising the standard of civility and learning among noble men and women.[45]

Chantry Schools. Finally, chantry schools come into view. Cultivated by philanthropy, chantries were memorials to deceased persons, and chantry priests were beneficed to offer masses for the repose of their souls. Always more popular in England than on the Continent, these chantries needed choirs for a high mass, so chantry priests trained boys for the choir; but along with, or in addition to, this training in liturgical music, they were in the habit of giving instruction in reading and writing. Evidence is lacking that chantry schools ever offered more. Specialized and restricted to boys with a talent for music, chantry schools were useful supplements in the broad design of medieval education.

The Medieval University

Without lower schools where some scholastic appetite was whetted, the great ornament to medieval education—the university—might not have appeared in the middle of the twelfth century. Unquestionably universities would have come sometime, but that they came so early is testimony to the soundness of the foundation for education laid in preceding

centuries. Accounts of the medieval university are both abundant and
excellent, so there is no need to repeat what has been done. But to
appraise the part universities played in medieval education, various sides
of university life—administration, teachers, curricula, and degrees—
should be examined.

From the middle of the twelfth century to the end of the fourteenth,
seventy-nine universities (called then *studia generalia*) were established
in Europe. Geography, scholastic custom, and variation in motivation for
advanced study affected the character of every school. North from the
Alps, university life and study were dominated by masters, but to the
south, students managed affairs of scholastic life in a way northern
schools never countenanced. Yet despite possibility for variation, a general picture of the university emerges, and this picture is the one we want to
see.

Academic Authority and Control. Although ecclesiastical authority
was exercised over all sides of medieval life, the Scholastic age encouraged
an open educational society. Masters and students could be orthodox or
heterodox and could enter into academic compacts at will to pursue
knowledge on any scholastic level. If trapped in heresy, they could be
severely penalized, although jurisdiction over academic freedom was usually vested in university masters.[46] If unlicensed teachers taught without
the supervision of a licensed master, their students were deprived of the
conventional privileges associated with the acquisition of knowledge. It
was important, perhaps essential, therefore, for masters and students to
observe the rubrics of educational administration and authority.

Without a civil state competing for educational authority, the
Church's position was supreme. Church officers granted masters on all
levels a license to teach, or they delegated this authority to kings or
princes. So the medieval university, whatever it might have been as a
legally unrecognized association of teachers and students, had its origin
with a charter. When a charter was granted by the pope, the school's
degrees were recognized throughout Christendom; royal charters gave
degrees legal standing in a kingdom. But any school, the source of its
charter notwithstanding, could have its teaching interdicted by a bishop.
Even the most advanced case of myopia could not cloud this vision of
educational authority secure in the maternal custody of the Church. And
because higher learning was considered to be both ornamental and important, and sometimes capable of threatening religious faith and discipline,
the Church's exercise of authority vis-à-vis universities was all the more
scrupulous and solicitous.

An exercise of authority often led to conflict. Masters and students
were indisposed to challenge the Church's place in education, but they

found it hard to tolerate an exercise of authority by ecclesiastical officers—usually the chancellor of the diocese where the university was located—that could award degrees to students whom masters refused to recommend or to deny degrees to students whom masters had approved. Such arrogance, masters declared, undermined the integrity of the scholastic enterprise.

University Teachers. Whatever disadvantage masters might have felt with respect to their autonomy as captains of the academic ship, they were unabashed specialists who arranged their professorial duty so as to stay close to their books and manuscripts. There is no reason to demean their scholarship, for it must have been abundant, but it was not revealed in *ordinary* lectures. These lectures were dictations from a master's book or manuscript, for which students paid directly to the master a fee set by the guild. Students used these dictated copies when they themselves began to teach.

Had ordinary lectures alone illustrated the scholarly pedigree of masters, a complaint could be registered. As it was, however, *extraordinary* lectures gave masters a chance to explain, elaborate, and embellish the content of ordinary lectures, and the ubiquitous (sometimes thought interminable) disputations afforded any master or student a platform to display intellectual acumen and academic prowess. Scholarship was the master's stock in trade and, in the absence of a means to record it (save in manuscript form where, even under the best circumstances, wide circulation was unlikely), evidence of erudition was reserved for the sermon, the disputation, or the public defense of advertised theses. In the absence of moveable type, an invention that gave the world of learning a new face but was still a long way over the horizon, scholarly publication was oral.

Enough has been said about tension over autonomy, but this might be added: when masters waged their battles with ecclesiastics, they were engaged in a contest of will and wit with their own kind, for according to most universities' statutes, masters were required to be in clerical orders and to remain celibate.[47] So however generous the Church might have been in maintaining an officially open educational society, its attitude toward higher education must, in the end, be interpreted as a gesture of generosity extended only to men of the cloth. Laymen were seldom formally excluded from university teaching, but formal exclusion was unnecessary; an inflexible tradition kept them on the sidelines. If a good face is to be put on restricting university teaching to clerics, it would have to be that it was a way of encouraging laymen to use their university education in the secular world, where clerics were either discouraged or prohibited from frequenting.

University Curriculum. When medieval masters first began to teach, they depended unavoidably upon reservoirs of knowledge that were not very deep. They had a few manuscripts, usually classical in content, although some may have belonged to an ecclesiastical literature that had been growing by leaps and bounds over the preceding centuries, and at first they went around the country reading them to anyone who would listen. More heralds than professors, they nevertheless kindled sparks of interest. Eventually seeing the limitation to this crude teaching (if indeed they were teaching), they organized into bands and began to offer in concert what earlier had been a solitary enterprise. As the ancient Sophists had done, these bands attracted students, and in this attraction the first universities were conceived.

The history of the first universities need not be recited for us to see what was occurring: the knowledge masters had in their possession—or in their manuscripts—was offered to students. Assuming that students were ready, a not altogether valid assumption in every case, masters gave them part of the legacy of learning by reading to them. The pedagogy was crude, so much is admitted, but it was the only one available and its shortcomings should not preoccupy us. What should be noticed, instead, is that students chose the readings to hear and, sometimes, to copy.

No doubt a good deal of hyperbole disguises the fact that even the most ambitious cadre of masters could not have possessed enough knowledge to fulfill the proud boast that *studia generalia* were schools for all knowledge for students from all parts. But however thin the resources of the first universities may have been, they never tilled old ground by duplicating the work of lower schools. The universities, with all presumption laid aside, were schools for specialists: they were professional schools, and so, the history of European higher education tells us, they remained.[48]

Now and then an eloquent master pronounced the inadequacy of his students. Some complained that students unable to read and write came to the university and attended lectures. John of Salisbury (d. 1180) adverted to this in the middle of the twelfth century and, moreover, in his famous *Metalogicon*, tried to redress it.[49] Neither he nor the reforming generation after him was entirely successful in immunizing higher schools from students unready for advanced study. Yet as universities became more common, the preparation of students for university study was upgraded by the influence of the universities themselves.

The principal schools preparing students for the university were conducted in conjunction with cathedral and collegiate churches, although some students cut their academic teeth in monastic schools or with tutors. Sometimes, either because these schools were deficient or because students were lazy and inattentive, their preparation was too meager for admission to the university. To repair these flaws, enterprising teachers opened schools near the university to ready students for it. Such schools sprouted in every university city and town, although a convincing record illustrates that they never incorporated with the university.

The most important, perhaps the only, requirement for matriculation in the university (and matriculation was nothing more than an oath binding students to university regulation) was knowledge of Latin. The test of latinity, we are led to believe, was at first made by the rector, but as universities grew larger and more complex, this humble duty was delegated. In any case, the record is ample and very likely accurate, the requirement was administered with a commendable degree of strictness, for the Latin fluency of medieval university students was about equal to the ability of contemporary American college students to use English.

The place where all students began university study was with arts; although the picture of the first universities includes the freedom of students to hear lectures of their choice, they had an obligation to be grounded in arts before tackling a specialty. Neither tradition nor regulation told them to specialize, for a degree in arts was entirely respectable; but if they did, their foundation in arts was solid. It was possible, in fact it may have occurred frequently, for students not to attend lectures or possess manuscripts on all the seven arts. They were, however, held accountable for knowing the artistic tradition in an examination given, not subject by subject or year by year, but at the very end of their studentship.

So far as anyone knows, the word curriculum went unused in medieval universities. Faculty was the term used instead. For a school to qualify as a genuine university, one of the superior faculties—law, medicine, or theology—had to be represented along with the inferior faculty of arts. No mystery surrounds the selection of these subjects for special attention: the professional faculties were responsible for a kind of knowledge that by any account was essential to contemporary society, and the faculty of arts contained skills of literacy and thought that, while important in their own right, were indispensable for an incursion into the professional disciplines.

The professional faculties gave the university its character, and even today, with the possible exception of theology, we expect a university to husband these disciplines. But the story in connection with the arts course has a different ending. Almost always the faculty with the most masters and students, and despite a commitment to the worth of the arts, the tendency to downgrade these faithful auxiliaries to learning was almost irresistible. Although students in the arts faculty were not usually perusing introductory books on grammar and rhetoric or for the first time wrestling logical propositions on cogency and classification, it was always hard to maintain that the intensity of their study was equal to the level of scholarship demanded in the superior faculties. Besides, toward the end of the medieval period, secondary education began to show signs of life. When secondary schools adopted a practice that had the blessing of tradition and organized their curricula in a systematic way, they borrowed subject matter from the higher schools. This put the integrity of the arts course in jeopardy, so universities began to reconstruct the inferior faculty. Giving up, or losing, grammar and rhetoric and the literary studies accompanying them, universities invested confidence in logic and inflated it to a complete course in philosophy. In consequence, we begin to see the foundation for a college or university curriculum, with an array of subjects once subsumed to philosophy, held together by a principle rejecting professionalism.

University Degrees. Then, as now, students expected to obtain recognition for hard work in school. The model of the guild was available to the universities and they followed it. Persons who passed academic muster were titled masters, and this title authorized them to practice or teach. The single title of "master" made any talk about university degrees illogical, for without various levels of academic accomplishment to be recognized, degree of accomplishment was meaningless. A master was a master. How long only one level of accomplishment (that of master) lasted is a matter for speculation, but the lawyers were the first to appropriate the title of "doctor," and in other fields, eager students who wanted recognition called themselves "bachelors."[50]

About equal parts of mystery and misinformation surround the origin and evolution of today's most common college degree, the bachelor's. The title, but not the degree, seems to have been introduced at Bologna, although there is no evidence that the title, to say nothing of the degree, was given statutory recognition there until 1432.[51] A professional and professorial status is alleged for the bachelor's degree beginning with Abelard's initiation to teaching in the school of a Parisian master.[52] According to law and custom, a person without a master's degree was either prohibited or discouraged from teaching unless a master supervised him, and this seems to have been the case with Abelard. Yet whatever truth may be lodged in Rashdall's assertion concerning Abelard's pioneering venture, the record of history, supported by the authority of etymology, is fairly clear on this point: a bachelor was an apprentice. He was studying for a master's degree and, along with his study, was tutoring students under the direction of a master. It was not until late in the medieval period, and then only at Paris and Oxford, that any sign indicated a bachelor's might have become a university degree.[53]

University statutes, while usually silent about any degree other than a master's, sometimes (as in the case of Bologna) provided for tutors or apprentice teachers (and stipulated salaries for them, because they were not allowed to give ordinary lectures and charge fees) who were to conduct extraordinary lectures and repetitions in the faculties of law and medicine.[54] If masters permitted a student to give a course of lectures (although the rule was strict and strictly enforced that these lectures could not compete with masters' lectures), the student was called a "bachelor." Eager and ambitious students who had this authorization from their masters, and if they had besides the funds to do so, enticed students to their lectures by offering them gifts or loans. It was never bad to have a reputation for being able to fill a lecture hall.

Although the faculties of law and medicine recognized students with four to six years of study as bachelors—if they were also academic helpers with duties to conduct reviews, to tutor, and to deliver extraordinary lectures—they made no provision for examinations or other tests of competence for bachelors. The examination was, of course, a universal requirement for the master's degree. Whenever it appears in any faculty, the station of bachelor was a step up the academic ladder, perhaps similar to the station of candidacy in the contemporary American university's doctoral program, but it was not a degree. It is, we think, a fruitless quest to search for the origin of the bachelor's degree in the superior faculties or to look for its first sign of life anywhere other than Paris and Oxford.

These two universities, although prizing the accomplishment of their superior faculties, placed a special emphasis on the education of young men in the faculty of arts. At first, of course, with a great need for teachers, it was usual to think of the master of arts as a prospective teacher and to equate the degree itself with a license to teach. But as opportunity for learning became greater and the faculties of these schools grew by leaps and bounds, it seemed unlikely that more than a few degreed students would become teachers. It was likely that they would aspire to study in one of the higher faculties and even more likely that they would leave the university to pursue some occupation whose relationship to teaching was remote.

Under these circumstances, could the appearance of the arts faculty as a professional discipline be maintained? When it became obvious that it could not, a distinction was made for study in arts: the master of arts was kept for those who wanted professional status; the degree of bachelor was introduced for students who wanted erudition but not a teacher's license. From this urge for a general or a liberal education, the arts curriculum was modified; and with this modification, the bachelor of arts appeared as a standard university degree. But whether this occurred early enough for the bachelor's to have been a genuine degree in the medieval university is a query whose answer, at least for now, eludes us. What is clear is that the bachelor's degree became in the fifteenth century a preprofessional degree and, as university students multiplied and as learning became less a preoccupation for a clerical population, a degree for a gentleman who could take his place in the company of educated men.

The Character of Medieval Education

The direction of education and the level of its success in the medieval period is illustrated best, but not alone, in the universities. The labor spent on a restoration and a rehabilitation of ancient wisdom was meant to give medieval thought vigor and appeal and to embellish it here and there, but not to alter its substantial compact with Christian conviction or to redefine the world God had made, but to accept and, with the array of knowledge available, to understand the world.

But a new wind was blowing from the south, and its velocity held aloft a new assessment of life's priorities. The gusts were too weak to capsize the Church or swamp devotion to God, but they were strong enough to carry a formula for living a fully human life. Preoccupied with the essentials, medieval scholars invested intellectual capital in them. Doing so, although not neglecting humanism entirely, they deflated it and, in the schools' curricula, neglected most of the legacy that survived in general literature.

Their successors, the humanists, found another answer to the vexing question of what knowledge is of most worth. They jettisoned huge parts of the medieval corpus of learning and in their place grafted to the curriculum a genre of classical literature portraying supremely human ideals. Certain of the efficacy of these ideals, they adopted imitation as a way for inculcating them. The shadows of medieval education, while becoming shorter, did not disappear at once. A new educational day—the day of humanism—with some rays of genuine brilliance was about to begin.

Chapter 7

The Great Renaissance and Educational Reappraisal

The temptation is strong to believe that the principal motives driving humanists toward their educational goal were satisfaction, greed, and pleasure. A total embrace of such motives would have led to an abandonment of religious conviction. When humanists undertook a leap back over a thousand years to search for a purer version of classical paideia, they were at pains to stress the good in the classical way of life, a good that was not related to or dependent upon religious faith, but they were neither antireligious nor un-Christian. Hundreds of illustrations can be brought to support an indictment of humanism for a rejection of religious belief and Christian value, but these are only illustrations of a shift in emphasis from paying attention first to the good of the soul to paying attention to the good of the person. They do not amount to a conviction of the humanists for apostasy, heresy, or secularism.

For the most part, humanists were religious persons, deeply dedicated to the truth of their faith and disposed to preserve it. But they were mesmerized by the idea that, first of all, men and women live in a temporal world, where they have a right to self-fulfillment and -satisfaction, to happiness, and some comfort, without being hampered by religious myopia to abandon everything human in a search for the solace of eternal prosperity. As much as anything else, this attitude dominated their perspective and, in the end, led to the articulation of an educational philosophy openly hostile to medieval educational assumptions and, anomalously, one frequently inconsistent with the way schools were organized and conducted.

The Genesis of a Humanistic Plan for Education

It is common to establish the forward boundary of humanism with the lifetime of Francesco Petrarch (1304–1374). Whether this boundary is correct, whether it should be earlier or later, need not be settled here. Still, since so much of Petrarch's energy was spent on recovering literary monuments, one should be careful not to equate the recovery of antique literature with the Great Renaissance itself.[1] Labor and talent were spent on the excavation of treasure in philosophy, medicine, and law, to say nothing of the arts, centuries before Petrarch entered the redoubt of classical literature. So interest in the past, and even the recovery of literature, must not be counted as the equivalent of humanism. What should be adverted to, however, is the kind of literature marked for rescue.

Petrarch's Humanism. In company with his humanist colleagues, Petrarch spent little time on those works associated with the specialties, and for which the medieval universities achieved fame. Disliking both lawyers and physicians, he was interested, as were his confreres, in a type of literature for which medieval scholars so often showed so much fear and disdain. And one wants to know why this kind of literature should have interested the humanists, when so obviously little in it was capable of fulfilling any, or many, practical needs.

If the answer to this question is to be found at all, it must be found in the canalization of humanist interest into those areas of classical literature capable of illustrating the good life. Humanism was generated and fueled by a cultural doctrine declaring that in order to discover the ideals, the values, and the human convictions propelling man's spirit, one must turn to the genre in literature that today is called fiction. This kind of literature, the doctrine dogmatically assumed, contains and discloses the substance of human aspiration. It shows how men and women lived, and it illustrates, besides, the motives inspiring and guiding their way of life. If their motives were human and noble, if they could be imitated and followed as guides for contemporary life, then the literature illustrating them should be revived, studied, and imitated.

So this assumption, rather than any antiquarian interest in digging up old ruins or raiding old libraries, launched the humanists on their expeditions of literary recovery. They wanted models of the good life to imitate and, from what they knew about classical literature, supposed such models could be found in it. Even if Petrarch and his associates had liked the old tomes on law, medicine, and philosophy, any effort to recover them was unlikely, for they did not contain the treasure the humanists were eager to possess.

For all his good work in elevating the classical legacy to a new level of scholarly consciousness, Petrarch's services to learning were only incidentally pedagogical, although implications therein point toward new educational principles. The principles, however, had to be translated into practice, and this was labor for which Petrarch had neither appetite nor special qualification. He needed instruction from no one on the significance of education, yet his disdain for the profession of teaching is almost too obvious to ignore, and it must have colored his appraisal of schoolroom method. Pedagogic technique is a subject he not only neglects but appears also to reject, and it is not hard to believe that a person so admired by his colleagues might have had a penetrating influence on their educational priorities. The work of teaching was beneath him, unworthy of his genius, and he was eager to tell talented men to forsake such work, if they were teachers, or if they were anticipating a career as schoolmasters, to alter their plans. "Let those men teach boys who can do nothing greater, whose qualities are a plodding diligence, a rather dull mind, a muddled intellect, ordinary talent, cold-bloodedness, a body tolerant of labor, and a mind contemptuous of glory, desirous of petty gains, and indifferent to boredom. . . . I . . . pity those who wasted nearly all their lives [teaching] in public school."[2]

To find the origin of humanistic education we should turn from Petrarch to Peter Paul Vergerius (1370–1444)[3] and Manuel Chrysoloras (1355–1415).

Education for Character

Vergerius was a teacher, as were most humanists, although some (like Petrarch) supported themselves as men of letters, as printers and publishers (like Aldus Manutius),[4] and as civil servants, who combined research and writing with their public duty. The word *humanist* either implied or confirmed the meaning of a teacher of the good, human, and liberal arts. What the Greeks had called "paideia," these teachers called "humanities." Whatever the nomenclature, they were talking about the liberal arts and thought them worthy of special attention. Battista Guarino (1434–1513), who may be understood as speaking the mind of his humanistic confreres, wrote, "To each species of creatures has been allotted a peculiar and instinctive gift. To horses galloping, to birds flying, comes naturally. To man only is given the desire to learn. . . . the pursuits, the activities proper to mankind."[5]

The question is obvious: What learning, pursuits, and activities are proper for the superior education of human beings? Undoubtedly, in asking this question, the interrogators were involving themselves directly in the enigmatic field of educational philosophy. Earlier authors, including Cicero, had talked about a perfect education and seemed to define it as knowledge of all things divine and human.[6] But this was an ideal which, while it could be aimed for, could never be reached. Humanists could praise the ideal and, at the same time, settle for something less. They settled for literature, moral philosophy and history, believing that the old specialties, so important to their medieval forebears, were incapable of producing free, civilized, virtuous, and sensitively aesthetic men and women. They eschewed universality in favor of specialization and never accepted a commission to teach everything; but they acknowledged the commission of humanistic teaching to transmit a legacy featuring Latin and Greek language and literature, history, and moral philosophy.

A Humanistic Curriculum. If Latin and Greek literature were to be mastered for the contribution it could make to a civilized use of leisure, the language rendering it would obviously have to be studied in a serious and scholarly way. So a great deal of time was spent on the careful study of both Latin and Greek, although the former was usually given the bulk of attention.[7] Logic might have been a great boon to contemplative scholarship, but humanists were activists, so ethics was mustered into service to teach the secrets of true freedom and to disclose the pathway leading to virtue rather than to vice. Ethics fortifies men with a knowledge of what should be done; history illustrates what has been done in the past and, in addition, may contain clues with respect to what should be done now and later. Finally, and not to be overlooked in any list of humanistic priorities, there is eloquence. The worth and place accorded eloquence and its handmaiden, rhetoric, have sometimes puzzled good scholars. Eloquence contributes to stylistic beauty, of course, and this is in itself good; but more significantly, it contains the means to persuade citizens to follow the lessons of history and the precepts of moral philosophy.

Physical Education. Citizens have an undoubted need for mental and moral training, but they need physical development as well. Every ancient political philosopher had recommended a refinement of physical skill for application to military activity. Either in armies or as solitary warriors, good citizens were expected to fulfill their duty to the state. Although some fourteenth-century humanists might have been afflicted with nostalgia (for they had surely sampled the antique political philosophy), it is not at all clear that the physical element in their educational program was intended to fulfill a military purpose. They thought, rather, of the harmonious formation of the person, and harmony was unattainable without some attention to sport.

Almost without exception, humanist writers gave unqualified endorsement to physical formation as a substantial part of any educational program, and there is no good reason to doubt their sincerity. In practice, however, although some humanistic schools came in time to stress gentlemanly sport, the curriculum of the conventional humanistic school tended to pay it scant heed.[8] This neglect might not have had a basis in a rejection of sport, but on the fact that with an extensive and burdensome literary syllabus to master, time for play could not be spared.

Vergerius: Character and Liberal Studies. The educational experiences most prized by humanists were illustrated and expressed in ancient literature. This conclusion was reached this way: If we are what our experience makes us, we should spend the bulk of our educational attention on the best experiences a curriculum can provide. The best of human experience, they assumed, was artistically recounted in ancient literature. No wonder, then, that the curriculum was filled by classics from which students were never allowed to stray.

This was the intellectual climate of which Vergerius was part, and these were the convictions he expressed in teaching and writing. His reputation as a schoolmaster was made before he began to till the soil of educational philosophy, so he was listened to. It is said, for example, that the little book for which he is best known—*De Ingenuis Moribus*—9 was possessed by good libraries for two centuries after his lifetime and in the sixteenth century was used as a textbook in the schools. It put him, it is said, in the mainstream of early Italian humanism.[10]

Born in Capo d'Istria, Vergerius spent several years at Padua before moving to Florence. He appears to have earned a master's degree in the faculty of arts at Padua and, for some reason, chose to specialize in logic. Sometime after 1397—Manuel Chrysoloras returned to Florence in 1396 as a city-paid teacher—he spent about three years attending Chrysoloras' lectures. But since Chrysoloras seems not to have taught in Padua, Vergerius must have studied with him either in Florence, Pavia, or Venice. Considering his humanistic sentiments, which must have been kindled early in his academic career and antedated his association with Chrysoloras, this concentration on logic is surprising, although we are told that his approach to the subject was innovative and well outside the tradition of medieval logic teaching.[11]

The mystery is compounded somewhat by his attention to canon and civil law. Obviously a professional study, something even the best humanists could not alter, law was outside the field of humanistic interest. Law had need for skillful scholars, and the contribution the arts could make to it is not in dispute; yet for Vergerius to have been engaged in its study is uncharacteristic of a dedicated humanist, although his clerical status could help explain an interest in canon law. How much of an investment was made in law's study is uncertain (he may not have stayed long with it), for when we meet him in 1391 in Padua, after his return from Florence, he has the titles of professor of logic, doctor of arts, and doctor of medicine.

Practical Logic. After about fifteen years as a professor of logic at Padua, Vergerius composed his famous humanistic educational manifesto,

On Noble Character and Liberal Study. Nothing in the book takes us into a classroom, and it is silent about how its humanistic recommendations are to be employed in practice. The only reference to pedagogy is in connection with logic: it should be practical. Vergerius could be indicted for creating a gap between medieval accomplishment in logic and the use anticipated for it in humanistic life, but this, it seems clear, is an indictment he expected and welcomed. He intended to break with the past. When he said logic should be practical, he meant that, in everyday life, men and women should have the ability to recognize and sort out the various problems facing them, and they should have enough intellectual skill to draw sensible, cogent, and socially sensitive solutions in connection with them. He was saying, to put it another way, that the logic of the past, aloof on a speculative and esoteric level, was antiseptic in an assertion of truth that had little or nothing to do with the way men and women lived.

Vergerius' Famous Book. Before Vergerius' book *On Noble Character and Liberal Study* appeared, considerable interest had been shown in the educational philosophy of ancient writers. Plato and Aristotle were known and read, and Cicero, of course, was a perennial favorite among a cadre of educators enamored of eloquence, but Plutarch's recounting of ancient educational doctrine and Quintilian's magnum opus, although extant in fragments, had not been recovered in complete editions.

Evidence of this background of knowledge about ancient educational philosophy permitted critics to allege that Vergerius was only recalling the work of his ancestors, rebottling old wine; but it is better to interpret his work as a studied reflection on the nature of his own teaching and not merely a repetition of what had been said before.

The observation is interesting, although not necessarily significant in connection with the composition of Vergerius' book, that it was written as a set of instructions to a young nobleman, Ubertinus of Carrara. Ubertinus was the son of a distinguished man, Francesco, the lord of Padua, so the advice given in *On Noble Character and Liberal Study* about his education could not reasonably be assessed as being applicable to the education of all children. This was the context prompting Vergerius to introduce his subject by telling his young reader (or more likely his father) that parents owe their children three things especially: an appropriate name, a good city in which to be nurtured, and a decent education.[12] Contemporary readers have little difficulty with the latter two admonitions, but the first one may be puzzling. Yet Vergerius goes on to say that even an "unlucky" name and a culturally impoverished city are shortcomings that can be redressed by "changing the one or quitting the other."[13] What can never be remedied, though, is the neglect of early education.

Because its importance is not subject to discount, education is the subject whereupon Vergerius will concentrate.

Early Education. The first purpose of early education, Vergerius is quick to say, is to develop sound, virtuous, Christian character. Intellectual finishing might pay a huge dividend (of that no humanist had any doubt), and it might contribute materially to the formation of character— for Vergerius was prepared to follow Plato's and Cicero's argument that right action could be promoted by right knowledge—[14] but the acquisition of knowledge, for all its implied worth, must always be subordinated to the discipline of moral excellence. "We call those studies *liberal* which are worthy of a free man; those studies by which we can attain and practise virtue and wisdom; that education which calls forth, trains and develops those highest gifts of body and of mind which ennoble men, and which are rightly judged to rank next in dignity to virtue only."[15]

Study of the Classics. Vergerius had come to believe, largely as a result of his own experience as a student and teacher, that classical study was a certain and dependable route to the formation of free, civilized, and perfect persons, but his commitment to the classics neither blunted his Christian zeal nor excluded a vast body of Christian literature from the school. In endorsing the classics, although not excluding Christian literature, he adopted the position (somewhat reminiscent of Clement of Alexandria's theory) that the classics contain a moral wisdom not materially different from the Christian ethic.

And at no other time in the history of education were scholars better equipped to read and interpret the classical literature than in the humanistic period. What seemed at an earlier time to have been offensive in the classics, and what was frequently proscribed in the schools, could now be criticized and analyzed in historical and literary context. The antique literature, so much feared for centuries and so often surrounded with safeguards, was viewed now with much less suspicion.

The point to be stressed, however, is not that the classics were embraced by humanists, but that, with their embrace, nothing in the citadel of Christian moral philosophy was suspended or rejected. Vergerius was, as were most of his humanistic confreres, a stable and faithful Christian who exhibited neither animosity nor indifference to the Church. Nobility of character was fed and sustained from two tributaries: classical literature and patristic theology.

Practical Knowledge. Liberal learning has Vergerius' warm endorsement, but a practical man knows something about life's many sides, and Vergerius was, above all, a practical man. He wanted to avoid both misunderstanding and narrowness. Liberal learning is good in itself, but it is not the only educational avenue young men can pursue. They might devote their lives to the profession of arms or some other honorable occupation, and so doing should be immune from criticism, but while they are engaged in these other things, their eyes should not be closed to the human benefit claimed from cultivating liberal disciplines.

At the same time, Vergerius wants his readers to recognize the practical values residing in liberal learning. For the public man, it gives an eloquence in speaking and writing "of no slight advantage in negotiation," and it provides a foundation for reading and understanding the documents and issues of public life.[16] Besides, there is the bonus of useful employment of leisure hours. Ubertinus would be foolish to follow the example of Domitian, the emperor Vespasian's son, who "was driven to occupy his leisure by *killing flies!*"[17] Unproductive use of leisure tempts one to distraction with unworthy or distressing themes, but such distraction can be redressed in the companionship of good books. Idleness may not be the devil's workshop, but it comes close.

The knowledge reaped from reading good books is a permanent possession, not liable to decay; it, like the inscription on a coin, has a kind of immortality. But knowledge's contribution is not of fact alone (although fact is important); it pays huge dividends to the shaping of cogent thought and felicitous expression as well.

Still, we have not come to grips with the principal subject of the discourse: What is to be studied? And to what end? It was common to suppose that an immersion into literature would make one conversant with the past, but would do little to prepare one for the future. This old caveat is discounted, for literature is "adapted to all times and to all circumstances, to the investigation of fresh knowledge or to the re-casting and application of old."[18]

The Trivium: Grammar, Logic, Rhetoric. Although Vergerius does not advert to language directly, the temper and tone of his book contains the clear implication that Latin must be first on the menu. Greek was coming into fashion, as the success of Chrysoloras' seminars attested, but whether Vergerius thought his schoolboys should have a mastery of the Greek language and literature is never clear. Supposing, then, that the student for whom Vergerius is writing has fluency in Latin, he must begin with a close and careful study of the rules of grammar. Without a solid foundation in the code of correct composition, any excursion into literature is bound to be flawed.

Next comes logic. Its two main functions are to "enable us to discern fallacy from truth in discussion" and in "setting forth the true method of learning, . . . [to] guide [us] to the acquisition of knowledge in whatever subject."[19]

Rhetoric is committed to the attainment of the art of eloquence.

Vergerius neglects the role rhetoric had played for centuries as a vehicle
for unraveling meaning in the classics to center attention on its practical
value in public discourse. He deplores the low state of contemporary
oratory, alleging that speakers were preoccupied with "speed, brevity,
[and] homeliness." His advice is an unmasked plea to return to the past
and to follow the oratorical models supplied by the great classical orators.

Additional Studies. With the traditional subjects of the "trivium"
accounted for, poetry, music, arithmetic, geometry, and "the science of
the Stars" (astronomy) are added as essential ingredients to the syllabus.
There is just enough time to mention the "three great professional Disciplines: Medicine, Law, Theology."[20] They should not be dismissed as un-
important, but Vergerius does not want anyone to think they are liberal.
Law, he supposes, might have a liberal side if it is studied as part of moral
philosophy. But he charges law, despite what it might be when studied
properly, with being hardly more than a trade. Medicine, an applied
science, is attractive to students, "[B]ut it cannot be described as a Liberal study." Theology, on the other hand, "treats of themes removed from
our senses, and attainable only by pure intelligence."[21]

The agenda is comprehensive, although its description is brief, but
Vergerius has told his readers what should be studied. He was right in
supposing it unnecessary to engage in a long description of the content of
these subjects. That had been done before, and no one was left in doubt as
to what Vergerius meant when he recited the essential parts of liberal
learning. Still, it was important for him to be clear on one point: No one
should expect total accomplishment in all these subjects. While wide
learning was both desirable and attractive, mastery of everything is impossible, although the well-educated humanist should be conversant with
all the liberal arts. "Most of us," he wrote, "must learn to be content with
modest capacity [in these subjects] as with modest fortune."[22] To be fully
accomplished in any one of the arts might be the occupation of a lifetime,
and Vergerius certainly wants students to concentrate their time and
attention on one discipline, depending upon their mental capacity and
interest; but for exceptional competence in any subject, it is essential that
it be seen in relation to the whole of knowledge. Specialization is warmly
recommended, yet it will result in distorted and defective understanding
unless it is supported by a strong foundation of liberal learning.

The Discipline of Study. The foundation of liberal learning will be
strong if teachers are carefully selected, with only the best being employed
for, perhaps especially for, the rudiments. But good teachers, for all their
worth, need help, and it comes (if it comes at all) from good books. Only
"those of first rank" should find their way into the syllabus. Now, however, there are two precautions to be observed: Students should not at-

tempt too much at once; and they should not "hastily [pass] from one subject to another, which is destructive of all steady progress."[23]

Taking up a book, they should stay with it until it is mastered and not sample a variety of books. Although this is meant to be good advice, it will be more useful when an order to study is obeyed, although Vergerius is silent about a correct order of study. It seems clear that he meant the curriculum to be organized and that literature should not be presented as an amorphous mass, but if this is what he intended, it must be said that long decades were to pass before such organization was achieved. Finally, if there are several good books on a subject, students must not be content with a mastery of but one. All should be read with care.

Perseverance in reading is praised, for the secrets a book contains are not discovered effortlessly, and one might have to read and read again. Perseverance, moreover, can be sustained by following a definite, regular reading schedule. Still, a day has many leisure hours which can be used by taking up a book, although distraction can diminish the worth of such effort. It is better to use a library where, with a clock placed so as to catch the reader's eye, the "swift lapse of time" will be a spur to greater accomplishment. In any case, libraries should be reserved strictly for the use for which they are intended.

All this is good advice, and despite obvious shortcoming and incompleteness as a comprehensive declaration on the discipline of study, it set in motion a new, and better, approach to pedagogy. It, in fact, ushered in the modern version of liberal education to which scholars and educators of succeeding centuries were indebted. The book ends with a relatively brief discussion of the place physical education should have in the formation of a noble person and some advice with respect to how persons of character should use leisure. Physical education and the utilization of leisure need attention, but "the larger the place we can allot to learning, the richer, the fuller, is the life we thereby secure to ourselves."[24] Vergerius set the pace; it was left to others to keep in step. Had others not toiled to cultivate humanistic education, it might not have survived the century of its birth. But before going down the trail blazed by Vergerius, some attention should be paid to the revival of Greek studies as they were husbanded by Manuel Chrysoloras.

Revival of Greek Studies

For centuries scholars and teachers from Greece had come to Italy. Some stayed only a short time and seem not to have influenced the schools; others had a long tenure as teachers and offered their scholastic skill on a variety of instructional levels. The fourteenth century followed this tradition of intellectual exchange, amending it only to put a greater emphasis upon obtaining knowledge of Greek culture.

Had it not been for this thirst for the literature of Greece, Chrysoloras could have come to Florence and left practically unnoticed. As it was, however, he turned out to be the right man at the right place and, among the many scholars and teachers from the East, the one who exerted the greatest influence on the humanists. Arriving in Florence as an ambassador some years before 1396, his personal charm, scholarship, and teaching talent were soon recognized and prized above his skill as a diplomat. He relinquished his diplomatic portfolio and began to lecture on Greek language and literature.

Eager and willing students in Florence, Pavia, and Venice flocked to his school and, we are told, most were mature men, many of whom held university degrees and professorships. Bitten by the bug of humanism, these students were determined to discover the mysteries hidden away in the Greek classics and to imitate them. To succeed on this expedition of discovery, they had to master the Greek language and find a method for literary exposition. Chrysoloras appears to have been of enormous help along both lines.

Chrysoloras the Teacher. Many of the technical details on Chrysoloras' teaching style were never recorded, for, apart from *Erotemata*, a manual on Greek grammar compiled for classroom use, he lacked either the time or the inspiration to write. Guarino Veronese (1370–1461), however, had a long and close association with Chrysoloras and endorsed his pedagogic code. Faithful accounts of Guarino's teaching practice illustrate the nature of Chrysoloras' approach. In addition, his pedagogical views and methods are in evidence in the writings of humanists who fell under his spell.

The principal plank in Chrysoloras' teaching platform was reading. It was to be wide, attentive, and analytical. In addition, it emphasized matter (content) over form (style), although form was never ignored, because it is essential for conveying meaning. Students were instructed to notice every apt or striking expression used by classical authors and remember them. But this put a heavy load upon memory, so repetition was called into service to aid it. This technique was intended to make correct and artistic use of language an indelible part of a reader's repertoire. Yet it had application to the content of the classics as well. As a reader worked his way through a classic, he was told to pay attention to and remember all the anecdotes, the descriptions of action, and the details of the story. In this way, it was supposed, students would be transformed to resemble the cultured men of fifth-century Greece. Put another way, they would become humanists.

Reading, noticing, and remembering everything of import is a huge pedagogical order, and it needed help to be filled. Chrysoloras was ready to supply it in two recommendations. Repetition, the first, should be conducted in a regular and orderly way. What was learned during the day should be recalled and repeated in the evening; and once every month there should be a general repetition. The second recommendation was to keep a notebook to record the substance of the reading to be memorized and to have an account of all previous reading if ever memory failed to do its work.

Such instructional practice was more appropriate for advanced students than for beginners, but only advanced students attended Chrysoloras' lectures. Yet humanists who thought about such problems in education must have known that the instructional preliminaries had to be handled before anything else could be done. Boys had to be able to read and write before they could tackle the Latin and the Greek classics. Even elementary education began with reading and then moved on to composition. Immature students read the easy authors and wrote short compositions on them. As they read and wrote, they were instructed to pay attention to a subject matter divided into two parts: *methodice* and *historice*. The former contained elements of style, including rhetorical forms; the latter was a body of general information. Even here in the elementary school, we have the impression that the humble auxiliary of instruction, the notebook, was present. At the end of any course it should contain a corpus of knowledge and an illustration of style consistent with a humanistic standard of culture.

All this was a theory of imitation, one based upon the proposition that what is experienced and assimilated will, in the end, have the effect of introducing a new and better style of expression and, more importantly, a new way of thinking and a new cultural background. Both were important to humanists, even though they may have fallen into the trap of believing that evidence of faultless style could be taken as a clear indication of culture. This trap caught many a humanistic teacher unawares and allowed, in consequence, a concentration upon style and a neglect of content. This was not what Chrysoloras taught, nor was it an outcome either he or genuine humanists endorsed; yet that it became the hallmark of humanistic education can hardly be denied. So despite his penetrating influence in erecting the stanchion for humanistic pedagogy, Chrysoloras was ignored almost as often as he was heeded.

Humanistic Schools and Educational Theory

The purpose and practice of humanistic education had been put in place by Vergerius and Chrysoloras, and the imprint of their influence was fairly clear. Still, more was left to be done, and other humanists were eager to lend a helping hand. Some in written discourse, and others by conducting schools, succeeded in elaborating a more complete picture of humanistic education. It is worth stressing, however, that throughout the fourteenth century and for most of the fifteenth, although humanism had the blessing of fashion, the schools were conducted as if the medieval age had never ended. Educational habit dies hard and nowhere was this exhibited more clearly than in these first two humanistic centuries.

On the university level, professors of rhetoric lectured in a conventional way and held their appointments, not because they were humanists, but because they were able to do a job that needed doing. Educated men who paraded their humanism as a credential certifying their academic worth were seldom found on university faculties, although they made more or less regular appearances at the universities to pronounce their views on the traditional subjects and were listened to because what they had to say appeared to be novel and interesting. But without permanent appointments and without a regular following of students, their work belonged more to the category of publicity than to instruction. They were, for the most part, heralds for a novel point of view rather than teachers of a discipline.

On the lower educational levels—and here a distinction between elementary and secondary instruction is not easy to make, because the two levels so carefully separated now were not always recognized—the same situation prevailed. With few exceptions, the ideals and practices about which humanistic educational writers wrote so optimistically were totally ignored in the schools. The exceptions, however, are noteworthy, for they help to reveal how humanistic educational conviction should be translated into practice. The exceptions were Guarino's school at Ferrara, in operation from 1429 to 1436, and Vittorino da Feltre's at Mantua, conducted from 1423 to 1446. Anyone who wants to study the educational practice of fifteenth-century humanism must concentrate on these schools, for if there were others, history has missed them. To regard these two schools as typical would be wrong, although they may have provided a model for the future.

Humanists were fairly certain that classical and Christian literature contained moral lessons and that some instruction in moral philosophy would pay dividends, but nothing could take the place of a basic piety and virtue instilled under the auspices of a good home. Parental care should be directed at the formation of character, an obligation not easily delegated. Should parents be unable or unfit to fulfill it, Vergerius, for example, told them to send children from the home at an early age.[25]

For reasons that must be readily apparent, mothers rather than fathers were the principal teachers, although, again, fathers were never authorized to abandon their responsibility. The first moral lessons had to do with instilling love of God, country, and home. Later there was time to include the qualities of respect and courtesy, and to pay attention to personal habits concerning eating and drinking, amusements and games, bodily carriage and dress, and, finally, the use of artificial heat.[26]

For the first five years of childhood, parental attention was expected to be most solicitous, for during these early years, the moral direction of youth was set, but the beneficial influence of a good home could never end. Yet despite all this attention to the place of the home in the early moral training of youth, one must not overlook the steadily increasing popularity of boarding schools. And humanism must share a good part of the credit or blame for this. Teachers stood *in loco parentis* and were usually vested with all the authority they needed in order to control students, but schools are not homes and teachers are not parents.

Nothing stands out more starkly in humanistic education than its commitment to liberal learning. How was this commitment honored in the schools? The best evidence comes from Vittorino da Feltre's (1378–1446) school at Mantua.

Vittorino's School

The details of Vittorino's early life are indistinct. In 1396 he matriculated in the University of Padua, where the spirit of Petrarch was still alive, although the poet himself had been dead for twenty years. Vittorino studied under such prominent professors as Giovanni Conversino da Ravenna and Guarino Veronese and was on intimate academic terms with Vergerius and Battista Guarino. From these associations, he obtained the essentials of Chrysoloras' teaching method and a good deal of the substance of Latin and Greek literary culture as well. He earned a master of arts degree, probably about 1400, and then invested some time in study of one of the superior faculties.[27]

Preoccupation with Vittorino's first years is unnecessary, for they do not enlighten us much as to the nature of the school he maintained in Mantua. But before going to Mantua, he had a good deal of experience as a teacher, first at the University of Padua and then as a private teacher of the arts in the university city.[28] The methods and practices of pedagogy that became famous at Mantua must have been honed during this period, and his reputation as a successful teacher must have been secure, otherwise there would have been no reason for the lord of Mantua, Gianfrancesco Gonzaga, to have invited him to become headmaster of the school.[29] This invitation was extended in 1423, and Vittorino assumed his duties almost at once.[30]

Humanist teachers (and Vittorino seems not to have been an exception) were, first and last, teachers of the classics. They wanted to produce students capable of reading difficult passages in the Latin and Greek literature and of writing, and perhaps delivering, an ornamental oration. If this objective satisfied the run-of-the-mill humanist, it did not satisfy Vittorino: he wanted his students to be well-rounded men and women, and this required a kind of education going beyond the classics.

The Study of Grammar. It began, however, with a preparation for using the classics, and this meant grammar. The ancient method of grammatical study—reading the classics themselves and learning rule from them—was followed. But it was supplemented by an introduction of textbooks wherein the rules were spelled out. The code of correct speech was learned, sometimes by rote and sometimes by analysis, but in the end it was immovably fixed in the student's mind. There is, in addition, the suggestion that Vittorino introduced translational exercises as aids in the study of grammar. The vernacular, Italian, was called into service to drive home the rules of accidence and syntax.[31]

Grammar was expected to open the gates to literature and to equip persons to understand and profit from reading the classics. In Vittorino's school, students were admonished to observe accent and enunciation. In practicing both, a good deal of time was spent on reading aloud. Besides, reading aloud was thought to be an aid to memory and a benefit to good health.[32] To record all the novelties literature contained, notebooks were kept. In them students entered both rules and illustrations of style in one category and, in another, fundamental and substantial ideas having to do with all kinds of important, especially moral, knowledge. When a notebook was full, it was supposed to contain a permanent reservoir of knowledge already stored in the mind. Vittorino expected his school to produce men and women capable of living successfully. The program of education was intended to allow students to relive antiquity and, thus, to assert their individuality.

Principle of Selection. This ambitious goal tended to conceal the fact that everything in the classics could not be taught, and that no teacher could go directly to the literature and carve from it all the principles needed for character building. Some selection was essential: Vittorino began with the seven liberal arts.[33] In their study, it appears, a good deal of variety was employed, reading aloud was a routine exercise, and memory and recitation were stressed. The vernacular, although it may have been used as an aid in the teaching of Latin and, in humanist pronouncements, was praised, was neglected in the Mantuan school. For the first time, history and ethics were taught as separate subjects: the latter as a guide to correct behavior and the former for the contribution it could make as a training ground for public life.

The School Day. Vittorino was both tutor and teacher. As tutor, he took the role of a parent and paid attention to morals, character, and deportment; as teacher, he undertook to teach what can be taught.[34] Filling both roles took a full seven-day week, and a school day consisting of seven or eight hours. The first half or so of the school day was used for direct instruction in literature and ethics; the second part of the day was given over to individual work, recitation, and personal counsel. In Vittorino's school, instruction and care were highly individualized: at one (perhaps unexceptional) time, forty-four students were attended to by twenty-one teachers.

Humanist Educational Theory

Humanists regarded moral formation more a matter of instilling habit than elaborating precept. Yet they never tired of mentioning the moral lessons illustrated in the classics and the precepts elaborated in patristic writing. Knowledge is not virtue; of that they were certain; but they were certain also that doing what is right is more likely when what is right is known. This was the basis for moral philosophy's place in the curriculum, and this emphasis upon action rather than precept elevated interest in ethics and depressed attention to metaphysics. All in all, one would have to admit, humanists tended to avoid complex issues in moral philosophy, skirted theoretical ethical foundations, and concentrated upon reverence, self-control, modesty, truthfulness, and courage.

Illustrations of these virtues could be supplied easily enough in classical literature. In any case, it would be short-sighted to discount their value in any of life's avenues, but it would be extravagant to attribute to humanism any profound philosophical disposition. Humanists were too impatient to invest time in speculative philosophy, although to their credit, the best of humanist teachers were not miserly when it came to spending time supervising the moral deportment of youth in their custody.

Physical Education. The old education with genuine classical ancestry had given full measure of attention to physical conditioning and development. The beneficiaries of this education were, first and foremost, citizens with a principal commission to defend their property or the state. It is unsurprising, then, to find the humanists, who in most respects wanted to imitate their classical ancestors, recommending a good deal of attention to physical education.

Attention to physical education had easy justification in schools closely associated with the courts and where students could be expected to follow the conventions of noble-class life. They had leisure to engage in many activities formerly part of the profession of arms or, occasionally, to enlist in that profession. But schools catering to the sons of merchants had a harder time fitting physical training into the curriculum and then justifying it as part of liberal learning. While humanism's appeal, it is perhaps true, was first to the upper class, its scope was broad enough to include others and to take into account general rather than special educational need.

Games, sport, physical education generally, could always be recommended for recreation, and this is something no humanist overlooked, but it was never the primary justification for training and conditioning the body. Dignity and grace of bearing were the first fruits of physical education, and both were closely associated with what the humanists meant by liberal education. Riding and swimming were accomplishments useful to soldiers, but they were beneficial to everyone, and humanist writers were careful to make this point.[35] Hunting, fishing, walking, hawking, and snaring birds are mentioned by one or another humanist as activities with merit, but they are the activities of adults, not part of a school course. What belonged in the school course were gymnastics and games. They were there because of their contribution to good health, mental accomplishment, and moral formation, in addition to everything else expected from physical activity. What we today praise as good sportsmanship was regarded by the humanists as security against indulgence, meanness of spirit, and selfishness. The humanists, therefore, recommended physical training and sport as handmaidens to moral formation. Sport might not lead directly to nobility of character, but experience with it could help form both disposition and habit to do what ought to be done.

The great enemy of humanistic education was narrowness, so in addition to all the other good justifications for stipulating the worth of physical education, its contribution to forming a well-rounded person was mentioned. This, one could argue, was probably the most practical justification for physical education being in the humanists' school syllabus. But it does not tell the full story. Despite all the good things humanists were disposed to say about physical education as a regular component of liberal learning—and there is no reason to suspect their sincerity, except for a few special schools (Vittorino's at Mantua and Guarino's at Ferrara, we are told)[36]—the recommendations with respect to physical education were neglected or ignored. Whether lack of time or lack of facilities for sport undermined this progressive view is hard to discover, but one thing is certain: physical education was to experience a poor and uncertain future in the schools.

The Education of Women. Humanism's educational perspective was to disregard gender. An ideal educational program could hardly withhold its reward from young women. This sharp, deep rupture in convention redressed the dogmatic assumption that women would have little need for learning or (if, indeed, need could be documented) that they had the ability to profit from an academic education. Whatever the practical accomplishment of humanism in promoting the education of women, the attitude was progressive and can be regarded as prophetic. It was not, however, a repetition of Plato's recommendation for parallel education. The subjects in the curriculum suitable for a young woman's study were, for the most part, the same as those recommended for boys. A humanistic ideal could not discriminate. Yet hardly any humanist, and surely not Leonardo Bruni D'Arezzo (1369–1444) in *De Studiis et Literis* (*Concerning the Study of Literature*)[37] or Mapheus Vegius (1405–1458),[38] meant to imply that men and women students should study the subjects in the same way, with the same intensity, or for the same purpose.

Although humanists elevated educational opportunity for women, they could not change the role of women in society. Home management, mastery of the social amenities, the care of children, and charitable and religious duties were among their first obligations. No educator was bold enough to hint that this convention should be altered. Yet for all this, a woman's role in the home and in society was expected to be productive and interesting. Women had intellectual qualities worth honing; they should not be regarded as only house-mothers. They had a right, most humanists thought, to an education in letters. Still, the clock of progress moves slowly, so any education in letters was supposed to stress religious regularity and decorum.

In their early education (especially, we should think, for girls from socially prominent families), the usual curriculum in Latin grammar was followed; otherwise there would have been no point to talking about a reading list for them. They would have to know Latin first. Then, as befits the propriety of liberal learning, their bibliography would be selected with care. They, along with their brothers, could read the classics, but preoccupation with the classics was discouraged. The books of the church fathers belonged on the reading list, and among them, Augustine was accorded first place.[39] Christian morality and character were worth the utmost care and respect, but the best Greek and Roman authors had said a good deal of worth about morals, too. They should not be neglected: the most noble of these writers had given good advice on continence, temperance, modesty, justice, courage, and greatness of soul.[40] In any case, a proviso with respect to the moral expressions of the ancient writers was clear and dogmatic: "Let religion and morals . . . hold the first place in the education of a Christian lady."[41]

Among the variety of subjects in a curriculum appropriate for the education of a "Christian lady," rhetoric is conspicuously absent. If Bruni was not speaking for all his colleagues when he declared, "Rhetoric in all its forms,—public discussion, forensic argument, logical fence, and the like—lies absolutely outside the province of woman,"[42] he was speaking for many. The record is fairly clear that in the schools catering to the education of women, with the possible exception of Vittorino's Mantuan school, those studies taking women into the public arena were discounted or proscribed. Even letter writing, although suitable for social exchange, was frowned upon when letters were written either on public matters or for public notice. The point is clear, women had a right to an education compatible with their talent, but since social convention kept them from the public arena, any studies meant for public application would be of no use to them and would, in fact, interfere with other studies of greater import.

Consistent with humanism's emphasis on education for character, and regarding this purpose as being important both for women and men, the school's curriculum and the reading list recommended in it were weighted in favor of moral and religious studies. But both women and men should aspire to true distinction and profitable enjoyment in life, so they were enjoined to study other things as well. For women, the list of these other studies was short, although it contained a type of literature capable of elevating mind and personality.

Women and men lived in the same world (although women were spared civic responsibility), and women, it was thought, should be conversant with contemporary affairs and public policy. History had no peer as a study for developing the comprehension of a studious lady. In addition, it gave her a basis for judging the course of contemporary affairs and it paraded a store of moral precepts. The historians mentioned by Bruni are Livy, Sallust, Curtius, and Julius Caesar,[43] but no humanist meant to stop with them. Parts of history were portrayed by the great ancient orators as well, and their eloquence was especially effective in extolling virtue and decrying vice. Driving history's lessons home, they communicated an invaluable style for writing and conversation.

Finally, a woman's education would be finished and polished by an immersion into literature. The range here was great; besides, this category of ancient writing had captured the bulk of humanist interest. At the same time, humanists remembered the old warning about the lies of the poets and their preoccupation with stories of spoiled love and sin. How were young women to handle themes that, in the past, had been so carefully expurgated or, sometimes, so completely proscribed?

Humanist commentators admitted to the danger lurking in the classical poets, but they pressed their case nevertheless. Alongside every lewd and lustful episode, they declared with supreme confidence, were illustrations of constancy and devotion. The good in classical poets outweighed the bad; the danger in them was exaggerated. Besides, properly educated readers were prepared to interpret fiction in a way to make it edifying. But what amounted to allegorical interpretation would have been needed for only an insignificant number of episodes compared to the "array of noble figures which stand forth from the pages of Vergil and Homer. . . . [It] is unjust criticism to ignore the beauty of any work of art and to call attention only to its blemishes."[44]

Moral, religious, historical, and literary elements dominated the curriculum recommended for women. These elements were intended to put women in the mainstream of a dignified life, but they should not be taken as evidence that a genuinely revolutionary charter on the education of women had been adopted. Women with knowledge, charm, and grace were superior to their sisters who lacked these qualities—of that there was no doubt in the mind of any humanist—but they were not being prepared to enter the public arena. The more a woman knew, the more charming she was; those who pursued the studies humanists recommended were better able to educate their own children, were better able to manage their homes, and were prepared to engage on a more nearly equal basis in the intellectual interests of their husbands. Despite the optimism exhibited in many humanistic tracts on the education of women, no humanist supposed that in fashion, manner, expression, gesture, conversation, or action women ought to be like men.

Church and State. Humanists were often uncertain about the respective claims of church and state for educational control. This turned out to be a vexing issue, but fourteenth-century states were too weak to assume responsibility for schooling or for directing the education of the people. Convinced that the purpose of education was broader than tradition proposed, some humanists recommended a loosening of the Church's grip on schooling. But this left them in a quandary, for if the Church did not encourage, and in some cases support, educational opportunity, what institution would do so? For all their uneasiness with ecclesiastical control over education, few humanists had any alternative to offer.

The Great Specialties. The specialties—theology, philosophy, law, and medicine—had grown to full stature under the influence of Scholasticism, and the effect of this influence turned out to be permanent. Against this background it is hard to understand why the humanists expressed such disdain for them. One does not have to read many humanists to sense their lack of aptitude and interest for philosophy. Even logic, philosophy's first cousin, was embraced only to the extent that it was turned into a practical discipline. And despite an undisguised interest in ethics, the moral philosophy promoted in humanistic teaching and writing was superficial. Humanists wanted conclusions confirming their preconceived no-tions about virtue and vice and were impatient with the difficult intellectual processes certifying these conclusions. It is surprising, therefore, that Plato should have attracted and held their attention, for their understanding of Plato, it is evident, was deficient. Humanists prized him for the eloquence and charm of his poetry, but they possessed hardly more than a schoolboy grasp of his philosophy. Aristotle, in an unenviable class by himself, used a bald style that humanists considered inartistic and unworthy of imitation.

Theology was a subject for clerics to pursue. It had significance for persons with a professional interest in the formal expression of religious doctrine but was outside the circle of knowledge considered important for laymen. Although not discounting theology's worth, most humanists were indifferent to it.

Law had a slightly different status. As a professional study, obviously outside the liberal fold, it had an undeniable relationship to daily life. How could one fulfill the multiple duties of citizenship without some knowledge of the law? While many humanists recognized this truth, they preferred to deal, not directly with the law, but with rhetoric, a subject in the artistic curriculum capable of rendering meaning from the ancient legal monuments at their disposal. Law, in consequence, was stripped of its independent status and made part of the study of rhetoric. It was studied along literary lines, and while this did not do much for the science of law, the literary approach had the effect of expanding a knowledge and command of ancient law. Humanists were not lawyers, but their superior linguistic and rhetorical skill enabled them to expose ancient texts and, in this respect, make some contribution to law. It should be added, though, that humanists who turned their attention to law were not pioneers. Medieval legal scholars had perceived the need for rhetoric in connection with the study of law, and their work along these lines had been rewarded. If humanists moved beyond them, it was because they were superior latinists.

Despite Petrarch's animosity toward physicians, an animosity shared by many of his successors, the modern world could not dispense with medical therapy. Men and women who were ill wanted relief. If they could afford doctors, they went to them. Still, in counseling a return to the ancient authorities, the humanistic attitude toward the study of medicine was unprogressive. Because of their undoubted literary skill, humanists were able to excavate new or fuller interpretations from the books of ancient medical authorities, and when they exhausted them, they turned to the lesser-known medical writers. In the hands of humanists, the corpus of medical knowledge, although restricted to the ancients, became richer.

Vernacular Language. A few humanists, Petrarch first and later Erasmus, exhibited a basic antipathy for any vernacular. It is said, for example, that Erasmus simply ignored anyone who spoke to him in any language other than Latin or Greek. On the level of educational practice, though, humanism was not so exclusive: the classical languages were culti- vated because they were the languages of learning, but when the vernacu- lars were dismissed from the school, it was because of their inability to bear the weight of scholarship and not because they lacked currency in the lives of the people.

Considering its commitment to ancient life and value, humanism would always have given classical language a prominent place in the cur- riculum, so there is no point in arguing that, had the vernaculars been stronger, they would have superseded Latin and Greek in the schools. Used in daily life, underdeveloped, and often abused, vernacular lan- guage was destined for popularity in the schools at a later time. Without prejudice against them, save for a few unusual cases, humanism did little or nothing to advance the fortune of vernacular language.

Erasmus' Recapitulation of Humanistic Educational Priority

Humanistic education had its genesis on Italian soil but was destined to achieve maturity elsewhere in Europe. Erasmus has the reputation for having raised humanism to its epitome, and the reach of his influence was nearly universal, so any study of his educational conviction is bound to be rewarding. But he was not alone. Other humanists in the north of Europe, inspired by the example of their southern confreres, took up the cause and melded it to the conditions of life in a society whose affinity to the antique cultural tradition was almost entirely literary. Italian humanism could count on some familiarity with remnants of classical values grafted to contemporary culture, and an oral tradition helped to keep them alive; but outside Italy, all this had to be learned in the schoolhouse. So al- though the humanistic menu featured the staples wherever it was found, these staples were prepared and consumed in a way that suited the cultur- al background and appetite of the English, the French, and the Germans.

Guillaume Budé (1467–1540), Peter Ramus (1515–1574), and Fran- çois Rabelais (1483–1553) were effective spokesmen for humanism in France; Thomas Linacre (1460–1524), William Grocyn (1466–1519), William Latimer (1460–1545), John Colet (1467–1519), Thomas More (1478–1535), Thomas Eliot (1490–1546), and Roger Ascham (1515–1568) were among the more prominent Englishmen who dedicated themselves to humanism; and in the Netherlands and Germany, we meet such humanists as Gerhard Groot (1340–1384), Alexander Hegius (1433–1498), Rudolph Agricola (1443–1485), Johann Wessell (1420–1489), Jacob Wimpheling (1450–1528), and Jacob Reuchlin (1455–1552). No country, it is said, could claim Juan Luis Vives (1492–1540), but Spain was the place of his birth.

This cadre of humanists, in one or another measure, influenced the course of education and helped it cross the threshold to the modern world. But for a synthesis of humanistic education and evidence of its permanent influence, Desiderius Erasmus (1469–1536) must be listened to. Although some hyperbole might be vested in the assessment, Bolgar calls him the most important man in the history of education.[45]

Christian Humanism. What Erasmus said about education had a basis in rational analysis and perceptive intuition, not in practical classroom experience. His many profound insights into the teaching of various subjects are worth heeding, yet one does not look to him for the detail of pedagogic technique. Even without a schoolmaster's credentials, Erasmus' service to learning included sound advice on the use of imitation in teaching the classics. *The Right Method of Instruction* and *The Liberal Education of Boys* were written for teachers who, when they consulted them, learned how the classics should be used to mold the spine of educational experience. Besides, he published several textbooks—some used for centuries—and study guides to help students scale the heights of classical scholarship. For all their worth, however, our interest drifts from them to his definition of humanistic education, where a connection between classical knowledge and style and the formation of character was finally and explicitly made. Characterized as Christian humanism, this definition put Erasmus in the mainstream of modern education, where his influence made a permanent mark on the meaning of liberal learning.

Earlier humanists, of whom Vergerius is probably the most prominent, had turned educational purpose toward the formation of character and, at the same time, had prescribed the classics as the most likely, but not the only, means for achieving this high aim. Their syllabus did not neglect moral lessons or the admonitions of Christian writers, but it was left to the classics to carry the principal weight of moral instruction. What these humanists neglected, however, was a justification for the assumption that a command of classical literature could cultivate moral virtue and noble character. Imitation correctly used, their vague recommendation asserted, could link the two, but almost nothing of consequence was said about imitation's correct use. Bruni and others introduced notebooks and told students to concentrate on linguistic and literary detail.[46] Their respect for strong memories and comprehensive erudition was unreserved. All this, though, was a long way from demonstrating the nature of the relationship between literature and character.

A Theory of Liberal Education. Erasmus was able to clarify what had so often been left vague, and his clarification amounts to a theory of liberal education. He acknowledged that erudition was too often merely ornamental but declared, nevertheless, his preference for knowledge over ignorance. Still, he wanted to express the worth, not just the ornamental character, of the treasures of wisdom reposing in classical literature. Why should decently educated persons have an abundance of knowledge? Why should they be able to read and understand their books? Why should they be able to think cogently and express their thought eloquently?

Erasmus' Christian humanism contained the lost pieces in a puzzle that had for more than a century perplexed humanists. He proceeded from this assertion: mankind's common experience attests to moral lessons illustrated in classical literature.[47] The best classical authors had always expressed ideals of human life, and these ideals complemented religious truth. The best minds, pagan philosophers and Christian Fathers alike, had contributed to an intellectual tradition wherein this assessment was endorsed. History, Erasmus explained, unerringly supported the first plank in his platform: The classics contained a moral wisdom that could be understood and should be imitated.

The second plank in the platform of Christian humanism established the discipline of scholarship as a link between learning and character. No one, Erasmus declared with supreme confidence, could achieve excellence in scholarship without dedication, determination, and perseverance. And this was all the more true in connection with a mastery of the classics. Classical languages were not easy to learn and the often subtle ideas in classical literature were not mastered without effort.

Students who did what was expected of them in school (that is, concentrated on their study and aimed for excellence) were at the same time developing a moral discipline. They were doing what, in their circumstance, ought to be done. And developing the general habit of doing what ought to be done had, according to Erasmus, direct transfer to the sphere of moral action. The school, and most of all its classical curriculum, had the ability to transform the practical virtues associated with scholarship into moral virtue. Ideals in classical literature were due a student's meticulous attention; of that Erasmus had no doubt, for he associated himself with the dogmatic assumption that the classics contained all worthwhile knowledge,[48] but he did not share the optimism of some moral philosophers who equated knowledge and virtue. What counted more was discipline: the habit of doing what ought to be done.

Erasmus remembered when others forgot: Men and women are to a great extent the products of their experience. They can rise above or fall below the impressions life makes, but they cannot escape them. If the classics illustrate the best of life's ideals, and all humanists were confident that they did, then the good experience contained in literature is bound to be influential. Every experience makes some impression on us, but the book we read, especially if it is artistic, eloquent, and convincing, has a penetrating and permanent influence.

Method for Study of the Classics. Three planks supported Erasmus' theory of Christian humanism to give it substantial standing in modern education where, especially in the secondary school, it secured for liberal learning a position of perennial respect. The theory was intact and, for the most part, convincing. It was, in addition, a complete and artful justification for filling the curriculum with the classics. But more needed to be done. Schoolmasters who listened to only this much of Erasmus' theory would not have known how to proceed. They would not have been much better off than before. Now the full weight of Erasmus' educational purpose comes to bear upon students who are to read all the Latin and Greek classics. But one reading was not enough. The first reading was for the story, for its ideas and inspiration. The second reading was to be intensive and analytical. With notebook in hand, students were expected to record appealing and useful ideas and expressions.

Using a notebook and taking notes, as any undergraduate knows, is a good deal harder than it sounds. What should be recorded and analyzed, and what should be left out? Students needed help for such a huge task. Erasmus was ready to give it. *De Copia Verborum et Rerum (Illustrations of Words and Ideas)* is a practical illustration of how to organize a notebook, how to set up the categories of words and ideas, and how to cite them under proper headings.[49]

Without a notebook, imitation could not survive the competition from other experience; with it, however, students could retain the gist of the classics and maintain a substantial identity with them in their speaking and writing. They were, to put it directly, mining classical treasures and storing them for their own use. Classifying, analyzing, recording, and, finally, memorizing the content of the notebook were all part of the doctrine of imitation, and it was this Erasmian method that almost alone allowed the classical heritage to become an integral and permanent possession of educated Europeans.

Safeguards to Study of the Classics. One is tempted to shrink before such high standards of classical scholarship and, at the same time, to inquire whether such a concentration on the mastery of classical literature could, in the end, produce persons of sound Christian character. Their intellectual diet, it is evident, was laced with paganism. Had humanists been un- or anti-Christian, this would not have been troubling. As it was, however, humanism was fundamentally Christian, so either to immunize students from paganism or to ensure the communication of a Christian ethical perspective, Erasmus erected safeguards. And these safeguards, not merely tacked on as afterthoughts, were substantial elements in his pedagogical theory.

The best guarantee that at the end of their course students would not be educated pagans without Christian conviction had nothing to do directly with the school. It was a moral foundation inculcated by the training supplied in a good home. With this foundation, students would be immunized from pagan contamination, but of even greater significance, they would be the beneficiaries of a bedrock of morality whereupon further education in virtue could stand.

The comprehensive classical curriculum to which students were exposed had, as any reader of the classics knows, an uneven quality. Some parts were antiseptic, suitable for students of any age; other parts elaborated mature themes whose introduction recommended care. On a level of principle, Erasmus rejected expurgation and suppression; everything was to be read; but certain books were to be read when students were ready to handle them. The safeguard was selection.

Erasmus took a more liberal view of the value of the classical heritage than his scholastic predecessors. The worth they asserted for this heritage allowed them to make certain types of technical information available to students, but dangerous ideas were suppressed. Erasmus, however, saw value in the ideas and refused to concede their danger simply because of their pagan origin. So selection, for all the confidence Erasmus placed in it, turned out to be one part of his plan more susceptible of interpretation and amendment. Fifteenth-century humanists were ready to accept the ancient literary corpus in its entirety, and bravely, Erasmus tried to follow suit, yet selection, even as he employed it, ended up by preferring certain authors and rejecting others. His educational heirs habitually used selection to pare the literary syllabus, thus making it more manageable for schoolboys and, at the same time, eliminating any classic with a reputation for being risky.

Selection, however, even in the case of the obviously preferred authors, might not always fill the bill, for some classical literature appears to contain passages that, in addition to being offensive to Christians, are morally reprehensible. If these passages could not be excised, what should be done with them? The safeguard here is allegorical interpretation, a way of finding a meaning in the passage that complements rather than contradicts Christian faith and value.

Finally, in concert with other humanists who distrusted and disliked philosophy, Erasmus excluded any formal study of philosophy from the school program. Logic, he agreed, should have a place in the school course, "but I refuse to go beyond Aristotle and I prohibit the verbiage of the schools. Do not let us forget that Dialectic is an elusive maiden, a Siren, indeed, in quest of whom a man may easily suffer shipwreck."[50]

With this classical school program and with safeguards supplied, Erasmus advanced a plan to govern the quality and decency of modern education. He had only to add strong recommendations for state support of education (he regarded school support as being on the same level of significance to the public good as military defense) and for all education to be aimed toward religious objectives. In the end, Erasmus clarified and completed an educational philosophy for Christian humanism, so he should be given principal credit for the intellectual and educational reappraisal conducted in the centuries following the medieval age.

St. Paul's School. The first school to test Erasmus' plan was St. Paul's in London. Founded by John Colet (1461?–1519?) in 1510, St. Paul's curriculum evidences an important amendment to the safeguard of selection. Colet, it appears, went beyond Erasmus in his concession to piety and was eager to eliminate from the list of classical authors any whose credentials were suspect and replace them with Christian writers. It is true, he may have been doing nothing more than pandering to a backward educational opinion; but if this were so, it must be said that he failed to recognize how the classics could be made morally innocuous when they were carefully selected and when emphases were put upon language rather than content. The credit for this discovery belongs to the heirs of Erasmus, mainly to John Sturm (1507–1589) and a generation of Protestant educational humanists.

At the end of this long trail, one should admit, Erasmus' humanistic prescription for education was aided and abetted by the development of moveable type. The printing press had an impact on education that was as broad and deep as any reconstruction of educational philosophy.

Chapter 8

The Evolution of Education in Modern Europe

Humanism's influence, although penetrating and lasting, was often concealed by contemporary social metamorphoses, chief among them being religious revolt and reform. A gratuitous assumption has circulated about Protestants and Catholics being enemies of humanism; while elements of truth are lodged in it, a more accurate assessment is that both Protestants and Catholics were eager and energetic in using intellectual and educational ammunition to forward denominational ends. It turned out that parts of the humanistic educational apparatus filled the bill; they welded them to educational practice and ignored the rest.

Neither Catholics nor Protestants ever doubted the efficacy of teaching as a means for maintaining persons in their faith, and they never discounted old doctrines asserting the indelible effect of early instruction in the home and school. Children should be taught, they were certain, but what and where should they be taught? These vexing questions needed answers, and for at least a hundred years, Protestant and Catholic educators were committed to wrestling them.

Despite humanism's impact on the life and mind of these centuries, other events exerted an influence and should not be neglected, although an intensive scrutiny of them is too burdensome for these pages. Suddenly and unexpectedly, the physical world almost doubled in size; imagination was staggered by the prospect of crossing unbroken frontiers to explore and inhabit the New World. Columbus and Magellan succeeded in giving geography a new face. Their work was matched in the literary and scholarly world by the invention of moveable type, for the printing press had the capacity to push back intellectual boundaries and to do for learning and education what indefatigable explorers were doing for geography. In addition, in 1543, the theory of heliocentricity supplied an urgency of motive for astronomers to explore and rechart the heavens the same way the voyagers had given geographers the task of redrawing old maps. In the wake of Nicolaus Copernicus' (1473–1543) *Six Books on the Revolutions of the Celestial Orbs*, the whole of natural philosophy was opened for reexamination and therewith began a longstanding conflict between science and Christianity.[1]

The extension of free cities and towns altered the political landscape, and this, coupled with the decline in influence and authority of the Holy Roman Empire, the deterioration of feudalism, and the substitution of principalities, altered the conventional position of civil *vis-à-vis* Church authority. And if all this were not enough, the economic conditions prevailing during these centuries left the common people in a state of unrest. A concentration of wealth in the hands of the few and mighty put most persons in a condition of subservient poverty. The fuel for running the generator of social and institutional reappraisal was being distilled in abundance. Only a spark was needed to light the fire of revolution. And this spark, as it turned out, was struck from the work and word of Martin Luther (1483–1546).

Religious and Educational Reform

A Sketch of Luther's Career. In 1505, only a few months after having been awarded a master's degree in arts at the University of Erfurt, Martin Luther entered an Augustinian monastery. Before two years had passed he was ordained priest. Nothing in his early life prefigured a vital role for him in the tempestuous course religion was to chart over the next several decades.

Luther's social pedigree was lower middle class, but his father, a coal miner, had planned an agenda for his son that, in addition to the usual primary and secondary schooling of the time, included attendance at the university. For the son of a miner to have attended a university, unless he aspired to holy orders, must have been extraordinary, yet it attests to a kind of educational opportunity that conventional chronicles are not always disposed to ascribe to a period of Church-dominated schooling. In any case, Luther turned out to be a precocious student; at the insistence of his father, he set his sights on the study of law and, according to dependable accounts, anticipated a civil professional career.

Able and energetic, and pious besides, Luther's progress up the ladder of monastic and scholastic preferment was rapid. By 1512, he held the doctorate in theology, and in the next year, as a professor of theology, he began to make his presence felt at the University of Wittenberg. Plagued by doubt, troubled by inner conflict, mortified by evidence of ecclesiastical abuse, and convinced that the pristine purity of Christian faith had been contaminated by the exertions of undependable, ignorant, or arrogant scholars and ecclesiastics, the five-year period after 1512 was, for Luther, a critical one. When it ended, he had adopted a course of action that, feeding on itself, could not be halted. In 1517, after nailing ninety-five theses to a church door in Wittenberg, Luther's rupture with the Church was too severe for repair. Offers were tendered to forgive and forget in exchange for recantation and submission to Church teaching and authority, but this was too high a price for Luther to pay for abandoning conviction of conscience. Besides, he entertained a justifiable skepticism about the genuineness of the offer of amnesty. Luther's and the Church's course had gone beyond the boundary of compromise. Revolt was inevitable.

   Religion and Education. Our purpose here is not to recount the history of religious revolt and reform, but one cannot be indifferent to religion's influence on education. Yet Luther was not the only religious leader to protest and revolt and, at the same time, to take the education of the people into account. Still, even taking due notice of John Calvin's (1509–1564) striking influence on schooling in some countries, Luther's pronouncements on education for those parts of Europe that followed his reforming creed are most illustrative of a new design for education. It is worth our time to see how, and to what extent, Luther's religious convictions affected education in Europe.

   At the outset, it seems fair to say, Luther neither preferred nor rejected any special mission for education. He had no professional investment to protect, so he could weigh the various sides to educational purpose and choose those most likely to accomplish the dual goals of serving the cause of religion and advancing the good of Germany. If medieval prescriptions were capable of fulfilling these objectives, he would put his immense influence behind them; if humanism filled the bill, he would endorse it; or if some combination of purpose seemed more satisfactory, it would be adopted.

   Luther's Educational View. Whatever Luther may have thought about the monumental educational task facing Protestants, one point must have been evident: the anti-intellectual attitude associated with Protestantism had to be suppressed. Otherwise, schools for supplying leaders for church and state could not be reestablished. And this took him directly to the question, What purpose should education be expected to fulfill? His answers, for the most part, are to be found in two seminal documents: *A Letter to the Mayors and Aldermen of the Cities of Germany* and the famous *Sermon on the Duty of Sending Children to School.*[2] The *Letter* is said to have been his first formal statement on education; the *Sermon,* his last. Both, regardless of their timing, can be interpreted as declarations with respect to educational purpose and, although they are not in every detail complementary, Luther's prescription for education.

Opportunity for education had declined precipitously and Luther expected the *Letter* to halt further erosion while, at the same time, laying a stronger foundation for more and better schools. The best chance, he thought, was to appeal to persons with the means for opening and maintaining them. These persons, as it turned out, were municipal officers who, over the years, had chafed under Church educational control. If the resources held by churches and monasteries were transferred to them, they, in turn, could supervise the design of an educational program that, on one hand, would serve pressing civic need, and on the other, satisfy the religious educational requirements of the reforming sect.

These requirements were two-dimensional: by this time Luther was promoting instruction in the vernacular for ordinary persons so they could follow the catechism of the new creed and read their German Bibles. This, however, was only one part, and probably the lesser part at that, of religious educational need. The other part involved the reconstitution of Latin schools wherein brighter and, possibly, more noble children could obtain a foundation for professional study. Among the professional studies, some, of course, were to fulfill an obvious civil purpose, but theology stood at the head of the list. It had to be cultivated if the purity of religious doctrine were to be maintained and if its subversion by Catholic theologians were to be halted. No one—and Luther knew this as well as anyone—could excavate treasure in theological mines without commanding Latin and other ancient languages and, generally, without the intellectual sustenance derived from a decent classical education.

The outlines of educational purpose are evident in the *Letter*, and though we should like more, this is about as far as Luther thought it necessary to go in articulating a plan for education in Protestant Germany. Despite the fairly obvious declaration with respect to educational purpose, what is more striking in the *Letter* is an apparent capitulation to civil authority on matters of educational import.

Civic Control of Education. Luther was apparently untroubled by turning over the tiller to the mayors and aldermen; henceforth, they would be the captains of the academic ship, and the ministers, who had so much at stake if Protestantism were to prevail, were enlisted only as subordinate officers. He must have supposed that the dedication of civil officers to religious rectitude would come close to matching his own. In any case, he argued with some confidence and conviction that civil authority has its genesis in, and derives its guidance from, a divine source. Princes, no less than ministers, were made responsible for the spiritual welfare of their subjects, and, it was evident, schools and education had an intimate and inevitable connection with spiritual welfare. The theory is clear enough, and though it did less for the good of education than Luther hoped, it nevertheless cultivated an attitude that in days to come achieved maturity in national educational control. Yet one should be slow (because the evidence does not lead unerringly in this direction) to assert that a surrendering of church authority over education to civil officers made Lutheran Protestantism responsible for the erection of systems of public education and that Luther was the prophet of popular education. Withholding this distinction from him, however, does not discount the merit in his conviction that educational opportunity in German principalities was in desperate need of resurrection. Participating in some way in a school survey conducted about 1527, Luther obtained first-hand evidence of a general ignorance, as well as an almost universal indifference to schools and learning, existing in the land. He was moved, due partly, one must suppose, to the weight of this evidence, to declare his support for schools and education in the *Sermon on the Duty of Sending Children to School*.[3] If religion were to flourish, and if the state were to prosper, schools had to be revived and children had to be compelled to attend them.

The Curriculum. Luther's plan for education flowed from his love of God and his affection for Germany. It took into account that worship of God and the prosperity of the state have imperative need for the presence of educated men. And this led him to elaborate in broad outline certain clear curricular preference, without which any educational recommendation would be flawed. The Bible, he declared, was the best means for inculcating genuine piety, but whether scripture was in Latin or German, its foundation in the languages of its origin could not be neglected. There must have been some reason, Luther supposed, for Divine Wisdom having selected Hebrew and Greek for communicating the fundamental deposit of faith; if it were to be understood in its fullness, scholars would have to be masters of the ancient languages.

Humanists had a long record of enthusiasm for the ancient languages, and there is a good deal of evidence of their promotion of them in the schools. They were, moreover, sincere Christians whose interest in scripture was genuine. They read the Bible regularly and devoutly as a religious exercise and not merely as a pleasant pastime. Under these circumstances, Luther could distinguish genuine humanism from humanistic educational practice, endorse the latter, and prescribe it for young men whose talent was high. At the same time, and taking into account the need any religious revival has for effective preachers, the study of rhetoric, a sturdy plank in the platform of humanism, was adopted. It could be pressed into service to ensure that the sermons of Lutheran ministers were persuasive, and it could be used, as well, by secular officers and businessmen who had to be able to express themselves clearly and correctly.

Lutheran education turned its back on Scholasticism, mainly because of Scholasticism's deep affinity with Aristotle, to make instead a cautious endorsement of humanism. But caution was stressed, and this meant that the appurtenances of humanistic education—grammar (including literature and the ancient languages), rhetoric, and logic, along with attention to new school subjects that began to find a place for themselves in the curriculum: history and natural science—were conscripted to provide an essential foundation for the study of scripture and, generally, for the advancement of religion. One must conclude that the outcome of this prospectus was not genuine humanism, despite (after several false starts) ringing endorsements of Latin schools.

Luther, we know, believed that the Bible in German should be in the hands of every citizen. And to achieve this end, a good deal of attention had to be given to the development of the German language and to its sound instruction as well. It is easy, therefore, to ascribe to Luther the stance of a zealous champion of the vernacular, and some historians have quickly leaped to the conclusion that the vernacular elementary schools so common to Europe's later generations were its direct descendants.[4] The evidence, however, once assembled and understood, sends one in another direction. The vernacular elementary school, when and where it flourished, tended to drain off both enthusiasm for and students from a study of Latin in the conventional classical schools. So in the last analysis, whatever Luther may have thought about the efficacy of vernacular primary schools for developing the piety of the people, he entertained a deep-seated fear that their cultivation would lead to the ruin of the more religiously useful Latin schools. At one time, he pleaded with parents (for example, in the famous *Sermon*) to send their boys to the classical schools, and at another time (because they seemed to be ignoring his admonition), directed civil authorities to close private schools conducted in the vernacular.[5] At best, the vernacular school was tolerated, but there is nothing of substance in Luther's expressions on education that ever gave it any hope of superseding schools wherein a Latin curriculum was given pride of place.

Philip Melanchthon's Educational Theory. With the fundamentals articulated, Luther was content to leave to others, principally to Philip Melanchthon (1497–1560), the more practical work of educational reconstruction. Having enlisted early in the Protestant crusade, Melanchthon possessed credentials of scholarship straddling humanism and scholasticism; recognizing Melanchthon's superior qualifications, Luther made him the primary spokesman on questions pertaining to Protestant educational practice.[6] It was Melanchthon, therefore, who succeeded more than anyone else in subordinating the scholastic conventions of humanism to an external purpose. His zeal for educational decency led him to expand the curriculum of the schools beyond a prosaic and somewhat humiliating task of serving religious need, although his liberal spirit, if the Saxon church-school ordinance reflects his conviction,[7] did not promote the study of any language other than Latin. But his devotion to Protestantism motivated him to stress knowledge and lucidity as qualities to be developed in students who, without being great men or ornamental scholars, would nevertheless be well instructed citizens and Christians. It is important to add, however, that despite the breadth of Melanchthon's educational vision and the vigor he mustered for educational recommendation, his prescription for humanism was followed only in faint outline.

Sturm and Cordier. Johann Sturm (1507–1589) and Mathurin Cordier (1479–1564), the former in Germany (although he must have framed the kernel of his educational plan when teaching in France) and the latter in France, translated theory into practice. Sturm and Cordier were teachers, not philosophers; but they were main characters in the saga of humanistic education as it was played on a stage whose fixtures were crafted by zealous Protestant schoolmasters. Sturm had a reputation for pedagogical skill and, beginning in 1537 at Strassburg, fashioned a school model (the classical gymnasium) for all of Germany. The school plan, detailed in *The Best Mode of Opening an Institution of Learning*,[8] had the effect of supplying an organizational structure for secondary-school study. The specifics of this structure need not detain us, although it might be said that despite all the pedagogical dullness they justified, Sturm's plan literally dominated secondary schooling in German lands and was vigorous enough to influence education throughout Europe.

One strays from the evidence in crediting Sturm with a genuine humanistic demeanor. The school's curriculum contained classical literature, to be sure, but it was a literature severely pruned and carefully selected to promote the Protestant religion. Nothing in the literary syllabus reminds us of the intense admiration earlier humanists had for the classics. Knowledge of Latin and an ability to use it fluently, without the accretion of the previous two centuries, was what counted most. Latin was taught as an idiom suitable for everyday use. And while it fairly dominated the curriculum (showing once again how the classics can be decontaminated when attention is paid to language rather than to literature), the first duty of the schoolmaster was to inculcate sound religious and moral principles and then to bolster them with material carefully selected from the classics. The arts of expression, all concentrating on a fluent and correct Latin, were to be taught in detail. The curriculum was narrowed to the point where broad and genuine literary scholarship was all but strangled.

Yet if Sturm succeeded in narrowing the curriculum to suppress the influence of literature, Cordier narrowed it even more. Cordier had taught in Paris for a long time, and while his sympathy with the religious reformers was a matter of common knowledge, he checked his enthusiasm for Protestantism in a way so as not to be offensive to Catholics. His career as a teacher was apparently free from attack.

Cordier achieved fame as a writer of textbooks, and his influence in the schools, lasting for decades after his death, extended well beyond the boundaries of France. But it was his tinkering with religious humanism that caught the eye of educators. His scholastic commitment was to a correct Latin, and the books he wrote for its instruction remind us of Alcuin's graded readers. To choose between them either in their dedication to accuracy or their ability to skirt the classical literature is not easy.

When instruction in Latin was over, Cordier assembled a course of study wherein selections from the classics were pressed into service. The basis for their selection was, of course, their ability to illustrate Christian morality at work. But even this was sometimes not good enough to satisfy Cordier's religious zeal: he resorted to pious pronouncement and the recitation of moral maxims. When this was not satisfactory, or if what was done failed to produce acceptable moral behavior, outright sermonizing found its way into the classroom. Humanism had indeed taken seriously Melanchthon's definition of subordination; it was the captive of religion.

Educational Work of the Jesuits. So far, we have paid attention only to the development of religious humanism in the hands of Protestant educators and teachers. Now is the time to look in the direction of the still hopeful Catholic educators who, embracing humanism, tried at the same time to cling to those elements in medieval education that had proved their worth. The roll cannot be called for everyone who labored in the vineyard of Catholic education during these hectic years, but among them, the stature of the Jesuits is evident and commanding.

In 1546, the Society opened a school at Gandia, but reserved it for the education of future Jesuits.[9] Two years later, the famous Messina school was ready to offer educational opportunity to secular youth.[10] The heirs of St. Ignatius of Loyola (1491–1556) knew, and capitalized upon, a pedagogical principle often neglected by their contemporaries: a course of study needed careful organization and presentation in the hands of capable, dedicated teachers. So, if one is to find the primary source of Jesuit success in the conduct of schools, attention must be given first to a cadre of Jesuit teachers who, prepared especially for their work as schoolmasters, were engaged in an apostolate. No myth surrounds the record testifying to the phenomenal success enjoyed by Jesuit schools.

The Jesuit educational plan is set forth in sensible proportion and detail in *Ratio Studiorum*, a part of the Society's religious constitution.[11] It provided for a selective reading of classical authors after the classical languages were mastered. Selection necessarily implied an organization of the material to be read and studied, so taking an almost amorphous mass of literature, it applied an order and a hierarchy. Yet, it would be a mistake to think that Jesuit education put a heavy emphasis upon a mastery of the classics or, put another way, assumed that literature contained some intrinsic merit. The authors were read and, it is not too much to say, mastered, not because they were good in themselves, but because they could contribute directly to the art of composition.

The human ability of expression was a prize to be won; literature conditioned students for the race. This assertion requires the candid admission that Jesuit education never accorded the humanities first place in the curriculum. They were cultivated because they could contribute to a higher educational purpose. As inferior studies, they were nevertheless consequential, even essential. In the final analysis, Jesuit and Protestant schools alike were remarkably successful in adapting humanistic education to the service of religion.

Religion and Humanism in Europe. Coming closer to a final appraisal of religion's relationship with humanism and, in turn, an application of this relationship to the schools, we see Germany and Switzerland dominated by a Protestant version of religious humanism. In Italy, although religious humanism remained largely ineffective, it was inspired to some action by the Jesuits. France, as it turned out, was spared the sharpest thorns of religious discord, so the religious humanism characteristic of the energetic Protestant lands had no great urge to mature. When humanism matured in France, it adopted an aesthetic orientation, one less likely to subordinate itself to religion.

English educational humanism followed an analogous, if not exactly parallel, course to the Continent's. The educational outcome of Henry VIII's religious policies was severe and shaking, and in the end, the schools adopted humanism; but Puritans and Catholics, uncomfortable with Anglicanism, sent their children to the Continent for an education. The British brand of educational humanism, absolved from educating saints or theologians, was at the same time freed from authenticating the assertion of sectarianism. It was commissioned instead to equip men to succeed in the world of affairs. Only mild enthusiasm was exhibited for a classical literature that would have put old-fashioned humanists in ec-

stasy, but the classics were culled for ideas with social and political implication. Hope was never abandoned that, with a thorough classical
education, men would find a way to solve the burning problems of contemporary life.[12]

By 1600, humanistic education had only a nominal reality. Yet its
exhaustion should not be read as failure. Humanism had been promoted
and cultivated because the elusive, although real, classical ideal captivated the allegiance of the educated. When this ideal lost its luster, humanism was embraced by Catholics and Protestants alike as another way
of paying allegiance to religion and piety. By 1600, however, classical
ideals and religious loyalties were made to compete with an new phenomenon unknown to medievalists and humanists: nationalism. The vocabulary of schools began to neglect humanism and religion as cohesive social
and political forces; patriotism took their place as the ideal to which
citizens should aspire. At the end of this long intellectual and scholastic
avenue, educational institutions of all kinds and on all levels were made to
answer a call to the aspirations of nationalism.

Realism's Influence on Education

Genuine humanistic education inured students so deeply to classical
lore that some Christian humanists—Philip Melanchthon and John Colet
(1467–1519) are good examples—worried about its practical effect unless
it were narrowed and amended. When their opinion was adopted, the
weight of the classical legacy in the schools was reduced. Linguistic excellence in Latin was almost the sole heir to Erasmus' bold program for
educational decency. But this impoverishment of the syllabus of classical
learning caused few educators much concern until they were shaken from
their complacence by an intellectual movement whose roots were buried in
a novel epistemology.

This movement, realism, prompted scholars to expand their vision of
the world and reexamine the educational assumption that for generations
had dominated all schooling: everything worth knowing can be found in
the classics. In the end, this dogmatic assumption was rejected, and realism had the first seat on a philosophical bandwagon carrying a new declaration: all knowledge is forged on the anvil of experience.

Humanistic Realism. Although dancing to different tunes, realism's
melody issued from a common source. Life itself was the great textbook,
so the educational question now was, How to read and understand this
textbook? One brand of realism was humanistic. It began by recognizing
the intellectual promise lodged in a careful scientific exploration of the

physical world. But as the infant sciences were cultivated, the knowledge accumulated had to be understood and communicated. For both objectives, a command of language was essential, so once again the appurtenances of humanism, the linguistic arts, were mustered into service. Without them as useful, but humble, auxiliaries, the progress of science would be halted. More exactly, it could never begin. No humanistic realist (a John Milton,[13] for example) could countenance a retreat from reality into a world of myth and fiction, but the myth and fiction of the classical legacy were too important to discard.

Social Realism. Social realists were less sanguine about finding solutions to the burning questions of the day by going to physical science. They recognized, however, that their scientific colleagues, for all the immaturity of their method, were getting closer to a kind of knowledge amenable to authentication by experimental technique. Although standing on the doorstep of positivism, it is unlikely that they recognized their position,[14] but they knew society was overburdened with problems. If it were possible to translate the method of science to the social arena, it might be possible to solve the most imposing ones. All social institutions were to become the object of their study, and they would scrutinize them using the techniques of their colleagues in physical science. This excursion into social realism set the first, albeit unsteady, foundations of the social sciences.

Sense Realism. Humanistic and social realism were bound to affect educational philosophy and practice, and the influence of both should be admitted; but sense realism spoke directly to educational practice and, in consequence, lay the foundation for an educational philosophy with elements of prophetic anticipation. Sense realists, among whom John Amos Comenius (1592–1670) was the most imaginative and eloquent, were almost indifferent to what was taught. Their interest centered instead upon methods of teaching and the extension of educational opportunity. Never outspoken enemies of humanism, they usually found it possible to meld their cultural values with those of their humanistic predecessors. At the same time, being zealous Christians, they wanted to ensure that nothing in education conspired to undermine religious piety and fervor.

Comenius' Plan for Education. In the hands of the sense realists who turned their attention to education, and especially the energetic and nomadic Comenius, the prescription for genuine religious humanism was melded with realism. One has no need to go beyond Comenius' *Great Didactic* to discover how much effort was spent on harmonizing humanism and realism.[15] Human beings should be learned, virtuous, and pious. This guiding principle could be applied in the schools only when an infallible program of teaching and learning was deployed. The centerpiece to this infallible program, it was confidently asserted, is sensory knowledge, wherefrom a rational soul can apprehend everything in God's universe. Without adverting to anything like *tabula rasa* (which, in any case did not find formal and philosophical definition until John Locke (1632– 1704) wrote the *Essay Concerning Human Understanding* about 1690), Comenius nevertheless stressed the necessity of experience if the intellect is to be formed. There was, moreover, no appeal to the Scholastic dictum that nothing is "in the mind unless it is first in the senses," yet this old axiom was implicitly affirmed by Comenius: "Whatever makes an impression on my organs of sight, hearing, smell, taste or touch, stands to me in relation of a seal by which the image of the object is impressed upon my brain. . . .[16] Those things, therefore, that are placed before the intelligence of the young, must be real things; and by the term I mean determinate, real, and useful things that can make an impression on the senses and on the imagination. . . . From this a golden rule for teachers may be derived. Everything should, as far as possible, be placed before the senses (for the understanding possesses nothing that it has not first derived from the senses)."[17] Although most realists would have preferred to give attention mainly to the physical world where what was experienced could be lifted and felt, the scope of experience could not be limited.

Comenius might have said that direct and vicarious experience is not only the best but the only teacher. Acknowledging vicarious experience, the whole of the classical legacy could qualify for attention in the school's curriculum. Experience is hospitable to everything: this was the sense realists' position when they adverted to the curriculum. Elevating experience to the level of a pedagogical imperative had implications for educational philosophy, but realists could be more explicit. Comenius, for example, is at pains to recommend the careful schooling of children from every social class, and almost without question, he distinguished himself in the history of education by removing all consideration of gender from his recommendation on educational opportunity. Probably for the first time, even taking into account Plato's declarations on the subject, there is a clear and explicit articulation of friendship for the schooling of women. One must be careful not to allow enthusiasm for Comenius' progressive attitude on women's education to cloud the provision he made for them. Schooling for girls ceased when the course in the vernacular school came to an end.

Although the recommendations Comenius offered in connection with pedagogical technique are often awkward and, sometimes, naïve, depending too much on analogy,[18] he must be credited with having provided a practical basis from which popular education could proceed. One is right in asserting his preoccupation with method and, at the same time, recognizing that the bulk of his accomplishments were technical.

Yet such occurrences as were to obtain in subsequent years, relative to the schooling of all the children of all the people, could not have been realized without some emphasis upon the naturalness of learning. So long as educational philosophy rested upon an ancient proposition that the conditions of learning are social station and the fortune of birth, the cause for popular education was sentenced to mark time. His theme, therefore, proclaiming learning as eminently natural and universally possible was heeded to the extent that barriers holding back educational opportunity for all were lowered. They did not disappear—that much is certain and would have been expecting too much—but accomplishment on the level of method allowed persons with educational good will to cultivate their optimism.

Some of Comenius' readers were cynical, as they had a right to be, about his praise for large classes. But schooling was not absolved from economic reality; the cost of instructing more than a few students was certainly an important obstacle in the path of popular education. Comenius was very likely wrong in supposing that the method he crafted could remove from schooling any impediments to learning associated with huge classes, but in an educational age eager for more schooling, lower quality scholastic accomplishment was often thought to be a fair price to pay for greater opportunity. When Comenius assured his audience that what is taught should be useful and that plenty of time should be allotted for practicing and applying what is learned, the sting of the large class was made more bearable.

This position put him in the company of the realists and it helped to enlist their support, for they thought models and demonstrations were pedagogical techniques with good credentials for taking precedence over words. Language was, of course, essential, but it should not be made an educational end in itself. And in the last analysis, whatever appraisal was made of the place language should occupy in the schools' priorities, his idealization of the vernacular as a practical objective had the effect of depressing the status of ancient languages in the curriculum and inflating the position of a mother tongue. In an age when nationalism and patriotism were becoming prominent, any promotion of a vernacular was bound to solicit support.

Comenius might have been the prince of schoolmasters.[19] His promotion of sense realism in schooling, in any case, was unmatched by any of his successors, but the point should be stressed that he had help in advancing, not only a theory of popular education, but the means to implement it as well. The Brothers of the Christian Schools and the Pietists have a place in this story of educational evolution, too.

The Christian Brothers. Given high rank by John Adamson as important contributors to modern education,[20] the Christian Brothers enlisted in realist ranks and remained long enough to refine a teaching method that had been around for centuries.[21] Some enthusiastic historians are tempted to credit the Brothers with the invention of simultaneous instruction (the class method of teaching), but anyone whose acquaintance with education's history is more than superficial knows where this assertion is flawed. Still, the luster of the Brothers' pedagogy is not dimmed in any way by setting the historical record straight. They took a pedagogical technique whose employment was at best erratic and commissioned it, in the hands of specially trained teachers, to provide effective instruction for an entire class of students. In their schools, where poor boys were given elementary instruction in a vernacular, the Brothers succeeded in providing modern education with an efficient pedagogy for keeping the cost of schooling within reasonable bounds.

Pietism. While the Brothers in their urban French schools were experimenting with method, the Pietists, in Germany especially, were stressing education as a handmaiden to piety and were recalling with enthusiasm a plank in Augustine's scholastic platform: belief must precede understanding. At first, this untamed theological assertion strikes us as being incompatible with any kind of educational progress. How could popular education find support in such a declaration?

The conviction evident in Pietism could lead to the formation of an epistemological cult wherein the operations of reason were discounted; but it could lead also, both in Pietism and Puritanism, to the dogmatic assumption that belief must precede understanding, and once a man has faith, he must undertake to understand as much as possible of the world God has made. Reason cannot take faith's place and supersede pure belief. Besides, some things always hidden from the mind are clear to the soul. Still, despite the inevitable weakness in reason, it is important for men to know the principles of their faith and to understand as much as possible about the divine plan. This interpretation of reason following in faith's footsteps sustained a drive toward the popularization, even, some would allege, the vulgarization, of knowledge and eventually a broadening of the boundaries of educational opportunity.

In the hands of August Hermann Francke (1663–1727), however, this apparent conflict between the realms of faith and reason was neglected in the interest of developing school programs which would be effective in teaching useful things for life and necessary things for eternity.[22] What is purely pedagogical in Pietism's connection with education centers on the preparation of teachers for people's schools (*volksschulen*) and on the development or refinement of teaching methods to serve the temporal and eternal objectives of deeply religious persons. On the level of teaching method, the Pietists did their best to certify and apply the principles of natural methodology bequeathed to them by Comenius. Besides, the Pietists (Francke especially) were instrumental in extending the principles of Christian charity to children of the poor and often fed, clothed, and treated them for illness while they attended religious schools and institutes. Yet, Francke's educational legacy, most educational historians aver, is to be found in his promotion of teacher education.

John Locke: Experience and Reason. The story persists, although it may be pure cynicism or clever hyperbole, that John Locke (1632–1704) was the sole genuine philosopher England ever produced. In any case, his preparation for a philosophical profession was long and intense. Tutored and schooled by the best Britain had to offer, he came close to making attendance at Oxford University a career in a twenty-year study of an array of subjects fitting him to examine the human condition.

For educators, *An Essay Concerning Human Understanding* (1690) is special, because it elaborates Locke's philosophical and psychological principles in connection with knowledge and learning. *Some Thoughts Concerning Education* (1693), although hardly a conventional educational tract and lacking thoroughness, reveals Locke's conviction with respect to the fundamentals of education and discloses some of his attitudes toward pedagogy.

Tabula Rasa. Locke spends considerable time in the *Essay* controverting the doctrine of innate ideas. To abandon innate ideas was one thing, but to replace them with something sturdier was another. If this was a conundrum, it did not trouble Locke. He forwarded a theory, *tabula rasa*, as hardly more than an obvious outcome of the functioning of common sense. Despite its later notoriety as a philosophical maxim, Locke offered it without pretension of novelty or profundity. What seemed evident to him, not, of course, from intuition, but from the crucible of experience, was that every person begins life with a clean slate. Experience and experience alone is capable of making an impression upon it.

With the doctrine of *tabula rasa* in place, the way was clear for an assertion of the significance of experience, a declaration of a fundamental equality of persons, and an acknowledgment of the precedence nurture has over nature. It is hard to imagine three propositions with a greater capacity for penetrating the abyss of educational philosophy.

Never blind to genetic inheritance (such inheritance was obvious to anyone as perceptive as Locke), he nevertheless persisted in being consistent: if experience fills the mind with data it otherwise could never have, then the process of obtaining that experience—nurture—could not be bargained away at discount. *Tabula rasa* generated a proposition about experience that no brand of logic could reject. But this was not the end of the story, a point not missed by Locke. The mind of every person absorbs data from experience, but what is done with those data once the mind possesses them turns out to be dependent upon the strength of that mind to weigh, assess, compare, and abstract from them. The conclusion is simple and direct: some persons profit from experience more than others.

The most tantalizing, and in some respects the most influential, of Locke's assertions was on the equality of persons. The ringing declaration—"all men are created equal"—can still be heard, and we wonder why its echo took so long to reach educational theory and practice. One could begin with a conjecture that Locke allowed philosophical doctrine *vis-à-vis* education to lie fallow. He seldom thought, wrote, or spoke about the education of anyone other than a gentleman. And the education of such a person, he declared, had various sides, some clearly having higher priority than others.

His list of educational objectives, while not long, was extraordinarily comprehensive: virtue, wisdom, good breeding, and learning. Although last on the list in any consideration of merit, learning was an essential condition for the realization of the more precious objectives, because it, more than anything else, exercised control over the development of reason. To separate reason from virtue, wisdom, and good breeding would leave them empty and fragile. Reason, the ultimate source and essential basis for human control and decency, could not be left to chance: sound instruction was imperative.

Where should this instruction occur and what should be taught? Locke seemed not to dispute the effectiveness of popular or public education for the communication of knowledge, but the students who concerned him most needed something more important than knowledge if they were to take their place in the company of educated and responsible citizens. Their character needed solicitous cultivation in the hands of capable schoolmasters in schools not overrun by a clientele whose virtue, manner, and character were already contaminated and vulgarized by the denominator of commonness. Public schools, because of the social infection endemic to them, were abhorrent to Locke, and while he might never have thought about leading a crusade of opposition to public education, his influence on the mind and thought of the seventeenth-century English-speaking world was great enough to siphon off affection from any proposal friendly to a more generous extension of educational opportunity for all the children of all the people.

The Doctrine of Utility. Locke's educational coin had another side:

while not conspiring to do so, it had the long-range effect of making school instruction more popular and more practical. It is unlikely that any theorist who labored in education's philosophical vineyard could match Locke in his embrace of curricular utility. We hear echoes of Comenius' recommendation that nothing in the curriculum should lack utility, but Locke translated urgent affirmation into doctrine. Nothing should be allowed in the curriculum of any school unless its use could be demonstrated.

Locke's astuteness, however, led him to recognize that the application of the doctrine of utility should be made person by person: what turns out to be purely ornamental knowledge for one person could, for another, be highly practical. Latin, for example, might be of little worth for a gentleman managing an estate, but a scholar could be confident of its value. Locke's doctrine of curricular utility never shut the schoolhouse door on any subject, although none was accorded pride of place. Whatever else Locke's doctrine of utility might have accomplished, it tempted schoolboys and -girls to enter the camp of practical knowledge. The seed of utility, once planted in the educational garden, bore fruit more eagerly sought after by the children of the common man.[23]

Eighteenth-Century Naturalism and Nationalism

It would be unpersuasive to argue that the eighteenth century was educationally aggressive and progressive, yet only a cursory examination exhibits exceptional educational ferment. The Enlightenment's idealization of reason, probably taking a leaf from John Locke's book, led to an assault on authority; its effect on education, although modest, was insidious. Jean Jacques Rousseau's (1712–1778) naturalistic creed was nurtured in antipathy to it; Étienne Bonnot de Condillac' (1715–1780) sensationalism and Claude Adrien Helvetius' (1715–1771) environmentalism followed in its wake; and Louis-René de la Chalotais' (1701–1785) promotion of national education and a suppression of religious schools were logical expressions of its assault on authority.

Meanwhile, the English slowly, painfully, and tardily entered the modern educational world by becoming enamored of Joseph Lancaster's (1778–1838) and Andrew Bell's (1753–1832) novel plan of monitorial instruction.[24] At about the same time (that is, toward the end of the century), Johann Bernard Basedow (1724–1790), a sometime disciple of Rousseau and then of la Chalotais, supplied the fundamentals for German dualism.[25] When the eighteenth century came to an end, Germany had a national system of education: all universities and schools were state agen-

cies; teachers were public officers; and the confessional school—which
had satisfied a variety of religious appetites for about a century—was
abandoned in the name of scholastic efficiency. Besides, this system contained an early recipe for compulsory school attendance.[26]

Jean Jacques Rousseau. Doubtless, Rousseau was on the side of
educational and social reform, and doubtless, too, under a veneer of
rationalism and flagrant negativism, the ideas generated in an agile, subtle mind were sincere. With the worth of education (but not schooling)
immediately apparent, he had no trouble defining its objectives: to remove obstacles social convention puts in the path of natural development,
and to fortify persons with an ability to attain natural, personal goals.
Society, he declared, should reject any commission to teach persons or
direct their scholastic course. Its role should be passive; nothing more
than an environment wherein the natural impulses of autonomous persons can find full satisfaction.

This gospel of social and educational anarchy was preached in an
idiom artistically contrived to appeal to emotion, and although much in
Emile is erroneous, little is patently dull. Studied with care and tested for
clarity and consistency, Rousseau's great book can be indicted for logical
lapses, an indictment Rousseau anticipated: "My words are often contradictory, but I do not think there is any contradiction in my ideas."[27]
Whether this disclaimer is sufficient to warrant the extravagant language
in *Emile* is a point for educational philosophers to debate, but this much
is clear: the book was not, and could never become, a handbook for
teachers. It was intended to set a new direction for education or, at the
very least, to realign conventional educational practice.

In the long run, it succeeded, yet for several decades after its publication in 1762, *Emile's* appeal was on the level of novelty, its message was
judged eccentric, and its author was classified as a social and political
revolutionary. The assertion that la Chalotais rather than Rousseau had a
quicker and more penetrating impact on eighteenth-century European
education is very likely sound. Rousseau's place in the history of education remains secure, but his influence on educational practice was en-
hanced by Johann Heinrich Pestalozzi (1746–1827), a pedagogical, not a
philosophical, disciple.

Pestalozzi the Schoolmaster. Almost every venture Pestalozzi undertook before trying his hand at schoolmastering withered, and even his
scholastic enterprises came close to suffering the same fate. Aspiring to a
reinvigoration of schooling by using the written word, his books were
misunderstood or, when understood, severely criticized.[28] His immediate
educational influence, it must be admitted, was slight. His educational
legacy, one capitalized by his followers, centered mainly on these ped-

agogical points: all subjects in the curriculum should be reduced to their most basic elements; everything in the curriculum should be organized into appropriate grades; object-lesson instruction should be employed; and oral instruction should have precedence over written lessons.[29]

Had Pestalozzi stopped here, his contribution could have survived. But he went on to stake a claim to at least the fringe of educational philosophy. The aim of education, he declared with considerable confidence, is the improvement of mankind: education should operate as a social panacea with an optimistic conviction that no social ill is immune to its healing balm. This aim should generate in schools an unshakeable commitment to humanitarianism, nationalism, and democracy. It was, indeed, an optimistic prescription for eighteenth-century education to embrace.

Surveying the educational landscape, Pestalozzi concluded that if education were to fulfill its promise, it would have to become scientific and, as a new science, illuminate such issues as order in teaching and learning, motivation according to principles of developmental and child psychology, and a complete and dependable analysis of object-lesson pedagogic technique. At the same time, he called attention to the nobility of the art of teaching and the preparation teachers should have before entering a classroom to direct and sustain students in their quest for intellectual and moral formation.

When the implications of Pestalozzi's declarations were taken seriously (this began to happen slowly and erratically), teachers could no longer be regarded as merely hearers of lessons. They themselves should be able to transmit dependable knowledge and, moreover, be skillful in employing the technique of cooperative artists. Whatever assessment is made of Pestalozzi's role in the evolution of educational practice, a place in the vanguard of professional teacher education should be reserved for him.

La Chalotais and National Education. Despite Pestalozzi's inspirational vision and a somewhat tardy influence on teaching and learning in the schools, national education, it is safe to say, was a condition for allowing pedagogic reform to occur. And the early promotion of national education owes a good deal to the sponsorship of the reckless, pedantic, and often plainly wrong Louis-René de la Chalotais.

Prominently associated with a religious–political coup that succeeded in expelling the Jesuits from France in 1764,[30] la Chalotais' *Essay on National Education* was an impressive, and often persuasive, brief for a state-controlled system of schools whose principal function was to cater to what he called "the nation's good." Considering that the temper of the time was favorable to educational reform and, besides, was mesmerized by anticlericalism, any assertion idealizing citizenship as an educational goal and raising the stock of laymen as teachers in the schools was bound to have an attentive audience. This part of the *Essay* must have contained its treasure, for as one reads on, there is not much worth excavating: "I claim the right to demand for the Nation an education that will depend upon the State alone; because it belongs essentially to it, because every nation has an inalienable and imprescriptible right to instruct its members, and finally because the children of the State should be educated by members of the State."[31]

Educational opportunity was restricted to persons with an evident need for it, because la Chalotais believed that schools in France were too plentiful and students in them, too numerous. A great educational danger, he declared, was to give the people more schooling than they needed for their station in life. To do so would not only threaten the common welfare, but would also undermine the happiness of the people.[32] On these grounds he declaimed against the schools of the Christian Brothers: they rescued poor boys from the streets and fed, clothed, and instructed them. But when they returned to their homes or hovels after having tasted learning, they were, or would become, infected with dissatisfaction, always an enemy of social harmony. After reining in educational opportunity, la Chalotais looked quickly in the direction of who and what should be taught.

At this point, there is no evidence of a reforming spirit and, moreover, no sign of Rousseau.[33] Naturalism was ignored in la Chalotais' projection for education. But this much is clear: antipathy was expressed for educational provision for common men, and moreover, the curriculum that for so long exhibited preoccupation with the classics was left untouched. In the last analysis, it was la Chalotais' idealization of national education that gives him status in the history of education.

National Education in Germany. Now some attention should be given to how this plan, expressed on the pages of a book, was put to work in the nations of Western Europe. Although England was slow to fathom the national benefit from educational reform and stood content with whatever liberalism resided in monitorial instruction, the inquisitive and energetic Germans were more progressive. In the first quarter of the seventeenth century, the Duchy of Weimar had adopted an extraordinary statute requiring girls and boys to attend school, and in Prussia, more than a half-century later, Frederick William (1688–1740) and Frederick the Great (1712–1786) followed suit. Even without a theoretical structure to support national education, elements which would eventually be intrinsic to it were utilized.

The theoretical structure responsible for compelling allegiance to national education in German lands was mainly the work of Johann Bernard Basedow (1724–1790), who, in turn, owed a huge debt to la Chalotais. But where the latter had studiously ignored Rousseau, Basedow paid him special heed. Yet Basedow's sympathy for naturalism is not now the point to be stressed; it is national education, and for that, we are led to believe, Basedow coaxed Germany to the forefront of educational reform. In a book published in 1768, *Representations to Philanthropists and Men of Wealth Regarding Schools and Studies and Their Influence on Public Wellbeing*, he convinced his readers that the state should undertake to establish, maintain, and support a system of schools tolerant of sectarian variety for a class-structured society and that these schools be controlled in almost every detail of their work by a "State Superior Council for the Supervision of Public Instruction."

This, though, is only part of the story telling how national education was adopted. In an age when the rights of the individual were being promoted by philosophers (here the work of Immanuel Kant (1714–1804) should be noticed) and when benevolent despotism was in vogue, the question of denominational latitude, if not freedom, was raised in connection with educational opportunity. German lands had, for a long time, embraced confessional schools that were intended to satisfy diverse denominational appetites, and these schools appeared to have the support of the people. But on one hand, they were, and would become more, expensive as schooling flourished, and on the other, they left a good deal of authority over education in the custody of religious denominations. This was a concession inconsistent with the direction national education was determined to take. In the end, in 1803, confessional schools were suppressed by law, and the last rung on the ladder of national education was fixed in place.

Nurturing national education, transporting it from the pages of theorists' books to practice, was, in Prussia, the accomplishment of the Minister of Justice, Culture, and Education, Baron C. A. von Zedlitz, who held this portfolio from 1771 to 1789. While it would be inaccurate to allege that von Zedlitz was the sole architect of a national education that is indelibly associated with Germany, one must admit to his leading role. Under his jurisdiction, it made a great leap forward; when he relinquished his office, almost conclusive steps had been achieved in finishing a national system wherein all universities and schools were state institutions.

National Education in France. Following in Germany's wake, France was quicker than Great Britain to embrace national education. And French theorists were more active than their British counterparts. La Chalotais has been noticed, but while he was in the vanguard for making the state responsible for the education of citizens and for assigning to laymen the role of teachers, others were eager to promote the same objective. Roland forwarded a plan in the *Report on Education to Parliament of Paris* (1768); Rousseau, an unlikely person to have a foot in the camp of national education, in *Considerations on the Government of Poland* (1772); Helvetius in *On Man* (1772); Turgot in *Memoirs* (1775); and Diderot in *Provision on Education* (1791).

All this testifies to considerable theoretical ferment and, under different circumstances, might have produced practical results, but fate, in her own way, called a halt: the French Revolution introduced new preoccupations. Still, even in revolutionary politics some hope for educational reform survived in the social-reform proposals advanced by Mirabeau (1749–1791), Talleyrand (1754–1838), Condorcet (1743–1794), Lakanal, Lepelletier, and Robespierre (1758–1794).[34]

As it turned out, Marquis de Condorcet's *Report on the General Organization of Public Instruction Presented to the National Assembly*, in 1792, contained recommendations that the French Assembly was tempted to adopt. The *Report* contained a long litany of reform: the church's educational authority was jettisoned in favor of the state; henceforth, the teaching cadre would be lay; schooling was to be universal, free, and compulsory; citizenship replaced religion as the main objective; five levels of instruction, beginning with the primary school and ending with the national university, were introduced; a uniform pedagogic technique was prescribed; and a new curriculum, one emphasizing natural science, history, geography, and citizenship, was instituted. With its adoption, the *Report* put France in the mainstream of national education.

The Science of Education

Crossing the threshold of the nineteenth century, we have the impression that, although much remained to be done, national education had become a reality. Our impression is very likely accurate, but promoting a national system of schools is one thing; making such a system work and wringing from it all of its prophetic anticipation is another. Were teachers and schools able to accomplish what was expected of them? From all appearances they were not, because, we are told, a science of education was either lacking or too immature to meet such a heavy responsibility. The spokesman articulating this dismal declaration was Johann Friedrich Herbart (1776–1841), a professor of philosophy and pedagogy at the German University of Königsberg.

Herbart and the Science of Education. Herbart's conception of philosophy's role is worth pondering, and had he been taken more seriously, it is likely that the hostility between the camps of modern science and modern philosophy would have been less acute. Epistemologically a realist, Herbart dismissed the possibility of having knowledge of the soul's nature, although (and with considerable enthusiasm) he adopted Locke's *tabula rasa*. At the same time, he restored educational philosophy to a position of dominance in the broad science of education and assigned to it the principal obligation of defining the nature of the person. To fulfill this obligation, philosophy, of course, would have to listen to the voice of psychology both for evidence pertaining to human nature and for articulating sound principles wherefrom a precise and scientific pedagogic technique could be developed. This psychology was new and different; and besides, while it could not discount the long legacy of rational psychology, it was also empirical and experimental.

In any case, philosophy (primarily ethics) and psychology were the bedrock for a science of education, and a science of education was imperative if the objective of national education—citizenship—were to be achieved.[35] Yet Herbart was always at pains to distinguish education's ultimate objective from the principal means—instruction—to attain it. Sound instruction should inform the mind and sharpen the intellect, for a blind will, unilluminated by the mind, would always be deficient in choosing the good over the bad or, in any given case, the better alternative.

When Herbart adverted to pedagogy, he spoke a language that national educators were eager to hear, for any national system of schooling had an imperative need for sound instruction, otherwise it could not be justified and would not be supported. And no one could ignore the fact that sound instruction required a corps of teachers thoroughly schooled in a scientifically supported pedagogic technique. More than anyone else in education's long history, Herbart promoted scientific teacher education as an essential plank in the platform for national school systems.

Nineteenth-Century Nationalistic Education

While Herbart was laying a foundation for scientific education, while Friedrich Wilhelm August Froebel (1782–1852) was introducing an avant-garde theory to extend elementary education downward to the kindergarten, and while other educators, now remembered or forgotten, were laboring in the vineyard of scholastic practice, the great European states—Germany, France, and England—were rearranging the pattern of national education. With more to gain or lose from a good or a bad system, their attention to it was by no means accidental.

German Education. The efficient cause for scholastic amendment in Prussia was the sting of defeat at the hands of Napoleon. In 1806, the outcome of the battles of Jena and Auerstedt empowered the French to impose a severe peace in the Treaty of Tilsit. But military defeat, rather than being an excuse for national resignation, became a spur for the resilient Prussians. Its sharp educational rowel ground into the side of public policy when Johann Gottlieb Fichte (1762–1814), in his *Address to the German Nation*, strapped it to the boot of nationalism.

He chose to concentrate on education as a principal means for resurrecting national strength, because first, the Treaty of Tilsit was silent about it and, second, Fichte was perceptive enough to foresee how schooling could be an effective instrument for achieving social, religious, economic, and political objectives. Education, he declared with supreme confidence, should be organized and managed to ensure social solidarity and national autonomy.

With this preamble to educational reform as a beacon, the organizational genius of the energetic Germans was enlisted to meld education's disparate elements into a national structure. To husband this delicate architectural undertaking, Friedrich Wilhelm von Humbolt (1767–1835) was appointed minister of education. Although his tenure in office was brief (only eighteen months), von Humbolt left permanent marks on German education.

Beginning by establishing a new university, the University of Berlin, von Humbolt recommissioned the higher learning to play a central and essential role in educational reconstruction.[36] The University of Halle, usually regarded as the mother house of modern higher education, had rendered the seventeenth-century version of academic freedom as an institutional guarantee of a professor's warrant to pursue and teach truth. Berlin embraced Halle's policy, but amplified it by giving the university the liberty to mange its own affairs, to control everything associated with research, study, teaching, and the administration of university life. This, indeed, was a generous and novel grant of liberty.

Encouraged by independence, the University of Berlin set new horizons for higher learning by emphasizing scientific research. Although a university cannot be a school unless it acknowledges a teaching function, the University of Berlin chose to regard as primary a goal of pushing back the frontiers of knowledge. Henceforth, and illustrating a remarkable adroitness at imitation, all German universities embraced Berlin's emphasis upon research. Doing so, they became the envy of the academic world.[37]

The German secondary school was not immune from the transformation occurring in the university. It, too, was amended from a school with a narrow classical course to one capable of more nearly meeting society's contemporary need. Since the time of Sturm, at least, the only secondary school commissioned to prepare students for the university was the *gymnasium*, but it was committed to an objective of literary and linguistic exactitude. Besides, *gymnasien* varied enormously, so it was frequently impossible to have any assurance about the quality of their graduates. This element of uncertainly was intolerable to von Humbolt, so to redress it, teachers' examinations were instituted, based on the conviction that, although teachers' examinations cannot eliminate poor teaching, they can discover teachers who lack mastery of their subject.

In consequence, the ranks of teachers were purged. The first to suffer were clergymen who, in addition to their pastoral duty, liked an association with a secondary school and regarded schoolmastering as a sinecure; but no unqualified person was immune to von Humbolt's clean sweep.[38] This move had the effect of raising the prestige and status of secondary-school teachers. And along with this upgrading of the teacher's position, the curriculum was broadened.

The traditional *gymnasium* was a classical school with an almost unalterable commitment to pure, idiomatic Latin; but now, wearing a new face, it approached the classics as repositories for an indelible human legacy. With this legacy in his possession, the serious student could probe for insight and ponder the burning issues of the day. Although German secondary education was prepared to pay allegiance to the classics, it was not mesmerized by them and, therefore, instituted two other secondary schools: the *realgymnasium* and the *oberrealschule*.

All three had common features. As schools for males, they had a nine-year prescribed curriculum, and a diploma from any one of them permitted students to enroll, without further assessment, in any German university. The normal age for graduation from the secondary school was twenty, despite the fact that most students entered at age nine. Without exception, the curriculum of these schools included religion, German language study, history, music, and physical education. The distinction among them came from curricular emphases. The *realgymnasium* gave attention to Latin, the classics, science, and modern foreign language; the *oberrealschule* abandoned Latin, Greek, and the classics and concentrated instead upon mathematics, science, and modern foreign language.

For students whose academic ability was unequal to the rigor of the full nine-year course or who, for other reasons, did not want to invest time, money, and talent in the conventional secondary school, six-year schools representing the various curricula were available. This realignment introduced considerable diversity to German secondary education without, at the same time, eroding its quality or altering its character substantially.[39]

The reforms on the elementary level, while far less dramatic, were

nevertheless consequential: all schools were public and free; school attendance from ages six to fourteen was compulsory; teachers, almost always
male, were selected with attention to their pedagogic skill for developing
the practical intelligence; and citizenship was established as a primary
educational objective. Once in place, this system of elementary schools
succeeded in rewarding Germany with almost universal literacy. Yet if
there was flirtation with educational democracy, it was quick and
abortive.[40]

Children went to an elementary school that suited their social station
and aspiration. *Volksschulen,* wherein reading, writing, arithmetic, and
religion were taught, were schools for the common people, and their
scholastic mission was simple and precise: to inculcate patriotism and
social solidarity. After a brief interlude of about five years in the elementary school, and for students who wanted more, terminal vocational
and technical schools were ready and waiting. The possibility of a student
moving from one of these schools to the halls of the university was so
remote as to be practically impossible.[41] But the coin of elementary
schooling had another side. For children whose social and economic station allowed them to aspire to secondary and higher education, there were
preparatory elementary schools. The national plan prescribed two tracks.
The schools of one track were expected to educate followers; the other was
commissioned to prepare leaders.

Education In France. When Napoleon grasped the reins of political
control in France, la Chalotais' theory of national education was both well
known and generally embraced. So the Napoleonic decrees of 1806 and
1808, making education a national monopoly, were no cause for alarm. Yet
the more perceptive and wary observer realized that they collided with
the ideals of traditional French education.[42] The University of France, a
bureaucratic monolith, was vested with absolute control over all French
schools, although this bureaucracy was largely indifferent to the operation of elementary schools. The University instituted an inflexible scholastic code: schools were conducted in a militaristic fashion; teaching and
learning, the twin treasures of schooling, were encumbered with myopic
and illiberal policies; the range and freedom of thought were curtailed,
for both, if left unchecked, could breed trouble; teachers and students
were subjected to a severe and often punitive discipline; and in the last
analysis, nothing lacking direct authorization in the regulations of the
University could be countenanced.

Despite the existence of the University of France, educational reform
or reconstruction marked time in France during the first quarter of the
nineteenth century. After 1830, however, leaders in the July Monarchy
(1830–1848), alert to the deflation of educational opportunity for the

common people, commissioned Victor Cousin (1792–1867) to investigate educational systems in other countries, to study the whole question of French education, and to produce recommendations for action. Cousin's first step was a study of Prussia's educational system, which culminated in the *Report on the State of Public Instruction in Prussia* (1831); and while he was so engaged, Guillaume Guizot (1787–1874), the minister of education, made a survey of elementary education in France. Guizot's survey revealed an almost total absence of public elementary schools. In consequence of these studies and the recommendations issuing from them, the Primary School Law was enacted in 1833.

From then until about 1875, French education stood still, apparently satisfied with what had been accomplished. But in 1879, when Jules Ferry (1832–1893) became minister of public education, the sights of national education were adjusted to accommodate a higher aim.[43] Ferry accepted private schools but inhibited them with state regulation and inspection: their face of freedom was severely altered. Yet this was only one side of the pendant. The other side upgraded and enriched elementary education; fees were abolished; higher-level primary schools, abandoned in 1850, were restored; and compulsory attendance legislation was applied to children between ages six and thirteen.

Secondary education, for so long classical and the exclusive preserve of the upper class, was reconstructed to make room for science. The classics were dethroned and Latin, while not jettisoned from the curriculum, became an optional study. Admission policies, moreover, were liberalized to encourage children who heretofore would not have thought of continuing their schooling beyond the elementary years to prepare for life in secondary schools. Seldom popular and never universal, French secondary education nevertheless began to show faint signs of democracy.

National Education in England. While Germany and France were tilling the soil of national education, the English appeared to be marking time. No less interested in the ascendancy of nationalism than their competitors on the Continent, the British sought to promote it by economic rather than social means.[44] Besides, the traditional principle, applied for centuries everywhere, was stamped indelibly on British education: each man according to his own means.[45] Educational decency was prized, to be sure, and Englishmen were fond of parading their erudition when they had it. But their perception of the worth of learning for the common man was not, as yet, keen enough to make provision for it a national goal.[46]

Still, blight on British mercantilistic practice as it applied to the care and training of the young was now and then recognized, and sometimes something was done to eradicate it. In 1802, for example, the Health and Morals of Apprentices Act, after restricting the apprentices' working day to twelve hours, enjoined masters to offer instruction in reading, writing, and arithmetic during the first four years of their training. But from all accounts, the law lacked vigorous enforcement. The Factory Act of 1833 was more progressive. It prohibited the employment of children younger than nine, made two hours of daily instruction in the common branches compulsory for children between ages nine and thirteen, and appropriated twenty thousand pounds for building schoolhouses for children of the poor.[47]

From 1833 to 1870, although it is probably correct to assert that English national education was a phenomenon of the twentieth century, the British erected a system of elementary schools open to all children, enacted statutes requiring attendance in school, and extended provision for secondary education to a point where it was no longer an exclusive preserve for the wealthy and socially prominent. This maturity was reflected clearly in the Elementary Education Act of 1870, sometimes called the Forster Act, and in the Education Act of 1891, wherein provision was made for free public schools.

The British were capable of making up a lot of lost educational ground, so by the advent of the twentieth century, it is right to speak of English national education, although the strict systemization of it with highly centralized control, so common to the nations on the Continent, is strikingly absent. At the same time, and illustrative of a deep affection for and an abundance of confidence in private schools, the British were careful to ensure the place of private schools. They were eligible for public support.

Despite an idealization of individualism and affection for tradition, the English could hardly avoid the metamorphoses in the modern world. In education they were most successful in escaping the intimidation of change in their universities and secondary schools; but the progress of the Germans and the French on national education, the remarkable success of the common school in America, the influence of the theories of foreign scholars, and the searching social inquiry of Robert Owen (1771–1858), along with the penetrating philosophical analysis of Herbert Spencer (1820–1903), were constant reminders of what was left to be done to hammer out an educational plan that would be "sound and cheap,"[48] preserve individual freedom, and promote the national interest.

At the end of this long educational trail, with religion, realism, and naturalism in its wake, we have seen some of the complexities surrounding European education as it moved slowly, steadily, and perhaps, inexorably to a confident, if not always comfortable, accommodation to nationalism in the twentieth century.

Twentieth-Century European Education

The respectable progress made during the nineteenth century in European education showed promise of continuing with the advent of the twentieth century. But preparation for war and war itself proved to be obstacles that responsible statesmen and educators could seldom hurdle. It is hard to imagine how, given the vicissitudes of war and the harsh human and material destruction associated with them, education in twentieth-century Europe prospered at all. Nationalistic disposition carried over from the previous century to dominate politics and proved to be unyielding before any philosophy of education that promoted a general educational good. National school systems became more energetic in shifting instructional objectives away from a traditional educational decency to an indoctrination of youth for national purpose and, perhaps, supremacy. In Germany and Italy, this shift was most evident; on the other side of the globe, Japan embraced an identical educational purpose. Neither France nor England was immune to nationalism, and neither shrunk from employing the schools for political ends, but neither was prepared to subvert the educational common good so completely to nationalistic goals as were Germany and, after bolshevism, Russia.

Italy's embrace of nationalism, and with it national education, lacked the zest of her northern neighbors mainly because the Kingdom of Italy, organized in 1861, was always more a federation than a kingdom. Regional or municipal allegiance superseded a national patriotic zeal. Italian educational tradition had more a municipal than a national foundation. Even so, the Educational Law of 1861 undertook to redress the shortcomings of Italian education by extending elementary educational opportunity, by providing more and better secondary schools, and by improving the universities. The law's sponsors entertained the noble goal of restoring Italy to its former place of prominence in the humanities and sciences. Despite its nobility, resources were needed to attain the goal, and Italy lacked them. When Italy succumbed to fascism, Giovanni Gentile (1875–1944) became Minister of Education in Mussolini's cabinet in 1922. A philosopher and scholar with an international reputation, Gentile launched a genuine educational reform that might have paid huge dividends had it not been for fascism's preoccupation with totalitarian politics that could only subvert educational progress. By 1931 all teachers were required to take an oath of allegiance to the fascist state and to follow its dictates. Mind control replaced intellectual integrity. Still, even a totalitarian state can benefit from an efficient educational program, and one was promised with the enactment of the School Charter in 1939. War, however, foreclosed any possibility the School Charter might have had in fulfilling its promise.[49]

Spain and Portugal followed parallel educational paths. Resting on a weak educational foundation inherited from an aristocratic past, twentieth-century education in these countries broke with religion and removed religious congregations and orders from the schools. To replace the teachers these religious communities supplied turned out to be an impediment to the success of the undemanding compulsory attendance laws (ages seven to ten) enacted in Portugal in 1911 and Spain in 1931. Fairness demands the admission that in the twentieth century educational progress was real in these nations where nationalistic zeal was tame, although candor requires the conclusion that it was slight.

Throughout twentieth-century Europe, where traditional classical educational remnants were most evident and most prized, the status of the classics was challenged, and the classical curriculum, for so long counted to be synonymous with educational decency, was made to compete, not only with vocational and technical curricula, but with both a thirst and a need citizens had for more extensive educational opportunity. Public resources to support schools increased and were used mainly to supply instruction for persons formerly neglected. Yet the traditional routes to secondary and higher education were not altered substantially.

Features of compulsory attendance that had been resisted in the nineteenth century were evident in every European nation. In the thirty years preceding World War II, compulsory attendance in schools was usually eight years in most European countries, except for the Soviet Union, where in 1930 it had been set at four years in rural areas and seven years in urban districts. In 1949, seven years were required throughout the country. After the war, the compulsory attendance requirement was raised to nine or ten years in the United Kingdom, France, West Germany, Belgium, and the Netherlands. Besides, some educational novelty was practiced: nursery schools and kindergartens, both somewhat suspect in earlier days, were accepted (although likely without genuine enthusiasm). And religion, since the sixteenth century a conundrum for any system of public, popular education, stood as a subsidiary, although important, issue, except in France, where it dominated the educational perspective of the Third Republic, and in the Soviet Union, where it was outlaw.

England entered the twentieth century without a commitment to national education. Her continental counterparts had adopted national systems while the British hesitated. Not until 1944 did England create a Ministry of Education, though before taking this step, England had moved cautiously toward supplying free schools for its citizens. In France, where centralized and nationalistic education had set a nineteenth-century pace, centralization was deflated, although by no means eliminated. France's most adventuresome action was an experiment in supplying free secondary schools, but tradition's crust, so hard to break, intimidated the experiment's success. Germany's dual system, along with the state control sustaining it, continued without abatement into the century. The century had hardly begun when Russia shed its ties with an aristocratic and imperial past and ushered in an entirely new political system with roots buried deeply in atheism and communism. Russian education had an immense amount of lost ground to cover before it could take its place alongside other twentieth-century European systems, and the argument could be made that Communist educational policy was a failure, but there were elements of success allowing for a conclusion that Russian education was better at the end than at the beginning of the century.

English Education. The Public Elementary School Code of 1904 illustrates the direction education in England was to take. The code recommended a general education for citizenship and, at the same time, proposed that qualified students from the elementary schools be given a chance to attend secondary schools. Local educational authorities were authorized to provide secondary schools with the stipulation that tuition be charged for attendance in them, although twenty-five percent of the places in these schools could be taken by students unable to bear the cost of tuition.

The Code of 1904 was followed by the Education Act of 1918 and, in turn, by the Education Act of 1944. Elementary education as a public enterprise was extended to age fourteen and was supplemented by continuation schools intended for adolescents and adults who would attend them part-time. Continuation schools featured vocational curricula. These acts cannot be interpreted as means to use education to generate social reconstruction. They were supposed to provide the lower classes with better instruction, not alter their station in life and society.

Secondary education was affected by law as well. Private secondary schools were granted government financial assistance. Public secondary schools were separated into two types: academic secondary schools were commissioned to prepare students for higher education in one of the nineteen English universities or one of the twenty-five universities in Great Britain; "further education" secondary schools, open to students who wanted and needed additional schooling but were not college-bound, offered a less demanding curriculum.

Twentieth-century English education is characterized by a high degree of uniformity and, on the elementary level, universal opportunity. Access to secondary schools is somewhat restricted. For the most part, achievement is the factor determining the character and length of secondary-school study available to a student. A diploma from a secondary school is not a guarantee of admission to a university any more than completion of elementary-school study opens the door to a secondary school. Entrance examinations are common for secondary schools, even public ones, and when places in secondary schools are limited, these examinations are highly competitive.

Tradition has cut a deep furrow in English society, and while no one should dispute the assertion that the British have a fundamental affinity for democracy, this furrow remains evident in the fertile field of educational opportunity.

French Education. 1875 to 1940 was the era of the Third Republic, a time when France was infected by a spirit of anticlericalism. In consequence, the education law of 1904 prohibited Catholic religious congregations from engaging in education and conducting schools. On both the elementary and secondary levels, these prohibitions created a vacuum that public schools, slowly coming into the picture, found hard to fill. In addition, the same law declared that private schools were to be suppressed after 1914.

Despite what has sometimes been characterized as a backward educational step in the suppression of religious and private schools, education in France benefited from some modernization, and along with modernization became more completely secularized. The early years of the century, however, exhibited internal social unrest and political disquiet throughout Europe, so anything in the way of genuine educational reform was destined to mark time. The First World War had a debilitating effect on France unmatched in other European nations, but commentators on French education maintain that there was a lesson to be learned. France's experience with war illustrated technical inefficiency, and this, it was assumed after the war, could be corrected by making a national investment in technical and vocational education. Both were promoted, although evidence of centralized educational control and stratification of educational opportunity accompanied this promotion.

In 1933, educational opportunity, while not assured, was improved by a law that abolished all fees for primary schools and set the legal school-leaving age at fourteen. And technical secondary education was upgraded to the point where it achieved nearly equal status with classical secondary education. Yet both technical and classical secondary schools were restrictive in their admissions policy, often requiring entrance examinations that were highly competitive, and made no pretense of being generally open to the people. As before, secondary education was regarded as appropriate to the upper social classes. Education, except for the teaching profession, was not a route to social betterment, because it tended to exclude from its higher levels the very persons who might have used it to improve their position in society.

In 1947, after World War II, educational reconstruction was proposed in the Langevin–Wallon Report. Forward-looking and progressive, the report stressed the imperative need for educational reform, for introducing genuine educational opportunity, for uprooting the traditionalism and formalism of French education on all levels, for providing diversity in educational experience, and for aiming instructional goals at the formation of personality rather than the accumulation of knowledge. The report was greeted with enthusiasm and praise, but candor requires the admission that its implementation was, at best, lukewarm.

While the general conditions surrounding French education were only moderately reformed after 1947, one kind of educational opportunity was improved: technical secondary education. Public technical secondary schools were made available to fourteen-year-old students from terminal primary schools. The length of the course in these schools was three years before and two years after 1963. An entrance examination governed admission when places in these schools were few, but all things considered, they were quite popular for young women and young men alike. Students who completed the course were awarded a certificate of professional aptitude. Some public technical schools, recognizing that a short course in technical education was incomplete, offered a more advanced curriculum of two years. Graduation from the advanced technical curriculum, with standard of accomplishment certified by a public examination, could afford students a chance to continue study in higher technical schools.

In addition to technical schools, vocational training centers were established for continuing and adult education. Correspondence courses were introduced and made generally available with the use of radio and television either to offer or to supplement instruction. For agricultural education, both vocational and technical instruction was provided under the direction of the Ministry of Agriculture.

Higher education, conventionally in the custody of the university, was most resistant to change. Advanced study in the sciences and the arts, in law and economics, in medicine, pharmacy and dentistry, had its integrity protected by state examinations and licenses and by a state doctorate. Admission to pursue university study in law, economics, and medicine was controlled by an admission examination. The clearest sign of modernization of French university education was the striking increase in the enrollment of women. At the outset of the twentieth century, a woman student in the university would have been hard to find; three-quarters of the way through the century, about half the students in French universities were women.

German Education. The structure for education in Germany was established by the end of the nineteenth century; the twentieth century witnessed no substantial change. Besides, the strong conservative educational disposition of the past was inherited and remained vital throughout the twentieth century.

Had Germany wanted to reject tradition in the early decades of the century, success would have been unlikely. Crippled by the Great War and the reparations imposed in the treaty of 1919, Germany lacked the resources to mount and sustain any consequential educational reform, so during the era of the Weimar Republic (1919–1930) past practice was accepted and change was incremental and marginal. The constitution of 1919 required the twenty-six German states to abolish the two-track elementary schools (*Volksschulen:* schools for common people; and *Vorschulen:* preparatory elementary schools for the upper classes) and replace them with four-year common elementary schools (*Grundschulen*). Yet this reorganization did not bespeak any serious rupture of traditional class education: after students completed four years in the common elementary schools, the conventional class-dominated design for schooling was maintained. Under almost any circumstance, it was difficult, if not impossible, for students from the lower social classes to gain admission to a secondary school (*Gymnasium*).

Nineteenth-century German education had remarkable and pervasive twentieth-century influence on neighboring European nations: the Low Countries, Scandanavia, Austria-Hungary, Poland, Switzerland, and the Netherlands. Religion, culture, and politics made Belgium a striking exception.

After 1930, under Nazi control, German education became an important spoke in the wheel of preparation for war. The Weimar revisions were allowed to remain, with the exception that educational control from preschool through the university was vested in the national state and exercised by a state ministry of education. State control was especially evident in the universities, where principal officers were appointed by the ministry. Appointment depended, of course, on their allegiance to National Socialism. University professors, always somewhat suspect by Nazis, were cautious about political expression, so while most retained their professorships, they took a safe, prudent course in stressing the practical aspects of their subjects and made them politically antiseptic. As public servants, teachers on all levels were expected to do the party's bidding. Women were discouraged from investing their talent in intellectual pursuits and the universities were almost entirely closed to them.

Indoctrination was substituted for education and no premium was put upon academic achievement. Physical conditioning replaced intellectual accomplishment as a scholastic objective. With misgivings about religion, Hitler's intention was to remove all religious instruction from the schools. Success along these lines was registered in the north of Germany, but the Bavarians resisted such extreme action. Religious instruction was permitted to remain in the schools of Bavaria, though with the proviso that it be scheduled as the last class of the school day and that examinations not cover the matter of religious instruction.

Education suffered during the brief period of Nazi control: anti-intellectualism became rampant; teachers were poorly educated and hard to recruit; standards of academic accomplishment, always a hallmark of German education, were depressed; and university attendance dropped precipitously.

After 1945, the primary goal of the "new" education was to denazify Germany, so educational programs were subject to intense scrutiny and to some amendment. Change in German education was dominated by two models: one Western and the other Soviet.

In West Germany, the allies insisted upon a decentralized state wherein education was to be a responsibility of subordinate jurisdictions. No general educational goal was required, although it was expected that the instructional program would cultivate attitudes rejecting both the Nazi past and the communism in East Germany. With so general a commission, it is perhaps unsurprising that West German education found comfort in reverting to traditional educational programs. The old system, adopting some of the provisions of the Weimar reforms but clinging closer to nineteenth-century practice, was reinstated. A four-year common primary school was followed by a three-track secondary program, each with its own length and standards. The *Gymnasium*, with a classical curriculum, was for the wealthy; the *Real-* or *Mittelschule*, for the lower middle class; and *Volksschule*—continuing elementary education—for children of the working class. Educational theory supported ancient assumption about what knowledge is of most worth for these social classes. Despite educational experiment occurring elsewhere in Europe, this plan for education in West Germany prevailed during the immediate postwar period and, indeed, prevails today. In 1970, a federal minister of education was appointed and the federal government began to play a more assertive role in education. In the same year, the ministry issued a plan for education in a document entitled *Report of the Federal Government on Education 1970*. It contains recommendations for change that may be profound—the verdict is not yet in—and may succeed in amending Germany's traditional scholastic allegiances and assumptions.[50]

East Germany's appetite for reform, for dismantling the Nazi structure, never matched that of West Germany. The purpose of education was, of course, different, but the structure imposed by the Nazis remained pretty much intact: centralization of control, comprehensive schools without social distinction, and a practical curriculum. The National Socialist ideology was excised and replaced with communist doctrine, and when East German educators looked for advice on all manner of educational matters, their eyes were riveted on the Soviet Union.

In the early 1990s, the reunification of Germany portends change for East German education. It is likely that the influence of West Germany on East Germany will not be limited to politics and economics but will be felt in education, too. If history is a good teacher, one might safely predict the reintroduction of traditional German educational policy and practice to a single German state.

Education in the Soviet Union. History, language, geography, climate, and cultural diversity imposed a weight on Russian education that was almost impossible to bear. Until nearly the end of the nineteenth century, Russia did not enter the world of modern education.

Despite early effort by Peter the Great (r. 1682–1725) to shift the country's attention to the West and to encourage the adoption of social, economic, and educational practice that had proved successful there, the Russian nobility was resistant and chilly to change. Even when Peter resorted to various forms of coercion, such as requiring literacy of nobles before they could marry, he was unable to persuade his countrymen to enlist in his cause. Somewhat less captivated by western models than Peter, Catherine the Great (r. 1762–1795) nevertheless encouraged, without much success, both social and educational improvement. It was left to Alexander I (r. 1801–1825), Catherine's grandson, to introduce national education. In 1802, a Ministry of Public Education was created, national control of education was prescribed, a new system of elementary and secondary schools was instituted, and three German-type universities were established.

The extent to which this embrace of nationalistic educational policy affected or improved Russian education can be debated. In the face of the nobility's distrust of what was called western learning—they thought it mere ornamentation—a coherent curriculum was hard to shape. In addition, during some periods of the nineteenth century, educational opportunity was forced to retreat before intense social and political unrest. And a class-conscious society, determined to keep persons on the right rung of the social ladder, could endorse an 1828 school regulation proscribing secondary-school attendance for children of peasants.

The first years of the twentieth century witnessed a Russia that was politically, socially, and economically unstable. Yet evidencing good will toward educational opportunity, a law of 1908 authorized compulsory attendance for children from ages eight to eleven. The law, however, was an exercise in educational flimflam: neither schools nor teachers were available for the children who might have attended them.

The Great War brought an end to the regime of the tsars; in 1917 the Bolsheviks assumed political control. Apart from other considerations that seriously question the substance of utopian bolshevism, the new masters hammed out an educational program that included universal compulsory education and an extension of educational opportunity with provision for kindergartens, colleges and universities, home education, scientific study on secondary and higher scholastic levels, and greatly improved teacher education. Besides, the centralization of educational control, characteristic for almost a century, was abandoned in favor of local educational control. There was more: all educational levels had as their goal an idealization of communism. To this general goal were added a commitment, not just to secularism, but to atheism; a new and profound respect for manual labor; investment in technical education; and, one would think inconsistently, an assent to a full and complete development of individual personality and talent. Although the schools were shameless laboratories for the cultivation of communism, Bolshevik policy remembered to include the formation of character. It was not first on the list, but it was there. Finally, exhibiting distrust for the nurture a good home (any home, for that matter) can provide, the policy undertook to immunize children from family influence and education and from parents. Schools and teachers, both with an undiminished allegiance to communism, were to replace them as the first and most important educators of youth.

All this was experimental, most of it was unsupported by any sound philosophy of education, a great deal in it was incoherent or contradictory, and whether it could have led to success in a society so paralyzed by tradition is a question that must remain forever on probation. The era of Stalin, beginning in 1928, was antagonistic to educational experiment and put an end to it. In any case, said the Stalinists, such educational innovation had amply illustrated failure. What was needed, they declared, was a collective educational doctrine clearly subordinating the individual to the common good and one completely disciplined in communist thought.

To achieve this purpose, the remnants of traditional education that had been tossed aside after 1917 were resurrected and restored, the schools were directed to discard goals accommodating personal development and to invest their scholastic capital in the mastery of subject matter. Technical education was endowed with a new luster, and secularism was even more firmly entrenched than before. Talk about equality of educational opportunity, which ought to have appealed to a society committed to collectivism, was suppressed in favor of undisguised meritocracy. Students who achieved in their academic programs moved up the scholastic ladder; those who did not were removed from the ladder altogether.

The Second World War visited almost unimaginable devastation on great parts of Russia. The country began the war with serious economic problems and in its aftermath found difficulty in alleviating them. Under the circumstances, educational progress since 1945 has been slow. Add to this the huge expenditures the Soviet Union felt compelled to make toward maintaining its war machine and to export communist ideology throughout the world, and it is understandable how limited resources cannot be stretched to include educational reconstruction. In the light of what portends to be a less hostile world where the Soviet Union can abandon its fear of being made to heel to Western capitalism and with what promises to be enlightened party leadership, the resources of material and intellect might move Soviet education from the status of no better than that in a second-world country to that in a first-world nation. Yet in the final analysis, all has not been bleak. There were Russian accomplishments for which its education must be given credit. At the outset of the century the language problem appeared to be insurmountable. Several discrete languages were used, and in the larger republics, the most popular language was the language of school instruction. In addition, dozens of dialects were extant. Nearing the end of this century, about one-third of Russia's population commands fluent Russian, a good omen for social solidarity. To a large degree, linguistic assimilation has succeeded, and for this, education deserves praise. Besides, the historical disadvantage rural people experienced in having access to schools, and even to more advanced education, has all but disappeared. Finally, in a society where women were largely outside the educational circle because, it was assumed, they could not profit from it or because it was unnecessary for them, educational opportunity for them has improved.

Chapter 9

The Advent of Education
in Colonial America

The seventeenth century, although not always so represented, brought men and women face to face with tumult in the modern world. Religion, humanism, and realism's fledgling science competed for allegiance and put conventional opinion in convulsion. In Europe, loyalty to fundamental value was often fragmented and sometimes inconsistent, but the brave pioneers who landed on America's shores during the first half of the 1600s, despite the vicissitudes confronting them, were fairly secure in their conviction about how the world should be faced. That they were courageous and competent is undebatable, but what is not always so clear is their commitment to the kind of life they wanted to lead and the social inheritance they were prepared to bequeath to their children.

As pioneers intent upon carving out a place for themselves in wilderness America, their adventuresome spirit was less evident in the cultural seed they chose to plant in the fertile soil of the New World. For the most part traditionalists, they had affection for the culture they themselves had imbibed, and while many were rustic and rough, many more were decently educated and fully prepared to promote the intellectual, moral, and religious values they had inherited. The word of their predecessors affirmed what knowledge was of most worth, and they wanted to be true to it.

If now and then, largely for reasons of religious appetite, they amended tradition, amendment was never so great or so penetrating as to alter the substance of their thought. Geographically and economically American, their allegiance to the colonies was firm, but this left them plenty of room to keep in step with the past. Whatever else they were, and whatever they might have become, they were first and foremost religious humanists, and they presumed this humanism contained values worth preserving and perpetuating.

223

The Colonial Inheritance and its Use

Religion. Despite what had happened to rupture the long Christian tradition, the seventeenth century is correctly characterized as an age of faith, but it was a faith infected with a sectarianism that was zealous, often intolerant, and usually exclusive. Religious truth could countenance neither tampering nor temerity, and no compromise could be forged between conflicting, or different, interpretations of religious doctrine. Under such circumstances, unsurprisingly, religious conviction cast a spell over all of life. Yet while religion might have been uppermost on a scale of life's priorities, it was by no means alone. Religion was prudent and practical, besides being essential, but men had other avenues of thought to travel and other duties to perform. Religion could prepare men and women for eternity, but the temporal world's requirements needed satisfaction, too.

Most early colonists had a traditional education that introduced them to grammar, rhetoric, logic, and literature. These subjects had value and could not be sold at discount. They were, moreover, eminently useful: they could clarify religious truth and persuade others to adopt it; they could contribute to a decent way of life; and under certain conditions, they could aid one in making a living.

New Englanders, for the most part, embraced Calvinism in its Congregational dress, but John Calvin (1509–1564), although often explicit with respect to religious dogma, left plenty of room for theological speculation and interpretation. This was work for the clergy. They were expected to explain the doctrine of piety to their flocks in a way that would be both instructive and edifying, and this emphasis on a systematic exposition of doctrine established the inflexible relationship between Congregationalism and education. It was "the portal through which ran the highway of intellectual development."[1]

In Virginia, James I instructed colonists to plant, practice, and preach the Christian doctrine along lines "now professed and established within our realm in England."[2] Virginia law gave Anglican ministers a yearly allowance of two hundred pounds and directed them to conduct religious services, instruct children in the creed, administer the sacraments, and keep vital records. The people, in turn, were expected to worship on Sunday. In the Middle colonies, save perhaps for Maryland, the colonists were more converts to mercantilism than to piety. Besides, they never aspired to create a Bible commonwealth. Generally and often enthusiastically Anglican, Southern colonists were seldom driven by religious motives and almost never recognized the relationship between religion and education so apparent to the New England Calvinist.

Humanism. Although religion was certainly important, it could not quench the colonists' thirst for humanism. The classical legacy had been cultivated selectively by medieval scholars, so the work of Petrarch (1304–1374) and his colleagues of the Renaissance should be regarded as a broadening, rather than a renewal, of interest in the classics. In any case, the best interpretation of educational humanism was made by Erasmus (1466–1536), but it appeared at a time in religious and educational history when sensitive Christians were certain that some check should be made on enthusiasm for the antique literature.[3] Wanting to be sure that the classics posed no threat to religion, they wanted, moreover, to be certain that everything in a school's program of study contributed to denominational rectitude. This conviction led both Protestants and Catholics to develop educational programs where a humanistic apparatus was used to support religion. Martin Luther (1483–1546), Philip Melanchthon (1497–1560), Johann Sturm (1507–1589) and Mathurin Cordier (1497–1564) took the vanguard among Protestant educators; the Jesuits (1534) led the Catholic educational march.

The noble auxiliaries of humanism—grammar, literature, rhetoric, and logic—were studies the Puritans adopted, and what they did was done by others in the New World. These studies were staples in the curriculum of colonial schools, and every schoolmaster paid them heed, but they fairly dominated the syllabi of grammar schools and colleges. Instructional method was traditional, too. Medieval scholasticism supported the authority of the Church and the pope, which disqualified it for Protestants; yet an outright rejection of Scholastic method was lacking (except when rejection served the end of religious polemic), and plans for its overthrow went unmentioned except when specific issues of ecclesiastical order and theology were in dispute. After Puritans made corrections on these points to suit them, they embraced the general corpus of knowledge and the method used to certify it—organized largely by the Scholastic process—as being only what all intelligent men recognized to be true.

The Doctrine of Piety. Despite affection for humanism, piety dominated Puritan emotional life. With an excess of zeal, it proscribed compromise and substituted belief and feeling for logic and reason whenever logic and reason failed to suit its end. But this embrace of piety did not at the same time ask for reason's abject surrender to belief, and it never doubted the worth of culture.

Piety could catch men in a thicket of inconsistency and breed intolerance, but it could also leave open a path to cultural respectability. Here, again, we find a narrow but satisfactory avenue leading to the culture and civilization of the mind. The character of our colonial ancestors, hardened by centuries of tumultuous experience, had an indomitable feature:

self-reliance. So the ever-present danger of ignorance, coupled with a profound confidence in personal capacity to interpret and judge all matters, recommended a condition of intellectual enlightenment that only a program of education could supply.

European Educational Models. There is no question that European school models influenced the direction of colonial education on all instructional levels, but these models did not prescribe direction, and an interpretation of them allowed room for maneuver. However interesting the history of European education, especially higher education, might be, it does us little good to stay too long with it here. The record of the first American colleges, especially those that survived, is long, full, and immensely interesting.[4] A study of these colleges, their successes, their failures, all the vicissitudes of colonial times that faced them, is rewarding. They might not now impress us much either with their scholarity, their resources, or their organization, but they were truly remarkable institutions. That they survived at all is testimony to the inflexible will of the people to secure the American wilderness from being at the same time a cultural and religious wasteland.

The Colonial College

Colleges of the colonies were small schools with few students and a president who served as the school's main teacher, religious director, disciplinarian, and academic manager. Had colleges the resources to engage tutors to aid the president in his instructional duty, there would have been scant need for them. Harvard's first class was hardly more than a dozen, and Harvard had to wait almost a full century before as many as a hundred students enrolled.[5]

The size, the poverty, the religious mission, and the demeanor of students are all part of the record of history, one clear enough to make repetition unnecessary. But for some reason or other, the myth persists that, for all their religious commitment (except in the case of the College of Philadelphia, which grew up from Benjamin Franklin's (1706–1790) Academy and matured into the University of Pennsylvania), these schools were centers for liberal culture and, despite their religious mission, were in the vanguard of a movement bringing a civilized and genuinely humanistic way of life to the New World. Many writers have contributed to the stability of this myth, so the most eloquent among them, Samuel Eliot Morison (1889–1977), Harvard's great historian, may be dispensed from special blame.

Morison, though, is unequivocal with respect to the college course and the justification for it. Harvard's curriculum, he wrote, and the curricula of schools tempted to use Harvard as a model, was the curriculum common to the higher schools—we cannot use the word *colleges* here—in Europe, and it infected students with a spirit of liberal culture.[6] The evidence mustered seems, at first blush, to be convincing. But examining and interpreting it carefully, we find a course of study that was not much different from the arts course in the medieval university. We see, too, that those accretions to the arts prompted by the influence of the Classic Renaissance were usually grafted to it. The point, then, appears to be persuasive: judged by their curricula, these schools were liberal in outlook. But is this the full story?

The College Curriculum. An analysis of the curriculum discloses that it followed almost to the letter the Scholastic paradigm: it organized knowledge the way the Scholastics had and used the same arguments to sustain it. But an allegation that the founders of colonial colleges enlisted in a crusade to perpetuate scholasticism could easily be disproved. The point is more subtle, and its roots are buried deeply in religious, not classical, humanism. Genuine humanists surveyed the classics, supposed them to contain all knowledge worth having, and in addition, became convinced, largely by their own arguments, that the classics contained models of excellence capable of making human life decent and harmonious. They might not always have wanted to educate princes, but they were convinced that education should first of all have a commitment to cultivating nobility of character.

No Puritan would have discounted the worth of noble character, but none would have depended very heavily upon the classics, or a genuine classical education, to obtain it. These men, fearing too much learning, depended too heavily upon piety. Yet amid all their reservations about too much learning, about honing the human ability of reason to a point where it could jeopardize religious faith, they knew that learning was essential. Religion could proceed without help from any school, and it never needed a college to sustain its claim on the spirit of humanity, but learning could be of considerable help to religion when tamed and made to submit to learning's inevitable limitations.

Puritan schoolmen—in fact, all those men of shrewd and sagacious religious sentiment responsible for opening and operating colleges in the American colonies—could have quoted Cassiodorus (480–575) with approval: The arts were instruments useful to divine learning, but they should be used without affection or love. No one, neither saint nor sinner, should make an investment in liberal culture for its own sake. The medal has another side: faith was reasonable even when filled with mystery, for it was a gift from a rational being, God. In order to plumb the reasonableness of faith, learning might be countenanced; it might even be encouraged. Yet it was learning for illuminating and explicating the truth men possessed, not as a result of reason, but as faith's gift.

Under the circumstances, liberal art could have utility but it could not have independence; no one in the first American colleges thought otherwise. Still, it would be hard to prepare men of accomplishment either for secular or sacred ventures without using some of the usual appurtenances of polite or liberal learning. And this learning had for centuries been part of conventional teaching in university lecture halls.

Grammar, Rhetoric, and Logic. Grammar was needed to understand the word of God as that word was contained in the Bible. With private interpretation of scripture now an article of religious conviction, who could deny to a saint the ability to read, interpret, and understand all that God had revealed? Rhetoric aims at clarity and persuasiveness in the use of language: Could religious persons of the seventeenth century afford to be without this skill? And logic, despite what the Puritans thought about Aristotle and deductive logic, had a supreme utility for churchmen and businessmen alike. Both the church and the state stood to benefit from its cultivation. The logic in the colonial college syllabus, however, was not the pure deductive logic of Aristotle, nor was it the newfangled induction paraded on the pages of Francis Bacon's (1561–1626) books.

Puritan mentality was not sufficiently sympathetic to the worth of science to put much stock in inductive logic, and despite Francis Bacon's popularity among our colonial forefathers, it ran counter to their religious vision of the world and their fundamental confidence in revelation to give them all the knowledge they needed. Aristotle had commissioned logic to discover knowledge. One had only to find the right place to begin the search. But this commission elevated too much the power of the intellect and thus failed to satisfy the taste of the colonists. Peter Ramus' (1515–1572) rewritten Aristotelian logic was more to their liking. Ramus discarded discovery as logic's role; he committed it to classification and organization of truth already in man's possession. Taking seriously the proposition that faith precedes understanding, the logic in the colonial college curriculum, with all its traps and thickets and all its artful reasoning devices that even Ramus did not strip away, was a logic of classification. As such, it could help, but never hinder, religious perspective and resolve.[7]

At the same time, we should remember, the colonial college was about as much a secondary school as it was anything else. To argue that the college course was liberal, in the light of its supremely religious context, lacks persuasion; and to argue, moreover, that it was an authentic college course, when in fact it largely duplicated European secondary schools in preparing boys for the university, does not have the ring of conviction.

Knowledge for Use. There is no need to abuse the colonial colleges or even those of the early national period, for they always did their best. From our vantage point, they give the impression of having been honest schools. They never pretended to be more than they were. But the point to notice is that they began with a charter for usefulness, for usefulness to religion especially, and it is this very utility, this commitment to studying what can be put to practical advantage, that planted the seed of electivism in American academic soil. It is true, of course, that no student in the early college was allowed to make any curricular choices for himself. His superiors, those who had responsibility for shaping him as a true son of the church and were supposed to know what was best, did this for him. Doing so, they organized a course of study with an inflexible commitment to those subjects judged efficacious, edifying, and useful.

A college experience was to be taken seriously, as the early regulations of the first American colleges attest; almost nothing was exempt from notice in the code governing student life and scholastic demeanor. When a boy went off to college—to Harvard, to William and Mary, to Yale, or any of the others—the authority of his parents was transferred along with him to college officers. Their role, conventionally described as *in loco parentis*, was to ensure diligence in study, soundness in character, and rectitude in religion. The chronicles of the time show us how the colleges prosecuted these responsibilities with rigor and vigor.

Another side to the story recounts how religious disposition and Christian character were cultivated. Neglecting that side here is not meant to discredit it, but our attention is riveted on the curriculum and its evolution on American soil, so at least a quick look should be taken at the regimen of college study.

Harvard's Course of Study. Probably the best example, very likely the fullest one, can be found at Harvard.[8] Morison's indefatigable enterprise led him to reconstruct Harvard's early course of study.[9] It was a three-year course; the four-year course came later, and the justification for it is easy to find: education in America's nineteenth-century common schools began in a modest way with a course of study that lasted for hardly more than three or four years; when schoolmasters and the public alike recognized that citizens needed more than rudimentary schooling, both years and subjects were added to the curriculum. They were not blazing a new educational trail. The same tactic had been employed by the early colleges: when the academic load became too heavy for three years, a fourth year was added. Any mystery remaining about the shift from a three- to a four-year college course is easily unraveled.

Coming to the college gates, boys were expected to read Cicero or other Latin authors of equal standing—such authors would have been hard to find—and to speak Latin in both verse and prose. In addition, they were expected to decline perfectly the paradigms of Greek nouns and verbs. The language of the first prospectuses allows for no exceptions to these qualifications for admission, and none may have been made, but the colleges were adroit enough to make a distinction between admission to the college course and attendance at the institution. A boy unable to meet collegiate requirements was seldom turned away: he was taught instead. When ready for college study, he was already on the premises. The transfer from an unofficial preparatory school to the college was negotiated easily and unobtrusively.

The schedule occupied thirty-three hours of a student's time for five and one-half days of a week. He entered the classroom or took a seat at his study-hall desk at 8:00 in the morning and stayed there until 11:00. After an interlude for dinner, rest, and recreation, he began again at 2:00 and either studied or attended class until 5:00. When students were not being instructed or engaging in recreation, they were studying under the sharp eye of the teacher. In the first and second years, eighteen hours a week were allocated for private study, but in the third year, study hours were reduced to thirteen a week.

Separate subjects were taken up day by day. Logic and physics, staples in the first-year course, were studied on Monday and Tuesday, Greek grammar on Wednesday, and religious doctrine—titled "Divinity Catechetical"—on Saturday. Rhetoric, history, and the nature of plants were in the curriculum, too. Time left over was used for disputation, declamation, bible reading in Hebrew, and "grammatical practice," the old fashioned name for composition. Attention to such things as disputation and declamation demonstrates how slowly the academic clock ticks, for these exercises, especially disputation, had their roots buried deeply in medieval university practice. But old or new, the theory dominating higher education was clear on this point: young men leaving the college should be able to express themselves cogently and persuasively, and they should be able to analyze and debate the burning issues of the day. The college exercise in disputation was intended to prepare students for the rough and tumble of life itself, and it mattered little whether it was a life destined for the church's or the state's service. The utility of eloquence was a stranger neither to the sacred nor the secular.[10]

The enthusiastic embrace of eloquence in writing and speaking explains rhetoric's prominence in the curriculum, yet its arsenal of rules, regulations, and technical appurtenances (including *chironomy*) might have been too complicated for first-year students. Starting with the second year, rhetoric's pride of curricular place went undisputed, and everything about this ancient linguistic science was taught with a zeal proving that the doctrine of detail still thrived. Rhetorical study was accompanied by ethics and politics, Greek grammar, Aramaic, and religious instruction. Besides, time was given to readings in Aramaic (almost certainly from the Bible), Greek poetry, and to a continuation of exercises in declamation and disputation.

Rhetoric's credentials were incontestable, so it appears again in the third-year course of study. Arithmetic and geometry are there, as are religious instruction (still called "Divinity Catechetical") and astronomy. Syriac was added; one is entitled to wonder how deeply students mined this esoteric linguistic treasure. Disputation and declamation were routine exercises. Readings in Syriac from the New Testament were made, and then (likely because Erasmus' pedagogic advice was still thought good) a subject called "Commonplaces" was introduced. Despite its name, this might have been a highly useful study. It concentrated on collecting words, passages, and references for oral and written composition; with a storehouse full of allusion, the writer or speaker had plenty of ammunition to make his case easily and effectively, but it is unlikely that any storehouse of allusion could have been of much help unless it were committed to memory.

For a long time, this was Harvard's conventional course of study, and with only minor adjustments, additions, and deletions, it was the course of study for most early American colleges. Any talk about changing the curriculum and any introduction of elective practice started by amending this basic and nearly universal regimen of study.

The Doctrine of Utility

By the time the colleges in America were born, the mainstream of educational philosophy, to which any kind of elective curricular practice was only a tributary, was fed from the doctrine of utility. Almost without knowing what they were doing, at least without any forthright endorsement of utilitarianism, the founders of America's first colleges adopted the thesis that learning should first of all be good for the soul; thereafter, the practical and pragmatic considerations of life could be attended to. Hardly anything had more utility than protecting doctrines of true religion from the contagion of heresy; and few things in life were more worthwhile than spreading the truth before minds disposed to acquire it. The point to be noticed, then, in connection with this educational disposition, is not so much what was studied, but that what was studied should be useful in promoting the primary stanchion of human life.

With a religious rather than an intellectual mission, the colleges of America's first years could not help but enlist in the ranks of utility. It would have been inconceivable for them to have been established in the first place had their commission been silent on the points of use and efficacy. So if this analysis is right, the roadbed was surveyed for an elective curriculum of later years by the doctrine of utility, and as the colleges of the country matured, all they had to do was learn novel educational techniques for rendering it passable. Reading, say, Thomas Jefferson's letter to George Ticknor (16 July 1823), Edward Everett's 1820 article on the "University of Virginia" in the *North American Review*, Francis Lieber's "On the Purpose and Practice of Universities" (1830), and J. Leo Wolf's "On German Academic Freedom" (1830) leads us to believe that nineteenth-century architects for higher learning were apt students in discovering them.[11]

John Locke's Influence. They had considerable help in discovering these novel educational techniques. One of the most influential helpers on the level of theory was the erudite empiricist, John Locke. If his colonial audience were not always sure of his reliability as a witness on matters of religion, it could nevertheless see the good sense in his emphasis upon using the evidence drawn from the data of experience before forming conclusions about reality and truth. For one thing, Locke's thesis, although unquestionably subversive of tests for religious truth, destroyed many of scholasticism's presuppositions and, for that reason alone, would have been worth a consideration just short of total embrace.

A principal plank in Locke's pedagogical platform discounted the disciplinary worth of the staple subjects in the school's curriculum. Some subjects were prized, but their worth was in their use, a use that could extend in some instances to the honing of reason. Such honing, however, was not indebted to a vacant claim about strengthening or improving the intellect: "An impression made on bees-wax or lead will not last so long as on brass or steel."[12]

Locke's educational commentary was abundant, although what appealed to higher learning was more implicit than explicit, and to a great extent, it was heeded in this good land. Nowhere, it appears, did he have a more attentive student than in Benjamin Franklin. Franklin liked Locke's tendency to dismiss the worth of Latin unless its study was undertaken by students whose professional aspiration was scholarship. In addition, he sided with Locke when Locke talked about the extent of the school's curriculum and the freedom students should have in choosing studies— ranging all the way from philosophy to gardening, fencing, and dancing— which would be most useful in their lifetime pursuits.

Locke's *Some Thoughts Concerning Education*, a compilation appearing in 1693, listed the subjects he considered worth the time and effort of study. Nothing, it appears, was excluded, not even the subjects

Locke despised; but nothing, on the other hand, was required except an unrelenting attention to the mother tongue. Locke transferred the elective principle, for a long time honored in European universities, to the lower schools. This transfer turned out to be appealing to the most progressive educational thinker in America. On most subjects, including education, Franklin was ahead of his time.

The first indication of Franklin's determination to pay attention to higher education is found in "Silence Dogood, No. 4: On the Higher Learning" in 1722.[13] At this time, Franklin might not have been familiar with Locke's educational theory, although when Franklin proposed a new approach to secondary education in America around 1749, he had mastered it.[14]

A Yearning for Cultural Independence. During the colonial period and for a long time thereafter, probably well into the nineteenth century, generation after generation of Americans listened to the voices of European philosophers.

Reading the lessons of an imported wisdom, our ancestors did their best to interpret it to suit themselves. Without cutting leading strings to the source of learning and culture, they nevertheless stretched the strings, allowing themselves a greater range. While it might be exaggeration to say that Ralph Waldo Emerson's (1803–1882) famous "American Scholar" address in 1837 was a declaration of American intellectual independence (especially if the declaration is taken to mean a report of accomplished fact), it is probably fair to conclude that Emerson's studied eloquence was about on the same level of significance as the political document drafted in 1776.[15] The Declaration of Independence, as every schoolchild knows, expressed a profound aspiration, but in itself neither recorded the existence of an independent nation nor by itself led to such a political accomplishment.

In any case, the hope for political independence, vague or otherwise, had been expressed in many ways before 1776. Emerson's address, in 1834, belongs to the same genre of optimism: the cultural independence it sought and the inspiration it whetted had been evident on the American scene for a long time. Promoters of cultural identity, who at the same time were eager to redress an American feeling of cultural inferiority, would make a fairly long list. Prominent on it are the names of Thomas Jefferson (1743–1826), Benjamin Rush (1745–1813), John Witherspoon (1723–1794), and Noah Webster (1758–1843). Jefferson's 1778 "Bill for the More General Diffusion of Knowledge"[16] was intended to provide a foundation for an educational program tailored for America; Benjamin Rush advocated, in a variety of plans and proposals, a fundamentally republican education;[17] John Witherspoon, in addition to supporting a kind of education capable of accommodating religious belief, was in the forefront of the movement to recognize a distinctive American English. Witherspoon's list of Americanisms compiled for the *Pennsylvania Journal* in 1781 bore little good fruit, but his work was prophetic. Noah Webster contributed a great deal to cultural self-confidence with the *Blue-Backed Speller* (1783) and went on during a remarkably productive career to cap his effort along this line with *An American Dictionary of the English Language* in 1828.

These men were famous in their own time and have remained so in ours, but the most eloquent among them was the versatile Franklin, called by some of his contemporaries the most civilized man in the whole of America.

Benjamin Franklin on Education for America. The final verdict on Franklin's stature in American cultural history was a long time in coming. For decades, fact and fiction about this famous man were melded. It took more than usual care to winnow one from the other. Sometimes taken to be only a frugal, eccentric experimentalist, Franklin's image could, on occasion, be altered to that of a statesman and philosopher or to that of a consistent, perceptive reporter of the basic values in American life. Now, with the long record of accomplishment unfolded, he is embraced as a man of many parts and, above all, one capable of brewing an alloy which, in the final analysis, tempered the metal for what was to become a distinctive, if not wholly indigenous, American intellectualism.[18]

This was a monumental accomplishment for a man of humble origin and limited opportunity. He and his biographers tell of an abbreviated interlude with formal education. While some of his biographers grieve over this, Franklin himself appeared to count it a blessing in disguise. For the most part, while it would be both exaggeration and poor logic to allege that he was self-taught, he was nevertheless mainly in charge of his own regimen of learning and intellectual development. Books were his teachers and constant companions; an almost unquenchable thirst for knowledge generated a discipline to keep them close to him. In maturity, he spoke with regret about the time spent with some books—mostly theological tract and religious polemic—not because they were useless (no book, in Franklin's opinion, could be useless), but because others would have been more beneficial to his formation.

What he read, though, was read because it was judged useful, although "use" was never defined narrowly. No one, save the authors read and his own good sense, helped him to make judgments about use. What was good for him (and this trait is common to self-made men) was, he supposed, good for everyone. Although everyone might not read the books he read, he was fairly certain they should be free to make their own selection. If this does not illustrate the elective principle, the elective principle must be too elusive to catch.

When Franklin read and reread the books he was lucky enough to obtain, he read in English, for his education cut him off almost entirely from the classical tradition. This English education may have tempted him to conclude that he had missed nothing of real value by skipping over the Greek and Latin classics in the original. In any case, there is ample personal testimony to persuade us that Franklin put slight value on the ancient languages; moreover, he was caustically critical of any school syllabus reserving an abundance of time for their study.

When the time seemed ripe to introduce a plan for education in a country as yet politically dependent but nevertheless feeling its regional mettle, Franklin published his essay on the "Ideal of an English School."[19] We need not stop to examine the details of the plan, but one thing stands out. Franklin wanted to promote a secondary school, different from the Latin grammar schools of the day, capable of doing two things: An important and distinctive element to the plan was that instruction be conducted in English and, moreover, that time and attention be given to study of the English language itself. Anyone familiar with the history of secondary education knows that the vernaculars were paid scant or no heed at all in conventional classical secondary schools. In this respect, American secondary education of the period was following a well-blazed trail. The other important element was that precedence should be awarded to useful subjects. Franklin knew and appreciated the finer things of life, the ornamental things, and he refused to repudiate them. But on his scale of value, they should always be subordinate to what could be demonstrated to be most useful.

To take this principle seriously means that Franklin was expressing an educational dictum used in later years to promote electivism. Use, by its very nature, must have a greater variety of meaning than ornamentation. Under such circumstances, any set of experiences, any school course or college curriculum, would have to have a range great enough to accommodate the various definitions of use. With an extensive range to any curriculum, and with a limited amount of time for formal instruction, Franklin's logic went a long way toward substantiating a curriculum where students would have the freedom to make a number of choices. It would be hard to read anything into Franklin's educational writing strong enough to support the free-elective principle that, with the ardent sponsorship of Charles W. Eliot (1834–1926), came to the forefront of educational practice in the late years of the nineteenth century, but there is enough there to convince us that Franklin's thesis supported an electivism of some kind.

Moving away from the "Idea of an English School" and the "Proposals Relating to the Education of Youth in Pensilvania," published in 1749,[20] to another side of Franklin's work, we find an intense engagement with science and a commitment to philosophical knowledge. Franklin was in the vanguard of an intellectual movement carrying with it the conviction that knowledge was still waiting to be discovered. He resolutely turned his back on the old cultural dogma that had buried knowledge away in classical tomes and made its exposition mainly a matter of literary excavation.

Almost from his youth he enlisted in realist ranks; the realists, always trumpeting the scientific method, were convinced that the corpus of knowledge was small compared to what it could be if proper scientific methods were used for discovery. Convinced of almost boundless data waiting to be discovered, Franklin was critical of the worth of conventional curricular paradigms. Confining knowledge rather than freeing it, they were retarding instead of promoting intellectual progress. With such a view, it is again impossible to believe that Franklin thought the curriculum of higher schools fixed. It was destined for expansion, and once expansion began (the eighteenth-century version of our "explosion of knowledge"), no student would have the ability or time to master even the elements of all knowledge. Selection of some kind was imperative.

Schooling and Instruction

Both in seventeenth-century Europe and in America, families continued the ancient tradition of educating their children. Yet in America and elsewhere, families were not always equal to the task of providing, in addition to moral and religious training, either an education or a training capable of fitting youth for life in society. Inevitably, both here and abroad, education came to have an extrafamily dimension.

British activity in connection with this kind of education was often confused and frequently inefficient, but in 1563, the Statute of Artificers, and in 1601, the Poor Law, helped to redress this situation.[21] Both laws, however, were directed more at reducing the incidence of poverty than at raising the level of learning, although both, it must be said, contributed to the advancement of literacy. This legal tradition quickly found its way to the colonies where Massachusetts Bay regularized it with the enactment of the famous laws of 1642 and 1647. Although both laws were important, neither, most scholars now agree, should be described as the cornerstone for American public education.

The proposition that New England's prompt attention to the means for education was dictated by liberal motive is seductive, but Merle Curti is almost surely right in asserting that education in New England and elsewhere in colonial America was intended primarily to sustain institutional religion and a class-structured society.[22] Had colonial leaders been aware, as they might have been, of a fragile democratic spirit in the world around them, they would have anathematized it. Yet they are conventionally credited with adopting the principle that education is an essential condition to good government and social prosperity. Putting this principle to work, they created a legacy from which later generations of Americans profited. At the same time, they managed to immunize education from the pernicious contagion of class status: schools of the colonies were open to all children without reference to social pedigree, although it would be plain hyperbole to allege that children from all classes found the time or opportunity to attend them.

Voluntary Schooling. Massachusetts Bay was in the vanguard enacting a law requiring some education of its inhabitants, but before taking this bold step the colony encouraged voluntary schooling. Such encouragement produced the Boston Latin School, possibly as early as 1635, although dependable records certifying this date are lacking. But the date of the Boston school's founding is a minor point: what counts is the excellence it achieved in the colonial period and maintained throughout its history. This school, moreover, had company, for Jernegan alleges that eleven New England towns had "voluntarily established, managed, and supported town schools."[23] In Boston and Dedham, for example, town land endowments were given to schools; in other towns, wealthy persons donated land for school support. Most of the schools generated from voluntary effort recruited students who could read and charged tuition for instructing them.

Early School Laws. But to return to early school laws: It is hard to be sure just what the people in New England towns meant by free, or public, schools, and we should be slow to attribute to them a contemporary meaning. Still, it is clear, the authors of the Massachusetts law of 1642 meant that every child in the colony should be instructed in reading, although they seemed not to care where—at home, in school, or elsewhere—such instruction was given. Morison, however, using evidence from Essex County, is convinced that the law of 1642 was enforced.[24]

Puritans could have had about as much difficulty understanding the scope of the law as we do, so they recommended its clarification in the Act of 1647, a law that defined town responsibility. The Old Deluder Satan Act—the popular name for the Act of 1647—required towns with fifty householders to engage the services of a schoolmaster capable of teaching reading and writing. Towns with one hundred or more families were expected to have a master who could prepare youth "as far as they may be fitted for the university."[25]

The record on compliance with the Act of 1647 is obscure, and legend clings to it. Educational directives in New England were written by an aristocracy, and aristocrats had some difficulty convincing others, for whom schooling was less than a burning issue, to comply with the law. So on the point of observance, historians disagree: some declare that the laws requiring the maintenance of schools were more honored in the breach than in the observance, while others hold that they were reasonably well enforced. Town records are not much help, and the testimony gathered from private schools—those Latin grammar schools that appeared almost spontaneously—is somewhat beside the point. Yet from fragmentary town and court records, it is clear that, before 1700, many New England towns tried to maintain schools, although some were negligent and exhibited great cleverness in evading the law. This much is certain: the law of 1647, although amended many times in subsequent years, remained on the statute books for decades, and during these long years, schooling and the means for education flourished.

South from New England, the Dutch appeared to be enthusiastic in their support for schooling. Kilpatrick and others tell how both religious belief and political allegiance supplied cogent justification for schooling in Holland, and they imply that this justification was transported to America.[26] In New Netherland, as definitely as in Massachusetts, the obligation to provide schools rested upon the colonial government, but it was an obligation easily neglected or artfully evaded. In 1657, a group of New Amsterdam religious ministers issued a report complaining of the widespread indifference to learning in the colony and, reciting the names of a half-dozen larger towns, declared "that so far as we know, not one of these places, Dutch or English, has a schoolmaster."[27]

William Penn introduced to Pennsylvania progressive policies relative to religion and government, so the stature of education and, at least, a nominal commitment to it was less imposing than, say, in New England. Yet Penn was at pains to stress the personal benefit accruing from learning, its contribution to social stability, and its ability to cultivate noble and virtuous character, while at the same time playing down the role schooling had in sustaining religious orthodoxy and promoting erudition. Children were, Penn knew, the future citizens of the colony, and a sound education, more than anything else, would help them to become good and effective.

Southern colonists evidenced considerable interest in education, and effort was spent to open schools for teaching the basics, but as often as not, such effort was hard to sustain. Abetting the encouragement of learning was an English confidence in the worth of knowledge for its own sake and for its efficacy in promoting religious and social stability. Prominent Southern colonists were themselves graduates of ornamental British acad-

emies and, constant in their determination to escape literary bankruptcy
for their children, were friendly toward schooling. But this attitude did
not lead them to invest the state with a responsibility for general school
support, and their definition of altruism absolved them from using their
own resources to educate the children of others. That exceptions to this
generalization occurred are, of course, evident in Southern educational
philanthropy, but the principle of educational support most often embraced was one making education an entirely private matter. Comfort was
found in what sounded like a good educational doctrine: "Every man
according to his own ability instructing his children."

Education in the Family. The colonial South lacked both a political
and emotional drive to repeal England's social and educational code. Most
colonists of the region, moreover, had neither the zeal nor the disposition
to amend the rules of society and religion. For the prominent and wealthy,
but for the rank and file as well, Anglican orthodoxy commanded allegiance, and they meant to follow it in and out of church. Their religious
temperament was moderate rather than fervent, and it allowed them to
distrust Puritans and despise Catholics without becoming zealots or fa-
natics. And while there was nothing in their outlook endorsing indifference to education, there was nothing in it recommending an alliance
between churches and schools.

Anglicans in the southern colonies were sensitive to the need for an
educated clergy, and their commitment to altruism, though often tainted,
was strong enough to make some provision for the training and teaching of
poor, neglected, and orphaned children. The church and societies associated with it were active in promoting scholastic philanthropy, but even
these examples are incapable of disguising the general conviction that the
obligation for the education of children rested first and foremost on parents. Should this conviction have been challenged, the geography of the
southern colonies and the diversity of their population discouraged any
disposition to imitate the educational activity of New England.

In New England especially, parents were commissioned to educate
saints, and the law of nature and of God stripped sentiment from this
commission. Parents knew that their own spiritual welfare and their
children's as well were at stake in the matter of education. No parent
could afford to neglect the instruction of his children, and a tradition of
long and honorable standing, authenticated by Francis Bacon (to whom
colonists paid close attention on educational issues), made reading the
gateway to learning. What was read had to be good for the soul. Reading
had a cultural side, too, one known and prized by most Puritans (and
other colonists as well); but reading's best recommendation was that it
could contribute directly to religious welfare. Eight laws of Massachusetts

Bay passed between 1646 and 1769 called for education, and five stressed "book" education. Instruction in reading, our sources say, was frequently given in the home.

The Need for Schools. Families were not always able to conduct the complete education of their children, so schools were recommended. But schools were expected to handle secular knowledge, although, almost inevitably, they developed the habit of casting a shadow over religious instruction. Still, schoolmasters were enjoined from intruding on family educational prerogatives even when the instruction they offered was thoroughly religious in content and tone. And in this connection, the most popular, and probably the best, instructional aid that schoolmasters had at their disposal was the *New-England Primer*.[28] It is hard to distinguish this schoolbook, and its subsequent companions, from catechisms, and some Puritans did not try. Despite the tradition that instruction in religion and morality belonged to the province of family and church, catechisms found their way to the schoolhouse. No very convincing evidence exists to show that this trend was ever questioned or repudiated.

Educational Theory in the Colonies. Education was expected to be an ally of denominational belief, and colonial educators were astute enough to recognize that such an affirmation needed support from theory. Francis Bacon (1561–1626) was likely the educational writer to whom colonial educators most often listened, and they read his *Advancement of Learning*[29] with attention and care. Born in London and educated at Trinity College, Cambridge University, he embarked on a political career in 1584 and managed to work his way up to the office of Lord Chancellor. A lawyer, scientist, and philosopher, Bacon wrote *On the Dignity and Advancement of Learning* in 1605 to promote, on one hand, a kind of knowledge unencumbered by the classics and tradition and, on the other, to introduce a novel epistemology that would counteract a creeping tendency to indict knowledge as an obstacle to civility and piety.

Out of religious conviction, the strictly orthodox American colonists harbored suspicion about antique learning, for religious reconstructionists had told them that the vaults of learning contained some contaminated wisdom. Although Bacon never went so far as to endorse their suspicion, he affirmed the proposition that conventional science and philosophy were filled with distortion. It was time, Bacon told his readers, to remove the shackle of tradition; the colonists, especially the Puritans, turned out to be an attentive audience. Learning in direct competition with piety was sure to lose, and colonial religionists tried their best to prove that a commitment to faith was not a ratification of ignorance.[30]

Bacon's book seemed to contain a formula for correcting the past's errors and promoting learning without undermining faith, piety, and civility. In Britain and America, Francis Bacon had achieved beatification for his belief in progress, for his utilitarian and empirical philosophy, and for his inductive method, which was heralded as the bulwark of traditional views in science and the universal means of acquiring truth. Considering the strength of his reputation, one might naturally suppose that his educational pronouncements would be well received. Small wonder, then, when colonial educators wanted assurance, when they looked for ways to justify their educational conviction, they turned to Lord Bacon and preferred him over all others.

The *Advancement of Learning* had the reputation of a book that all educated men read, so it is easy to see why colonial savants consulted it. It is harder to understand their uncritical embrace, for nothing in the book—or for that matter in Bacon's philosophical outlook—could have been interpreted as supporting the rigid platform of Puritan religious policy and polity. They either succumbed to tolerance or were inattentive readers (neither of which sounds plausible), or were so desperate for sound educational advice that those parts unpalatable to religious taste were neglected. Being unable to fathom either their motive or temporary lapse into tolerance, a conjecture that colonial readers were prompted to take good advice wherever found and to treat wounded conscience with the balm of good intention is allowed to stand.

Ancient Greek philosophy, Bacon declared, might be used with commentary pruned, and the words of its authors could be studied with impunity, although not always with a good dividend: "As to the point of usefulness, the philosophy we principally received from the Greeks must be acknowledged puerile, or rather talkative than generative—as being fruitful in controversies, but barren in effects."[31] But Bacon demurred, as did his colonial readers, despite reservation about ancient philosophy's worth, from discrediting the intellectual inheritance, so he complimented the best of the ancient authors but refused to embrace commentary on them: "The intellectual sciences . . . sometimes appear most perfect in the original author, and afterward degenerate." This assertion, the starting point for his thesis in *The Advancement of Learning*, illustrated his conviction that knowledge had been corrupted and learning had been paralyzed.

The boldness of Bacon's indictment was untroubling to colonial readers, for they, too, had lingering doubt about much that was in the corpus of learning, and they were friendly to revision that appeared to be progressive so long as it did not intrude on fundamental faith. But if they read on they should have been distressed at Bacon's concession that among contemporary scholars engaged in redressing learning's sterility, the best were the Jesuits. Puritans counted this hated society an unmitigated evil; if its genius in education could not be ignored, it should not, in any case, be praised.

After the introduction, Bacon elaborated a carefully reasoned and highly perceptive philosophy of education. The colonists' disposition toward learning took schooling into account but always ranged beyond schooling, so Bacon's philosophy of education, while paying heed to schooling without being curtailed by it, complemented their own educational conviction. The family, the church, society generally, were commissioned to teach youth. Colonial educational leaders were confident of this principle, so Bacon's endorsement of what they themselves held was further testimony to his soundness. In the last analysis, confirmation, rather than conversion, helped to maintain Bacon's reputation for educational orthodoxy, and his readers, instead of seeking instruction from him, might have found support for a standard they had already erected. But this is conjecture and does nothing to subvert Bacon's stature as an authority to whom colonists listened.

The Advancement of Learning had another side recommending its reception in the colonial world. While Bacon deplored unreasonable dependence upon ancient authority or upon knowledge stored in hoary tomes, he illustrated a conversance with the classics and the Bible. Hardly a page in the book is without classical reference or scriptural allusion, and this was not overlooked by readers ready to pay allegiance to both. An author who knew his sources so well and used them so effortlessly, and one who appeared to count upon the authority of the Bible, was worth attention. They must, however, have skimmed over Bacon's principal declaration that old storehouses of knowledge and the authors who filled them were, at best, undependable. His colonial audiences might have had grounds for refusing to subscribe to *The Advancement of Learning*, but they had better grounds, they thought, for adopting the prescription it contained.

One important part to educational perspective, however, was left untouched and unmentioned by Bacon. Colonists tried to settle it themselves, although the record of history confirms their lack of success. From the outset in the colonies, conflicting theories relative to public and private education had some currency, and while it is true that the phrases "public education" and "private education" were far less precise then than they were to become in the twentieth century, this question, nevertheless, was posed: Is education (which meant schooling) a collective or personal responsibility?

Tradition was on the side making education a personal, at least a family, obligation, and one has a right to be surprised that a question about schooling could have been framed at all. Yet there were faint but persistent signs that all was not well with tradition; the citadel of personal educational responsibility was under assault. The best, but not the only, evidence is found in the early colonial acts enjoining communities to make some provision for schooling and, on occasion, although always permissively, to contribute some support for the employment of a teacher or the maintenance of a school.

The collective principle had a precarious genesis, and for a long time, no one would have endorsed the whole of the concept; but it refused to go away. So when one looks for the roots of conviction with respect to what American public education was to become, they can be found in the tentative, and always insecure, embrace of educational collectivism in the colonial years. This conviction matured to the point where, by the late years of the nineteenth century, citizens took for granted the social policy that provision for public education is among the most significant responsibilities of government.

The colonial climate was not especially conducive to scholastic growth, although more than anyone has a right to expect was accomplished on the collegiate level. Following the lesson of history almost to the letter, American education developed from the top down. Yet lower schools were indeed extant, although it would be exaggeration to say that they flourished.

Colonial Schools. The history of American dame schools and the existence of any general theory sustaining them are hard to report. Such enterprises, humble, erratic, and ephemeral, seldom capture the attention of chronologists. But they and their counterparts, the petty schools of the South, offered educational opportunity to children who otherwise might have been neglected. Their character and the credentials of the persons conducting them justify certain assumptions: their curriculum was simple, consisting of the alphabet, a little spelling, reading, and moral and religious instruction. If girls attended, and good reason for doubting their attendance is lacking, they learned some sewing and knitting in addition to ABCs and reading. Town schools, it appears, sometimes set reading skill as a prerequisite for attendance, and when this prerequisite was enforced, it helped to keep dame and petty schools alive.[32]

Consistent with the attitude of Puritan parents that in loving their children too much, they would be tempted to ameliorate discipline and abandon sternness, thus depriving their offspring of a saintly education, they packed their children off to boarding schools that began to appear on the colonial scene. In other colonies, geography recommended that children be sent from home to live at school, for homes were scattered, and even a central place for a school would have been out of reach for most students. It is hard to know exactly what prompted the boarding-school movement in early America, and it is unlikely that these were the foremost factors, but they played some role. In any case, boarding schools, sometimes for elementary instruction but more commonly for secondary education, came into being and remained as a permanent part of the American scholastic landscape. Elementary or secondary, however, these schools forwarded an attitude toward education that gained nearly universal support when they respected gender differences in provision for schooling.

Town schools (stimulated, we should think, by the Massachusetts Act of 1647) made a fairly regular appearance in the New England and Middle colonies. In New England they stayed close to the church's official orthodoxy; but in the Middle colonies, religious diversity recommended a less strident expression of sectarianism, and the schools, while never nonsectarian institutions, were prepared to fly a flag of tolerant sectarianism.[33] Both teachers' skill and instruction's material varied greatly from school to school; any assessment of general quality is bound to be flawed. But these town schools, wherever found, were elementary, with a concentration upon reading, although writing and arithmetic sometimes and in some places found their way into the syllabus. In New England especially, schoolmasters were usually aspiring ministers waiting for a pulpit, but elsewhere clerical pedigree was uncommon.

Secondary education was accounted for in some town schools and in private Latin grammar academies. Wherever secondary education was found, it was designated as an education in grammar, and the first American secondary schools usually succeeded in maintaining a classical course of sorts, intended at first as a complete education. They were destined, however, to become preparatory schools for colleges.[34] Town secondary schools tried to be classical too, and sometimes they succeeded, but good teachers and willing students were not easy to find. Still, the stated purpose of the town secondary school was to fit youth for the university.

At the end of the colonial period, education's character was fairly clear, and support for it, while more often implicit than explicit, was evident, too. That there was a dearth of mature educational philosophy, and that it did not alter much the stride of traditional educational practice, is admitted. Still, an educational philosophy coupled to social and political aspiration was in the process of generation. There is a temptation to call it prophetic, for as it matured in the decades following the colonial years, it began to promote the development of an educational program for the people, one capable of serving the interest of this good and energetic society.

Chapter 10

Education for Citizenship

Before the Revolution was over, even before it began, Americans had commenced to wean their social ideals and institutions from the mother country. Not bold enough to declare a cultural independence to complement a newly-won political sovereignty, because they were sensitive to the indignity in becoming cultural orphans, our ancestors nevertheless complied with an urge to translate old cultural convictions and values for the novel condition of their infant nation. Translation, it should be admitted, was inevitable and would have occurred whether or not Americans encouraged it, for a complex of social and political value nurtured for Europe could not have survived in the progressive climate of this good land.

For a long time, the class distinction defined by social convention was in jeopardy; even with a social philosophy temperamentally accustomed to it, a frontier society learns this lesson in the anthropology of personal experience: social pedigree is a discounted currency for the bargains to be struck in the stark conditions of pioneer life. Yet pockets of civility were evident in colonial society, and aristocratic pretension and the manner wedded to it reminded common men to beware of declarations about equality among persons. Social privilege had worth, and those who possessed it were not disposed to give it up without a struggle. But a residue from pioneer experience refused to respect the boundaries of the frontier and was virile enough to infect even the most intransigent theories relative to the perpetuation of a class society. Old social theories that convention had protected began to disintegrate even when they were not repudiated.

At the same time, and in about the same way, the force of religion in society was weakened. It had been for a long time a dominant factor in shaping society's character, and it would be plain hyperbole to declare that its strength was suddenly and unexpectedly sapped, but divergent and competing sects undermined religion's grip on the minds of men and women. Variety kindled doubt about which denomination held the keys to the kingdom of heaven, and doubt was enough to intimidate without displacing religion's heretofore pervasive influence. Religious liberalism was as yet some distance over the horizon, and secularism's sounds were ugly and discordant, but the days of a Bible commonwealth were over.

American society began to reflect a new image, one that eventually affected education and schooling and, in turn, was affected by education and schooling.

Political Independence and Educational Transition

It might have been true that the colonies severed from Great Britain were unready for independence, but suddenly independence was a reality to which they had to accommodate. Although loyalist sentiment— especially among a codfish aristocracy in New England—was ready to redress the political course introduced by revolution, independence soon began to make its own urgent demand. The time came, probably after 1812, when a reversal of political course was unrealistic and unthinkable. Americans had no choice but to come to terms with the political reality facing them. They had to make provision for national existence; for an infant state, this was far from easy. Every part of society, every institution, every theory, was enlisted in a crusade to make the republican experiment work. History records how hard this prescription was to fill.

Promoting Nationalism. Nationalism was on the march in Europe, so our ancestors were in a position to profit from the European nationalistic experience. They were at least aware of the influence a vernacular language, a national literature and history, and a program of education could have in cultivating social sinew for a national state. Promoting the production of a national literature and history, and reaping political benefit therefrom, is a slow process, but while progress was made, neither history nor literature comes quickly from hope and need.

Both take time to mature, and both, if they are to be didactic, require a sensitivity to and reverence for place: their content and form must be indigenous. Along the same line, language cannot be reconstructed in a day and systems of schools do not spring suddenly into being. Yet language and schooling can be accelerated, while history and literature take their own natural pace and cannot be hurried. In the end, then, the builders of the American nation, the architects of a genuinely avant-garde society, were motivated by practical necessity to support a reconstruction of language and a program of education.

American English. Tradition can be chilly to change, and language enjoys no special immunity, but the fact that, even in the late eighteenth century, English was a retarded vernacular must have been a blessing in disguise. What in British English was correct; what was the standard for orthography, punctuation, and syntax? Authors and orators, comfortable in their conviction that they were the beneficiaries of English's golden age, followed their own lexicon and supposed the rules they invented could be used by all others as well, but men in the schools and on the streets were not so easily converted. To introduce a distinctive American English, or to try to do so, was, while by no means easy, not impossible. Eloquent voices began to speak in favor of jettisoning linguistic dependence. Some went so far as to ostracize the ancient tongues, to recommend an outlawing of British English, and to invent an entirely new language, but the more moderate and, as a result, the more successful exponents of linguistic autonomy spoke in favor of creating an American English whose prescriptive convention could eventually succeed in interdicting British English.

Benjamin Franklin and, before him, Francis Bacon had idealized utility in knowledge and schooling. If the principles surrounding the utility they pronounced were sound, as they appeared to be to an American public, why should Americans cling to a language, or languages, whose credentials of utility were suspect? Franklin wanted the schools to use English as a medium of instruction and give it official curricular status, but although he might have been willing to settle for traditional English, some of his successors, all more avidly committed to nationalism than he, wanted to strike a better linguistic bargain. Noah Webster (1758–1843), as it turned out, was the most illustrious and most successful among them.

Noah Webster. With sober scholarship, and at first with a small, friendly audience, Webster began by reciting the danger in imitating foreign educational models and in sending American students abroad for their schooling. In either case, he declared, national pride and native political institutions would be wounded. He warned, moreover, that the primary fuel for running the engine of American government and society—an American language—would be deprived of an indigenous energy that could make it vigorous, responsive, and effective. With characteristic courage or stubbornness, and in the face of opponents who thought him either arrogant or ridiculous, Webster declared America's linguistic independence.

He proposed an American standard, one independent of any foreign model, and urged it as a staple for the schools and schoolmasters of the country. Appealing to national pride and patriotism, he wrote: "Our honor requires us to have a system of our own, in language as well as government. Great Britain, whose children we are, and whose language we speak, should no longer be *our* standard; for the taste of her writers is already corrupted, and her language on the decline. But if this were not so, she is at too great a distance to be our model, and to instruct us in the principles of our own tongue. . . . Several circumstances render a future separation of the American tongue from the English necessary and unavoidable. . . . We have therefore the fairest opportunity of establishing a national language and of giving it uniformity and perspicuity, in North America, that ever presented itself to mankind. Now is the time to begin the plan."[1]

Webster's logic and eloquence were persuasive enough to enlist support for his doctrine on language. The result was that, from about the time of the adoption of the Constitution to the end of the second decade of the nineteenth century, the American language changed more than at any other time from the first colonial days to the period of great western expansion.[2] Metamorphosis in vocabulary—the introduction of Americanisms—was most pronounced, but the canons of use were affected as well.

Cultural Values. Despite all this activity in connection with language, and despite, too, an obvious determination to become an independent nation with a political and social system cut from New-World cloth, we should be cautious about jumping to any conclusion that our forefathers were ready to abandon their fundamental convictions about life's meaning and its basic values. The aftermath of the Revolution, for all the common ground it uncovered, did not produce social and political equilibrium, and the lessons contained in a traditional wisdom penetrated the minds of Americans with a characteristic stubbornness.

There was brave, and sometimes irresponsible, talk about political, intellectual, and literary independence; but in the end, most Americans were intellectual children whose ideals had been shaped and tested in an inherited legacy. For all their courage, Americans were not eager to blaze entirely new intellectual trails and, for the most part, saw no imperative need for them. They were faced with a practical problem of social and political organization. It most of all needed their solicitous attention, but they were not always sure that pondering theory or engaging in philosophical discourse would lead to its solution. Intellectual autonomy, a separation from the intellectual legacy of the past, was prized and praised and sometimes tested, but in the end, it was a luxury they could not afford.

Enlightenment Influence. By the middle of the eighteenth century, bookshops in America were stocked with the latest editions of European scholars who were in the habit of promoting attractive Enlightenment propositions, and curious colonists read them, always with attention and frequently with approval. American writers began to make a name for themselves by adopting a similar literary and philosophical stance. By the end of the Revolution, Enlightenment thought was an intellectual medium of exchange. It was circulated in newspapers, magazines, tracts, and popular books.

Anyone who could read had, to some degree, been infected by what was often Enlightenment propaganda, and while such propaganda did not much affect a man's daily life, it almost certainly altered the measure of his thought. The basic thesis of the Enlightenment was that authority is evil; the only warrant for action is unvarnished reason, always unadulterated by convention, tradition, and authority. If this was a hard lesson to learn, it was enormously more difficult to apply.

The Enlightenment idealized reason, but it was not in reason's elevation that the highest dividend was paid. The scientific method, somehow joined to Enlightenment doctrine, led to the discovery of knowledge which under no circumstance could have been unearthed by a further excavation of traditional literary mines. Sir Isaac Newton (1642–1727), William Harvey (1578–1657), Robert Boyle (1627–1691), René Descartes (1596–1650), and Francis Bacon were in the vanguard of a scholarship that added to science's respectability and, at the same time, whetted the intellectual appetite of their immediate successors: Rutherford (1749–1819), Cavendish (1731–1810), Bergman (1735–1784), Priestly (1733–1804), Lavoisier (1743–1794), Galvani (1734–1798), and Volta (1745–1827).

While the best of the scientific scholars were enthusiastic in their search for knowledge, they were never unrealistic. They knew that science was unequipped to answer every question that a curious mind might ask. But this reservation often went unheeded by persons who had strained for so long under humanism's and religion's leash.

Science was on the march, but its path was frequently blocked or impeded by old adversaries: humanism and religion. Both exerted about equal influence in Europe and America, one usually strong enough to keep science a safe distance from the schoolhouse door. In America, Franklin expressed his friendship for science and had a hand, too, in promoting Enlightenment spirit among his erudite confreres. Some joined with him in founding the American Philosophical Society as early as 1769, but for all the Society's good work, it did little to promote any fundamental reconstruction in education; and as it turned out, despite the pronouncements for educational reform coming from home and abroad, nothing of consequence was done on the level of schooling.

The schools continued to function as before, and even the colleges, where one might have expected more intellectual curiosity, stuck to their old ways. Still, something on the horizon would severely alter the traditional approach to schooling. Enough has been seen of colonial schools for us to know that they had served two masters: an aristocratic social order and denominational religion. The new educational theory coming from Europe, always put in the context of Enlightenment aspiration, set in motion new ways of looking at educational purpose. The man most responsible for this, for sending the message to America, was John Locke (1632–1704). His credibility was good among educated Americans because he said so many things about politics that coincided with or confirmed American political opinion. If Locke's political doctrine were sound, and they supposed it was and, to a great extent, had adopted it, was it not logical to attribute the same soundness to a program of education that could ensure the implementation of political theory?

Locke's educational theory, though somewhat diffuse, stood on a foundation challenging both theological and humanistic conceptions of human nature. Arguing from the position of a deist, he rejected pietism, a doctrine that probably originated with Augustine and one appealing to Calvinists and Puritans, as being nothing more than myth. Jettisoned, too, were propositions friendly to innate ideas and self-evident propositions. Knowledge, he declared with supreme confidence, has but one source: experience. The traditional corpus of human learning, he went on, needed careful reappraisal and considerable pruning; everything in it—especially theology and philosophy—had to be confirmed by reason. Any part of knowledge failing reason's test was abandoned.

Equally audacious and likely more consequential was Locke's assertion that at birth a person's mind is blank: *tabula rasa*. Assuming the validity of *tabula rasa*, it follows as night follows day that the environment wherein persons must live and learn is more important than anyone heretofore had imagined. Experience alone is capable of making impressions on the mind, and experience can be had nowhere but in the environment. What anyone is to become depends not upon divine interference or the acting out of a predetermined master plan, but upon the richness of experience and the mind's ability to do something with it. If Americans were disposed to embrace self-reliance, *tabula rasa* supplied them with ample justification, but it justified as well the proposition that in the last analysis the fullness of human life is to be realized by first using the environment and then learning to control it.

This was the way to put the conditions in place for the production of noble persons and effective societies, and an important, likely indispensable, condition for the improvement of human beings is education. If men and women become what their environment makes them, if their reasoning ability is to be sharpened to a point where it can distill dependable meaning from experience, that part of the environment amenable to scholastic organization and transmission cannot under any circumstance be ignored.

No one was in the habit of discounting the worth of schooling. Education was high on the list of the imperative human needs, although it was all too frequently left to wither on the list. A long and honorable tradition certified the good sense in cultivating human talent. But never before had a philosophical–psychological doctrine declared so unequivocally for schooling.

It would be exaggeration to aver that American educators and the public at once perceived the full import of Locke's thesis, and it would be incorrect to allege that once the implications were recognized, the scholastic enterprise was amended to comply with it. All this took a long time and was, perhaps, not fully exploited until well past the middle of the twentieth century when theories of environmental determinism began to swamp educational practice, but enough was mined from the doctrine to inspire and inform the school reform advocated by Horace Mann (1796–1859) when be began to lead the common school crusade in Massachusetts.[3]

Another dimension to Locke's *tabula rasa* theory, again only imperfectly understood in the late years of the eighteenth and the early years of the nineteenth century, was the support it offered for a policy of universal education. No person's mind has at the outset an experiential advantage; everyone begins the race of life from a common starting line. Such a proposition ends up ratifying the principle of equality of educational opportunity, a principle recognized and promoted by one of America's most progressive social theorists: Thomas Jefferson (1743–1826).[4] On the level of theory, he asserted the importance of universal education for the realization of an effective political democracy.

Finally, Locke gave credence to an idea whose time had come: knowledge is useful and, moreover, powerful. But when Locke and his disciples spoke of knowledge, they meant to endorse only that part of its corpus supplied and validated by empiricism. Anything outside empiricism's ambit was dismissed as undependable. This bold program and the formula whereupon it depended were so ambitious as to be unrealistic: from an entirely practical point of view, how much of the total body of knowledge would be left after empiricists finished pruning it?

What prudent mind could embrace without reservation or amendment a doctrine abandoning those parts of reality, such as love, hate, greed, and sympathy, which are as real and influential as anything produced by empirical technique but cannot be assessed, tested, or explained by it? And what would be left in a school curriculum, if at every turn of the road the empirical test had to be made? Had the experience of the human race nothing to contribute to the treasury of knowledge? The whole of Locke's thesis was easy to embrace but impossible to apply, so enthusiastic theorists took from it what could be used and neglected the rest.

They settled for utility and thus introduced an epistemological convention, one not entirely inconsistent with a pragmatic tendency affecting Americans, that authorized filling the schools' curricula with useful knowledge. This convention was slow to mature, but evidence of its making headway can be found in the Report of the Yale faculty, a famous document intended to curb academic utilitarianism that would not have been written at all, had traditional liberal knowledge not been under assault.

For the most part, Locke's educational views were melded in an American social theory only then coming of age, but there was another side to Locke's advice to educators that, while attractive and appealing to a minority, was eventually either ignored or repudiated by the rank and file: good evidence, one supposes, to maintain that as Americans worked to erect an educational citadel capable of serving society, they were never mere imitators. Locke discredited public education and poked fun at popular schooling.[5] He was content to perpetuate a British tradition giving gentlemen the first call upon schools. All others were left to fend for themselves.

Locke's admirers are tempted to apologize for what they call simple oversight, or they acknowledge the anomaly in his stance; whatever the source of Locke's myopia, the historical fact is that American educational theory repudiated this plank in his educational platform. After this, it was ready to erect a foundation for American education that owed Locke a great debt.

Impediments to Educational Theory. One has a right to be impressed with the amount of thought directed at national education during this period of transition when Americans were struggling to salvage the best of past theory and weld it to something new and more promising. Their success is evident to the historian, but it was by no means assured during the late years of the eighteenth and the early years of the nineteenth century. At the same time, one is struck by the fact that for all this wrestling with theory, with an examination of the doctrines of deists and empiricists, and with a yearning for a better society, almost nothing on the level of educational practice was accomplished. Action was paralyzed in the absence of theory, and while theory matured, the schools marked time.

Tradition's crust is hard and not easily penetrated. Besides, education was not the only issue facing our ancestors and, one has a right to conclude, was seldom if ever a burning one. Other vexing issues were current, and some had been around for a long time. Americans, along with their European cousins, were uncomfortable wearing the yoke of restrictive religious dogma, although (except as a minority view) the place and worth of religion were understood and acknowledged even among the faithless. But seeds of doubt were scattered by the wind of freedom; when they germinated, all but the most orthodox religious temperaments were affected.

Doubt was never meant to swamp men and women in atheism or to anathematize their relationship with God, but only to repudiate irrational sectarianism. The straight road of religious orthodoxy was permanently bent as new characters began a parade in the drama of religion in America: deism, Unitarianism, and Transcendentalism. Their lines were prophetic: God's plan was adumbrated. His apercu of humanity left his creatures to find their own way. If they were to have a good society, if they were to articulate ideals and seek to achieve them, they would have to devise their own plan. God would not do man's work. So as battles were fought over the custody of the human spirit, the cause of religious liberalism was aided by infusions of scientific knowledge fast becoming more abundant.[6] It was beginning to be obvious that any social order would have to be designed and directed by the hard-won lessons of human reason. This revelation contributed directly to the rise of a social and secular religion called humanitarianism.

Humanitarianism. Enthusiastic and optimistic, and possibly influenced by the romantic naturalism of Jean Jacques Rousseau (1712–1778), American humanitarians, without adverting to it, were the beneficiaries of Christian altruism. Embracing a spirit of humanity, trumpeting the betterment of mankind, their creed (if one can call it that) was usually more emotional than rational and never called for much help from philosophy or theology. It would be unfair to allege antipathy to religion or favoritism for a kind of strident secularism in the humanitarian outlook, and in any case, its exponents were not disposed to fight old battles; for them, the battlefield was not the church but society, and their ammunition was social theory, not religious dogma. Humanitarians wanted a society sensitive to the welfare of the people; they wanted to help all manner of men and women lead more satisfying and productive lives; they wanted to create a family of humanity.

History reports that humanitarians were more successful in defining the dimensions of the social problems than in resolving them; lack of success slowed but never halted their crusade. Still they were faced with an immense problem: social altruism is easy to pronounce but hard to prescribe, and those conditions that lead either to its realization or, at least, to the amelioration of social shortcoming are exceptionally elusive. The litany of humanitarian objectives for American society was long and, taken together, added up to social reform, with education always first on the list. So easy to promote but so difficult to achieve, educational reform of the first order had to wait for the vested educational interests to identify, and sometimes to amend, their principal social and educational convictions.

As a new nation began to find its place in a modern world, the social and political theory securing its foundation needed clarification and articulation for the development of consistent national objectives. Such theory has its genesis in conviction with respect to what has worth, a judgment of value. And in this good land, for all its promise for the poor and oppressed, sharp difference in value was evident and inevitably affected pronouncement of worth on such matters as education. Who should be offered opportunity for schooling and how much instruction should they have? Where should curricular priorities lie, and what knowledge should the curriculum contain? What knowledge is of most worth, and what balance should be maintained between intellectual accomplishment and moral standard? There was nothing pedantic or trivial about these questions.

With the advent of national existence, it soon became evident that two social theories were competing for precedence. One, fundamentally aristocratic, had Alexander Hamilton (1757–1804) as its foremost spokesman. The other, far more democratic in essence and application, was promoted by Thomas Jefferson.

Social Theory

Aristocratic Social Theory. Disdaining romantic naturalism as nothing more than catering to folly, and discounting humanitarianism as a warrant to reward weakness, Hamilton and other aristocrats identified the principal source for human motive: avarice and ambition. Nature's order allows the strong to command the weak and thus to maintain a dependable and stable society wherein they might ensure the success of their ambition.[7] Power and authority in all matters applying to society and government should be vested in "landowners, merchants, and men of the learned professions," for with power and authority at their disposal, they can protect the interest of property.[8]

This social thesis was bound to affect education: the masses were distrusted, for given the chance, they would choose evil over good and, with such a dangerous predisposition, could never be capable of or trusted with self-government. If these defenders of the right of property over persons possessed any altruistic inspiration, it must have been hidden away in a conviction that persons of wealth, prominence, and position have an obligation to protect the masses from their own weakness and indiscretion. Poor and uneducated people have a limited place in society: they are to be governed. This fundamental distrust of democracy led unerringly to a recommendation that any program of education be designed to check "the turbulent, uncontrollable and imprudent" disposition of people who formed the bulk of the population. Support was not withheld totally from schooling of some kind for all the children of all the people: aristocratic self-interest, if nothing else, dictated a level of instruction for the inculcation of docility in the masses and therefrom some assurance that the established social order could be kept intact.

This theory of social control, perhaps too harshly represented in Hamilton's rhetoric, was out of step with progressive opinion. It needed softening if it were to have any chance of acceptance, and the man who undertook to blunt some of its thorns was John Adams (1735–1826). Though his language conveyed a tone of compromise, the theory he pronounced reflected the fundamental assumptions of Hamilton's. Adams never doubted that most persons were permanently corrupted by original sin and by their own natural meanness. He was convinced, moreover, that on the common man's scale of value, reason is always subordinate to the drive of self-interest. Finally, he supposed, a universal human condition prescribed an aristocracy of ability that could be unerringly predicted and convincingly demonstrated along class lines. Persons ascend to the upper class because they are able. Position, power, and privilege were stripped of all mystery.

Political authority should, according to this interpretation, be vested in persons clearly able to lead, otherwise anarchy would prevail, for the wild disposition of the underclass could never contribute to the maintenance of an orderly society. Still, the underclass should not be ignored, for this, too, could be dangerous. Without surrendering any of its authority, the upper class should, out of self-interest, make some concession to the poor, allowing them enough latitude and giving them enough help to make a life for themselves and not be a burden upon society. By implication, at least, Adams was ready to lend some support to a program of education for the people.

In the end, neither Hamilton nor Adams was persuasive enough to convince his countrymen that oligarchy was preferable to democracy, although it should be acknowledged that a residue from this oligarchical theory lingered for a long time in America and was too often successful in slowing the pace of educational progress. It might be said, as well, that a cadre of revisionist educational historians have adopted an interpretation wherein this theory and its application to education was never abandoned. They aver that it was simply concealed in an educational policy that, while appearing to endorse broad, even universal, schooling as a means for personal and social welfare, was actually a conspiracy to ensure social control.[9]

This is probably neither the place nor the time to debate the revisionist thesis. What is clear is that the letter of the social-control theory was not adopted, whatever may be said about its spirit, and in its place, the more open, optimistic, and humanistic social theory of Thomas Jefferson was given a sympathetic hearing before the bar of American political opinion.

Democratic Social Theory. Jefferson essayed to promote a philosophy of humanity that made men and women capable of guiding their own destiny. Human nature was not deprived, it most certainly was not depraved, and it had within it the seeds for social and political responsibility. Justice, law, reason, and truth were superior to force and the exercise of arbitrary authority. The bedrock of Jefferson's social theory was composed of equality and inalienable human right, and both fed those institutional tributaries whereupon the right of property was allowed to float but never to maroon personal right, opportunity, and equality before the law.

Jefferson never went so far as to discount ability, and he presumed that it should be rewarded, but he refused to countenance any doctrine predetermining ability along class lines. When he turned his attention to education, he declared that all citizens should have the means to realize whatever ability they possessed and, with a cultivated intelligence and enlightened minds, be ready to exercise the responsibility of self-government. Public policy, he said, should be shaped by public opinion, but if public opinion is to be responsible, it must be aided and abetted by a program of education and a plan for schooling equal to the task of keeping public opinion informed. No argument could convince Jefferson that an educational program should aim at social control, and the record of his achievement in the educational arena would appear to contain evidence that dissimulation never clouded his expression of support for a system of universal schooling.[10]

Jefferson's social, political, and educational positions had special appeal for persons whose experience in frontier society persuaded them that equality was no myth and that arrogant elitism was archaic. But their honest optimism with respect to the promise for mankind in this new nation was met with skepticism and derision by persons who had something to lose should democracy carry the day. Still, almost any way one reads American social history, it appears clear that the class system was always in some jeopardy in a land with abundant natural resources, with a rising and aspiring middle class, with the separation of church and state, and with a stronger voice in political decision for the common man. Although this might be true, one should be careful about assuming that hostility between social dogmas abated, that the oligarchy surrendered without exhausting its most powerful ammunition, or that a democratic social philosophy secured a foothold without the expenditure of dedicated and determined effort.

While the war of theory was waged, American educators, sensitive to the need for schooling and the contribution it could make to society at large, were reviewing philosophies of education that had been around for centuries. They hoped to discover in these treasuries of ancient educational wisdom clues to guide them in their quest for an American educational plan. But whether or not they were successful in excavating old educational mines is somewhat beside the point. What is clear is that theory was either too weak or too imprecise to be of much help in supplying the motive force to produce the schools the country needed. Politics, not educational philosophy, contained the answer to the problem of schooling, and the question was put this way: Who should be educated and what kind of instruction should they have?

Education: A New American Creed

Anticipating the need American society would have for a kind of education fitting citizens for self-government, public leaders, just before and just after the adoption of the Constitution, began to till the soil of educational discourse. Franklin and Jefferson are best known for their educational manifestos, but hundreds of others contributed to the public debate as well. In concert they proclaimed the worth of educational decency and urged upon the new nation a policy for ensuring it. For the most part, however, they were not tempted to adopt the old-world model of centralization. The European school systems that over the years had been designed to serve national purpose had achieved good results, and Americans were by no means ignorant of them, but the citizens shaped by such national school systems were not engaged in self-government, and the proposition of popular sovereignty had, for them, a reality reserved largely for the pages of the philosophers' books.

Educational Plans. There had been some talk about a national university, and for a while such an institution solicited a fair amount of support, even from George Washington (1732–1799).[11] In the end, however, the idea was abandoned and with it, too, any disposition to adopt the idea of a centralized, or a national, school system.

It would be a mistake to assume that the educational problem facing the new nation was not taken seriously. The record rejects such an as-

sumption. And the details of Franklin's and Jefferson's educational proposals are preserved for study.[12] What are not so well known are the
national educational plans solicited for a contest sponsored by the American Philosophical Society. Benjamin Rush (1745–1813), whose considerable acumen added substance to the educational debate, developed a plan
which can be taken as illustrative of centralized education for America. In
addition, its rather striking differences from Franklin's and Jefferson's
educational ideas give it historical distinction.[13]

Benjamin Rush. Rush undertook to meld the goal of universal
schooling—to be gained through state-supported elementary schools—
with a program of instruction exhumed, it would seem, from the Latin
grammar school. The business of education, he wrote, "has acquired a
new complexion by the independence of our country. The form of government we have assumed, has created a new class of duties to every American. It becomes us, therefore, to examine our former habits upon this
subject, and in laying the foundations for nurseries of wise and good men,
to adapt our models of teaching to the peculiar form of our
government."[14]

Rush wanted the schools to help prepare good and effective citizens,
but he wanted them to pay close attention to morality as well. The best
way to do this, he proposed, was to recognize that the "foundation for a
useful education in a republic is to be laid in religion." Jefferson must
have been horrified when he read Rush's plan, especially its affirmation
of religion, for Rush was not declaring for any general religious sentiment
or a religion of humanity, but for Christianity.

Proclaiming that "a Christian cannot fail of being a republican," he
went on to prescribe the role the Bible should have in the curriculum of
the country's schools: it should be read and explained to students. For all
its worth, however, the Bible could not stand alone, and here Rush is at
pains to endorse what he considered to be the best elements of traditional
humanistic education. "[T]he learned or Dead languages" were to be well-
represented, but Rush's justification for them must have been prospective: he thought their primary value was the aid which knowledge of them
could give to the teaching of English and as a corollary to the ability of
American youth "to read and write our American language with propriety
and elegance."[15]

Careful to establish a principle of educational opportunity without
subscribing to Jefferson's doctrine of universal education, Rush was on
the side of government action for the inauguration of a school system
wherein the country's children could be readied for a new social order he
saw coming over the horizon.

What sounds like a proclamation in "Thoughts upon the Mode of

Education Proper in a Republic" was articulated more fully in "A Plan for the Establishment of Public Schools."[16] But before taking a closer look at Rush's plan, it should be recognized that public men in eighteenth-century America had intimations of the meaning of public education—a meaning that had matured over the years as an addendum to colonial law—and could sense its implications for the future. Rush's eloquence in advocating public schools should discourage historians from leaping to the conclusion that public schools were the invention of the middle years of the nineteenth century without any leading strings to the past, and that they sprang full-grown from the fertile mind of Horace Mann.

Beginning with a solid justification for educational opportunity, Rush went on to assert that learning is useful to religion. There is, however, no sign of commitment to sectarianism in the schools, although there is a reasonable analysis portraying intellectually responsible religion as an instrument for stamping out prejudice and superstition.

Realizing that democracy is fragile, likely helpless without good will and intelligence to sustain it—and borrowing from Rousseau the phrase that without education "men become Savages or Barbarians, and where learning is confined to a *few* people, we will always find monarchy, aristocracy and slavery"—Rush despaired of its prospect in the absence of a system of schools. Learning is the foundation for law and justice, for equitable and effective government, and for a civilized society; when it is lacking, elements essential to human decency inevitably will be impaired.

He called for the institution of free elementary schools the country over, and while he is silent about such things as compulsory attendance, he wanted all children to attend them. For those who evidenced talent and disposition for more advanced study, provision was made for classical schools and colleges. Yet he was unready to cast a common educational mold and demurred from endorsing any school plan that would erase religious, ethnic, and linguistic distinction. Such distinction, he believed, was valid justification for voluntary scholastic segregation, and he counted these differences to be strengths to be capitalized and cultivated rather than eliminated by a common, undifferentiated school program.

Rush was education's good friend, although he was not alone in advocating its essential compact with democracy. Yet he can be taken as illustrative of public men who regarded schooling as a pressing American social and political problem, one in need of prompt resolution. Any recounting of educational progress during this period of transition must, however, give to Thomas Jefferson the guerdon for educational vision.

Thomas Jefferson and Free Schools. Jefferson had supreme confidence in the ability of the men of his generation to institute a system of good and responsible government to serve, not master, citizens. His evident hostility to established religion's intrusion on civil affairs is too well known to warrant repetition here; but in connection with education, it is worth reporting that he had confidence in the ability of citizens to govern themselves if they were literate, informed, and prudent. But these necessary conditions for self-government were dependent upon a broad and generous distribution of educational opportunity. In the absence of schools wherein intelligence could be cultivated, the realization of popular sovereignty was impossible.[17]

The plan for education proposed by Jefferson, especially its free-school feature, enabled the people to stand as the safe depositories of their liberty. At the same time, it revealed Jefferson's fundamental educational philosophy: universal education is essential to civic virtue, and citizenship is education's primary objective. In time, this philosophy was translated into a political–educational policy making elementary instruction an entitlement, but the educational calendar turned slowly in the late eighteenth and early nineteenth century. Jefferson's plan and the philosophy of education it expressed were premature. Both were either rejected or postponed. But universal education as a corollary of democracy and republican government could not be discredited even by neglect, and Jefferson's bold plan and ambitious theory captivated the thought of nineteenth-century educational leaders who adopted popular education as their cause.

Popular Education. With all the force they could muster, nineteenth-century social reformers led a crusade for the common man's cause and, with an almost unmatched display of altruism, undertook to tailor public policy to his interest. But causes embraced by crusaders are always controversial (otherwise a crusade for their adoption would be redundant), so progress was frequently erratic and always unpredictable. As this crusade cut a path through the underbrush of reactionary conviction, it hoisted one banner as high or higher than all the rest: educational opportunity. This solicitous attention to education, these social activists declared, was justified, for it, more than anything else in society, was an essential condition for securing natural right and ensuring the progress of mankind.

For all its appeal, however, this declaration was contested by a tradition going all the way back to early colonial days that schooling was very likely a personal or private, and not a public, responsibility.[18] Any quick review of this tradition would have told the reformers who essayed to make education their special cause that law could demand literacy and say nothing about schools, or it could encourage the establishment of town and district schools and be silent on support for them.

Buried deeply in the recesses of an attitude toward education was the assumption, sometimes (but seldom successfully) challenged, that government could exercise authority over education, yet this assumption was paralyzed by a precedent of inactivity that could be interpreted as having rescinded it. At the same time, there was the conviction, far from universal but nevertheless common, that whenever government intrudes upon the province of education, it exceeds its proper authority. To authorize a plan for public education capable of finding its way through this labyrinth of conflicting conviction required an expenditure of intelligence, persuasion, and effort almost without equal in American social history. And, as it turned out, help came suddenly from a most unlikely source when the Continental Congress inaugurated a land policy in the Northwest Ordinances of 1785 and 1787.

The Northwest Ordinances. Pursuant to the Articles of Confederation, states with title to land west of the Allegheny Mountains ceded it to the national government. Congress, in turn, authorized a survey of the Northwest Territory in the Ordinance of 1785, and in consequence of the survey, the territory was organized into townships. Townships were six miles square and, divided into sections one mile square, had thirty-six sections. Section sixteen of every township was reserved for the support of education. Such reservation was intended to withhold the section from private ownership and to use the income derived from it for education or, should it be sold, to use the proceeds for educational support.

Shortly after the enactment of the ordinance, Congress sold two immense tracts of land to settlement companies and, to ensure attention to the support of education in the Northwest Territory, granted to each company one township for the support of a college, section sixteen of every township for the support of schools, and section twenty-seven for the encouragement of religion. In 1802, when Ohio became a state, Congress granted to the state section sixteen of every township for school support.

As states were thereafter admitted to the Union until 1850, with the exception of Texas, Maine, and West Virginia, Congress designated every section sixteen as the school section. After 1850, beginning with the admission to statehood of California, the land grants became more extensive. California was given two sections of every township, and Arizona, New Mexico, and Nevada were given four sections of every township for the encouragement and support of education.

A national policy friendly to education is evident in the disposition of huge parts of the national domain, but this policy was in its infancy, and one should be diffident in asserting that the ordinances of 1785 and 1787 illustrate anything more than a brave beginning. The land granted to the states helped them to create permanent school funds to which the local districts could appeal for financial assistance, yet it is clear, too, that land was cheap and the policy evidencing friendship to education was inexpensive. But cynicism should give way to good sense: the policy was progressive and stood as a prominent reminder of education's compact with national aspiration. The vigorous language of the preamble to the Ordinance of 1787 stands as an eloquent reminder of this: "Religion, morality, and knowledge being necessary to good government and the happiness of mankind, schools and the means of education shall be forever encouraged" in the Northwest Territory.[19]

The State and Education. Precedent for federal and state action in education in the early years of the national period could not make much of a story, for state experience was too brief, and federal action in connection with land policy was easily misconstrued because land was plentiful. Colonial tradition had at least implied a collective educational responsibility, but these implications lacked the vigor to give direction to practice. Oratorical eloquence promoted an ambitious educational idealism that eventually paid a good dividend, and plans for a system of popular education were abundant, but social and political inertia turned out to be imposing obstacles to educational progress.

The Tenth Amendment to the Constitution ("The powers not delegated to the United States by the Constitution, nor prohibited by it to the States, are reserved to the States respectively, or to the people."), now interpreted as a commission to states to manage affairs of government not specifically reserved to the federal government—such as education—contained little in the way of educational incentive. It is unlikely that any of the framers of the Constitution had education in mind when they made this delegation of authority to the states; moreover, it is hard to believe that when the states adopted the first ten amendments, they were convinced that education was a matter being reserved to them.

Despite all the bold rhetoric proclaiming the import of educational decency *vis-à-vis* popular sovereignty, the lack of any direct reference to education in the country's basic legal document is a remarkable and, some might aver, an ominous oversight. One is left to conclude that the founding fathers, for all their prophetic intelligence, were satisfied with the educational status quo. They left responsibility for the country's schooling in the weak and unsteady hands of religion and philanthropy.

As the nation matured, the educational bandwagon began to gain speed, so it was not long before the states began to fill the vacuum the Constitution left, although they did so with some hesitation and equivocation. In 1800, only seven of sixteen states made constitutional reference to education, and among those that did, Massachusetts, Vermont, and New Hampshire were most precise.

Without making provision for public schooling, they nevertheless enlisted the states' good will in education's cause. They praised wisdom and virtue, declared knowledge essential to the preservation of right and liberty, and encouraged the generous distribution of educational opportunity. Finally, setting the compass on a course that all states were eventually to follow, they assigned to their respective legislatures responsibility for promoting schools of all kinds and learning in general. From such modest and uncompromising declarations came the more explicit and universal constitutional command to state legislature to establish and maintain systems of public education. But tailoring this command took time, and a command, when given, was often inaudible or unheeded.

Legislative action or inaction in connection with constitutional directive was both praised and blamed. In the face of doubt that any action the legislature might take relative to education was a legitimate exercise of state authority and not an invasion of parental right was bound to make legislatures timid. For the most part, they skirted this basic legal issue, allowed it to go unresolved, and tinkered instead with the safer matter of establishing a state structure for educational administration: commissioners of education, state boards of education, and commissioners of state school funds began to appear.

Political and legal principle were confused in these years on the point of authority, and although the states did something, they always stopped short of creating a genuine system of public education. Attention was riveted instead on instituting some mechanism for helping local communities with schools to support them. This, too, was a conundrum. In a long and honorable tradition of altruism whose roots were buried in Europe, the practice persisted of helping persons unable to help themselves. Public support for education could be interpreted as alms intended for the weak and indigent, and such interpretation stood in the way of the development of free public schools. Parents who could afford to educate their children refused to be stigmatized by having them attend public schools and, it might be added, resented being required to contribute their wealth for schooling children other than their own. Public education had to redress a tradition of pauperism that, although it sounds like fiction today, was nevertheless extant during the early decades of the nineteenth century.

Chapter 11

A Record of
Educational Accomplishment

By 1828, with the election of Andrew Jackson (1767–1845) as president of the United States, the political foundation for republican government was secure, and most states, having abandoned property tests, had provision for universal male suffrage. Proposing and debating theories of education was fodder for agile minds, but a determination of public policy by public opinion had become a political fact, and inattention or indifference to public education could no longer be countenanced. The engine to drive republican government needed fuel from a more dependable source than private, religious, and philanthropic educational effort, however dedicated and sincere. Prescient educational spokesmen began to lead a campaign for public control and support for education, and as it turned out, they succeeded in translating their progressive conviction into practice. This exercise in translation, however, proceeded at an unsteady pace: there were pockets of exceptional activity elsewhere matched by rude neglect.

Educational Leaders

The work of men who were in the vanguard of popular education is amply recorded on history's ledger, but to neglect the principal expositors of the common school movement here would be unpardonable. That what they urged upon the nation would have been achieved sometime is plausible conjecture, but it is no warrant for ignoring or discounting their achievement.

Horace Mann. In recounting this achievement, one can do no better than begin with Horace Mann (1796–1859). Located in Massachusetts, a state whose educational legacy provided a good springboard, Mann utilized every means at his disposal to convince the people to enlist in a crusade to ensure basic schooling for the children of the commonwealth.[1]

As a public officer, first as a member of the legislature and then as Secretary to the State Board of Education, Mann's zeal for the common school frequently led him into controversy from which he refused to shrink. Educational tradition in Massachusetts appeared to endorse a practice of leaving educational control largely in the hands of towns and school districts; this was a tradition that he had first to reverse. While a theory of state educational authority was embraced, few public officers wanted to expose themselves to the thorns in the thicket of local control and allowed the local communities to believe that educational authority was vested in them. But such autonomy, Mann declared, was myth, and it intimidated the application of a standard throughout the state for ensuring a decent education for responsible citizenship. He rejected what amounted to educational anarchy and proposed, instead, a state board of education capable of exercising genuine control.

To strip from local communities prerogatives that appeared to belong to them was unpopular, but more difficult was the matter of redefining the purpose of public education for citizenship rather than for religion. And any such redefinition unavoidably put Mann at loggerheads with persons who were convinced (and to a great extent their conviction had the support of tradition) that the school's curriculum should accommodate sectarian instruction. But such instruction, Mann said, could end up accomplishing only one thing: the destruction of the common school. The point is debatable but, very likely, Mann was right. At the same time, however, despite pronouncements of Mann's detractors to the contrary, his conviction that the Bible should be read without comment in the common schools, shows that he was never religion's enemy.[2] The Bible, he supposed, contained an essential foundation for moral education. Despite evident success in shaping the character of common-school education in Massachusetts, the road Mann chose to follow was rough and treacherous.

James Carter. Less well known, but hardly less effective, was James G. Carter (1795–1849), also in Massachusetts. His *Essays upon Popular Education*, published in 1826, was widely read and exceptionally influential in soliciting support for the improvement and popularization of schooling. His work riveted attention on common schools, what today are called "public elementary schools," and was instrumental in shaping a public attitude regarding the elementary school as the "university" of the common man.[3]

The educational platform he adopted was shared by many others, so if one wants to discern the distinctive contribution Carter made to the common-school movement, history's page should be turned to the education of American teachers, where Carter's figure looms large. He, more than anyone else at the time, saw the imperative need for improving instruction by introducing to the common schools a cadre of teachers skillful in pedagogic technique. Nothing so important as educating teachers for America's schools could be accomplished quickly or effortlessly, and Carter's investment began by paying only small dividends. Yet he deserves praise for having made a brave beginning in establishing state normal schools whose commitment was precise and clear: they were to prepare teachers for the common schools.

Uneven in quality, the normal schools that appeared as a result of Carter's zealous effort were seldom ornaments to scientific pedagogic technique and never substitutes for the conventional college, yet they literally swept the country in the second half of the nineteenth century. One is right to conclude that the modest but important accomplishment of the common school in educating America's children was due, in large part, to the better preparation for common-school teachers afforded in the normal-school experience.

Henry Barnard and Others. Evidence supports the conclusion that common-school activity was intense in Massachusetts, but elsewhere, too, prominent riders could be found on its bandwagon. Henry Barnard (1811–1900), a scholar, administrator, and, in 1867, the first United States Commissioner of Education, left a permanent record of accomplishment in the thirty-two volume *American Journal of Education*. His mark on the common school was made in Rhode Island. In North Carolina, Calvin Wiley (1819–1887), and in Indiana, Caleb Mills (1806– 1879) were leaders in the common-school crusade; their industry, along with that of hundreds of others, advanced the prospect for the common school.

The Common School

This prospect, however, depended to a great extent upon the further development of state educational control and support. The states had tinkered with educational control and had assumed that it belonged to their province of authority, but at the same time, they hesitated to cultivate it. An integral part of the common-school crusade was to rescue this dormant state commission and to stimulate the states to take action with respect to state boards or commissions of education, superintendents of public instruction, regulations governing the qualifications of teachers, and definitions of a legal school curriculum.

A Policy of Nonsectarianism. For the most part, this rescue mission succeeded, and spurred on by crusaders and the public alike, state educational policy with respect to control began to mature. Perhaps all elements of control were hard to realize, for the local communities had for so long been in the habit of taking their own direction in matters of education, but the one element that created the greatest and most acrimonious controversy was sectarian teaching in the schools.

We know enough about the place religion occupied in early American education; we know, too, how much influence religious sects had in determining the content of instruction. Promoters of the common-school movement were too often branded as antireligious and sometimes were charged with repudiating the moral fiber of American society when they declared that sectarian common schools could not thrive in a nineteenth-century climate.

Interpretation varies among sober scholars, but educational leaders who adopted a stance of nonsectarianism were very likely right. The common school could not have survived had it been burdened with the weight of teaching sectarian religion in a society fast becoming denominationally heterogeneous. At the end of a long and bitter debate over the status of public education, the common school became officially nonsectarian, although it should be noted that, in most states, bible reading continued either as a permitted or required exercise.[4]

Financial Support for Education. In spite of an abundance of regulation and legislation relative to state educational control, control alone, and especially in the absence of public support, was unable to erect a system of public education in any state. Now the scene of battle shifted, and again, educational leaders were required to demonstrate their stamina and talent for molding public opinion. Rate bills, a form of tuition in most public schools of the early nineteenth century, defrayed part of the cost of instruction and sometimes paid other bills as well. And pauper schools, which we have met before, were evident in many parts of the country. So long as pauper schools survived, citizens shied away from publicly supported schools and the genuine public school marked time. Finally, the most intransigent attitude of all had to be amended: Why should one person be taxed to pay for the education of another person's child? The argument forwarded by educational leaders, one eventually endorsed throughout the nation, was that tax support was alone capable of maintaining a system of common schools adequate to the scholastic need of nineteenth-century America. This position, although taken for granted now, was adopted slowly and cautiously.

As public education—illustrated best in the common school—gained ground, active opposition to it relaxed: tax support was grudgingly accepted, permissive laws were enacted allowing local communities some latitude in ways to support their schools; pauper schools were abandoned; and rate bills, although still employed, in New York, for example, as late as 1867, lost favor. Along the same line, state control, while not greeted enthusiastically, was accepted without sharp complaint and a state educational bureaucracy began to articulate and enforce educational standard.

Progress in the Schools

Despite evident gain, the pace of progress for state educational control and support was slow, and the translation of gain to the level of school practice was slower still. Common schools appeared in the 1830s; thirty years later, all states had some kind of public school system. Yet in none was the percentage of youth attending common schools much higher than in 1830, and few schools had earned enviable reputations for providing good instruction. At the same time, probably because of the energy directed at promoting common schools, upward extension of scholastic opportunity was seriously neglected.

The academy, likely an invention of Benjamin Franklin, was in place and more often than not superseded the high school, an indigenous American school unit, that appeared about 1821. Educational disappointment could be stated for every part of the nation, and differences in educational commitment on a regional basis were hard, if not impossible, to discern. Even where schoolhouse doors were open to students, few students were disposed to enter. Those who did enter attended irregularly. This erratic picture was redressed somewhat with the enactment of a compulsory school attendance law in Massachusetts in 1852, but sixty-two years passed before all of the first forty-eight states enacted such statutes.

The educational picture, however, was not entirely bleak. The colonial town school, which appears to have been a prototype for the common school, had an abbreviated and rudimentary curriculum, a dearth of instructional material, a group of students classified neither by age nor grade, and a teacher whose credentials were more often than not defective. The shortcomings of this model soon became obvious, so as part of the common-school crusade, determined effort was made to lengthen the school course, add substance to its rudimentary character, encourage the production of textbooks accommodated to pedagogic technique,[5] and redress the academic chaos illustrative of ungraded and unclassified students by introducing the graded elementary school. By 1848, Quincy, Massachusetts, could boast of a graded eight-year elementary school, and with it, one could maintain, the common school graduated from its formative stage. Graded instruction became the standard of elementary schooling, although the number of grades varied from eight in the North to seven in the West and nine in the South.

In the three decades before the Civil War, the educational thrust was clearly in the direction of elementary schooling; this thrust was justified on the basis that elementary schooling was an essential condition for democratic government. Energy and expenditure were preoccupied with what was called "public education," but few persons were ready to broaden the definition of public education beyond elementary instruction. In consequence of this restrictive definition, students who aspired to secondary and higher learning had to satisfy their ambition in private academies and colleges. But in America, the thirst for education was hard to quench, so signs that the definition of public education might be applied to secondary schools and colleges began to appear. At first indistinct, they soon became clearer.

Secondary Education. In 1821, the Boston English Classical School, sometimes credited with having been the first American high school, was established to offer young men a kind of practical schooling that neither Latin schools nor academies were disposed to sponsor. Shortly thereafter, other cities and towns the country over began to open high schools; when they did, it is hard to believe they were imitating the Boston school. They had, rather, their own local educational situation in mind and were cultivating their own interest.

What, more than anything else, dominated the high-school movement was the conviction that the country's educational need could not be fulfilled by common-school education alone and that the opportunity for secondary education, restricted as it was mainly to private effort, had to be liberalized if the nation were to fulfill its political, economic, and social promise. At the same time, one should not miss an American disposition to achieve practical objectives which, some educational spokesmen began to say, could not be met in the conventional secondary-school curriculum.

Scholars have been in the habit of calling the American high school an accident of history, but they would be on safer ground in looking for its origin in an interpretation of the doctrine of utility that was becoming equivocal about the worth of a classical curriculum. The question asked so often before was asked again: What knowledge is of most worth? Expositors for the high school were ready to play their trump card, and the trademark of practical schooling was stamped all over it.

Secondary Education for Women. This philosophy of secondary education was avant-garde when it recited the educational outcomes that society needed but could nowhere be found in the prospectuses of Latin schools and academies. Yet despite progressive elements, secondary education heeded a tradition that paid almost no attention to the scholastic appetite of women. It is true, of course, that normal schools had redressed what could be called educational discrimination against women when they encouraged young women to matriculate, but one would have to be extraordinarily myopic not to see that the normal-school course had neither the academic status nor stature to qualify as genuine secondary education.

It took almost another half-century before post-elementary instruction for women was perceived as important enough to promote, and then it was not in the new high schools where this perception was allowed to mature, but in special schools where vocational curricula appealing to women were offered. The first among these special schools was opened under the auspices of the Women's Educational and Industrial Union in 1877. With a membership of thirteen and $185 in its treasury, this Boston union undertook to apprise the public of women's need to be prepared to work outside the home. It sought to provide a model by introducing professional curricula to its school where women could be instructed in nursing and teaching, but its main impact was on a lower educational level: in a curriculum of dressmaking and homemaking.

This early illustration of vocational education for women was duplicated the country over and, no doubt, paid good dividends, but however optimistically one reads the history of secondary education for women in the United States, the conclusion is inevitable: all this effort produced an effect that was always in the rearguard of activity directed at the high school education of boys. And, it must be admitted, the schools for women that could trace their genesis to a vocational consciousness were secondary only in a most general sense, and never matched the instruction offered in Latin schools and academies or, for that matter, in the high schools whose primary clientele was male.

The American High School. Whether women were included or excluded from secondary education, the high school gained support. One might be tempted, in fact be well advised, to discount some of the myths surrounding high-school origin, but the record of history is clear on some points. The states began, first in Massachusetts in 1827 and later in other states, to make high schools a legitimate part of public education. They did not always perceive the dangerous legal ground they were treading.

Boston chose to remake its high school along lines distinct from its Latin school, but this was a practice seldom followed elsewhere. The high schools that came into existence as a result of state legislation endeavored to be more comprehensive. Most local communities could not afford two types of secondary education—one for the classical course and another for the English course—so they tried to meld the two. Successful or not with such an audacious instructional experiment, the high school movement gained momentum.

The Massachusetts High School Act of 1827 directed towns with five hundred or more families to conduct schools to teach the common branches: history, bookkeeping, geometry, surveying, and algebra. Towns with four thousand or more inhabitants were required to have teachers capable of teaching Latin, Greek, history, rhetoric, and logic. The author of this act, James Carter, was trying to strike a balance between a practical and a classical course, but such a balance was hard to obtain, and further legislative action became necessary. Almost certainly, considering the traditional affinity of the classics with secondary education, practical curricula were choked in such a compromise.

Either following the lead of states like Massachusetts, New York, and Michigan, or acting entirely on their own, states, one after another, began to make provision for high schools. In many cases the legislative enactments for high schools had a permissive character: school districts were authorized to establish high schools if they wanted to.

The high schools that came into existence, however, did not have the full certification of public institutions, and the public responsibility owed to them was far from clear. They began, nevertheless, to exhibit a slow but steady growth. Whether one looks to the high school of the East, the South, or the West, it tried to offer vocational and practical English study alongside or, in some melding, with the traditional classical course. Progress was made, but what kind of a school was being promoted? And some communities, well ahead of the time, opened these new high schools to women. One has the impression that a good deal of satisfaction was felt among the American people with all the progress that had been made in educational opportunity. Still, few, even among the most optimistic, would have predicted, say, in 1860, that high schools as they were known then would become a standard for American secondary education, that they would experience much success in overtaking academies and Latin schools, or that they would ever become real public institutions.

Progress in the Colleges

During this period of educational ferment, attention was given first to the common school and then to the high school. Somewhat out of sight (because so few persons attended it) but not forgotten was the college. And now, because the American appetite for education was great, the public college began to be noticed in novel ways.

Georgia, North Carolina, and Vermont, early in the century, were in the vanguard of public higher education, but the universities created in these states, and in the states that followed their example—say, Virginia in 1825—were for a long time destined to take a back seat to the private colleges dominating the higher educational landscape. A plausible argument can be made attributing to the Dartmouth College decision a leading role in the cultivation of state colleges, but repeating the argument adds nothing to its weight.[6]

Yet even adopting the proposition that the Dartmouth College decision abetted the state-college movement, it is evident that the public attitude was comfortable with a familiar road to higher learning. Evident, too, is the fact that the battle to extend public higher education was fought principally on other fronts. The relationship between civil government and common-school instruction was amply demonstrated by 1850, but no such demonstration had been made, or could have been predicted with confidence, in connection with higher education. So in the last analysis, the growth of public higher education must be attributed to a perception that such schools could do some good in expanding the boundaries of knowledge and, at the same time, contribute to the general welfare. But how were these objectives to be translated into college purpose? On this point, and for a long time, the colleges were remiss. If private colleges in which the public seemed to have so much confidence were still preserves for an elite, if they catered still to a traditional, polite learning for a gentleman, could one realistically expect public colleges to be much different? It was hard to be optimistic, although change was evident, but change was never so dramatic or rapid as to warrant crediting nineteenth-century colleges as trail blazers in reconstituting higher learning.

Change was propelled from an expected source. In an era ready to put confidence in the utility of knowledge (a lesson taught early by Bacon's *Advancement of Learning* and learned well), the colleges, never immune to the expectation of the society surrounding them, were literally forced to discount their traditional preoccupation with the training of ministers and the instruction of gentlemen. Without really wanting to, they began to heed persistent social and economic voices telling them to introduce professional, technical, and scientific curricula to their programs of study. In the end, although always with some sign of reluctance and a conviction that something of worth was being discounted, they abandoned culture and began to invest in use.

Because they were closer to the people and thus better able to assay their hunger for practical knowledge, the state colleges were always at the forefront of curricular expansion. While unready to jettison academic convention, public higher education was tempted to amend it, and it was at these amendments that the framers of the Yale Report directed their rhetorical barrage.[7] They said the college way of life was in jeopardy and that the course of study, for so long containing what most educated persons acknowledged to be true, was being eroded and fragmented.

The Report was a statement of higher-education philosophy and a plea for the retention of decent learning and dependable academic standard. It declared that the colleges should reject the temptation to become practical and vocational institutes and should cling to a traditional commitment to cultivate, discipline, and strengthen the power of the mind. No curricular avenue, the writers declared with zeal, could do this better than the traditional one.

As it turned out, a majority of college leaders applauded the Report and endorsed its findings. They might have been sincere and honest in their appraisal of it, but the weight of social pragmatism was too heavy to resist. The colleges ignored the Report's most fundamental recommendations, and by 1850, it was hardly more than an interesting document tucked away in the archives.

In the wake of the Report there appeared the kind of realignment of educational purpose that it had condemned. Institutes, schools, and departments began to promote a "new learning," and the most prominent among them were Rensselaer Polytechnic Institute (1824), the Sheffield Scientific School at Yale (1846), the Lawrence Scientific School at Harvard (1847), and the Chandler Scientific School at Dartmouth (1851). But they were not alone. Agricultural, industrial, mining, and engineering schools and departments made their appearance in colleges and universities all across the country. American higher learning was ready to shed its old ways, and by the end of the fifth decade of the century, public colleges evidenced a determination to become associated with the economic and industrial prospects in American society. The untroubled waters of academic solitude were no longer attractive. Colleges wanted to be part of what they perceived to be real life.

Higher Education for Women. This effort on the part of public and private colleges to offer what the public wanted should not be interpreted as a sign of boldness. In any case, boldness was uncharacteristic of early nineteenth-century American higher education, except in one area where some were truly daring: coeducation.

In 1833, Oberlin College in Ohio admitted women to the full college course and held out to them the prospect of earning a bachelor's degree.[8] This brave experiment signaled the beginning of something new, and however little progress was made in the conventional private college, coeducation progressed by leaps and bounds in the state colleges. State universities—Michigan and Indiana, for example—and almost all state colleges established after 1850 opened their doors to women on an equal basis with men.[9]

What was done in public higher education, allowing women access to the higher learning, gave schools for women some confidence that they, too, could transform themselves into respectable colleges. Private schools for women had been in the habit of offering a kind of polite education that they thought was suited to women. Although they were temperamentally opposed to becoming coeducational institutions, the examples around them of colleges admitting and educating women on the same basis as men prompted infant women's colleges to upgrade their programs of study and henceforth comport themselves as genuine colleges. This was never an easy undertaking to manage, because there was a residue of opinion maintaining that the education of a woman should be fundamentally different from the education of a man. Almost as often as not, colleges for women succumbed to this opinion and, at the same time, tried their best to belong to the same league of higher learning as colleges for men. Not until myth relative to female education was exposed could colleges for women begin to establish themselves as genuine intellectual centers.

By 1900, nearly eighty-five thousand women were enrolled in postsecondary institutions. They made up about a quarter of all students attending regular colleges and an estimated forty percent of the total student population, if normal schools are included.[10]

The Land-Grant College Act. The great impetus for the development of public higher education, however, is to be found neither in a theory of utility, in a new approach to the education of women, nor in some revelation with respect to the obligation a democratic society has to the refinement of its citizens, but in federal action. The Land-Grant College Act of 1862 offered the states financial means and motive to engage in the establishment of public colleges. According to the act's provision, any state opening a school of agriculture and mechanical art, including, if it chose, the liberal arts and sciences, could qualify for a land grant equal to the representation the state had in Congress: thirty thousand acres for each senator and representative. With proceeds from the sale or use of the land, state legislatures either established new colleges or assigned the revenue from the land grant to existing colleges.

Federal stimulation was the great boon for public higher education, and it allowed these new colleges or new departments in old schools to concentrate upon technical, vocational, scientific, and professional curricula. With its enactment and the states' response to the land-grant act, American higher education began to wear a new face. Looking for the principal force generating public higher education in the United States, preoccupation with the Dartmouth College decision should be abandoned and, instead, attention should be paid to the Land-Grant College Act.[11]

The Education of Teachers

Despite their articulation of academic principle to which they only infrequently paid heed, and despite, too, their tendency to tinker with practical education, the colleges missed one area where educational need was pressing: the education of teachers. Colleges proved their response to social need could be selective. But to heap all the criticism on them for what can be called nonfeasance might, in the end, be unfair. The colleges would likely have instituted programs for the education of teachers had their students wanted them. But throughout most of the nineteenth century, a college clientele, whatever other vocational aspiration it might have had, was indifferent to the pedagogical need of the common school. If common-school teachers were to be given a professional preparation for their work, it would have to be obtained outside the gates of the regular colleges. And in this respect, the record of public and private colleges is alike.

A good omen for common-school teachers' preparation is evident in Samuel Hall's private normal school in Vermont. Hall's school, opened early in the 1820s, illustrated how teachers could be fitted to fulfill their pedagogical role in a quick and inexpensive way. In consequence of this pioneer work, hundreds of schools modelled after Hall's appeared throughout the nation, although it would be exaggeration to assert that Hall's model contained the full pedagogical charter for the public normal schools that appeared in the fourth decade of the nineteenth century. What can be called the prototype for the public normal school, a school opened in Lexington, Massachusetts, in 1839, was the result of James Carter's dedicated effort to improve instruction in the common schools.[12] Before the end of the century, every state had public normal schools and common-school teachers were expected to have attended them.[13]

Normal schools were good enough for preparing elementary-school teachers, but the high schools needed teachers, too, and where were they to be prepared? Now the record of the colleges becomes somewhat better, though hardly ornamental.

For a long time, the academies had engaged in a kind of teacher preparation, and it was generally assumed that an academy graduate could handle the instructional responsibilities of high-school teaching. But as the high schools began to depart from their original purpose—that is, a kind of practical English education—and become more and more preparatory schools for college, a more intensive classical education than the academies could offer became essential. Here, without any precise commitment to the education of high-school teachers and almost by accident, the colleges began to play a larger role. Some of their graduates might decide to enter the teaching ranks. But this was not good enough, and before the end of the century, the teachers college came into existence. Going beyond the normal school and incorporating into its syllabus everything that the science of education had to offer, it essayed to prepare teachers for both elementary and high schools.

Educational Theory

Our ancestors liked to think themselves prudent and wise, and so they were, but they were not well schooled in philosophy and, except for logic, which was recognized as a useful and necessary intellectual instrument, chose to disregard it. They could afford to be unphilosophical because they had, they believed, a reservoir of truth in theology. But as time passed and as the theological citadel was assaulted by dispute and defection, philosophy was resorted to as a unifying discipline capable of supplying coherence and meaning in a world that, without it, would have been chaotic. An attitude of cordiality toward philosophy became evident in the early years of the nineteenth century, due largely to the missionary work carried on by a cadre of American philosophers calling themselves Transcendentalists.

Transcendentalism. Transcendentalists essayed to substitute philosophy's emphasis upon reason, scientific method, and immutable laws of nature with a doctrine wherein human nature was recognized as the primary source of motive and behavior. Their essentially spiritual vision of human nature put it in harmony with a universal spirit, sometimes called God. Human spirit transcends the body and all material reality: thus the name, Transcendentalism.

Such a definition contained paradoxical elements illustrated by a disposition among Transcendentalists to ignore nature and its laws as objects for study and, indifferent to the scientific method, to be obsessed with nature and invest it with spiritual character. Its cordial assessment of God and an outright rejection of materialism put Transcendentalism in a friendly relationship with orthodox sectarians, but in the declaration that God was oversoul and impersonal, much of this good will evaporated. And to make the Transcendental relationship with orthodox theology even more unsteady, the authority of the Bible was abandoned.

Looking back, one can see signs that Transcendentalism's chance to enter the mainstream of American philosophy was slight. Its foremost scholars, good and capable men—Theodore Parker, James Marsh, Caleb Sprague Henry, and Ralph Waldo Emerson—had admirable ideals and high aspirations; its theories were tolerantly nonsectarian without being antireligious; and it could appeal to the intellect without being a secular philosophy or a brand of theological rationalism. But if these were its strengths, they were never quite good enough to outweigh a stubborn neglect of a scientific method that could produce positive knowledge. In the end, Transcendentalism gave way to a more vigorous idealism.

Idealism. Philosophical idealism was filled with implications for social uplift and for the development of an American social order wherein the best capacity of men and women could be given a fair chance for realization. Flying a banner of optimism, idealism fell heir to the position religion had in former years occupied in supplying direction for grappling with the human condition. Besides, because idealism could speak directly about the fundamentals of education, it became, and during most of the nineteenth century remained, the guiding force behind American education; one must admit, though, that its practitioners tended to remain aloof from practical issues of schooling.

A principal exception was William T. Harris (1835–1909), whose career illustrates a melding of philosophical scholarship and educational leadership.[14] Others, too, always in sufficient number to make a difference and with good talent, promoted a philosophical cause they thought noble. Some among them invested their philosophical talent in education, and with them the discipline of educational philosophy was revived in many of the nation's leading colleges and universities.

Realism. While Transcendentalists and idealists pondered the mystery of human spirit and its relationship to a divine essence, another philosophical system with historical and intellectual credentials equal to idealism's began to assert itself: realism. Realism's main appeal was its affirmation of material and spiritual reality. Employing dependable methods of investigation and submitting what is discovered to the arbitrament of reason, dependable knowledge about reality can be attained: Mystery abounds but is never completely unfathomable. What realists found unacceptable and unreasonable was a dependence upon intuition for revealing meaning and truth about nature, man, and society.

Realism could subscribe to a dualistic philosophy of human nature, thus leaving intact traditional religious commitment, but it could, as in the case of the evolutionary hypothesis sometimes grafted to it, turn toward materialistic monism and define human beings as products of the evolutionary process, more complicated than other forms of matter but not essentially different from them.

Idealism could be friendly to a kind of evolution where, acknowledging the spiritual character of human nature and an association with the Absolute, human beings could fulfill the promise of their capacity, but this was not the kind of evolution that made its appearance with the publication, in 1859, of Charles Darwin's (1809–1882) *Origin of Species* and, in 1871, *The Descent of Man.* Had it not been for an embrace of the theory of evolution, introduced now in a systematic and scientific way, realism might have become America's philosophy, because it conformed so closely to what most educated Americans already assumed to be true.

Toward Popular Education

Taking into account such phenomena as urbanization, industrialization, immigration, and the translation of biological Darwinism into social Darwinism, the monumental task facing American schools can be sensed. History's record shows that it took an abundance of educational wisdom, and some luck, for America to accommodate to a new social face; and it took even greater wisdom, and more luck, for American education to play an effective role in reconstructing the social order and bring to heel the rugged individualism that had become a hallmark of economic policy and practice. At this point in the country's development, educational leaders riveted attention, not on reconstructing the social order, but on expanding and organizing schools and making an educational program, assessed to be satisfactory, available to a larger number of the nation's youth.

Compulsory Attendance. Now law was called upon to help in the achievement of a social good. Compulsory attendance statutes had their inception in 1852 in Massachusetts, and a pattern of adoption was illustrated by other states. But not without some intransigent opposition. Thundering against compulsory attendance law came from persons who harbored the sincere conviction that parental right was being put in jeopardy; from those who argued from the position of natural right: that a person should be free to elect ignorance; from the studied rejection of the principle that public money could be used for the support of schools; and from teachers who, surprisingly enough, were disposed to take the position that instruction would become more difficult when children who lacked ability or interest were required by law to attend school.[15]

In the end, however, despite the relentless battle waged by opponents of public education, and especially compulsory attendance, in and out of state courts, the policy of compulsory attendance gained social, political, and legal sanction. From 1865 to 1920, forty-six states enacted compulsory attendance laws, but the tardiness of state action (Massachusetts and New York having enacted such statutes in 1852 and 1853, respectively) must in part, at least, be attributed to social and political unrest preceding, accompanying, and following the Civil War rather than to the strength of the opposition to an extension of opportunity for schooling.[16]

Broadening Elementary Education. Confident that public policy was on its side, nineteenth-century elementary education began to extend its horizon. First, its regular course was lengthened to the point where the eight-grade elementary school became an American standard, and then in a downward extension, the kindergarten was grafted to it. Despite the appearance and, in some places, the modest popularity of kindergartens, their standing as regular parts of public education was achieved slowly, cautiously, and somewhat erratically before the advent of the twentieth century.[17]

As elementary education the country over became more energetic, and as kindergartens began to capture the fancy of educators, private elementary schools received renewed and somewhat unexpected attention from religious denominations. Commitment to educational decency accompanied religious scholastic effort, but it was not uppermost in the minds of advocates for private, religiously-related schools. The success of the common school depended extensively upon the elimination of sectarianism from its syllabus, and it was the abandonment of religious instruction that troubled educators who associated themselves with private, religious schools.

In order to safeguard the foundations of faith, many religious denominations undertook to establish elementary schools of their own, declaring them essential to political and religious freedom. Operating from this platform of conviction, the establishment of Catholic parochial schools became a matter of Church policy, and over the succeeding seventy-five years matured into the largest private school system in the country.[18]

Public elementary schools had come of age, but it was becoming obvious that the regimen of learning in them was insufficient to prepare citizens for a role in society that was far more complex than the fathers of the common schools could ever have imagined. It was this very complexity that put a heavier burden on the schools and recommended a further extension of educational opportunity.

Maturation of Secondary Education. Secondary education, for so long in the hands of the academies and private preparatory schools, began to have an appeal that could hardly have been forecast a quarter of a century earlier. The constitutional provision in most states usually obliged the legislature to establish and maintain a system of public education, and for a long time it was convenient to interpret the phrase "public education" as elementary-school instruction. But now some state legislatures began to give the phrase a broader interpretation. They enacted permissive legislation authorizing school districts to open and support high schools, and this, some persons alleged, was an impermissible and unconstitutional interpretation of the phrase "public education" which, they argued, meant elementary, not secondary, instruction.

The future of the American high school was determined in the court-room. The precedent-setting case had its origin in Kalamazoo, Michigan, in 1872. In 1874, Michigan's supreme court rendered a verdict wherein the meaning of "public education" was declared to be a system of schools beginning with the elementary level and extending all the way through the state university.

Report of the Committee of Ten. With the legal status of the high schools settled,[19] another, perhaps even more important, question was asked in connection with high schools: What should be their purpose? Should they concentrate on the traditional objective of secondary education and prepare students for college, or should some other legitimate purpose be assigned to them? While the Committee of Ten, appointed by the National Education Association in 1892, was not specifically commissioned to answer this question, as things turned out, it did.

The *Report of the Committee of Ten* (1893) supported a conventional secondary-school curriculum for all high schools, but played down its college preparatory function in favor of preparation for life.[20] With this commission in their portfolio, American high schools entered the mainstream of popular education.

The American University

With an eight-year elementary school and a four-year high school, the paradigm for American education appeared to be complete. But educators were not satisfied. They recommended the introduction of a junior high school and later, largely because of what was occurring in the new American university, proposed a junior college.[21]

Earlier, however, in 1862, the Land-Grant Act had generated activity throughout the country to create public colleges or universities. The state college, by no means a novel phenomenon, could, its proponents alleged, alter the direction of conventional higher learning. And this, they declared with a good deal of confidence, was exactly what was needed. The old college, with its commitment to the classical course, or even amendment to that course, despite the protest to amendment in the Yale Report, spoke to an age that had passed. What society needed, it was said, was a kind of higher education that could engage professional and practical study and, in addition, make a genuine commitment to research, scholarship, and specialization.

Land grant colleges could carry most of the load for practical education, but professional and scholarly objectives, now thought to be characteristic of genuine universities, were cultivated first in private institutions. Although the college community, presidents and professors alike, was well represented in this effort to alter the character of American higher education, the leader was Daniel Coit Gilman (1831–1908), president of Johns Hopkins University. Founded in 1876, Johns Hopkins was America's first genuine university.[22]

Electivism. Some schools of higher learning persisted in their traditional way and catered to undergraduates, but most American colleges at the outset of the age of the university set their sights on achieving some level of university status. A few private and public colleges became effective and ornamental universities. But even they were not absolved from academic strife and from the pain of institutional growth. Among the many novel issues plaguing them, the most notorious was electivism.

About the time Johns Hopkins was establishing itself as a university prototype, Harvard, led by its often controversial but always energetic president, Charles W. Eliot (1834–1926), introduced curricular reform. Basic to this reform was the conviction, most articulately expressed by Eliot, that a university should be concerned with universal knowledge.[23] All knowledge, not just so called liberal learning, should be the business of the university, and students and scholars alike should be free to pursue the special objects of their study and research.

This unfamiliar tune—electivism—was played first at Harvard, but before long it became an informal or formal concert in most American colleges. No longer was there only one lyric reciting the pedigree of the bachelor's degree or one clear melody accompanying the question, What knowledge is of most worth? The traditional thesis that higher learning should be welded with a common bond of cultural knowledge and value was victimized by electivism. Never again would American colleges exhibit a common curricular face.

However much college presidents and professors debated the direction of curriculum, they were not, it must be conceded, asking the burning educational question of the day. Other questions pressed for attention and resolution. Federal activity was increased with the creation of the Department of Education in 1867. Although the department was mainly a clearinghouse for information during its early years, its first commissioner, Henry Barnard, had the standing to make the department consequential. Still, federal activity in education could not then be an educational preoccupation. Educators riveted attention on something else.

The Science of Education

Conceding a traditional reverence for learning, the American people were disposed to invest confidence in the schools they supported and the teachers they employed. One could argue that this confidence was misplaced; teachers, often uneasy and fretful about the vacuum in dependable pedagogical knowledge, might not have disagreed. In any case, they were ready and eager to embrace a science of education if one could be erected. By then, plenty of illustrations were extant of science speaking directly to social issues. Could science speak to education too?

The litany of activity and accomplishment *vis-à-vis* scientific pedagogy is long, and a full recitation is not necessary to make the point: Education as a discipline, a subject fit for scholarship and study, made its tardy appearance first, as we have seen, in normal schools, then in teachers colleges, and finally in colleges and universities.

Over the centuries, education had commanded the attention of good minds, although as an academic subject for special study with a stature recommending it as a discipline in its own right, it played second fiddle to philosophy, politics, and psychology. So long as education lacked credentials of a genuine science and an academic discipline, an independent scholastic record was hard to make.

The first step on education's long road to academic respectability lay in the ability of its proponents to demonstrate that it was worthy of collaborating with traditional disciplines in the syllabus of higher learning. The universities where this infant discipline of education was promoted should not be credited with having had a special wisdom, for they benefited from the accident of having certain scholars on their faculties who, with an almost missionary zeal, engaged in teaching and research and, with unrelenting enthusiasm, preached the gospel of education as a science. These schools—Teachers College, Columbia University; the University of Chicago; and Stanford University—gained the reputation for being oases from which pedagogic knowledge flowed, but they soon had imitators. Public and private colleges alike fell in step and began to introduce academic programs for the preparation of teachers.

Educational Standard and Control

Despite all this ferment, one battle was left to be fought: How much control could states exercise over education? School surveys had become almost a way of educational life, and while not exercising control directly over the schools, they introduced elements of standardization that were justified by educational experts. Regional accrediting associations appeared, too, and, though always falling short of exercising control, exerted enormous influence over the quality and character of schools of all kinds. Beginning in 1885, with the formation of the New England Association of Colleges and Preparatory Schools, regional accrediting associations covered the entire country by 1918.[24] But the kind of control that had real muscle came from the state, and by now all interpretations of public educational policy justified this stance. But were there any limits to state educational control?

Worried about the growth of private schools and implying that somehow private schools paid less allegiance to the common good than public schools, various groups throughout the country began to inveigh against nonpublic education. It was charged with being undemocratic.

The matter came to a head in the famous Oregon law, passed in 1922 by initiative action, that required all "normal" children of compulsory attendance age to obtain their instruction in public schools.[25] The law was challenged under the property provision of the Fourteenth Amendment and was declared unconstitutional by the United States Supreme Court in 1925. Although the court acknowledged the states' general and legitimate authority to control education within their borders, its judicial interpretation withheld from them the authority to require parents to send their children only to public schools.[26]

Along the same line, although a few years earlier, Nebraska and nine other states passed laws prohibiting the teaching of languages other than English in public and private elementary schools. The legal issue was joined in Nebraska in 1919, when a teacher in a Lutheran parochial school taught German to his students. He was arrested and punished according to the statute. On appeal in 1923, the law was declared unconstitutional, because it deprived a citizen of the right to pursue a lawful occupation under the liberty provision of the Fourteenth Amendment, and the teacher was absolved.[27] In consequence of constitutional protection, private schools were secure in their legal right to exist, and parents could choose schools for their children to attend and select the subjects they should study. The court, however, was careful to maintain states' authority to set curricular standards consistent with the common good.

Chapter 12

Educational Purpose in a Democratic Society

From colonial days to the end of the Civil War, American temperament and character reflected the anthropology of rural experience. The country and the people changed in the decades following the war, but schools and colleges, although playing a role in moderating change, were not responsible for introducing it. By the advent of the twentieth century, a perception of the meaning of the good life, although not ignoring totally rural value and temperament, was shaped by new aspirations hammered out in a society fast reacting to realities imposed by urbanization, industrialization, and a slow but steady settlement of the vast region west of the Mississippi River to the Pacific Ocean. American society began to wear a new face. Yet amid amendment to perspective and ideal, growth was accompanied by the blight of ignorance, poverty, inequality, and avarice. A democratic society, a haven for the common man's hope, deserved praise for its accomplishments, but sensitive social and educational philosophers saw unfulfilled much of the prophecy it implied. For perhaps the first time, schools were recruited to participate as partners in a work of social reconstruction.

Schools and Society

World War I, an unsettling experience for Americans who recognized a shrinking political world and perceived fault in the old declaration eschewing entangling alliances with Europe, was hardly more than an interruption in the progressive political and economic policies proclaimed by President Woodrow Wilson (1856–1924). Almost without realizing what was happening, educators were swept along with a progressive tide. The faith citizens had in their country and an implicit belief in its promise was translated to education.

Those who call education "America's secular creed" might be right; if

285

they are, the creed was learned and recited by educators and citizens alike. The confidence invested in education, even supposing it to be a panacea, would have bewildered their American and European fore-bears.[1] It could, they imagined, remove social blight, improve economic station, and provide for upward social mobility. Contemporary critics are disposed to declare them either wrong or excessively optimistic, but history contains enough lessons to demonstrate the extraordinary power of education. It might not have remade American society along idealistic lines, but it was responsible for shaping the direction of millions of lives. The time might come when luck was the main ingredient for success, but during the early years of the twentieth century, both native born and naturalized Americans counted on schooling as a way of bettering themselves and their children.[2]

America's faith in education, some scholars allege, was misplaced: rather than freeing both native-born citizens and those who since the late years of the nineteenth century had been landing on the shores of this good land prepared to face the uncertainties of the future, conventional education molded them to suit the expectation of a dominant social class. Advanced under the guise of an unmitigated social good, it was an education for servitude, not freedom. The relationship of social theory to educational practice, and the validity of a thesis defining American education as repressive rather than progressive, is worth assessing, but it cannot be done here.[3] What can be done is to recount the principal educational steps taken in the early years of the twentieth century to ensure education's contribution to the shaping of a society wherein men and women might succeed in their quest for the good life.

By the first decade of the twentieth century, all the rungs for the American educational ladder were in place. And while high schools and colleges were far from being popular institutions, they attracted a larger and larger clientele. Still, the majority of educational attention was given to the elementary school, where most children of compulsory attendance age were expected to be. Was their time in school well spent? Were they prepared to meet life in American society?

Progressive Education. A full recitation of progressive education's allegations against traditional schooling is unnecessary to illustrate its response to these questions. Schools and the pedagogy employed in them were hauled up for indictment and, for the most part, found guilty of conducting children through an ineffective or defective educational experience. The shift progressive educators promoted was from the subject-centered school, where children were expected to master a specific body of knowledge and skill, to the child-centered school, where the curriculum was shaped by the child's experience and interest. Progressive educators were idealistic, humanitarian, and optimistic. They aspired to the realization of a better society, and education, they predicted, could lead the way.

Reviewing pronouncements of leading progressive educators, or reading Lawrence Cremin's *The Transformation of the School: Progressivism in American Education, 1876–1957*,[4] leaves one with the impression that neither progressive educators nor the methods they promoted were inspired by an evil or conscious anti-intellectual motive. More likely, excessive optimism led the theory's expositors to misread the compass on the nature of learning, the preservation of culture, and the structure of society, and this led in turn to a neglect of an important question that progressivism's opponents, along with intelligent outsiders, began to ask: How can schools whose attention is riveted entirely on the subjective desire of pupils handle a common core of basic knowledge essential to life in society? Without a common intellectual ground as a meeting place for minds, communication, the essential requirement for social decency, is impossible. But progressive educators, too long saddled, they thought, with a prescriptive curriculum and myopic pedagogic techniques, refused to heed the signs of danger.[5]

Francis W. Parker. Leading the parade and carrying the banner of progressivism, Francis W. Parker (1837–1902) was a herald for scholastic innovation. Although more a man of the nineteenth than the twentieth century, Parker's pedagogic reform had the effect of revolutionizing American elementary education and, some contemporary scholars allege, stamped upon the schools the indelible mark of "soft" pedagogy.[6] As a teacher in the schools, an army officer during the Civil War, and a keen student of schooling on an extensive European excursion, Parker served his novitiate for the superintendency of the Quincy, Massachusetts, public schools, an office he assumed in 1873. Quincy's schools were criticized by the board of education for having permitted low standards in reading, writing, and spelling, and the board commissioned Parker to repair them.

Repair began with the schools abandoning conventional ways of teaching. A member of the school board reported how old books on grammar, reading, and spelling were jettisoned in favor of magazines, newspapers, and student accounts of their own experience; and how arithmetic and geography were studied in practical and natural settings. The curriculum was formed from student experience rather than being mined from archaic schoolbooks.[7] Parker's magnetic personality and optimistic spirit enlivened the Quincy schools. Teachers were said to be enthusiastic about new levels of achievement, and students were praised for their excitement about this personalized approach to learning.

Parker's plan, hailed as a success and soon imitated, was called progressive education. Although Parker demurred from inflating the importance of the Quincy experiment, he identified a point whereupon progressive education later was to stand or fall: what children study should be exciting and personally consequential. Implicit in the point, however, was the almost inevitable disposition to downgrade the content of learning and inflate the significance of utility.

Parker's curriculum and the progressive curricula following in its wake idealized utility, and the pedagogic technique recommended depended for its authenticity upon the child-centered doctrine. But likely the most consequential oversight was the abandonment of the thesis that a fundamental body of knowledge and skill exists, and that persons who expect to function effectively in society should possess a common core of experience. The traditional epistemology making effective communication dependent upon a common cultural core and, in turn, serving as a bedrock for a solid, productive society was discounted.

For reasons not entirely clear, Parker's stewardship of Quincy's schools led to controversy, so Parker left. For a brief interlude he was a school supervisor in Boston. From there he went to Chicago to become principal of the Cook County Normal School.

John Dewey. While Parker was promoting a new approach to education in Quincy and Chicago, John Dewey (1859–1952), at the universities of Minnesota, Michigan, Chicago, and, later, Columbia, was tilling a philosophical field to produce a distinctive, coherent American philosophy—pragmatism. Dewey's reconstruction of philosophy paid such heed to education that some scholars regard pragmatism as essentially a philosophy of education. In any case, Dewey's appetite for educational change was whetted at the University of Chicago, where he held a professorship in philosophy, psychology, and pedagogy, and where, in establishing the famous Laboratory School, he essayed to test philosophical principle. First and foremost, however, the school was committed to excellence in elementary instruction.

The first principle of learning, Dewey correctly declared, is discovery. Employing it artfully in a rich environment for learning, with talented teachers and students of superior ability, personal curiosity prompted students to learn, and the record confirms the exceptional success of Dewey's school. But an educational program suited to genius, educators should remember, may be close to useless for the rank and file.

Although never adopted universally, progressive education soon became known the country over, and in the opinion of many a teacher was a long-lost recipe for unraveling the mystery of school learning. As progressive education gained momentum, its exponents were eager to enlist Dewey, and probably Dewey's philosophy, for their cause. But Dewey demurred and over the period of a long and productive academic career steered clear of any intimate or official association with progressivism. By 1938 Dewey called progressive education a failure.[8]

Progressivism in Secondary Schools. Progressive education had its greatest impact on elementary education where, promoters said, it was most beneficial, or where, detractors declared, it was most harmful. On a somewhat more modest scale, secondary education was affected by progressive ideology. The *Report of the Committee of Ten* (1893) might have anticipated a progressive direction for high schools, although good examples of progressive secondary schools are hard to find. One example, scholars say, was the Gary, Indiana, plan, introduced by William Wirt. Wirt, a student of Dewey's, followed progressive practice by appealing to utility in learning and capitalizing on the interest and ability of students to direct curricular reconstruction. They were, to put it directly, authorized to build their own curriculum.[9] The plan's dominant theme was personal reward from learning, and permitting students to set their own educational gait was its principal technique.

Progressive Education in the Colleges. In colleges and universities, although courses in educational philosophy and method were frequently infused with progressive doctrine, progressive practice was largely ignored. Progressive educators aspired to a rebuilding of the whole of American education, but the college curriculum was unreceptive to hasty amendment.[10] Because its public foundation was relatively recent, elementary education was most susceptible to progressivism, whereas secondary schools and colleges, with a more secure historical structure, were in a better position to resist innovation.

The curricular expansion in the colleges was an outgrowth of electivism and had nothing to do with progressive influence. The staples paving the way to a bachelor's degree were losing status, but social pressure for professional and practical college study, not infiltration of progressive doctrine, was responsible. At the same time, college doors were open to students who theretofore could not have entertained the prospect of college study, but this, while having a progressive appearance, had a genesis in social change rather than progressive education's theory.

Progressive Education and Revisionist History. If the educational reform cultivated by Francis Parker, John Dewey, and Marietta Johnson (1876–1938),[11] for example, did not illustrate the core of progressive education, it nevertheless whetted an appetite for a kind of education powerful enough to remake persons and reconstruct society. This idealism led to enlistments in progressive ranks and promoted a philosophy of schooling rather than a philosophy of education. Affinity to schooling is illustrated effectively and ornamentally in Lawrence Cremin's *The Transformation of the School.* But prominent revisionist educational historians tend to play down scholastic reform and build a strong, even alarming, case against progressive education for not being progressive at all.[12]

Acknowledging progressivism's genesis to have been inspired by an urgent idealism, they see the vigor of idealism drained away when it was captured by, and held hostage to, special economic and social interest. In the end, progressive education turned away from its original radical educational mission, one intended to promote popular educational sovereignty, to feign an allegiance to the common good.

Whatever the merit of these revisionist representations of progressive education, its impact on school practice should not be neglected. Students in teachers colleges and university departments of education were schooled in the progressive creed, and many, like converts to religious faith, embraced progressive education. Their conversion, ratified by a sensible acknowledgement that education is more than book learning, led to an indictment of conventional schooling for harboring a reactionary social and cultural agenda. Besides, driven by enthusiasm with the prospect for making pedagogy a genuine science, they abandoned the ancient abstraction about teaching being an art to declare instead for making teachers competent, skillful pedagogical technicians capable of applying scientific knowledge to the instruction of children.

Embracing, moreover, the child-centered doctrine and pronouncing an allegiance to "teaching children not subjects," they adopted, without always recognizing their model, the naturalistic thesis of Jean Jacques Rousseau: superior education must be consumed entirely by the burning personal interest and desire of the child.

The theory (if it deserves the name) was often consistent with the generally progressive attitude of parents. They themselves having been schooled in conventional ways, and remembering more pain than pleasure in their experience, were eager to have something better for their children. To discount the idealism of progressive teachers would be wrong and to characterize them as incapable of generating enthusiasm for their educational conviction would be incorrect. But idealism and enthusiasm, while probably essential for provoking innovation, are poor substitutes for the painstaking work essential for articulating and implementing a coherent pedagogical theory. So the more ambitious and able progressives began to work along these lines.[13]

Progressive education suffered decline in the 1950s. Had the well of enthusiasm run dry; had excessive zeal in promising more than could be delivered undermined its credentials; or had the voices condemning it as educational flimflam finally been persuasive? Saddled from the first with an indictment for soft pedagogy, progressive education never gave a convincing explanation that child-centered schooling represented more than a fundamental disrespect for the validity and stability of knowledge; and the charge that discipline, authority, truth, and tradition were sacrificed in the name of pedagogic innovation was hard to deflect. Essentialists had ammunition to mount an assault on progressive education.

Essentialism's Opposition to Progressive Education. Essentialists could find plenty of fault with the schools and, as eagerly as progressives, wanted reform. Yet they argued with one voice for introducing reform by commissioning schools to teach a common core to basic culture. Teachers, moreover, should possess a substantial foundation in liberal learning along with enough technical skill to direct instruction effectively. Learning, often hard, could not always be pleasant, and for any degree of excellence in achievement, discipline is imperative. Besides, recognizing the primacy of discovery in learning, essentialists endorsed activity as a sound principle of learning. In the end, though, the school's fundamental function is cultural transmission, and this function, essentialists declared, was neglected in progressive education.

Although essentialists had various educational priorities, they agreed on one: a basic curriculum—reading, writing, arithmetic, history, and English—must be taught and student achievement must be demanded. Leading a brigade of essentialists was William C. Bagley (1874–1946), a professor at Teachers College, Columbia University, the oasis of progressive doctrine. As early as 1930, Bagley called attention to the shortcomings in progressive education and to its threat to decent educational standard.

Essentialism's ideals could match those of progressivism and, enthusiastic about the prospects for American society, prized personal dignity and spoke in favor of school programs wherein ingenuity and freedom could be cultivated. But the difference between being free and being able was recognized: some freedom must sometimes be sacrificed to secure ability. Still, despite a basic friendship for solid learning, essentialism was often cast in a negative role of appearing to raise obstacles to educational change. When essentialists defended instructional standard, a solid regimen of learning, and strict discipline, they were caricatured as reactionary and mean, indifferent to the welfare of children.

The temporary successes of progressive education were always enough to keep essentialists active. Nicholas Murray Butler (1862–1947), president of Columbia University and a keen critic of progressive education, deplored the decline in academic standard and, to make his case for the neglect of learning in the schools, cited regular or social promotion. Using stronger language, Bagley accused progressive schools of contributing to a general decline in the nation's morality. The jails, he declared, were filled with examples of scholastic neglect, and he attributed the rising crime rate to the feeble discipline and vacuous teaching in schools with a progressive infection. Other essentialists adverted to a dismal level of accomplishment in the history of the republic, knowledge of geography, and basic facility in science and mathematics. Under any circumstance, such indictments were alarming. So educational matters stood when America entered World War II.

Postwar Issues. During the war, educators and the public alike, otherwise preoccupied, called a halt to educational dispute. At war's end, and probably because they assumed their work in elementary education was done, progressive educators riveted attention on secondary schools. In 1946, five regional conferences, convened under the sponsorship of the United States Commissioner of Education, John W. Studebaker, were asked to consider the status of vocational education in secondary schools. These conferences recommended an extension of vocational secondary education with a concentration on "life adjustment education."

In 1947, a Commission on Life Adjustment of Youth issued a report appearing to give progressive education a charter to "promote life adjustment, a kind of education designed to equip all American youth to live democratically with satisfaction to themselves and profit to society as home members, workers, and citizens."[14] The commission wanted secondary schools to promote "active and creative achievements as well as an adjustment to existing conditions; [for life adjustment education] places a high premium upon learning to make wise choices, since the very concept of American democracy demands the appropriate revising of aims and means of attaining them."[15] The commission was active to the end of the decade and prepared reports assessed to have had some influence upon the character of secondary education. If life adjustment education for secondary schools was a progressive educational thrust, it was likely also its last.

Almost silent during the war, essentialists renewed their assault on progressive education and noticed especially its assignation with life adjustment. Essentialists, who in former years were at a disadvantage from being a loyal educational opposition, now received support from unexpected sources. During the war, school construction was almost halted, but now more school buildings were needed, and the public wanted to know how they were to be used. Was life adjustment education worth supporting when what was needed were schools that could prepare persons skilled in conducting the serious business of America? Essentialists had new grounds for assaulting progressive education, and they used them.

Criticism leveled at progressive education from the essentialist camp has a contemporary ring. Education's faults must be perennial, for they were recited again in the 1980s. In any case, essentialist writers were skillful and persuasive in parading them in books and articles, some of which merit notice here. Bernard Iddings Bell's *Crisis in Education* indicted the schools for a failure to encourage sound and decent learning, for coddling youth, and for promoting educational mediocrity. Besides, he alleged, schools had lost sight of their principal function—teaching what can be taught—only to indulge in a variety of activities more properly the responsibility of parents, churches, and social service agencies.

Along the same line, Mortimer Smith, in *Madly Teach*, charged educationists with moral and intellectual nihilism and cultism: "If anyone will take the trouble to investigate, it will be found that those who make up the staffs of schools and colleges of education, and the administrators and teachers whom they train to run the system, have a truly amazing uniformity of opinion regarding the aims, the content, and the methods of education. They constitute a cohesive body of believers with a clearly formulated set of dogmas and doctrines, and they are perpetuating the faith by seeing to it, through state laws and rules of state departments of education, that only those teachers and administrators are certified who have been trained in the correct dogma."[16] Discharge educationists, he wrote, and replace them with persons who understand and respect schools as moral and intellectual teachers.

In the early 1950s, Albert Lynd's *Quackery in the Public Schools*, Arthur Bestor's *Educational Wastelands* and *The Restoration of Learning*, Robert Hutchins' *The Conflict in Education*, Paul Woodring's *Let's Talk Sense About Our Schools*, and Mortimer Smith's *The Diminished Mind* appeared in quick succession. A summary of these books is a taxing exercise, but their general thesis may be fairly stated: Schools should reclaim a legitimate intellectual purpose and provide all citizens with a basic education; scholarship rather than pedagogy should have precedence in the education and certification of teachers; and, finally, control of schools should be exercised by parents rather than professional educators. Hyman Rickover, in *Education and Freedom*, declared war on progressive education and professional educators alike: "Parents are no longer satisfied with life-adjustment schools. Parental objectives no longer coincide with those professed by professional educators."[17]

Philosophy of Education

Preoccupied with curriculum and method, neither progressive education nor essentialism matured into a genuine philosophy of education. Yet both raised substantial educational questions, thus contributing to a revival of interest in the most ancient subject in the study of education: educational philosophy. While battles raged over what knowledge was of most worth or, if any existed, how it should be taught, philosophers shifting attention to education began to sharpen their intellectual tools.

Idealism. Philosophy was always on speaking terms with education, but for most of its history, educational philosophy was wedded to general philosophy—especially to ethics and politics—and usually appeared as a footnote in philosophical disquisition. With the advent of the twentieth century, however, and with education high on the list of contentious social issues, educational philosophy reasserted itself and was cultivated as an independent academic discipline.

Even among scholars tempted to discount educational philosophy as an intruder, general philosophy was accepted as a discipline worth intellectual effort, and for generations the dominant general philosophy in America was idealism. Whether American affinity to idealism was lodged in idealism's long and ornamental history as genuine philosophy or to its intimate association with theology is hard to say, but idealism's influence on American education is clear. A reasonable case could be made, moreover, to the effect that progressive education was mainly a reaction to idealism. Idealist epistemology affirmed the possibility of discovering dependable knowledge and, sometimes, absolute truth, a thesis always at odds with a progressive assumption of truth being too elusive to grasp.

If progressives were uneasy with idealism, essentialism, it might be argued, was idealism in disguise. Yet while idealists might have infiltrated essentialist ranks, the principal writings of essentialists conceal any direct allegiance to idealism. The most prominent of twentieth-century educational idealists, Herman H. Horne (1874–1946), in *The Democratic Philosophy of Education*[18] took John Dewey's *Democracy and Education* and almost line by line reinterpreted it to suit the temper and principles of idealism. Although often sounding like an essentialist, he demurred from enlisting in essentialist ranks. Despite Horne's exceptional erudition and eloquence for dressing idealism in fine literary garments, he could not restore its former eminence as the philosophy with a charter to direct American education.

Idealism, even when cultivated by such prominent scholars as Horne, was largely responsible for its own demise. With a decline in allegiance to strict religious orthodoxy, the bond between idealist philosophy and theology was weakened, for idealism's inflexible adherence to an absolute spirit or idea, which persons of religious disposition could translate as God, usually kept it on friendly terms with theology. But equally important, idealism departed from the common-sense explanation of reality and advanced a metaphysical principle wherein reality was essentially spiritual.

In twentieth-century America, with the evolutionary hypothesis in its wake and with materialism fast becoming a secular religion, no philosophy—not even idealism with its almost impeccable historical credentials—could be convincing in asserting a principle almost certainly contradicted in the daily experience of men and women. There was more: for almost as long as any philosopher could remember, idealism had entertained an internal and logically consistent intellectual doubt of ever arriving at truth from sense experience and, instead, declared that truth comes, if it comes at all, from intuition and cultural immersion. The senses supply, at best, a reflection of reality, and while this reflection might establish, in Plato's language, a foundation for right opinion, it should never be confused with truth.

Philosophical principle should not be dismissed in connection with the decline of idealism in America's philosophical vocabulary, but so far as idealism's connection with education was concerned, the coin had another side. If internal experience were not conclusive, evolution and its accompanying materialistic outlook had made persons acutely aware of their physical nature, and by this time the psychological literature was filled with talk about the interaction between mind and body. Idealists, however, continued to speak mainly about education's responsibility for intellectual development and seemed not to care whether children came to school with their bodies.

Concentrating upon the development and refinement of the intellect, idealists recommended an educational process projecting an image of discipline and difficulty. They called for a curriculum filled with a wisdom stored in the books and were, it appeared, ready to jettison the new instructional techniques revealed by empirical investigation into the nature and conditions of learning. People with long memories were unready to turn back the calendar, and idealism, while it continued to solicit academic interest, lost its place as the driver of the educational bandwagon to new educational philosophies coming down the road.

Pragmatism. Almost from the first settlement of the New World, pragmatism was grafted to an American attitude to resolve the issues of life by doing what needed to be done, without ever becoming a genuine philosophy; and relativism, almost as old as philosophy itself, hovered in the intellectual environment, but it lacked the credentials of principle and system to make it an authentic philosophy. Yet, either as a general outlook putting confidence in result or as a principle rejecting absolutes, pragmatism was durable enough to thrive in an American climate, although it had to wait for cultivation by Charles Sanders Peirce (1839–1914), popularization by William James (1842–1910), and systematization by John Dewey before it became a genuine philosophy with enough vigor and appeal to dominate American philosophical thought.

Capitalizing on a foundation supplied in the positivism of August

Comte (1789–1857) and the evolutionary hypothesis of Charles Darwin (1809–1882) (both of whom called up for doubt a theistic definition of human nature) and an indigenous pragmatic American disposition, pragmatism's architects put the philosophical world in ferment. Beginning with Peirce, whose pragmatic credentials were later discounted, an intellectual effort was made to bridge the epistemological gap between philosophical subjectivity and scientific objectivity. To his own satisfaction, Peirce succeeded and supplied pragmatism with a criterion: the meaning of an idea is determined, not by a rational process, but by testing it. An idea's meaning is revealed in consequence.[19]

William James, an eloquent and perceptive philosopher–psychologist, although never a fully credentialed pragmatist, enlisted in pragmatism's ranks, found its principles useful, and popularized them in *The Will to Believe and Other Essays on Popular Philosophy, Varieties of Religious Experience, Pragmatism, A Pluralistic Universe,* and *The Meaning of Truth.* John Dewey put pragmatism on the philosophical map. His journey was long and complex. As a realist first, he turned away briefly to idealism and, finding it wanting, invested his considerable talent in making pragmatism a systematic, coherent philosophy.

Pragmatism stood on two solid but debatable piles driven into the bedrock of twentieth-century philosophy. The first, and probably the most important, was evolution; that the meaning of a philosophical declaration is derived from tested experience was the second.[20] Reason had been the conventional test of philosophical principle, but excessive dependence upon reason sometimes swamped philosophy in rationalism and immunized it from the burning questions of daily life, the very questions philosophy was supposed to answer. Schools, Dewey said, were where philosophy's principles should be tested; in consequence, educational philosophy was catapulted to the highest rung it had ever occupied on the academic ladder.

Pragmatism's enthusiastic embrace of evolution put it in conflict with modern philosophies who accorded to human nature a status distinct from other kinds of matter. Besides, to square evolution with a theological interpretation of human nature's origin and destiny, while not impossible, was never easy. Pragmatism took men and women to be highly developed material organisms, and was ready to jettison unscientific dogmas about God having created a special kind of matter. Like all matter, human beings are the products of an evolutionary process, but this process is complex, frequently unpredictable, and always fluid. It begins for human beings on a biological level, advances to a higher psychological stage, and from there moves on to sociological development.

At the end, because of accelerated evolutionary progress, men and women are accidentally, but not essentially, different from other matter. The genius of education, the pragmatists could declare, is to make them active agents in a changing world, upgrade them from private, subjective experience, and introduce them to social relationships where they learn to be responsible and useful members of society.[21]

Blazing a new philosophical trail, Dewey adopted what critics have called pragmatism's only absolute: change. Everything is in flux; nothing remains the same. Dewey anticipated the bold assertion of Ludwig Wittgenstein (1889–1951) that metaphysics, apart from the mental exercise it affords, is a waste of time;[22] and if Dewey was right about the inevitability of change, then investigating the meaning of reality in general, looking for what is ultimate in substance and essence, is pointless. At the same time, pragmatism abandoned the age-old search for truth, a preoccupation of philosophers since the time of Plato, to depend instead upon tested hypotheses. So in this respect, the pragmatic criterion invented by Peirce was woven into pragmatism's fabric: in order to determine the meaning of an idea, it must be put to work. Its outcome constitutes its meaning. All this could be interpreted as ponderous, erudite, or outside the ken of educators, and it might have been natural to inquire what it had to do with how and what students are taught in the schools.

Dewey tried to make clear his conviction that philosophy is expressed finally in a pedagogic creed. It has a responsibility to explain human nature, knowledge, and reality in a way making for social efficiency, and in turn, schools must organize tested experience to conform to the explanation. The schools were commissioned to deal with empirical reality, not with antiquated prescriptions of a reality buried away in old philosophical and theological tomes. Educators following faithfully the pragmatic code were quick to perceive the futility of trying to state educational objectives with precision or even to build a structured curriculum. For them, knowledge is not an educational goal, though effective experience is, and were quick to add that the best learning comes from experience. It prepares persons for uncertainty and, moreover, makes for social efficiency.

Pragmatism and progressive education shared some common ground: the pedagogical techniques used in progressive schools were compatible with a pragmatic conception of reality and instruction, and an experimental method capitalizing on personal interest was supposed to stimulate a reorganization of experience. Along with the progressives, and with enthusiasm, pragmatists endorsed child-centered pedagogy, but progressives, habitually regarding the content of experience with indifference, were out of step with Dewey. He demurred from endowing curricular content with inherent and permanent value, yet experience needs predicates. Some experiences are better than others, and for Dewey, the best test of experience is durability. The traditional corpus of knowledge cannot be dismissed with impunity, although the problem-solving method should be used in connection with it.

Such a prescription for education, Dewey averred, produces persons capable of thinking effectively.[23] The best schools ready students for living effectively by immersing them in life. These pronouncements were appealing to teachers and students, so pragmatism's reception in the schools was usually cordial. Yet, strange to say, as the educational community's attraction to pragmatism increased, its flirtation with progressive education declined.

Realism. Although pragmatism gained considerable mileage from an intimate association with the schools, its command never ranged over the whole of educational philosophy. There was stiff competition, mostly from realism. The roots of realism, buried as deeply in the history of philosophy as pragmatism's, had been subject to more intensive cultivation. Pragmatism stood on the fringe of philosophical scholarship until the twentieth century, whereas realism originating with Aristotle was almost as old as speculative philosophy itself. Attributing independent existence to physical reality—an almost incontestable position on the scale of common sense—made realism attractive because it squared with what most thoughtful people believed to be true. From direct contact with reality, dependable knowledge, although never guaranteed, is possible.

Realism made a claim on philosophy by reasserting a challenge to idealism and, when pragmatism became more prominent, by staking out a position in clear opposition to it. Eventually realism separated into New Realism and Critical Realism; as it turned out, the latter camp expressed an educational philosophy controverting pragmatism and most nearly satisfying the educational appetite of essentialists.

Realist educational philosophers were remarkably effective in parading their distrust of "soft pedagogy," but it would be wrong to suppose that realism's strength was nurtured by broadsides against pragmatism. Realist educational philosophy, represented most ably by Henry C. Morrison (1871–1945), Frederick S. Breed (1876–1952), Ross L. Finney (1875–1964), Harry S. Broudy, and (if an essentialist can be counted) William C. Bagley, was full of substance. Although asserting personal emphases in interpretations of human nature, reality, and knowledge, and applying these emphases to education, realists usually circled the same tree of philosophical conviction.

Beginning with a decent respect for empiricism, and stressing the worth, stability, and dependability of knowledge, they unreservedly subscribed to a universe of structure whose design is revealed in natural law. Acknowledging change (who could deny it?), they nevertheless refused to countenance the pragmatic representation of a world in constant flux. Change occurs within the limit of natural design. Men and women must therefore live within the limit imposed by nature's law, and this led realists to prescribe a kind of education with a commitment to the transmission of dependable knowledge about how the physical and human worlds function. Although often concealed, the law of nature is not unfathomable, and by using dependable processes for discovery, much of its mystery can be disclosed. Dependable knowledge is the only chance persons have for conducting a society wherein a decent life is possible. Without it they would be helpless.

Despite an abundance of good sense, realism could not scale every philosophical hurdle. Realism began with a phenomenalistic definition of human nature, affirmed material and spiritual reality, but usually rejected supernaturalism. Its evident materialism put it at loggerheads with an American cultural tradition respecting, and sometimes embracing, theism, so trust in its educational philosophy was siphoned off. Yet this shortcoming was redressed somewhat in a careful empirical analysis of the phenomenon of human behavior: women and men are capable of rational thought and responsible action. Their unique and natural, albeit material, capacity deserves a kind of cultivation that only a program of education can supply. Educational decency must stand upon a bedrock of truth.

Influenced over the years by Alfred North Whitehead (1861–1947) and Bertrand Russell (1872–1970), realist educational philosophers acknowledged the need to establish educational objectives along lines compatible with bodies of dependable knowledge accumulated by a long, careful, scientific study of the physical world and a careful and thorough appraisal of human nature. It is possible to discover the kind of knowledge men and women need if they are to lead effective, responsible lives and contribute to the conduct of a humane society. The history of the race had, in any case, already established the fact of human capability. Schools should select dependable knowledge certified by both scientific and rational test and put it in the curriculum. Such knowledge, the basic culture of learning, should be transmitted in a way to ensure its assimilation and preservation.

The educational process, essentially one of communicating dependable knowledge, is never immune from personal interest, yet it is responsible for teaching students what they need, not what they want, to know in order to equip them to live effective personal and social lives. So training, instruction, and discipline headed the list of realist educational objectives. Pedagogical technique to sustain, promote, and ensure solid learning was never sold at discount, but mastery of necessary knowledge was encouraged by every realist who, almost in the same sentence, deplored progressive and pragmatic educational programs as being pointless and profitless. Recognizing the psychological soundness of learning by discovery, realists observed, nevertheless, that life is too short to allow students to follow uncertain and unmarked routes to learning.

Humanism. The philosophical record of the first decades of the twentieth century attests the prominence of pragmatism and realism. It demonstrates how idealism was losing ground, but it reflects as well a resurgence of humanism and its often eloquent expression of educational purpose.

The record also illustrates the allegiance educational philosophers had to systems, or schools, of thought; but as time wore on, especially during the second half of the century, affection for philosophical systems atrophied. Identifying an educational philosopher as, say, a pragmatist, idealist, realist, or humanist became increasingly difficult, and philosophers themselves eschewed such classification. Allegiance shifted to analysis. Adopting analysis, educational philosophers took as their commission finding meaning in what educators said, how schools were conducted, how curricula were organized, and an appraisal of controversial educational issues. An embrace of analysis should not, however, conceal the stark fact that any philosophical system worthy of the name always employs analysis as an essential intellectual tool.

Either anticipating or reacting to analysis, at least subscribing to the proposition that extant educational philosophy was unrepresentative of the entire corpus of educational ends and means, humanism hoisted its philosophical flag. Humanism was neither a philosophical nor an educational novelty, and for centuries it had employed a common vocabulary for educational discourse that when used now concealed obstacles to philosophical unanimity. Educators who liked to call themselves humanists found it hard to agree on a single definition of human nature, truth, and culture, and this discord was probably more important than the point whereupon they agreed: that the "new pedagogy" was defective and undermined a legacy of educational decency. So although humanism is often represented as an organic educational philosophy, calling it a composite of humanisms—literary, rational, and Christian—is closer to the truth.

Cultivated by Nicholas Murray Butler (1862–1947), Mark Van Doren (1894– 1972), and Norman Foerster (1887–1972), to name its most prominent expositors, literary humanism stressed the significance of cultural permanence and paid close attention to the obligation schools have for perpetuating the literary tradition. Characterizing literary humanism as nothing more than elitism in disguise, critics indicted it for undermining social democracy.

Rational humanism, represented best in the work of Robert Maynard

Hutchins (1899–1977) and Mortimer Alder (b.1902), emphasized the import of a trained reason and unequivocally subscribed to educational programs whose goal was intellectual development. Christian humanists, operating mainly (though not solely) within a framework of Catholic educational tradition, endorsed intellectual and cultural refinement as being consistent with the development of distinctive human ability—thought and expression—and, to illuminate the dependence human beings have on their Creator, gave religion an essential place in the school's syllabus. Thomas E. Shields (1862–1921), William F. Cunningham (1885–1953), but most prominently Jacques Maritain (1882–1973), spoke for these humanists who, critics often said, had one foot in the camp of rational humanism and the other in theology.

Opposition to naturalism (frequently called "materialism") made for strange bedfellows and, in this respect, humanism was unexceptional. Yet humanists, although frequently taking different philosophical routes, were in general agreement on educational purpose. Difference was acute on the role of theology for illuminating educational decision, but common ground, if not common agreement, was found for metaphysics and epistemology. As dualists, humanists appeared to share common philosophical ground with realism.

Humanists concurred in the proposition that education's principal purpose is a cultivation of the distinctive human abilities—thought and expression—although harmony was lacking when curricula and methods were selected to hone these abilities. All humanists affirmed the existence of truth, the possibility of achieving it, and the need for schools to communicate it. In addition, ready to acknowledge the existence of intellectual truth, they forthrightly pledged allegiance to moral knowledge, which, while lacking the precision alleged for the former, is nevertheless real. Moral knowledge was accorded a legitimate place in the curriculum, and schools were expected to create an environment for its inculcation.

Humanists of every persuasion made the schools moral and intellectual agencies and pleaded with them to acknowledge the superiority of liberal study. Yet attention, though riveted on liberal study, was not restricted to it; humanists were not engaging in conspiracy to turn back the pedagogical calendar, or to lead students in retreat from the contemporary world. But persuaded that education should be based upon a bedrock of intellectual and moral truth, they knew the demands of social and economic life and declared that without a prescribed and rigorous educational program, society and its members were being shortchanged. They wanted educational excellence and intellectual discipline and (seldom giving this view the prominence it deserved) abandoned any affinity with insensitivity, harshness, and brutality in the schooling of children. A necessary condition for the realization of excellence—discipline—they charged, was absent in pragmatic and progressive schools: without discipline any degree of excellence is impossible.

Philosophy and Methods of Instruction

Within the context of substantial issues of educational ends and means, the importance of pedagogic technique became more obvious. Whatever philosophers might say about how instruction in the schools should proceed, teachers supervise and direct learning. In this respect, progressive educators had made some important and lasting contributions, but it was left largely to pragmatism to relate pedagogic technique directly to educational principle. Dewey had recommended problem solving as the ideal style for promoting learning and declared correctly that all learning begins with a problem. One of his disciples, William Heard Kilpatrick (1871–1965), took the lead in translating this declaration for school practice.

William H. Kilpatrick. Following a short interlude as a schoolmaster, Kilpatrick undertook graduate study at Teachers College, Columbia University, earned a doctor's degree, and thereafter joined the Teachers College faculty. The time of his enlistment in progressive ranks is unclear, but his early, still consulted scholarly work includes books on the Dutch schools of colonial New York, Montessorian methods, and the kindergarten theory of Friedrich Froebel (1782–1852).[24]

Shortly, attracted to the connectionistic psychological theses of Edward L. Thorndike (1874–1949) and education's social objective as promoted by John Dewey, Kilpatrick began to invest his considerable talent in the development of a problem-solving method. Progressive education had flirted with job-analysis curricula wherefrom students could learn special skill for social efficiency, but job analysis was susceptible to a charge of being traditional and, in any case, had little to do with problem solving. Something different was needed, and in 1925 Kilpatrick supplied it in *Foundations of Method*, a book permanently attaching problem solving and project methods to progressive education.

Following Dewey, Kilpatrick adopted the thesis that schools should create a superior social environment allowing students to learn what they live, and then proceeded to excoriate traditional school method for stunting moral and social formation: "Our schools," he wrote, "have in the past chosen from the whole of life certain intellectualistic tools (skills and knowledges), have arranged these under the heads of reading, arithmetic, geography, and so on, and have taught these separately as if they would, when once acquired, recombine into the worthy life. This now seems to me to be very far from sufficient. Not only do these things not make up the whole of life, but we have so fixed attention upon the separate teaching of these as to at times starve the weightier matters of life and character. The only way to learn to live well is to practice living well."[25]

Kilpatrick recommended the project method for allowing students to grapple with problems from their own experience and, in solving them, to engage in the finest kind of learning. Teachers were expected to act as resource persons, ready when asked to supply help and advice, but were never authorized to intrude when students selected the kinds of experiences important to them.

Kilpatrick, however, demurred from releasing students to proceed without some guidance. The project method had four sequential parts: identifying a problem lodged in personal experience with the intention of solving it, designing a plan for solving it, testing the plan in direct application, and evaluating the outcome. The features of the method had a merit not easily neglected; psychology of learning confirmed them, but they tended to discount a substantial and essential legacy of learning. This was enough to give all but the most zealous progressives pause about putting the total weight of learning upon what even the most eloquent opponents of progressive education recognized as a sturdy beam: direct experience.

In advancing the worth of the project method, Kilpatrick appealed to the record of the Laboratory School and to Dewey's praise for it as a way of facilitating learning. But Dewey's praise was partial and selective. Critical of traditional methods, he wanted schools enlivened by issues from contemporary life, but he wanted to retain scholastic structure and design as well. Dewey could be critical of conventional curricula without abandoning them, for they contained a heritage formed from social experience and could not be dismissed peremptorily or neglected entirely. Kilpatrick, however, found fixed subject matter wearisome, an intruder upon effective learning, and invested confidence, instead, in school programs whose problems arose in a student's personal experience. To say the entire cadre of American teachers converted to Kilpatrick's approach to method is exaggeration, but only blindness concealed its influence in the country's schools.

A popular writer and an influential teacher, Kilpatrick became progressive education's foremost spokesman. But in concentrating upon technique rather than theory, Kilpatrick allowed the ship to sail without a rudder. In making method supreme, Kilpatrick's imbalanced approach put progressivism in jeopardy. Even sympathetic critics agreed that, for all its luster, Kilpatrick's idealization of method left the educational enterprise without coherence or stability and, moreover, without a substantial

theory to support social reconstruction.[26] Bode expressed these sentiments when he wrote, "Unless we know where we are going, there is not
much comfort in being assured that we are on the way and traveling
fast. . . . If education is to discharge its rightful function of leadership, it
must clarify its guiding ideals."[27]

Counts broadened the argument and defused the spark of pedagogic
technique by commissioning schools to engage in the serious business of
social reconstruction. They should, as the title of his book implied (*Dare
the School Build a New Social Order*), lead a crusade to change the
American social order to ensure the realization of a complete and effective
democratic society. Because students, depending upon limited experience
and a variety of social motive, could hardly have been in the vanguard of
such an idealistic movement, teachers were recruited to become social
activists. If they were to be effective leaders, something more than re-
sponding to student need was necessary.

Chapter 13

Educational Policy
in Twentieth-Century America

Disposition for social reform, an almost indigenous characteristic of American society, was nurtured in the Great Depression, but whether Depression inspired optimism or cultivated despair relative to the principal social and economic stanchions of the country is unclear. Unclear also is the effect of economic catastrophe on the schools. Schools remained open, operated with limited budgets, and possibly, although not certainly, displayed a greater interest in social studies without ever becoming agencies for social reform or converts to social activism. They were expected, however, by encouraging students to remain longer in school, to help moderate a bleak picture of unemployment.

A cause and effect relationship between school organization and economic conditions is at best obscure, although in the decade after 1930 the school reorganization movement reached an apex. Junior high schools increased in number by leaps and bounds, and junior colleges—baptized as democracy's colleges—were greeted with enthusiasm, especially in states west of the Mississippi River. The effect of junior high schools on a labor market is hard to discern, although motive for additional study might have been kindled in them, but junior colleges, especially those with a terminal function, were designed to teach saleable skill and, in keeping persons longer in school, to reduce unemployment.

Besides, so students could afford to continue in school, various federal programs were instituted, among them the National Youth Administration and the Public Works Administration. In these humble auxiliaries to opportunity, the prospect for federal aid to education was nurtured.

Government and Education

With the entrance of the United States into World War II, many of the economic problems besetting the country were postponed, as were most of the items educational reformers had on their list. However, the war deferred, without altering substantially, America's commitment to education. A review of education's record from the founding of the Republic to the end of World War II solicits an acknowledgment of monumental progress, but perceptive Americans knew there was more to do.

Federal Policies on Education. Unprecedented federal legislation—the Serviceman's Readjustment Act of 1944—offered veterans a variety of benefits, including opportunity to continue their education in colleges, schools, and training programs. About eight million veterans availed themselves of the educational benefit provided in the law.[1] One argument prompting the enactment of the law predicted social and economic benefits to the nation from having better educated citizens; this argument, with its implicit cogency, embellished America's fundamental faith in education. And this faith was amply illustrated in the educational policies promoted by the Fair Deal, President Harry Truman's (1884–1972) redefinition of the New Deal.

For the first time on such a large scale, the federal government adopted a policy to promote higher learning and justified it by stressing the social and personal benefit that was bound to accrue. Every high-school graduate should have an opportunity at public expense to complete at least two years of college study. Most students, it was expected, would go to local public junior colleges, but public and private four-year colleges were sketched into the portrait too, and federal subsidy encouraged the introduction of a variety of programs intended to help them improve and expand.

A public appetite for higher education was whetted by national policy, and national policy was wedded to national security: higher learning, especially in science and technology, enjoyed not only pride of place, but the more generous support, although fairness recommends the observation that hundreds of millions of dollars were made available for other programs as well. Higher education experienced a period of unique, unexcelled prosperity. Having lived most of their institutional lives in near poverty, the colleges reaped a reward of financial plenty, and this, it might be argued, led them to drift from their original educational mission. Seduced by unfamiliar wealth, higher learning in America began to lose its way, and schools that should have husbanded resources for work consistent with their personality and history began to imagine themselves capable of competing with universities whose resources and experience recommended their engagement in highly specialized and exceptionally expensive educational and research programs. But a new dictum began to pervade educational discourse—equality of opportunity—and this dictum, although praiseworthy when properly applied to persons, was trumpeted for institutions as well.

The principle of human equality, expressed so eloquently in the Declaration of Independence, was all too frequently neglected in social policy. After World War II, however, the principle of equality was understood literally, and signs soon appeared that schools were violating it. Throughout most of the nineteenth century, Americans were optimistic about their chances for success, and for the most part, their optimism was justified in the experience of both native-born and naturalized citizens. Hard work, along with some good luck, had allowed them to climb the social and economic ladder. Although earlier generations had a modest educational investment whose dividend only infrequently contributed to their improved condition, they were nevertheless eager to have greater educational opportunity for their children. But for millions of Americans, despite what appeared to be accepted social principle, equality of educational opportunity was foreclosed.

Equality of Educational Opportunity

Equality of educational opportunity was endorsed in clear and precise prose in the 1947 report of the President's Commission on Higher Education, *Higher Education for American Democracy*: "If education is to make the attainment of a more perfect democracy one of its major goals, it is imperative that it extend its benefits to all on equal terms."[2] The statement was intended to be prospective, in setting the direction for the future, and corrective, in rescinding laws and customs that withheld equality of opportunity in and out of schools on a basis of gender, race, religion, or national origin. This form of discrimination, sometimes with the blessing of law—such as the famous *Plessy v. Ferguson* (1896) Supreme Court decision—[3] was a formidable obstacle to constitutionally protected civil rights enshrined in the Bill of Rights and the Fourteenth Amendment and, in 1964, afforded statutory recognition in the Civil Rights Act.

Effort to redress educational discrimination had a long, uneven, and generally unsuccessful history, especially in state courts, and the legal theory issuing from *Plessy v. Ferguson* held bleak prospect for the future. Yet this legal theory was ruptured by an unlikely source: the federal judiciary.

In *Sweatt v. Painter* in 1950, the United States Supreme Court, in a unanimous opinion, enjoined the University of Texas from conducting a separate law school for a black student and rejected the University's assertion of equal academic quality in the separate school opened for him.[4] The court appeared to follow the precedent of the Gaines decision of 1938, where the state of Missouri, although not required to admit Gaines, a black, to the University of Missouri law school, was directed to provide an equal legal education for him.[5] So in 1950 the separate but equal doctrine, although faltering, was still alive, but not for long. *Brown v. The Board of Education of Topeka* (1954) declared separate schools inherently unequal and directed school jurisdictions throughout the United States to proceed "with all deliberate speed" to desegregate public schools.[6]

Constitutionally, equality of opportunity is clearly established—citizens enjoy equal protection of law and public services may not be withheld arbitrarily—but this is only part of the story. What does equality of educational opportunity mean? The answer is in dispute. Over the centuries, opportunity for education was afforded in various ways. Sometimes privilege, either social station or wealth, conferred upon persons the benefit of schooling. But in the United States, although privilege probably never disappeared entirely, the time came when public resources were used to open and maintain schools and, after 1954, when all schools were open to all children, slow but steady progress was made to interdict discrimination and establish a unitary, integrated school system.

Despite society's idealization of education, resources to support schools and various programs in them are limited. Even with the elimination of artificial factors such as gender, race, religion, and national origin, this question bores to the core of democratic education's meaning: To what part of society's educational resource is a citizen entitled? Unsurprisingly, the question tests the acumen of educational and social philosophers.

Allocation of Educational Resource. The empirical fact is that persons are unequal in various ways: opportunity afforded to one person might be used effectively, while for another the same opportunity might be wasted. The place to begin is with a forthright acknowledgment that a common attribute of human beings is inequality and therefrom to proceed toward a policy for allocating educational resource. Objection is muted when educational opportunity is based on talent—persons should have the kind and amount of education from which they can profit—but a definition and identification of talent is harder than it sounds. When capacity to achieve is unequal, inequality in educational opportunity is both prudent and just.

Fairness, it is assumed, will be explicit in the identification of talented persons. But what should be done when talent is buried by social and educational disadvantage? Persons should have a fair chance to demonstrate capacity for achievement in their early education, thus allowing for an unequal allocation of resources later.

The matter of allocation *vis-à-vis* equality of opportunity is compounded by philosophy and psychology. Talent, hereditarians maintain, is lodged principally in genetic endowment, and genetic endowment, while amenable to shaping and refining, cannot be altered substantially. Environmentalists read the other side of the coin. The significance of genetic endowment upon intelligence and the fact of individual difference are freely admitted, but neither, they assert, plays more than a part in the determination of talent. Environmental factors, always more important, should be equalized, thus allowing persons an equal chance to capitalize on genetic capacity. If environmental factors were equalized, variation in talent would be determined entirely by genetic endowment and alone affect performance. Hereditarians and environmentalists alike acknowledge genetic intelligence but differ sharply with respect to its dominance and development.

But the goal of equality of educational opportunity is not equality. Although persons should have a fair chance to hone their talent, its development and employment will inevitably disclose differences in achievement among persons and therefrom will come inequality in education, status, and income. And this is a logical outcome of equality of educational opportunity. If the goal of equality of educational opportunity is not equality, how can it be forwarded as a fair and just policy for education in a democratic society? The goal anticipates that the procedures employed to select persons to occupy different positions in society will discount factors other than talent and, when this is done, will allocate equal resources to equal talent.

If the goal of equality of educational opportunity is acknowledged to be consistent with the values of a fair and just society, it becomes necessary to identify those conditions that militate against the realization of basic capacity. These conditions, it can be assumed, are found either in schools where resources for decent learning are absent, thus intimidating intellectual development during the early years of schooling, or in families' background and the nurture they cannot supply to enable children to profit from the benefits of schooling. The first of these conditions can be removed by equalizing resources for schooling from one to another community, for it is evident that some communities, even with an abundance of good will toward education, simply lack the economic strength to support superior educational programs.[7] The second condition resists removal, although its effect can be inhibited by compensatory education. This, the proponents of equality of educational opportunity aver, is the prescription for a society motivated by justice and fairness to follow.

Despite its inherent appeal, equality of educational opportunity has doubters and detractors. Some educational and social philosophers, while admitting to obvious inequality among persons, declare that racial, religious, ethnic, and gender differences cannot be evidence of inequality. There are various differences among persons, including ability to learn, but the essential question asked is whether these differences can be translated into a clear policy with respect to the allocation of society's educational resources. The answer is that they cannot.

So as education in the United States moves toward the twenty-first century, a fundamental disagreement with respect to the use of society's educational resources hovers on the horizon. One side of debate holds that opportunity for education should depend upon two factors: the ability of persons to profit from the opportunity offered and the need society has for the kind of talent they possess. Ability varies in social worth and social priorities change. Society, then, must identify the kind of talent it wants to support. This, on the other side of the debate, is alleged to be meritocracy in camouflage: simple justice requires an equal share of society's educational resource for everyone. Talent of one kind cannot make a more legitimate claim than another; talent of all kinds must have a chance to thrive. A just society, moreover, will not allow ephemeral need to stand as an obstacle to a distribution of economic goods for the realization of equality in education. A pressing social need for, say, physicians and engineers cannot justify a withholding of educational opportunity from persons with other talent. Everyone must share equally in society's resources for education; how they are used in an individual case is a personal decision.

Affirmative Action

Although cogent theory could be advanced to defend equality in education on one hand and equality of educational opportunity on the other, translation of either theory to the level of practice turned out to be a vexing and controversial matter. Even when translation was made, another issue, tangential to equality of opportunity, was raised in connection with affirmative action programs instituted in many, especially professional, schools.

Affirmative action, intended to compensate for earlier discrimination against certain minority groups, could be turned on its head and result in reverse discrimination, its critics declared. Dispute over affirmative action policy was moved from the street to the courtroom when, in 1971, Marco DeFunis, Jr., asserted injury from being denied equal protection of the law, a right guaranteed to citizens in the Fourteenth Amendment. The University of Washington law school refused to admit DeFunis, although minority students, alleged to be less qualified, were admitted to places reserved for them. A state court intervened, ordered DeFunis' admission, but the Washington Supreme Court reversed the lower court's decision. The case at controversy was appealed to the United States Supreme Court where, in 1974, because DeFunis had in the interim completed his legal study, it was declared moot and the court refused jurisdiction.

A prediction by some Supreme Court justices that a constitutional question relative to affirmative action would soon reappear turned out to be accurate. Allan Bakke applied to the University of California at Davis medical school first in 1973 and again in 1974. He was rejected both times, although minority candidates, alleged to have academic records inferior to Bakke's, were admitted to the school's special program where sixteen places were reserved for them. Bakke claimed the school's policy was in violation of the equal protection clause of the Fourteenth Amendment, the California constitution, and Title VI of the Civil Rights Act of 1964.

The Court's 1978 decision, although ordering Bakke's admission, fell short, constitutional scholars agree, of being a definitive declaration.[8] Without a single opinion representing a majority, six separate opinions were produced, and only two were joined by four justices each. This lack of unanimity led to a 5–4 majority that found affirmative action as practiced in the school unconstitutional and to another 5–4 majority holding some form of race-conscious admission policy to promote diversity in a student body constitutionally acceptable and consistent with a First Amendment protection of academic freedom. Taking into account the complexity of the issue and its fundamental relationship to equality of opportunity in a free society, it is likely, because of the equivocal position of the Supreme Court in *Bakke*, that litigation will continue with respect to affirmative action in schools. The constitutional question awaits a clear and precise answer.

State Educational Authority

A consideration of educational opportunity should take into account the availability, control, and support of schools. And any accounting of educational resource in a free society should include private as well as public effort. Enough is known about the genesis of education in this good land to recognize at once its private foundation and to recognize, too, how several decades passed before provision for schooling was accepted as more a collective than an individual responsibility. But while collectivism was marinating, private schools buried their roots in America's educational soil.

By the advent of the twentieth century, the educational enterprise had matured into a partnership of public and private schools. At the same time, public schools throughout the nation, supported by the public treasury, were open to all children, and resting upon a tradition of evident good to the nation, the foundation for private education appeared secure. As it turned out, appearance was deceptive.

The authority of the state to exercise control over education within its borders was challenged from time to time, mainly by religious denominations with schools of their own. The first of these challenges arose in connection with compulsory attendance statutes when Massachusetts in 1852, and other states later, enacted laws requiring children of certain ages to attend school. Contemporary vision sees nothing oppressive in these early laws. Demanding little and often ignored, they nevertheless asserted the state's authority in education, and this led to trouble. If the state could use its police power to compel children to attend school, how much more could the state do in education?

By the middle of the nineteenth century, state educational authority had been illustrated in various ways, probably most significantly in compulsory attendance, and this, it was said, eroded parental control. For the next fifty years, states were busy getting their authority affirmed in the courts, and at century's end it was fairly clear where authority over education in the United States lay: limited only by the Fourteenth Amendment, the state, not the local community, held the reins of educational control.

This authority was demonstrated in these legal principles: state legislatures have authority to control public schools except as legislative action is limited by federal and state constitutions; constitutional provision and statute make plain that authority over education is not inherent in local government; organization for education proceeds at the discretion of the legislature and school districts can be distinct from other branches of local government; and even in the absence of an exercise of educational control, the authority of the state in education remains intact. The states have an extraordinary commission to control education within their borders, but is this commission unrestricted? Two impregnable United States Supreme Court decisions demonstrate that it is not.

English in the Schools. Between 1917 and 1921, ten states enacted statutes making English the language for school instruction. A 1919 Nebraska law read, "No person, individually or as a teacher, shall, in any private, denominational parochial or public school, teach any subject to any person in any language other than the English language."[9] A teacher in the Zion Parochial School, Meyer, taught reading in the German language to ten-year-old Raymond Parpart, who had not finished the eighth grade. Arrested, tried, and convicted under the Nebraska statute, Meyer on appeal to the state supreme court challenged the law's constitutionality under the liberty provision of the Fourteenth Amendment.

The court held the law to be a reasonable exercise of state police power and adverted to conditions during the First World War. Thousands of men from foreign-language-speaking homes and schools, the court wrote, had entered the armed forces "unable to read, write, or speak the language of their country, or understand words of command given in English." Besides, the opinion continued, anti-American and alien sentiments were fostered in schools where English was not the medium of instruction. In the court's opinion, the Nebraska law was neither an unreasonable interference with individual liberty nor an infringement of the liberty provision of the Fourteenth Amendment.[10]

In 1921, Iowa's and Ohio's supreme courts, considering the constitutionality of statutes similar to Nebraska's, adopted as precedent the Nebraska decision to hold constitutional the state's "right to adopt a general policy of its own respecting the health, social welfare, and education of its citizens."[11] There was, the courts said, no inherent right to instruct children in German, especially if such instruction were inimical to state interest. The constitutionality of acts proscribing foreign-language teaching, the Ohio court declared, depended upon whether the general welfare required such legislation, and on the point of ensuring general welfare, the legislature is the best judge.

Without exception, state courts found no fault in laws restricting the teaching of foreign language, holding them consistent with the liberty provision of the Fourteenth Amendment. But these decisions were put in jeopardy when the decision of the Nebraska Supreme Court was forwarded on appeal to the United States Supreme Court. It was asked to decide whether the Nebraska statute infringed on liberty or property without due process of law. In 1923 (*Meyer v. Nebraska*), the Supreme Court found the Nebraska statute an unconstitutional infringement "of the calling of modern language teachers, with the opportunities of pupils to acquire knowledge, and with the power of parents to control the education of their own."[12]

The court acknowledged the authority of the state to "go very far, indeed, in order to improve the quality of its citizens." It can "compel attendance at some school and . . . make reasonable regulations for all schools, including a requirement that they shall give instructions in English . . . ," but was at pains to assert the fundamental rights of individuals: "The protection of the Constitution extends to all, to those who speak other languages as well as to those born with English on their tongue." There might be considerable advantage to society, the court wrote, "if all had ready understanding of our ordinary speech, but this cannot be coerced by methods which conflict with the Constitution—a desirable end cannot be promoted by prohibited means."[13]

Compulsory Attendance in Public Schools. In 1922, by initiative measure, the state of Oregon adopted a compulsory attendance law requiring, with four exceptions,[14] attendance in public schools of all normal children between ages eight and sixteen. Anticipating the effect of the law's enforcement to be the demoralization or destruction of private education in the state, the Society of Sisters, a Roman Catholic religious community, and the Hill Military Academy challenged its constitutionality under the property provision of the Fourteenth Amendment. The law, appellees alleged, conflicted with the "right of parents to choose schools where their children will receive appropriate mental and religious training, the right of the child to influence the parents' choice of a school, the right of schools and teachers therein to engage in a useful business or profession. . . . And, further, that unless the enforcement of the measure is enjoined the [corporations'] business and property will suffer irreparable injury."[15]

Defending the law's reasonable intent, proponents recalled how the nineteenth-century common school had been characterized as a principal bulwark of democracy, and went on to assert the superiority of the public school for inculcating civic duty and responsibility, for reducing juvenile delinquency, and for neutralizing religious prejudice and hostility. Public schools, they maintained, were better able than private schools to instruct children, especially immigrant children, about America's government and institutions. The public good, moreover, would benefit from having children from all social classes attend public schools. But the primary plea was for patriotism, which could be best cultivated in public schools; without the law, the state would be stripped of means to prohibit the subversive teaching of bolshevists, syndicalists, and communists.

Citing the Nebraska decision, the court reaffirmed the state's right to "regulate all schools, to inspect, supervise and examine them, their teachers and pupils; to require that all children of proper age attend some school, that teachers shall be of good moral character and patriotic disposition, that certain studies plainly essential to good citizenship must be taught, and that nothing be taught which is manifestly inimical to the public welfare."[16] It declared, nevertheless, that the "Act of 1922 unreasonably interferes with the liberty of parents and guardians to direct the upbringing and education of children under their control. . . . The fundamental theory of liberty upon which all governments in this Union repose excludes any general power of the State to standardize its children by forcing them to accept instruction from public teachers only. The child is not the mere creature of the State; those who nurture him and direct his destiny have the right, coupled with the high duty, to recognize and prepare him for additional obligations."[17] Oregon's law was struck down. In affirming parents' right in the education of their children, the Supreme Court's Nebraska and Oregon decisions established almost unshakeable precedent, but the Oregon decision contained an additional bonus. Before 1925, the year of the Oregon decision, private education in the United States stood on a foundation of tradition that lacked any explicit legal confirmation. The decision supplied private education with a charter and a constitutional warrant.[18]

Public Money and Private Schools. Before the advent of the twentieth century, and especially when public schools were in their infancy, the use of public resources for private schools was a fairly common practice. But as public schools prospered in the wake of favorable popular sentiment, and as religious temperament became more sensitive, state after state passed laws restricting the use of public money to institutions under direct public control. For the most part, private schools, especially private religious schools, were barred from receiving public money. This led private school advocates to cry foul: they sent their children to private schools, paid tuition, and at the same time paid taxes to support public schools from which they received no direct benefit.

The level of support mustered by this argument is impossible to measure, but regularly and vigorously repeated, it elicited sharp rejoinder from persons who saw it as an attack upon public education and a conspiracy to undermine the principle of separation of church and state and the democratic charter. Public schools were represented as the stanchion for social unity, while private schools, whatever educational value might be claimed for them, were portrayed as being socially divisive. If they could not be suppressed, they should not under any circumstance be helped by the public treasury.

Appealing to social unity and democracy, the fault in private education was paraded and the virtue of public education was extolled. Opposition to private and religious education in what appeared to be an argument favoring a public education monopoly was pronounced by John L. Childs,[19] Hollis L. Caswell,[20] and James B. Conant,[21] who rejected the traditional proposition whereupon public–private dualism had stood and, moreover, ignored a long and impressive record of private schools' contribution to education.

Public–Private Dualism in Education. Dualism was justified both in tradition and law, because a pluralistic American society recognized the right of responsible individuals and groups to maintain schools of their own: a free society proscribing the existence of private schools would be an anomaly. Yet this right was always to be exercised without expense to the common good, to values fundamental to American law and life, and to standards of scholastic accomplishment. Within these reasonable limits, parents were free to exercise choice with respect to the education of their children and the character of the school they would attend. Nothing in American educational tradition or law recommended a public education monopoly, and nothing in the history of American private schools justified the conclusion that they were either divisive or deficient.

The history of American private education is, in fact, fairly ornamental. Normally enjoying more flexibility that public schools, private schools were able to introduce innovation in curriculum and method, to mount scholastic programs and develop pedagogic practices that arrived only tardily in public schools. It is reasonable to say that private schools were in the vanguard with respect to normal schools, progressive education, schooling the handicapped, the kindergarten, and junior colleges.

Yet neither pronouncement in support of private schools nor their record of impressive accomplishment was entirely persuasive. In the years immediately following World War II, prominent spokesmen for public education declared private education an impediment to the realization of a good society and argued, moreover, that public–private dualism was a prescription for peril: without a monolithic public school system, the democratic core would rot. Private schools were called undemocratic because they kept apart children of various ethnic, religious, social, and economic backgrounds. Scholastic separation could have but one result: rupturing the essential bond of social solidarity whereupon a democratic society depends.

Despite its eloquence, the voice of opposition to private education and to a mature compact of dualism was not persuasive. Americans were unready to jettison private education on the basis of the case made against it. Yet private education began to wither during the two decades after 1950. Immediately following the war, private schools, especially religiously-related schools, showed marked gain in number and enrollment but soon found themselves caught in an inescapable financial web. The relentless economics of education were more powerful than social theory: private schools, so expensive to maintain, closed by the hundreds. In the last analysis, then, and by default, public education succeeded in dominating the American educational scene.

In the two decades after 1970, thoughtful Americans, no longer heeding arguments, when they were made, about private education being inimical to social unity, worried about the precipitous decline of private education as a threat to the fabric of a democratic society. Early in the century, the pendulum of public opinion was swinging away from private education, but late in the century, it tilted toward the preservation of public—private dualism.

Church—State Relations and Education

In the nation's formative years, education was expected to heed and promote religious doctrine and piety. During the colonial and early national periods, education was, and was expected to be, religious in content and purpose. Throughout the seventeenth century, it should be recalled, every colony in New England (save Rhode Island) and most of the colonies elsewhere had an established church. Americans supported the status quo.

As the decades wore on, however, religious allegiance became less fervent, and the influence of the church on government was reduced, making more plausible the declarations of Benjamin Franklin and Thomas Jefferson in opposition to religious establishment, to the application of religious test in political life, and to the intrusion of religion in schools and colleges. All, both argued, intimidated religious freedom. Yet, it should be noted, Jefferson, the author of the 1779 Virginia Act for Establishing Religious Freedom, expressed a minority view. The people were not quite ready for the separation of church and state.

Education and Religion. Before the Constitution could be ratified, the framers had to add ten amendments (the Bill of Rights), the first of which severely limited the range of federal authority vis-à-vis religion: "Congress shall make no law respecting an establishment of religion or prohibiting the free exercise thereof." Care recommends the observation that the First Amendment spoke to the Congress and the federal government, not to the states, and, moreover, even taking into account the whole of the Constitution, made no reference whatever to religion in education. Had the founding fathers the prescience to foresee the erection of a public school system, they might have given the federal government some role in education and might even have barred religion's intrusion upon pedagogy. But this, although having the ring of plausibility, is conjecture. When the First Amendment was adopted, no one hinted at its being a wall of separation between church and state or an insulation of education from religion.

The First Amendment, it might be noted, was never appealed to when the states (for example, Massachusetts in 1827) proscribed denominational teaching and sectarian materials of instruction in common schools. What Massachusetts did in 1827 was done dozens of times in other states before the Fourteenth Amendment (1868) applied the Bill of Rights to the states. Without the Fourteenth Amendment, the educational action of the federal government in the years between 1950 and 1970 with respect to civil right and the extension of educational opportunity might not have had a constitutional basis, but the record of history does not point unerringly to an interpretation of the First Amendment as a barrier to religion in education. At the close of the eighteenth century no one was confused about the meaning of "an establishment of religion," so a persuasive case for the proposition that, on its face, the First Amendment made religious teaching in public schools illegal is hard to make. But this should not be taken to mean that contemporary policies immunizing public schools from denominational influence are wrong and should be rescinded. If history teaches anything, it is this: had public education in the United States not adopted a policy of nonsectarianism, it would have been a failure.

Public Support for Private Schools. Religion in public education is one side of the church–state issue. There are others. Long before this good land had anything faintly resembling authentic public schools, institutions ranging in character from denominational Latin grammar schools to nonsectarian academies sometimes received public funds and land grants. Even after state laws interdicted sectarian teaching in public schools, private religious schools continued to receive, although less regularly and generously than before, support from public sources. And in those instances when private schools were denied public support, it was not always because they were private or denominational. In Massachusetts, for example, a law prohibited academies from public land grants when other schools existed nearby; and, of course, the Massachusetts law of 1827, in proscribing the teaching of denominational doctrine in the common schools, was silent about the use of public money for church-related schools.

An interpretation of the First Amendment as prohibiting the disbursement of public funds to support denominational purpose in private schools was by no means evident when President Ulysses S. Grant twice urged the adoption of a constitutional amendment to prohibit the use of public money in church-related schools.[22] The proposed amendment failed, but advancing it for consideration illustrates the point: public money had been and was being used to aid private and religious schools. As much as anything else, it focused attention on a practice fast losing public support, so state after state, in constitutional provision and statute, began to limit the use of public money to clear and specific public purpose.

In some states, the language of statute or constitutional proscription was directed at religious institutions. In the end, then, legal precedent restricting the use of public resources and excluding religious institutions and schools from them was neither introduced nor ratified in the first years of the Republic. And whether the language and intent of the First Amendment imply such prohibitions can be debated by reasonable persons. In any case, it should be clear, statute had in many cases and many places prohibited the diversion of public funds for religious purpose in an out of schools without ever making any appeal to the First Amendment.

Denomination influence in public education and public support for private schools account for only some of the vexing issues relative to religion and education in American schools: Bible reading, prayer, and denominational instruction are others.

Bible Reading in the Schools. Throughout the colonial years and for most of the early national period, teaching reading was the school's main commission. Even before schools were extant, reading was the first rung on education's ladder, and in homes and elsewhere the Bible was the book usually enlisted for teaching this humble but essential auxiliary to learning. No primer rivaled its popularity.

Naturally enough, when public schools were properly organized, the Bible had an important, almost irremovable place in schooling. Besides being an instrument for secular instruction, it had the recommendation (one not easily discounted) of being good for the soul. The nearly unassailable status of the Bible in education was left undisturbed when the first state law banning denominational teaching in common schools was enacted. For its moral and intellectual worth, Bible reading was required, but in order to eliminate the introduction of sectarian doctrine, interpretation of Scripture was barred. The states thereafter handled Bible reading in various ways, and plenty of evidence supports the assumption that it seldom led to controversy.

Bible reading in public schools was simply not a burning issue. By 1963, thirteen states required its daily reading in public schools, although without comment or discussion; twenty-five states had permissive statutes, leaving Bible reading decisions to local school districts; eight states, regarding the Bible as a sectarian document, enjoined it being read in public schools; and four states maintained statutory silence.

In 1952, a New Jersey statute requiring the reading of five verses from the Old Testament as an opening exercise in public schools was challenged in the courts. Lower courts found no fault in the statute and the United States Supreme Court refused jurisdiction.[23] But this was only the beginning. In 1963, two cases—one involved a Pennsylvania statute requiring "at least ten verses from the Holy Bible shall be read, without comment, at the opening of each public school on each school day. Any child shall be excused from such Bible reading, or attending such Bible reading, upon the written request of his parent or guardian; . . . ", and the other, a regulation of the Board of School Commissioners of Baltimore, prescribing an opening school exercise of the "reading, without comment, of a chapter of the Holy Bible and/or the use of the Lord's Prayer. . . ."—were heard by the Supreme Court.[24]

The court found that schools following the statute and the regulation were imposing exercises, under the provision of compulsory attendance in school buildings under the direct supervision of teachers, that were, and were intended to be, religious ceremonies. The Bible, the court wrote, is an instrument with a religious, even sectarian character, and the Pennsylvania law and the Baltimore regulation required religious exercises in direct violation of the rights of the persons who initiated the litigation. Permitting students to absent themselves from these exercises was not, the court declared, a defense to the assertion of unconstitutionality. Required Bible reading in public schools was a violation of the establishment clause of the First Amendment.[25]

But in banning Bible reading, the court was careful to maintain the Bible's scholastic status. Judicial notice was taken of the Bible's literary and historical character, and the court demurred from enjoining school study of either the Bible or religion when it was conducted objectively as part of a secular curriculum, instead recommending such scholarship as essential for academic integrity and a competent understanding of the history of Western civilization. In declaring for a strictly secular rather than nonsectarian approach to such study, the court's decision antagonized persons who opposed the introduction of any religious document to the schools, while failing to mollify friends of religion in education. Rather than settling dispute, the court's decision likely raised the issue to a higher level of controversy and encouraged a campaign for a constitutional amendment that would allow for religion's return to American education.

Prayer in the Public Schools. Despite the court's decision with respect to the place of the Bible in public education, law and tradition as well as the temperament of the people—as evidenced in their affinity for organized religion and their participation in religious service—testify to America's profound respect for religion. Nothing in the Constitution can be interpreted as declaring war on it. And for much of the nation's educational history, it is fair to say, the schools were understood to have a close relationship to religious and moral formation. Nothing was unusual about the recitation of prayer in early schools or, as in the case of the famous *McGuffey Readers*, the teaching of morals.[26] Yet American schools drifted away from both prayer and moral teaching.

In 1951, this drift was reversed slightly when the New York State

Board of Regents proposed the recitation of a prayer in the public schools: "Almighty God, we acknowledge our dependence upon Thee, and we beg Thy blessings upon us, our parents, our teachers, and our country." Public reaction to the prayer bordered on indifference; only about ten percent of the state's school districts chose to adopt it.

Whatever the extent of its reception, the constitutional status of this officially adopted prayer was challenged, and the challenge worked its legal way to the United States Supreme Court where in *Engel v. Vitale* (1962) the practice was declared to be an establishment of religion by government, impermissible under the First Amendment.[27] An optimistic and uncritical reading of the decision lead enthusiastic religionists to suppose the court outlawed school prayer only when it was composed and proposed by government, or when the state invaded the neutral ground of religious conscience, but a closer reading made clear that *Engel v. Vitale* forbade all prayer in public schools whatever its source or auspices.

Denominational Instruction in Public Schools. Constitutional questions about bible reading and school prayer were asked and answered in the 1960s, so the record would appear complete. But in the two decades before these decisions were rendered, religion was reintroduced to public education along different lines and constitutional questions were raised for adjudication.

In the 1940s, two Illinois school districts introduced programs of religious education by inviting representatives of various religious denominations to enter school buildings during the regular school day and conduct classes in religion. Attendance was voluntary, and the teachers of religion were not compensated by the schools. When legal challenge was mounted, state courts declared for the practice, but the United States Supreme Court found it a violation of the First Amendment: "To hold that a state cannot consistently with the First and Fourteenth Amendments utilize its public school system to aid any or all religious faiths or sects in the dissemination of their doctrines and ideals does not . . . manifest a governmental hostility to religion or religious teachings. A manifestation of such hostility would be at war with our national tradition as embodied in the First Amendment's guaranty of the free exercise of religion. For the First Amendment rests upon the premise that both religion and government can best work to achieve their lofty aims if each is left free from the other within its respective sphere. Or, as we said in the *Everson* case, the First Amendment has erected a wall between Church and State which must be kept high and impregnable."[28] This 1948 decision emphasized the use of tax-supported public-school buildings for the dissemination of religious doctrine and concluded that the state's compulsory attendance statute was, in effect, supplying pupils for classes in religious instruction. This, the court declared, violated the principle of separation of church and state.

Yet, to illustrate how complicated questions relative to religion and public education can be, a New York State law permitted public schools to release students from school upon parental written request, during the regular school day, to attend classes in religious instruction or participate in religious exercises. Neither public funds nor buildings were used, but students exercising their option to engage in the program were under the jurisdiction of the school and subject to compulsory attendance.

In the wake of the *McCollum* decision the pot of controversy boiled, and a constitutional test of the New York law was inevitable. The charge of unconstitutionality was clear and direct: the New York practice was an establishment of religion and public resource was used for sectarian purpose. But in *Zorach v. Clauson* (1952) the Supreme Court demurred: released time was permissible under the First Amendment doctrine because it neither prohibited the free exercise of religion nor made a law respecting an establishment of religion.[29]

The court, moreover, abandoned the metaphor "wall of separation," so prominently introduced in *McCollum*. It preferred to explain precisely the meaning of separation of church and state: "There cannot be the slightest doubt that the First Amendment reflects the philosophy that Church and State should be separated. And so far as interference with the 'free exercise' of religion and an 'establishment' of religion are concerned, the separation must be complete and unequivocal. The First Amendment within the scope of its coverage permits no exception; the prohibition is absolute. The First Amendment, however, does not say that in every and all respects there shall be a separation of Church and State. Rather, it studiously defines the manner, the specific ways, in which there shall be no concert or union or dependency one on the other. That is the common sense of the matter. Otherwise the state and religion would be aliens to each other—hostile, suspicious, and even unfriendly. Churches could not be required to pay even property taxes. Municipalities would not be permitted to render police or fire protection to religious groups. Policemen who helped parishioners into their places of worship would violate the Constitution. Prayers in our legislative halls; the appeals to the Almighty in the messages of the Chief Executive; the proclamations making Thanksgiving Day a holiday; 'so help me God' in our courtroom oaths— these and all other references to the Almighty that run through our laws, our public rituals, our ceremonies would be flouting the First Amendment. A fastidious atheist or agnostic could even object to the supplication with which the Court opens each session: 'God save the United States and this Honorable Court.'"[30]

The concept of separation, the court wrote further, would have to be pressed to the extreme to nullify the New York law and "nullification would have wide and profound effects. A Catholic student applies to his teacher for permission to leave the school during school hours on a Holy Day of Obligation to attend a mass. A Jewish student asks his teacher for permission to be excused for Yom Kippur. A Protestant wants the afternoon off for a family baptismal ceremony. In each case the teacher requires parental consent in writing. In each case the teacher, in order to make sure the student is not a truant, goes further and requires a report from the priest, the rabbi, or the minister. The teacher in other words cooperates in a religious program to the extent of making it possible for her students to participate in it. Whether she does it occasionally for a few students, regularly for one, or pursuant to a systematized program designed to further the religious needs of all the students does not alter the character of the act."

Released time might be shown to be unwise or improvident, it might offend individual preference, but these objections, said the court, are not constitutional standards. The constitutional standard was set in the *McCollum* case where classrooms and the force of the public school were used to promote religious instruction. "Here . . . the public schools do no more than accommodate their schedules to a program of outside religious instruction. We follow the *McCollum* case. But we cannot expand it to cover the present released time program unless separation of Church and State means that public institutions can make no adjustments of their schedules to accommodate the religious needs of the people. We cannot read into the Bill of Rights such a philosophy of hostility to religion."[31]

The effect of the Supreme Court decisions was to insulate public schools from direct sectarian influence and to ensure that public resources were not used directly for the benefit of any religious denomination. Yet students attending private and religious schools are citizens and are entitled to equal protection of the law. This principle, now clearly recognized, took time to define, and the definition antedated the Supreme Court's decisions on Bible reading, prayer, and released time.

Students' Rights as Citizens. A Louisiana law permitted the state to supply textbooks to children in public, private, and religious schools alike. A question of constitutionality was raised in the allegation that the law either aided or advanced sectarian religion, but the United States Supreme Court in *Cochran v. The Board of Education of Louisiana* (1930)[32] upheld the law, because in promoting a public purpose its furthering of a private end was merely incidental. And in *Everson v. The Board of Education* (1947),[33] the *Cochran* decision was noticed and ratified.

The *Everson* case introduced a constitutional challenge to a New Jersey statute authorizing local school districts to supply transportation for children attending private nonprofit, and, mostly, church-related schools. Answering the allegation that the law contravened the First Amendment, the court said the "wall of separation" between church and state was not breached by such benefits, because children received them as citizens of the state, not as students attending certain types of schools.

The state, the court declared, is obliged to ignore the child's creed but not his need, and the New Jersey statute, in contributing to the safe and expeditious movement of children to and from school, fulfilled a public purpose even when private schools reaped an indirect benefit. These decisions made auxiliary educational services available to all children without regard to the school attended, and a variety of such services—textbooks and other instructional material, health care, lunch programs—have found their way to private and religious schools. Care should be taken to observe, however, that states have discretionary authority to extend or withhold these benefits. The constitution neither requires nor prohibits them; states may or may not make children in nonpublic schools beneficiaries of such services.

Educational Standard and Reform

Control and support of education and religion's place in the schools accounted for a great deal of ferment in the first three-quarters of the twentieth century, but following World War II other important issues competed for attention. For a long time, except when temporarily distracted by progressive education, citizens were satisfied with the standard of instruction maintained in the schools, although, fair to say, debate about what knowledge had most curricular worth in high schools and colleges never subsided entirely. But debate about the curriculum was projected to a new level of significance in 1957 when the Soviet Union launched *Sputnik*.

Praised as a scientific achievement of the first order, the invasion of space by a hostile nation was at the same time a bad omen hinting that American educational ineptitude was undermining American power, influence, and security. Almost at once, the schools were called up for scrutiny and reforms were recommended to improve them, especially in science and mathematics. The federal government, in almost unprecedented action, and in the name of national defense, mounted program after program to support an upgrading of education in science.

Retreating somewhat from ideological skirmishes, educators began to line up on the side of sturdy academic standard, but for the most part their attention was riveted on science. And this made them susceptible to the charge that a concentration on scientific study unbalanced the curriculum to the point where the breadth of decent learning was being sacrificed to hasty and premature specialization. Without questioning the legitimate role scientific study should command in the curriculum, a responsible argument was made in support of the humanities.

The extent to which this argument was heeded is debatable, but this burst of enthusiasm for scholastic excellence began to wane, and as teachers and students looked for other ways to satisfy scholastic appetites, schools began to return to their former more comfortable standards.[34] They were aided and abetted by two uncomplementary sources: the Vietnam War and a new epistemology idealizing relevance. The former put schools and colleges in convulsion, and the latter raised to the level of principle the novel assertion that reason is irrelevant and commitment is profound.

Protest and Relevance. What had for so long been taken for granted—that students in schools and colleges would support the country at war—[35] was rudely rejected as the United States became more deeply involved in Vietnam and as justification for a war so far from home became less persuasive. College student disaffection all too frequently turned into strident protest and then, by force, to an interruption of academic functions. At the same time, and in almost the same way, students assessed college curricula and declared them deficient and irrelevant. Driven more by emotion that by reason, and by a less than prudent analysis of the corpus of knowledge, they intimidated boards of trustees, school committees, administrators, teachers, and professors who, under unfamiliar assault, bargained away their legitimate authority to define educational purpose and content and the integrity of the educational process.

The history of education is filled with episodes of student activism, complaint, and sometimes insurrection, so what occurred lacked the ring of novelty, but history offers little solace to schools under siege. Historians recounting these years of revolt might conclude that student activism introduced a necessary catharsis to American education, and their conclusion might contain elements of truth, but they might find a basis for concluding, too, that these irruptions, untempered by common prudence, infected with political motive, and marred by violence, retarded the introduction of legitimate reform and downgraded the quality of the educational process. They might assert, as well, that the proposition making students the final judge of educational content and standard demeans any rational epistemology and surrenders responsibility for educational decency to interest, demand, fad, and whim. Still, however long the shadow of discontent, the cloud that cast it might have had a silver lining.

Concealed by frantic negativism, protest, unconventional dress, appearance, and manner, a fundamental idealism flourished. Probably in a better position than any previous generation of students to afford idealism, students in the 1960s formed a solid corps of support for the civil rights movement and for equality of educational opportunity. Their enthusiasm accelerated a progress that, over the years, had been painfully slow. Compensatory education, Head Start, Higher Horizons, Upward Bound, bilingualism, mainstreaming, and affirmative action became idioms in the vocabulary of education.

Improving the Schools. In the wake of school desegregation, concerted action was undertaken, often required by the federal courts, to integrate the schools. But at almost the same time, in a genuine response to concern for the quality of the educational process, state after state introduced methods for assessing minimum competence both for students and teachers. In concert with state action to correct what were perceived as deficiencies in schooling, several reports were issued by various groups to define the dimensions of scholastic reform. Some gave attention to the educational process, while others focused on the improvement and, in some cases, the restructuring of teacher education.[36]

The Education of Teachers

However much attention is visited on the organization and the curriculum of the schools in order to secure reform and thus higher scholastic standard, both history and philosophy of education speak to the central role teachers play in directing instruction. Instructional materials have been refined and a variety of instructional aids have been introduced with a salutary effect on teaching and learning, but in the last analysis, teachers supply the educational process with an integral vigor. While the student's place as the principal agent must not be neglected, the teacher is an essential auxiliary. This conviction has led educators and the public alike to pay special heed to the qualification and status of teachers whenever the educational agenda includes the elevation of standards and the initiation of reform in American schools.

Throughout most of American educational history, professional status was withheld from teachers. Their rank on the economic and social ladder was inferior to physicians, lawyers, and engineers, and in many communities their compensation was lower than for policemen and firemen. When teachers were mainly 'hearers of lessons', the public showed no sign of alarm, but as schooling in the nation underwent drastic metamorphosis, the old-fashioned teacher, only modestly educated and usually temporarily employed, became an anachronism.

Expectation relative to a teacher's qualification for directing instruction was raised, so the public, no longer content with teachers who had spent some time in a normal school, began to demand college degrees for teachers. Step by painful step, teachers improved their status in American society, yet all this effort did not confer genuine professional status. Teaching was burdened by being viewed as an occupation, and whether the public's perception has been amended is a strikingly interesting, and debatable, question.

How much reform or redefinition will occur in connection with teachers is unpredictable, but it is evident that, either as a profession or an occupation, teaching has been subject to remarkable evolution. Teachers were always underpaid, too often their tenure was temporary, their work was hard, and they were without any or many of the benefits offered to workers in industry. Most of this grim picture has been altered. Tenure affords teachers stability in their position; salary schedules and benefits remove uncertainly from economic life; but the unanswered question is whether Americans are prepared to reward teachers who are agents in a process to which allegiance is paid.

Teaching is a complex combination of science and art, and the nature of learning has still some mystery surrounding it, so precision in assessing the work of a teacher eludes exactness. Yet in recent years, teachers have felt compelled to demonstrate their productivity, and this has led them to endorse, although with some hesitation and caution, the phenomenon of accountability: What did pupils achieve? How much and how well did they learn? The public, understandably interested in knowing what the educational dollar has purchased, tends to be enamored of accountability. And it would be hard to argue convincingly for a proposition making teachers immune to any assessment of performance. Despite the force of this common-sense position, it is far from clear whether the practices of accountability, borrowed for the most part from commerce and industry, will function effectively in the schools or whether teachers will be benefited or harmed by them.

The education of teachers is a popular contemporary issue. No one doubts that teachers in the 1980s had more schooling than their earlier counterparts, but the central question was not the amount of schooling they had, but the level of intellectual competence it represented, and this point speaks directly to a philosophy of teacher-education, something whereupon the educational community seldom finds much agreement. Contemporary report and recommendation, moreover, tend to skirt philosophy, although the basic question is easy to articulate: Should teacher-education be liberal, with a clear commitment to cultural insight and adequacy, or should it be professional and technical, preoccupied with communicating the skill teachers should possess?

The College Curriculum

Any appraisal of education should take into account the three levels of schooling. For a long time, the college course stood relatively immobile: it contained the kind of knowledge most educated people thought to be true and, moreover, worth having. If sometimes it appeared to lack direct utility, ornamentation and culture were not discounted as a load too heavy for the educated person to carry. But in the last half of the twentieth century, and urged on by an appeal to democratize higher education, the traditional college course was subject to searching scrutiny and, eventually, to amendment so severe that a nineteenth-century professor would have had trouble recognizing it.[37] In addition, junior colleges (sometimes called "community colleges") were added as downward extensions, and graduate schools were grafted to the top.

The character of American higher education has been subject to substantial change, but has change been beneficial or detrimental? Over the past three decades, critical scholars have pointed to the deficiencies in preparatory education for college, to the low requirements for admission in all but a minority of the nation's elite colleges, to the undemanding and often unacademic courses in the curriculum, to inflated assessment of student achievement, to the apparent inability of college graduates to handle basic English and mathematics, and to the abject surrender of higher education to the exigencies of the marketplace.[38]

A perhaps praiseworthy hunger for higher education has tempted students to flock to the colleges (too often, critics say, without solid preparation),[39] and the colleges' urge to be genuinely democratic (and sometimes not unmindful of profit) aided and abetted them. Besides, economists persuaded the public of the financial benefit that accrues to persons with academic degrees. In order to offer something in the curriculum for everyone, standards were discounted and courses were introduced that, some scholars allege, could not be justified either by method or content. No one, critics declared, could predict with any confidence what standard of learning a college degree represented, and even more serious, persons who were supposed to be educated lacked any common foundation of knowledge as a basis for communication. The traditional core to the college experience and the conventional norm of educational decency were absent.

This infection of liberal education led to a latitude in the colleges that turned out to be worrisome. But the infection did not come suddenly; it had been festering since the end of the Great Depression in the 1930s. Recognizing something amiss in the college course, college presidents and professors began to seek for its rehabilitation. At the University of Chicago, Robert M. Hutchins undertook to reconstruct the undergraduate experience by introducing the Great Books program and a two-year bachelor's degree. In 1945, the Harvard College faculty issued a seminal report: *General Education in a Free Society*.[40] But neither Chicago nor Harvard produced a definition of liberal education whereupon educators could agree. The college course appeared to be impervious to reform, but tantalizing questions of standard and stability refused to disappear from the lexicon of intelligent outsiders and the notebooks of concerned academicians.

In 1977, Dean Henry Rosovsky of Harvard College, realizing the college curriculum was in jeopardy, tried to restore a genuine core curriculum in the college. Some success, most commentators agree, accompanied his effort, and the bewildering array of 2,600 subjects from which Harvard undergraduates could choose their studies was reduced. But uneasiness remained in much of the academic community about the health of the undergraduate curriculum. That this is a persistent and, for the most part, an unresolved problem is illustrated best by the reception such recent books as Earnest L. Boyer's *College: The Undergraduate Experience in America*,[41] and Allan Bloom's *The Closing of the American Mind* have had in the late 1980s.[42]

Yet with all the unresolved educational issues, ranging from access to the schools to the standards maintained in them, American education must finally be praised for its monumental achievement. From almost nothing, a vast and various school system was erected, and the record of history reports high marks for its service to American society.

Notes

Chapter 1

1. Plato *Protagoras* 319b.

2. Plato *Laws* 7. 810c–811b; Plato *Republic* 2. 377a–392b.

3. *Histor* meant search or inquiry and had nothing to do with recording the past. Eventually, however, the quick Greek mind perceived the worth of a record of past deed and event, and transformed history's meaning and purpose.

4. Bury, *A History of Greece to the Death of Alexander*, 72.

5. Isocrates *Areopagiticus* 44–45.

6. Xenophon, *Banquet* 3. 5, is one witness to the story that every cultivated Greek had a copy of Homer at his bedside. He quotes Nicoratus: "My father, wishing me to become an accomplished man, made me learn the whole of Homer, so that even today I can still recite the *Iliad* and the *Odyssey* by heart."

7. Plato *Phaedrus* 245a.

8. For example, Homer *Iliad* 9. 524; Homer *Odyssey* 1. 30, 40, 296; 3. 306.

9. Aristotle *Politics* 4. 1279b, 16–25.

10. Plato *Laws* 7. 793–794.

11. Xenophon *The Constitution of the Athenians* 2. 10.

12. Aristophanes *The Clouds* 964–965.

13. Ibid., 1002–1019.

14. Euripides *Autolycus*.

15. Pindar *Nemeans* 3. 57–58; Pindar *Olympics* 8. 59–61.

16. Aristophanes *The Clouds* 986.

17. Aristophanes *The Clouds* 1009–1014.

18. Forbes, *Greek Physical Education*, 40–44.

19. Aeschines *Against Timarchus* 9.

20. Euripides *Iphigeneia Among the Taurians* 2. 584.

21. Plato *Republic* 7. 451e–452b.

22. *Herodotus* 8. 75.

23. Freeman, *Schools of Hellas*, 66–69.

24. Plato *Politics* 7. 277e–278ab.

25. Aristotle *Politics* 8. 3. 1.

26. Plato *Protagoras* 326.

27. Aristophanes *The Wasps* 656.

28. Plato *Protagoras* 325–326.

29. The school's name, always puzzling, must have had something to do with music's place of prominence in Greek life. Plato, *Laws* 2. 654ab, puts the case for music bluntly: "Anyone who cannot take his place in the choir (as a singer or dancer) is not truly educated."

30. Plato *Laches* 197a; Xenophon *The Constitution of Lacedaemon* 3. 1.

31. Plutarch *Antony* 33.

32. Aristotle *The Constitution of Athens* 42.

33. Sweet, *Sport and Recreation in Ancient Greece*, 112.

34. Lynch, *Aristotle's School*, 96.

35. Aristotle *The Constitution of Athens* 42.

36. Aristotle *Politics* 7. 13.

37. Plutarch *Lycurgus* 1. 293–297.

38. Xenophon *Cyropaedia* 1. 2. 15. Xenophon expressed his admiration in both literary and practical ways: at least one of his sons was sent to Sparta to be educated. Although this was unusual, and aliens could not become citizens, Sparta sometimes allowed the sons of prominent outsiders to take the full training course.

39. Isocrates, *Panathenaicus* 2. 209 and 251, says the Spartans were illiterate, although Plutarch, *Lycurgus* 1. 257, claims they had just enough literary skill to "serve them."

40. Jaeger, *Paideia: The Ideals of Greek Culture*, 1:82–83.

41. Plutarch *Lycurgus* 1. 257–259.

42. Plutarch *Lycurgus* 1. 247–249.

43. Plato *Protagoras* 319b.

44. Isocrates *Antidosis* 2. 235.

45. Isocrates *Against the Sophists* 2. 3.

46. Plato *Sophist* 222–224.

47. The history of sophistry and the record of the best Sophists cannot be given here. A dependable, sometimes thought definitive, account of the Sophists can be found in Untersteiner, *The Sophists*. Jaeger, *Paideia*, 1:286–331, is well worth consulting as is Jarrett, ed., *The Educational Theories of the Sophists*.

Chapter 2

1. These issues are amplified considerably in Robert J. Bonner, *Lawyers and Litigants in Ancient Athens*.

2. Xenophon, 3:231.

3. See Plato's *Apology*.

4. Ibid.; and see Xenophon 3:231ff.

5. Kenneth J. Freeman, *Schools of Hellas*, 180.

6. H. F. Cherniss, *The Riddle of the Early Academy*, 236–238.

7. Edward J. Power, "Plato's Academy: A Halting Step Toward Higher Learning." *History of Education Quarterly* 4 (September 1964): 155–166.

8. Werner W. Jaeger, *Paideia: The Ideals of Greek Culture*, 2:200–203.

9. Plato *Republic* 7. 558.

10. Ibid.

11. Plato *Laws* 6. 776.

12. Plato *Laws* 7. 804.

13. Plato *Republic* 2, and 3; *Laws* 7.

14. Plato *Laws* 1. 643.

15. Plato *Republic* 7. 526b.

16. Ibid., 3. 410c–412.

17. Ibid., 2. 367e.

18. Ibid., 2. 514a.

19. Ibid., 2. 367e.

20. Ibid., 7. 298.

21. Plato *Laws* 7. 810.

22. Plato *Republic* 7. 298.

23. Ibid.

24. Ibid., 7. 302–303.

25. The comment is made at the close of Plato's *Phaedrus*.

26. Isocrates *Against the Sophists* 21.

27. Isocrates *Antidosis* 271.

28. Ibid., 30.

29. Ibid., 95–96. This must have put a heavy burden upon teachers, for moral excellence is not easy to discern. To help them with this burden, Isocrates told teachers to watch boys at play, for on the playground, he thought, boys would display the true metal of their character.

30. Isocrates *Areopagiticus* 115; *Against the Sophists* 163.

31. Isocrates *Nicocles* 79–81.

32. Isocrates *Antidosis* 87–88.

33. Ibid., 277.

34. H. I. Marrou, *A History of Education in Antiquity*, 85–86.

35. Isocrates *Antidosis* 183–185.

36. Edward J. Power, "Class Size and Pedagogy in Isocrates' School." *History of Education Quarterly* 4 (Winter 1964): 22–23.

37. Isocrates *Panathenaicus* 519.

38. Isocrates *Nicocles* 80–83.

39. Aristotle *Against the Sophists* 34. 7.

40. Opinion on this point varies. Some scholars believe Aristotle wrote a book on educational philosophy, but others are confident that no such book was ever written.

41. John Patrick Lynch, *Aristotle's School*, 90.

42. Ibid., 88.

43. Aristotle *Politics* 7. 17.

44. Ibid., 7. 13.

45. Ibid., 8. 1.

46. Plutarch *Moralia*, 8, 10.

Chapter 3

1. Isocrates *Panathenicus* 32–33.

2. Demosthenes *On the Symmories*.

3. Bury, *A History of Greece*, 724–725.

4. Bury, *The Hellenistic Age*, 40–60.

5. Marrou, *A History of Education in Antiquity*, 242; and Gruen, *The Hellenistic World and the Coming of Rome*, 1:250–260.

6. Bolgar, *The Classical Heritage and Its Beneficiaries*, 43–44.

7. Plato *Republic* 2. 401d–c; Aristotle *Politics* 7. 15.

8. One convenient source for these examples is Diogenes Laertius *Lives and Opinions of Eminent Philosophers* 2, 5, 7, 9.

9. Ibid., 2. 72.

10. Eby and Arrowood, *The History and Philosophy of Education*, 472.

11. Gruen, *Hellenistic World*, 1:317–318.

12. Quintilian *The Education of an Orator* 2. 17. 41.

13. Diogenes Laertius 7. 52–53.

14. For a fuller treatment of these and other Hellenistic educational theorists, see Power, *Evolution of Educational Doctrine*, 16–24.

15. Marrou, *History of Education*, 104.

16. Plato *Republic* 7. 526b; Isocrates *Nicocles* 1. 80–83; and Aristotle *Politics* 7. 17.

17. Jaeger, *Paideia*, 1:298–299.

18. Marrou, *History of Education*, 147.

19. Plutarch *The Education of Children* 7CD, 8B, 9DE, and 11CD.

20. Marrou, *History of Education*, 137.

21. Ibid., 141.

22. Quintilian 1. 1. 24.

23. Marrou, *History of Education*, 150.

24. Plato *Protagoras* 326d.

25. Marrou, *History of Education*, 157.

26. Quintilian 1. 1. 18.

27. Ibid., 1. 3. 14.

28. Ibid., 2. 5.

29. Marrou, *History of Education*, 164.

30. Quintilian 1. 4. 3.

31. Dionysius Thrax *On Grammar* 7. 8–10, 15–20, quoted in Marrou, *History of Education*, 171.

32. Quintilian 1. 9. 1.

33. Ibid., 1. 9. 6; 2. 1. 1.

34. Euclid *Elements of Geometry* 1. 5.

35. Ibid., 7–9.

36. Rostovtseff, *The Social and Economic History of the Hellenistic World*, 1088–1095.

37. Marrou, *History of Education*, 193.

38. O'Leary, *How Greek Science Passed to the Arabs*, 170–173; and Strabo, *The Geography of Strabo*, 8:35.

39. Ibid.

40. Rhetorical instruction repudiated change. The same syllabus was followed in Rome. See Bonner, *Education in Ancient Rome*, 68.

41. Quintilian 2. 5. 19.

42. Ibid., 9. 2–3.

43. Ibid., 11. 3. 100.

44. Marrou, *History of Education*, 206.

45. Plato *Gorgias* 450c.

Chapter 4

1. The imperial policy of Rome, once taken for granted, is now a subject of scholarly debate. A body of respected opinion holds that Rome engaged in conquest more to defend herself than to extend her sphere of influence. See Gruen, *The Hellenistic World*, 1:7–8.

2. Tacitus *Dialogue on Oratory* 28.

3. This distinction is confirmed in the work of Stanley F. Bonner, *Education in Ancient Rome*, xi.

4. The *Dialogue on Oratory*, attributed to Tacitus, gives Roman mothers special attention and praise in connection with the education of children.

5. Pliny *Letters* 2. 8. 14.

6. Dionysius, *Roman Antiquities* 4. 20. 13, supplies some information on the role of censors.

7. Gwynn, *Roman Education from Cicero to Quintilian*, 17.

8. Cicero *Laws* 1.

9. Tacitus *Dialogue on Oratory* 34.

10. Bonner, *Education in Ancient Rome*, 27.

11. Suetonius *Of Grammarians and Rhetors* 1. 3.

12. How or why Romans came to use the term *ludus*, (play) to designate a school is a puzzle that is partly unraveled by Bonner, *Education in Ancient Rome*, 56–57. He relates how ancient etymologists "were fond of explaining that word-meanings could be derived from contrary ideas." Quintilian and others accepted the story that a school was called a *ludus* because it was the very opposite of a place for play. Others asserted that the term was used to attract children to school. Bonner offers this interpretation: In ancient times, Romans commonly conducted training interludes preliminary to military service, and since this training was entirely physical, depending a great deal upon games for exercise and conditioning as practice for battle, the place where this training was given was called a *ludus*, a training ground. Since the training given in a school was also a preparation for the give and take of public life, especially in the Forum and arena, the name adopted for the school was, naturally enough, *ludus*.

13. Quintilian *The Education of an Orator* 1. 1. 9.

14. Ibid., 1. 1. 8.

15. This view is confirmed in Gwynn, *Roman Education*, 31. For expressions of the same disdain for primary teachers, see Tacitus *Annals* 3. 66. 4; and Florus *Was Virgil an Orator or a Poet?* 3. 2, in *Epitome of Roman History*.

16. Cicero *Laws* 1. 23. 59; and Augustine *Confessions* 1. 13.

17. Quintilian *The Education of an Orator* 1. 10. 35.

18. Ibid., 1. 4. 2, 1. 2. 14.

19. Juvenal *Satires* 157. 203.

20. Now and then a grammar master was disposed to business or commercial ventures. If income from teaching was invested prudently, with some luck a *gram-*

maticus could become a rich man. Remmius Palaemon, a successful teacher of grammar, owned a clothing factory and a vineyard from which he profited, although he may have been engaged in both ventures before he opened his school (Bonner, *Education in Ancient Rome,* 153–154).

21. Cicero, *The Orations of Marcus Tullius* 1. 18. 34.

22. Juvenal *Satires* 6. 452.

23. Quintilian *The Education of an Orator* 1. 8. 13.

24. Cicero *De Oratore* 1. 187.

25. This division of labor was practiced in Quintilian's time, but though he deplored it, his objection, apparently, was paid scant heed. Quintilian 1. 9. 1; 6. 2. 1–8; and 6. 4. 1.

26. Quintilian 2. 6. 1–2.

27. Quintilian 2. 3. 7.

28. Cicero *De Oratore* 1. 20. Despite Cicero's deflation of it, the literary oration was retained as part of Roman rhetoric and was commonly used to sharpen a student's wit. A student might be assigned a topic like this: The law states that if a woman has been seduced, she can choose either to have her seducer condemned to death or marry him without bringing him a dowry. A man violates two women on the same night. One wants him put to death, the other chooses to marry him (Seneca the Rhetor *Controversiae* 1. 5, quoted in Marrou, *History of Education,* 287).

29. Suetonius *Of Grammarians and Orators* 1. 8. 13.

30. Roman law was held by Edward Gibbon, *The History of the Decline and Fall of the Roman Empire,* 44 (4:446, 457), "to surpass in genuine value the libraries of Grecian philosophy," although he conceded that Roman law was polished and improved in the seventh century by an alliance with Greek philosophy. [Gibbon's chapter number is given in the citation and in parentheses the volume and page number.]

31. Cicero *Brutus* 305.

32. The pleader is sometimes represented as the equivalent of a district attorney, but this is not quite accurate. A pleader, or an advocate, could have been either the prosecutor or the defense attorney. In neither case was this a state office. Bonner, *Education in Ancient Rome,* 66–68, gives a good account of the role of pleaders.

33. Cicero *De Oratore* 1. 5.

34. Ibid., 1. 6.

35. Ibid., 2. 22.

36. In *Brutus* 33. 126–127, Cicero identifies the orators he most admired and tried to imitate.

37. Ibid., 3. 19–35.

38. Ibid., 2. 5.

39. Ibid., 1. 20–21.

40. Cicero *Oratoriae* 120.

41. Cicero *De Oratore* 3. 142–143.

42. Quintilian *The Education of an Orator* 12. 1. 1.

43. Spain was sometimes a Roman province and we have Plutarch's assurance, *Sertorius* 14. 2–3, that the sons of influential Spaniards were given a genuine Roman education in Latin and Greek by teachers imported from Rome.

44. The Latin title, *Institutio Oratoria*, is sometimes rendered *The Training of an Orator*. The work is organized into twelve books, or parts.

45. Quintilian *The Education of an Orator* preface 4–9.

46. Ibid., 1. 1. 9.

47. Ibid., 3. 8. 47.

48. Ibid., 1. 1. 4, 7–8.

49. Ibid., 1. 1. 9.

50. Ibid., 1. 1. 15–19.

51. Ibid., 1. 1. 36.

52. Ibid., 1. 4. 22.

53. Ibid., 1. 1. 20.

54. Ibid., 1. 1. 18.

55. Ibid., 1. 10. 34–49.

56. Ibid., 1. 4. 6–7.

57. Ibid., 1. 10. 35.

58. Ibid., 1. 1. 1.

59. Ibid., 2. 1. 1.

60. Ibid., 10. 1. 72–82.

61. Ibid., 10. 1. 105.

62. Ibid., 1. 4. 13–17.

63. Ibid., 2. 3. 7–8.

64. Ibid., 1. 1. 36.

65. Ibid., 10. 3. 10.

66. Ibid., 1. 3. 14–17.

67. Ibid., 1. 1. 1.

68. Ibid., 2. 1. 1–18.

69. Ibid., 1. 2. 12.

70. Bonner, *Education in Ancient Rome*, 328; and Marrou, *History of Education*, 299, 301.

71. Marrou, *History of Education* 301–302.

Chapter 5

1. Laistner, *Christianity and Pagan Culture in the Late Roman Empire*, 59–61.

2. MacMullen, *Christianizing the Roman Empire*, 12; and Wilken, *John Chrysostom and the Jews*, 110.

3. Eph. 6:4; Col. 3:21.

4. Although Pierre Riché's account deals with the episcopal schools extant at the end of the fifth century (*Education and Culture*, 124–128), there are good reasons for supposing that the conditions he describes were in evidence for centuries.

5. Cassiodorus Senator, *An Introduction to Divine and Human Readings*, 2. preface 5, and 2. 1–13, is a good witness here.

6. According to Eusebius of Caesarea, *Ecclesiastical History* 2. 3. 3, Origen had such authorization. It is not clear, however, that he exercised it in the Alexandrian School. (De Faye, *Origen and His Work*, 25–26.)

7. Riché, *Education and Culture*, 124–128

8. In some cases, we are led to believe, bishops were satisfied when candidates to the priesthood could read, although St. Caesarius of Arles is reputed to have refused to ordain deacons unless they had read the whole of the Bible four times (Marrou, *A History of Education*, 335).

9. Ibid., 323.

10. David C. Lindberg, "Science and the Early Church," in *God and Nature*, David C. Lindberg and Ronald L. Numbers, eds., 22–29.

11. Jaeger, *Early Christianity and Greek Paideia*, 86–102.

12. Lindberg and Numbers, *God and Nature*, 24; and Clement of Alexandria, *The Writings of Clement of Alexandria*, in *The Ante-Nicene Christian Library*, 1:359.

13. St. Jerome, "Lives of Illustrious Men," in *A Select Library of Nicene and Post-Nicene Fathers of the Christian Church*, 3:349.

14. According to Jaroslav Pelikan (*The Excellent Empire*, 44), Jerome and Origen are ranked as the most accomplished scholars of the early Christian world.

15. The classics were one source of danger to faith, and Chrysostom warned Christians about them, but faith was put in jeopardy as well by Christians who observed Torah and attended synagogue. Wilken, *John Chrysostom*, 78.

16. Lindberg and Numbers, *God and Nature*, 25.

17. *Selected Letters of St. Jerome*, 16:125–127.

18. Both Hellenistic and Roman secondary schoolmasters had employed a practice of appropriating style from classical authors while neglecting the story (Bonner, *Education in Ancient Rome*, 49–50), but there is no evidence that they elevated this practice to the level of pedagogical doctrine. Although the record lacks confirmation, Jerome may have adopted this early practice, and if he did, some of the luster of novelty vanishes from the doctrine of formal study.

19. Marrou, *Saint Augustin et la Fin de la Culture antique* (Paris: Vrin, 1949; Paris: E. De Boccard, 1958), 187–197.

20. St. Augustine, *Works*, 2:554.

21. Deut. 21:11–13 was the basis for this advice, quoted countless times by all manner of writers.

22. Bolgar, *The Classical Heritage and Its Beneficiaries*, 35–36, 50–54, 57–58.

23. It is unlikely that the warning was always heeded. Boys aspiring to the priesthood seem to have attended grammar schools. Thereafter, "in the service of the Church . . . they learned their trade." The study of sacred science was an entirely private matter. (Riché, *Education and Culture*, 8–9).

24. Julian, called the Apostate because he rejected his Christian nurture at about age twenty, undermined Christianity in a variety of ways: the clergy were stripped of immunity, bequests to the Church were forbidden, Christians were discouraged or prohibited from studying grammar and rhetoric, military and civil positions were foreclosed to members of the Church, and Christians were obliged to make restitution for the pagan temples they had destroyed. Had it not been for his early death, Gibbon concluded, Rome would have become involved in a religious war. (Edward Gibbon, *Decline and Fall*, 21 (2:395); 23–24 (2:432–519). Gibbon wrote *Decline and Fall* between the years 1776 and 1788.).

25. *The Rule of St. Benedict*, 58.

26. Ibid., 38.

27. Ibid., 48.

28. Riché, *Education and Culture,* 122. Despite lack of promotion, profane culture was cultivated and kept alive. See, for example, W. Lourdaux and D. Verhelst, eds., *Benedictine Culture: 750–1050.*

29. Chadwick, *John Cassian,* 24.

30. Marrou, *History of Education,* 333.

31. *Rule of St. Benedict,* Prologue, 45.

32. Quoted in Marrou, *History of Education,* 323–324.

33. Riché, *Education and Culture,* 128.

34. The best witness here is Cassiodorus (*Introduction,* preface), who, along with Pope Agapitus, tried to organize a school for higher study in Rome. The project did not succeed.

35. St. Augustine, *Works* 2:554.

36. Often regarded as a Christian martyr, Boethius was known as St. Severinus. Although reared in a Christian family, the status of his faith when he wrote *Consolation* is uncertain.

37. Patch, *The Tradition of Boethius,* 24.

38. Cole, *Later Roman Education,* 16. Commentators on Capella's book often call it "little." In print it runs about 350 pages.

39. See *The Marriage of Philology and Mercury,* trans. William H. Stahl and Richard Johnson with E. L. Burge, in *Martianus Capella and The Seven Liberal Arts.*

40. Quoted in Rand, *The Founders of the Middle Ages,* 239.

41. Riché, *Education and Culture,* 112.

42. Cassiodorus *Introduction* 67.

43. Ibid., 1. preface. 6 is one example.

44. Ibid., 2. preface. 4–5.

45. Ibid., 1. 27. 1; and 1. 28. 3.

46. Ibid., 1. 10. 1–2.

47. Cassiodorus' diligence in collecting books for the library in Vivarium is illustrated especially in ibid., 1. 8. 9; and 1. 29. 2.

48. Riché, *Education and Culture,* 162.

49. Bolgar, *Classical Heritage,* 57.

50. Gregory *Letters,* 11. 34.

51. Riché, *Education and Culture,* 312.

52. Carney's *Studies in Irish Literature and History* supplies evidence of the abundance of literature; and see Hyde, *A Literary History of Ireland*, 243, 584–585.

53. Gwynn and Hadcock, *Medieval Religious Houses: Ireland*, 2

54. For a description of these glossaries, see Riché, *Education and Culture*, 470, n. 146.

55. Bolgar, *Classical Heritage*, 94.

56. In the seventh century, the principal monasteries were Derry, Bangor, Armagh, Kells, Clonard, Kildare, Linsmore, and Cloyne. See Riché, *Education and Culture*, 310.

57. Quoted in McCormick and Cassidy, *A History of Education*, 222.

58. Ibid.

59. West, *Alcuin and the Rise of the Christian Schools*, 90.

Chapter 6

1. Several authors, Riché especially (*Education and Culture*), assert that the classical heritage, although severely bruised, from the seventh through the ninth centuries was not entirely destroyed.

2. Rashdall, *The Universities of Europe in the Middle Ages*, 1:75–76.

3. Roman law remained alive throughout the Dark Ages, but it would be exaggeration to say that it was studied. The *Institutes* was an introductory textbook to Roman law; the *Code*, a compilation of imperial edicts; the *Digest*, commentaries on the law by the great classical jurists; and the *Novels*, the fourth part of the *Digest*. Without the *Digest*, any serious study of Roman law was bound to be deficient.

4. For centuries before law became prominent at Bologna, and for a long time thereafter, good scholars were convinced that law and rhetoric were two parts of one science. The conventional division of rhetoric into three branches—demonstrative, deliberative, and judicial—allowed law to enter into the curriculum of the seven arts. See Cassiodorus *Introduction* 2. 2. 8.

5. Castiglioni, *A History of Medicine*, 292–294. Rashdall, *Universities*, 1:76, is of the opinion that Salerno, a medical school, anticipated both Paris and Bologna. Yet the school seems not to have had any special indebtedness to classical sources in its early years.

6. For a fuller yet brief account, see Edward Grant, "Science and Theology in the Middle Ages," in Lindberg and Numbers, eds., *God and Nature*, 49–70.

7. Salerno, perhaps an exception, enacted fairly severe regulations for its physicians: In addition to eight years of study, five in medicine, they were to advise the poor *gratis*, visit their patients upon request, and not sell their own drugs. Rashdall, *Universities*, 1:83.

8. Ibid., 1:80.

9. The influence of rhetoric was, of course, either reversed or obliterated by the twelfth century. No less an authority than John of Salisbury, *The Metalogicon of John of Salisbury*, 2. 10, laments the preoccupation with logic and in doing so seems to realize that he is advocating a losing cause.

10. Rashdall, *Universities*, 1:40–49, is tempted to attribute logic's lofty position to its connection with theology. While this connection cannot on any account be discounted, logic's growth to prominence before Abelard was prompted by strong secular motivation (Haskins, *Studies in the History of Medieval Science*, 223–234).

11. Murray, *Abelard and St. Bernard*, 95.

12. Woodward, *Vittorino da Feltre and Other Humanist Educators*, 104.

13. Haskins, *The Renaissance of the Twelfth Century*, 101–102. John of Salisbury's account of the school he attended confirms this comprehensive, almost encyclopedic, thirst for knowledge (*The Metalogicon*, 1. 24).

14. Thierry's *Heptateuchon* is the best example. See Rashdall, *Universities*, 1:38; and Haskins, *The Renaissance of the Twelfth Century*, 376–377.

15. Gilson, *Heloise and Abelard*, 1–2.

16. Rashdall, *Universities*, 1:52.

17. Bolgar, *Classical Heritage*, 151.

18. Pierre Abailard, *Sic et Non: A Critical Edition*.

19. The techniques of proposition, opposition, and solution, Abelard assumed with supreme confidence, could lead to truth, but they could also disclose weakness in long-accepted conviction and tend to undermine authority. See Haskins, *Renaissance of the Twelfth Century*, 355.

20. Rashdall, *Universities*, 1:36.

21. Bolgar, *Classical Heritage*, 208, gives Helias credit for introducing dialectic to grammar. Haskins, *Renaissance of the Twelfth Century*, 137–138, gives attention mainly to Alexander and Evrard.

22. The principal old books were based on *De inventione* of Cicero, the *Rhetorica ad Herennium* of disputed authorship, and the *Ars poetica* of Horace.

23. Rhetoric's use for textual exposition has a contemporary illustration in Mortimer J. Adler, *How to Read a Book*, revised and updated edition (New York: Simon and Schuster, 1972).

24. Conrad lists the authors that were, he claims, regularly read: Donatus, Cato, Aesop, Avianus, Sedulius, Juvencus, Prosper, Theodolus, Arator, Prudentius, Cicero, Sallust, Boethius, Lucan, Horace, Ovid, Juvenal, Homer (*Iliad* in Latin), Persius, Statius, and Virgil.

25. Quintilian *Education of an Orator* 1. 8. 13; 2. 5. 4.

26. Quoted in Bolgar, *Classical Heritage*, 216.

27. Hugh of St. Victor, *Didascalicon*, 3. 8. 92. Allegorical expression is a way of representing experience, otherwise hard to describe, by using figurative language. Allegorical interpretation is a way of deriving moral, intellectual, or spiritual lessons from a source that does not seem to contain them.

28. Rashdall, *Universities*, 1:103–104.

29. While Rashdall, ibid., 1:120–121, alleges that Irnerius taught the entire *Digest*, these notes are more frequent in the *Code* and *Institutes*.

30. Rashdall barely mentions Bulgarus, but Bolgar, *Classical Heritage*, 145–147, pays him special heed.

31. Ibid.

32. Accursius' *Glossa ordinaria*, while probably the best illustration of scholastic method applied to law, was by no means the last of the legal glosses to appear. These glosses, or interpretations, allowed legal principles to be applied to contemporary issues. See Haskins, *The Renaissance of the Twelfth Century*, 202; and Rashall, 1:256–258.

33. Scholastic philosophy has its historians and interpreters. See Copleston, *History of Medieval Philosophy*. The excellence of their work cannot be summarized here, nor need it be, yet this much should be said: the Scholastic spirit in philosophy was whetted by the relationship philosophy necessarily has to theology and abetted by the recovery and translation of Aristotle's authentic works.

34. The full title of Alexander's work is *Summa Universae Theologiae*. See Copleston, *Medieval Philosophy*, 160, for a summary of Alexander's theses.

35. *Metalogicon* 4. 13.

36. Hugh of St. Victor, *Didascalicon*, 3. 1. 83.

37. McCarthy, *Educational Thought of Vincent of Beauvais*, 151–152.

38. Tobin, *Vincent of Beauvais' "De Eruditione Filiorum Nobilium"*, 150.

39. This decree is reproduced in Leach, *Educational Charters and Documents*, 37.

40. This decree is quoted in Rashdall, 1:279 n. 2.

41. The capitularies are quoted in Mullinger, *The Schools of Charles the Great*, 97–99.

42. Leach, *Schools of Medieval England*, 71–75.

43. Thrupp, *The Merchant Class of Medieval London*, 164–167.

44. Salzman, *English Life in the Middle Ages*, 202.

45. Education in the court had changed remarkably over several centuries. While earlier courts had by no means neglected training for life in court, literary instruction, if obtained at all, was a domestic rather than a court function. See Riché, *Education and Culture*, 239.

46. William J. Courtenay, "Inquiry and Inquisition: Academic Freedom in Medieval Universities," *Church History* 58, 2 (June 1989): 181. Bolgar, *Classical Heritage*, 180–181, recounts the case of Amaury of Bène—although his account is disputed (ibid.)—whose students suffered more than their master from his alleged heterodoxy. After his death, Amaury was convicted of heresy, so his corpse was removed from consecrated ground and his students were apprehended and punished.

47. Rashdall, *Universities*, 3:396.

48. They were not, as Stephen C. Ferruolo maintains, either narrow or utilitarian in their specialization, and "they [managed] to serve the interests both of the university and of their society rather well" ("'Quid dant artes nisi luctum?': Learning, Ambition, and Careers in the Medieval University," *History of Education Quarterly*, 28, 1 (Spring 1988): 1–22).

49. *Metalogicon* 3. 1.

50. Rashdall, *Universities*, 1:19.

51. Ibid., 1:215.

52. Ibid., 1:284.

53. Ibid., 1:220–221.

54. Ibid., 1:220–221, 247.

Chapter 7

1. At the time of Petrarch's death, it is estimated that his library—the best of the day—contained two hundred volumes of the classics. Those in Greek, although he could not read them, were especially prized.

2. Francesco Petrarca, *Letters on Familiar Matters*, bk. 12, no. 3 of 1, 143–144; quoted in Grendler, *Schooling*, 3.

3. The dates of Vergerius' birth and death are uncertain. Most scholars appear to accept the dates given here, but Woodward, *Humanist Educators*, 93, says Vergerius was born in 1349. He is silent about the date of his death.

4. Aldus, one of Venice's most prominent printers, was a scholar turned printer. Like most humanists clinging to the fringe of the academic world, he took the opportunity that came his way. See Lowry, *The World of Aldus Manutius*, 52. This fascinating book illustrates the compact between business (printing) and scholarship in the fifteenth century.

5. Battista Guarino, *De Ordine Docendi et Studendi (Upon the Method of Teaching and of Reading the Classical Authors)* in Woodward, *Humanist Educators*, 177.

6. Cicero *De Oratore* 3. 142–143.

7. Greek was regarded as essential to genuine humanism, for without it, the best in Greek literature could not be sampled. Yet its popularity was always lower than Latin. Western Europe's cultural affinity to Greek was both profound and traditional; but Italians, the midwives of humanism, tended to harbor cultural reservations about Greek, and Greek was an enormously difficult language to learn.

8. We are assured, and the assurance appears to be sound, that not until the sixteenth century did humanistic schools outside of Italy cater to sport. Eugene F. Rice, in Foreward to Woodward, *Humanist Educators*, xii-xiii.

9. The full title of the work, although early editions vary, seems to have been *De Ingenuis Moribus opus praeclarissimum et Liberalibus Studiis*. McManamon, however, asserts precedence for *De ingenuis moribus et liberalibus studiis adultescentiae* (John M. McManamon, "Pier Paolo Vergerio (The Elder) and the Beginnings of the Humanist Cult of Jerome," *The Catholic Historical Review* 71, 4 (July 1985): 355). The usual rendering in English is *On Noble Character and Liberal Study*.

10. Ibid.

11. Woodward, *Humanist Educators*, 93.

12. Ibid., 96.

13. Ibid.

14. Ibid., 97.

15. Ibid., 102.

16. Ibid., 104.

17. Ibid.

18. Ibid., 107.

19. Ibid.

20. Ibid., 108.

21. Ibid., 108–109.

22. Ibid., 109.

23. Ibid., 110.

24. Ibid., 118.

25. Ibid., 101.

26. Declamation against the use of artificial heat in schools was not distinctive of humanists. They must have adopted the position of their medieval predecessors on this point, for medieval teachers in both lower schools and universities had an almost fanatical opposition to the use of artificial heat. Their opposition, one supposes, had its origin in the fact that churches, monasteries, and scholastic halls could not in any event be heated. It was better, then, to stand on the principle that artificial heat is bad for students.

27. Woodward, *Humanist Educators*, 5.

28. Ibid., 8.

29. The Gonzaga family was engaged, as were many other prominent Italian families, in maintaining culture and education in the court. This is amply demonstrated in Simon, *A Renaissance Tapestry: The Gonzaga of Mantua*.

30. Woodward, *Humanist Educators*, 22–23.

31. Ibid., 40–41.

32. Battista Guarino, in ibid., 174, has this to say: "Apart from its value mentally, reading aloud is physically beneficial, in the opinion of the experts in medicine. . . . Shouting . . . must of course be avoided, or injury to the throat results."

33. Woodward, ibid., 195–234, explains the school's curriculum in considerable detail.

34. Ibid., 201.

35. Vergerius and Guarino, in ibid., 114 and 246.

36. Ibid., 245.

37. This short work, sent as a letter to Baptista di Montefeltro, is probably the first humanistic tract on education dedicated to a woman. It is reproduced in Woodward, *Humanist Educators*, 123–133.

38. *De Educatione Liberorum et Eorum Claris Moribus (On the Education of Boys and Their Moral Character)*, in Vincent J. Horkan, *Educational Theories and Principles of Maffeo Vegio*.

39. Bruni, in Woodward, *Humanist Educators*, 127.

40. Ibid.

41. Ibid.

42. Ibid., 126.

43. Ibid., 128.

44. Ibid., 131.

45. Bolgar, *Classical Heritage* 336.

46. Bruni, *De Studiis et Literis*, in Woodward, *Humanist Educators*, 124.

47. William H. Woodward, *Desiderius Erasmus Concerning the Aim and Method of Education*, 159.

48. Erasmus, *De Ratione Studii*, in ibid., 164: "For I affirm that with slight qualification the whole of attainable knowledge lies enclosed within the literary monuments of ancient Greece."

49. See Desiderius Erasmus, *On Copia of Words and Ideas*.

50. Erasmus, *De Ratione Studii*, in Woodward, *Erasmus*, 165.

Chapter 8

1. Thomas Kuhn, *The Copernican Revolution*, 191–197.

2. Both are reproduced in Eby, *Early Protestant Educators*; and Painter, *Luther on Education*.

3. Painter, *Luther*, 269–270; and Eby, *Early Protestant Educators*, 149–150.

4. For example, Painter, *Luther*, 168; Bruce, *Luther as an Educator*, 299; and Lindsay, *Luther and the German Reformation*, 238.

5. Painter, *Luther*, 269–270; and Eby, *Early Protestant Educators*, 149–150.

6. Manschreck, *Melanchthon, the Quiet Reformer*, 95–97; Adolf Sperl, *Melanchthon Zwischen Humanismus und Reformation*, 71–73; and Steinmetz, *Reformers in the Wings*, 73.

7. Henry Barnard, *German Teachers and Educators*, 169–171.

8. Singer, *Furstenspiegel in Deutchland in Zeitalter des Humanismus und der Reformation*, 271–286.

9. Farrell, *The Jesuit Code of Liberal Education*, 16–17.

10. Ibid., 25.

11. Ibid., 357–359.

12. See Alice T. Friedman's article, "The Influence of Humanism on the Education of Girls and Boys in Tudor England." *History of Education Quarterly* 25 (Spring-Summer 1985): 57–70.

13. Milton, *Areopagitica*, 1–68; and Milton, *Milton on Education, the Tractate Of Education*, 51–64.

14. The great exponent of positivism, Auguste Comte (1798–1857), *Positive Philosophy*, asserted scientific credentials for the social sciences and especially for sociology. There are laws, he declared confidently, governing social and political action in the same way that there are laws governing physiology, chemistry, physics, and astronomy. The work of science is to discover these social laws so persons can function harmoniously with them.

15. Despite its store of pedagogic wisdom, *The Great Didactic* never received the attention it deserved. Its neglect by educators was due mainly to the history and the linguistic inaccessibility of the book itself. Written in Czech in 1632, translated into Latin in 1657, the first complete English translation of *The Great Didactic* appeared in 1896. Keatinge's *Comenius* is a reprint in somewhat abbreviated form of his fuller translation of *The Great Didactic*.

16. Comenius, *The Great Didactic*, 197.

17. Ibid., 336–337.

18. The operations of nature and of learning, he declared, were parallel: nature observes a suitable time, prepares material before giving it form, develops from within, proceeds from the universal to the particular, moves without leaps step by step, and compels nothing to advance save by internal energy (Comenius, *The Great Didactic*, 112–141).

19. Ibid., 98.

20. Adamson, *Pioneers*, 212.

21. These schools had their origin in the early eighteenth-century educational work of Jean de la Salle (d. 1719). Battersby, *De La Salle, A Pioneer of Modern Education*; and Fitzpatrick, *La Salle, Patron of All Teachers*, give competent accounts of the work of La Salle and the Brothers.

22. Literature on Francke is neither recent nor abundant. One might consult Kramer, *A.H. Francke's padagogische Schriften*; Barnard, *German Teachers and Educators*; and Eby, *The Development of Modern Education*, 247–260.

23. One should note that while utility was a trump card in the contest for schooling, parents in England and on the Continent were not always ready to play it. They thought it likely that children could have more important things to do than go to school. In this connection, see Maynes, *Schooling*.

24. Kaestle, ed., *Joseph Lancaster and the Monitorial School Movement*.

25. Dualism was a two-track system of schools. One track, for the common people, essayed to prepare persons to be good and docile citizens; the other track, for an intellectual and social elite, undertook to prepare leaders. This policy of designating schools for followers and leaders eventually became so rigid that transfer from one to another track was virtually impossible.

26. Despite the school reformers' enthusiasm for them, compulsory attendance laws often met with open hostility from the very class they were supposed to
benefit. (Maynes, *Schooling*, 86–90).

27. Rousseau, *Emile*, 72.

28. For example, Herbart, *Outlines of Educational Doctrine*, 91.

29. This is the way Pestalozzi described the object–lesson method: "When a
confused conglomeration of objects is brought before our eyes, and we wish to
dissect it and gradually make it clear to ourselves, we have to consider three
things: (1) how many things and how many kinds of things there are before our
eyes, i.e., their number; (2) what they are like, i.e., their form; (3) what they are
called, i.e., their names" (Pestalozzi, *How Gertrude Teaches Her Children*, 47).

30. La Chalotais' *Constitutions of the Jesuits* was a literary indictment of the
Society charging its members with unfitness for conducting secondary schools.
They were unfit, la Chalotais argued, because with primary allegiance to the
Society, the pope, and the Church they could not prepare their students for
citizenship. See la Fontainerie, *French Liberalism and Education in the Eigh-
teenth Century*, 4.

31. Quoted in la Fontainerie, *French Liberalism and Education*, 53.

32. This is what Maynes, *Schooling*, 38–40, calls the obscurantist position
and demonstrates that it was common among aristocrats in France, Germany, and
England.

33. The story persists that la Chalotais despised Rousseau and refused to
mention his name or his educational proposals even when, on some points, such as
sense education, he appeared to agree with Rousseau.

34. Barnard, *Education and the French Revolution*, 68–80; 166–178.

35. "The one and whole work of education," Herbart wrote, "may be
summed up in the concept of morality" (Herbart, *The Science of Education*, 57).
Educators who embraced national education were quick, and very likely correct,
in interpreting morality to mean citizenship.

36. Paulsen, *German Universities and University Study*, 114–115.

37. McClelland, *State, Society and the University in Germany, 1700–1914*,
123–132; and Konrad Jarausch, "The Social Transformation of the University,
The Case of Prussia, 1865–1911," *Journal of Social History* 12 (Summer 1979):
609–636.

38. La Vopa, *Prussian Schoolteachers*, 23–28.

39. Paulsen, *German Education, Past and Present*, 280–281.

40. Douglas R. Skopp, "The Elementary School Teachers 'Revolt': Reform
Proposals for Germany's Volksschulen in 1848–1849," *History of Education
Quarterly* 22 (Fall 1982): 341–361.

41. While the testimony is hard to assess, the general estimate is that hardly more than one in ten thousand students was successful in moving from this scholastic track to the one leading to university study. See Ringer, *Education and Society in Modern Europe*, 29–31.

42. Kandel, *The Reform of Secondary Education in France*, 66–71; and Moody, *French Education Since Napoleon*, 9–10.

43. Maynes, *Schooling*, 143.

44. Mary Jo Maynes, "The Virtues of Archaism: The Political Economy of Schooling in Europe, 1750–1850," *Comparative Studies in Society and History* 21 (October 1979): 611–625.

45. Smith, *Class Formation in English Society*, 192.

46. Silver and Silver, *History of a National School*, 4.

47. Wardle, *English Popular Education, 1780–1975*, 64.

48. Maclure, *Educational Documents: England and Wales*, 70.

49. Cook, ed., *The History of Education in Europe*, 86.

50. Bündesminister fur Bildung und Wissenschaft, *Report of the Federal Government on Education 1970*, 30.

Chapter 9

1. Miller, *The New England Mind*, 21.

2. Quoted in Cremin, *American Education: The Colonial Experience*, 150.

3. Todd, *Christian Humanism and the Puritan Social Order*.

4. For example, Tewksbury, *The Founding of American Colleges and Universities before the Civil War*; Rudolph, *The American College and University*; and Ernest, *Academic Procession*.

5. Morison, *Harvard College in the Seventeenth Century*, 1:140.

6. Morison, *The Puritan Pronaos*, 30.

7. Graves, *Peter Ramus and the Educational Reformation*, 21–25.

8. See Rudolph, *Curriculum*, for a general exposition.

9. Morison, *Harvard College in the Seventeenth Century*, 1:140–143.

10. One should note as well the role literary and debating societies played in cultivating this objective. See Rudolph, *American College*, 138; Ernest, *Academic Procession*, 82–84; and Thomas J. Wertenbaker, *Princeton: 1747–1896*, 203.

11. Reproduced in Hofstadter and Smith, *American Higher Education*, 1:266, 199, 297, 308.

12. Locke, *Some Thoughts*, par. 176.

13. In Franklin, *Benjamin Franklin on Education*, 165–171.

14. Franklin, *Papers*, 3:397–421.

15. Emerson, "The American Scholar," in *Emerson: Representative Selections*, 64–70.

16. Jefferson, *Papers*, 2:526–533.

17. Rush, "To Friends of the Federal Government: A Plan for a Federal University" [1788], in *Letters of Benjamin Rush*, 1:491–495.

18. Wright, *Franklin of Philadelphia*, 349–360.

19. Reproduced in Franklin, *Benjamin Franklin on Education*, 165–171.

20. Franklin, *Papers*, 3:397–421.

21. Jernegan, *Laboring and Dependent Classes*, 177.

22. Curti, *Social Ideals of American Educators*, 4–5.

23. Jernegan, *Laboring and Dependent Classes*, 82.

24. Morison, *The Puritan Pronaos*, 69.

25. The act is reproduced in Knight, *Education in the United States*, 105.

26. Kilpatrick, *Dutch Schools*, 38; for a recent and readable account of life in the colony, see Van der Zee, *Story of Dutch New York*.

27. Kilpatrick, *Dutch Schools*, 124.

28. Harris, [*The Protestant Tutor*], *The New-England Primer*.

29. Bacon, [*On the Dignity and*] *Advancement of Learning*.

30. Morgan, *Godly Learning: Puritan Attitudes*.

31. Bacon, *The Advancement of Learning*, 11.

32. Cremin, *American Education*, 174.

33. Pointer, *Eighteenth Century Religious Diversity*.

34. Carter, *Letters to the Hon. William Prescott. . . on the Free Schools of New England*, in Sizer, ed., *The Age of the Academies*, 155.

Chapter 10

1. Webster, *Dissertations on the English Language*, 20–23.

2. Mencken, *The American Language*, 12.

3. Kaestle, *Pillars of the Republic*, 75–82.

4. Jefferson, *Crusade Against Ignorance*, 83–92.

5. Locke, *Some Thoughts*, par. 94.

6. Tyler, *Freedom's Ferment*, 25–29.

7. Padover, *The Mind of Alexander Hamilton*, 13.

8. Ibid., 16.

9. "[A]lthough the educational system may have been structured to exert social control," Joel Spring concedes in *The American School 1842–1985*, 181, "that goal may have been modified by other social forces." Besides Spring, other illustrations of revisionist educational history are Katz, *The Irony of Early School Reform*; Katz, *Class, Bureaucracy, and Schools*; Tyack, *The One Best System*; and Karier, *Shaping the American Educational State*. Ravitch, *The Revisionists Revised*, is eloquent, and often persuasive, in rejecting revisionist hypotheses.

10. Lee, *Crusade Against Ignorance*, 83–92, 102, 145–146.

11. Washington, *Writings of George Washington*, 30:493–494.

12. Jefferson, *Crusade Against Ignorance*, 83–92; and Franklin, *Papers*, 3:397–421.

13. Between 1786 and 1800, in addition to Rush, Robert Coram, Samuel Knox, Samuel Smith, James Sullivan, Noah Webster, Nathaniel Chipman, and Du Pont de Nemours wrote the most notorious essays deploying an educational plan for America. The fullest one-volume treatment of these plans can be found in Hansen, *Liberalism and American Education*.

14. Rush, *A Plan for the Establishment of Public Schools and the Diffusion of Knowledge in Pennsylvania*, 28.

15. Ibid.

16. Ibid., 3–12.

17. The details of Jefferson's school plan for Virginia are widely reported and shall not be repeated here. See, for example, Honeywell, *The Educational Work of Thomas Jefferson*, 201–205; "A Bill for the More General Diffusion of Knowledge," in Jefferson, *Papers*, 2:526–533; and Cremin, *American Education: The Colonial Experience*, 438–441.

18. By the nineteenth century, the question of educational responsibility was often a matter of political doctrine. See, for example, the analysis in Kaestle and Vinovskis, *Education and Social Change in Nineteenth-Century Massachusetts*, 208–232.

19. Poore, *The Federal and State Constitutions, Colonial Charters, and Other Organic Laws of the United States*, 1:431.

Chapter 11

1. Scholarly work on Mann is both good and extensive. See, for example, Messerli, *Horace Mann: A Biography*; Culver, *Horace Mann and Religion*; Hinsdale, *Horace Mann and the Common School Revival*; and Williams, *Horace Mann, Educational Statesman*. Mann's own work should not be overlooked, especially the *Annual Reports*, partly reproduced in *Republic and the School*.

2. Mann, *Republic and the School*, 106.

3. Carter, *Essays upon Popular Education*; and for another appraisal of Carter's work, Jonathan Messerli, "James Carter's Liabilities as a Common School Reformer," *History of Education Quarterly* 5 (March 1965): 14–25.

4. Apparently in the vanguard of state action, Massachusetts, in 1827, enacted a law declaring that "[school committees] shall never direct any school books to be purchased or used, in any of the schools under their superintendency, which are calculated to favor any particular religious sect or tenet" (Laws of Massachusetts, 10 March 1827, chap. 143, sec. 7).

5. Activity in the production of such textbooks for the elementary school was intense, and more books appeared than anyone would want to recite here. Still, a few might be mentioned. In the wake of Benjamin Harris' *The New-England Primer* [*The Protestant Tutor*] there came Noah Webster's *American Spelling Book*, published first in 1783 but reprinted and revised several times, as the most popular. Warren Colburn's *First Lessons in Intellectual Arithmetic* appeared in 1821 and remained as a staple text for forty years. Goodrich's *History of the United States* and Webster's *History of the United States* competed for dominance in the schools. Introduced, too, were books on children's literature that, so far as American writing was concerned, formed a new genre. (See R. Gordon Kelly, "American Children's Literature: An Historiographical Review," *American Literary Realism* 6 (Spring 1973): 88–90; and Estes, ed., *American Writers for Children before 1900.*) The one subject left uncultivated by American writers of schoolbooks was grammar, still left in the somewhat unsteady custody of British writers. But for all their worth, none of these books matched William Holmes McGuffey's *Eclectic Readers* in capturing the affection of Americans. As reservoirs of essential information, as a foundation for general education, and as a standard source for moral knowledge, the *Readers* essayed to produce good and ethically sensitive citizens. Between 1836 and 1922, about 122 million *Readers* were sold. See Mosier, *Making the American Mind: Social and Moral Ideas in the McGuffey Readers*, 167–170. For a general account of schoolbooks, see Johnson, *Old-Time Schools and School-Books*.

6. John S. Whitehead and Jurgen Herbst, "How to Think about the Dartmouth College Case," *History of Education Quarterly* 26:3 (Fall 1986): 333–349. The Dartmouth College case is too complex for summary, but the principal issue was whether the New Hampshire legislature could alter the charter given to the college by the King of England. The legislature, in 1816, changed the charter

and the college contested its action. The United States Supreme Court, in the Trustees of Dartmouth College v. Woodward, 4 Wheaton 555–600 (1819), held for the college. A common interpretation of the court's "inviolability of the charter [contract]" doctrine is that with charters private colleges were secure and that this sense of legal security led to the expansion of private colleges and weakened the state-college movement. But the coin has another side: if the states wanted to have a voice in higher education, and enjoined from intruding upon private college effort, they would have to establish their own colleges.

7. "Original Papers in Relation to a Course of Liberal Education." This document is reproduced in Hofstadter and Smith, *American Higher Education*, 1:276–291. Lane, "The Yale Report of 1828 and Liberal Education: A Neorepublican Manifesto," *History of Education Quarterly* 27:3 (Fall 1987): 325–328, is not so sure that the Report was either a response or a reaction to drift in the college curriculum. He appears to conclude that it was mainly a redefinition of liberal education for application in nineteenth-century America.

8. Fletcher, *A History of Oberlin College*, 2:718.

9. Brubacher and Rudy, *Higher Education in Transition*, 171.

10. Burke, *American Collegiate Populations*, 215–216.

11. For pertinent excerpts from the act, see Hofstadter and Smith, *American Higher Education*, 2:568–569.

12. Cyrus Peirce, *First State Normal School in America*, 227–245. This school was relocated in Newton, Massachusetts, about 1840, and later moved to Framingham, Massachusetts, where, titled Framingham State College, it continues to function.

13. Dearborn, *Oswego Movement in American Education*, 94–106. It should be remarked that schools concentrating on the education of teachers, and called normal schools, were still in existence in many states in the 1940s. Thereafter, although the schools remained, they tended to broaden their curricula and were titled state colleges or universities.

14. Curti, *Social Ideals of American Educators*, 310–336; and Leidecker, *Yankee Teacher: The Life of William Torrey Harris*, 83–84.

15. Joseph L. Tropea, "Bureaucratic Order and Special Children: Urban Schools, 1890s—1940s," *History of Education Quarterly* 27 (Spring 1987): 29–53.

16. The standard work on compulsory attendance is Ensign's *Compulsory School Attendance and Child Labor*.

17. Although restricted largely to St. Louis, Troen *The Public and the Schools*, 101–104, recounts the hard, early years of public kindergartens.

18. Buetow's *Of Singular Benefit* is the standard work on the history of the Catholic school system in the United States.

19. 30 Michigan Reports 69 (1874–1875). Clearly, the decision of a Michigan court could not bind other states, but a firm precedent was established. Krug, *Salient Dates in American Education: 1635–1964*, 91–95.

20. National Education Association of the United States, *Report of the Committee of Ten on Secondary School Studies*, 51.

21. The point is debatable, but there are signs telling us that the junior college idea had its genesis with William Rainey Harper, president of the University of Chicago, in *The Trend in Higher Education*, 382.

22. Gilman, *Launching of a University*, 41–43; and Brubacher and Rudy, *Higher Education in Transition*, 178–182.

23. Eliot, *Educational Reform*, 1.

24. Butts and Cremin, *History of Education in American Culture*, 444.

25. Although this action in opposition to private education enlisted the support of various groups, the Ku Klux Klan is alleged to have had a major influence in the enactment of the Oregon law. Wade, *The Fiery Cross: The Ku Klux Klan in America*, draws a revealing portrait of political extremism in America. Michigan, a few years earlier, had experience with a referendum that would have accomplished the same purpose as the Oregon law. Acting to a great extent upon the advice of the Michigan attorney general, who interpreted the proposed measure to be unconstitutional, the voters rejected the measure.

26. Pierce v. Society of Sisters and the Hill Military Academy, 268 U. S. 510.

27. Meyer v. Nebraska, 262 U.S. 390.

Chapter 12

1. Perkinson, *The Imperfect Panacea*, 12.

2. Jencks, et al., *Inequality*, 14–18. To be fair, one should observe that Jencks and his colleagues were reassessing the sixth and seventh decades of the twentieth century.

3. Katz, *The Irony of Early School Reform*; idem, *Class, Bureaucracy, and Schools*; and idem, *In the Shadow of the Poorhouse*, is a principal exponent of the repressive thesis, one reexamined and, to a great extent, rejected by Vinovskis, *The Origins of Public High Schools*. In "The Origins of Public High Schools," (*History of Education Quarterly* 27:2 (Summer 1987): 241–258), Michael Katz, Edward Stevens, Jr., and Maris Vinovskis debate the two theses.

4. (New York: Alfred A. Knopf, 1961).

5. By no means a new idea, since it had been advanced by the essentialists to counteract the popularity of progressivism, this position is persuasively and intel-

ligently stated by Hirsch in *Cultural Literacy*. The appendix contains a catalogue of what literate Americans know and is represented as the foundation upon which effective communication depends.

6. Although not alone, Arthur E. Bestor, in *Educational Wastelands*, was eloquent and persuasive in taking this vanguard position. In their retrospective essay, "Arthur Bestor's Educational Wastelands," Theodore R. Sizer and Molly Schen (*History of Education Quarterly* 27:2 (Summer 1987): 260), characterize *Educational Wastelands* "as the most important of a genre of critiques of the schools that emerged in the early and mid-fifties." The book was reissued in 1985 with an afterword by Arthur Bestor and commentaries by Clarence Karier and Foster McMurray.

7. Cremin, *Transformation of the School*, 129–130.

8. Dewey, *Experience and Education*, vi–vii.

9. Cremin, *Transformation of the School*, 154.

10. Two books are especially instructive on the American college curriculum: Butts, *The College Charts Its Course*; and Rudolph, *Curriculum: A History of the Undergraduate Course of Study since 1636*.

11. Johnson, *Thirty Years With an Idea*.

12. Katz, *Class, Bureaucracy, and Schools*; and Tyack, *The One Best System*.

13. The list of progressive educators who undertook this work is too long for recitation here, but it should certainly contain these names: Harold Rugg (1886–1960), George S. Counts (1889–1975), John Franklin Bobbitt (1876–1956), William Heard Kilpatrick (1871–1965), Caroline Pratt (1867–1954), and Boyd H. Bode (1873–1953). The founding of the Progressive Education Association (1918–1955) implied for progressive education a unity and an orthodoxy, but progressive educators had their own priorities. The association was unable to represent and unify all of them.

14. United States Office of Education, *Vitalizing Secondary Education: Report of the First Commission on Life Adjustment Education of Youth*, 1.

15. Ibid.

16. Smith, *Madly Teach*, 7.

17. Rickover, *Education and Freedom*, 189.

18. Horne, *The Democratic Philosophy of Education* (New York: The Macmillan Company, 1932).

19. Peirce, *Collected Papers of Charles Sanders Peirce*, 5: par. 9.

20. John Dewey, *Democracy and Education*, 392–395.

21. Dewey, *Experience and Education*, 99–103.

22. *Tractatus Logico-Philosophicus*, 4:003.

23. John Dewey, *Logic, The Theory of Inquiry*, 105.

24. For a brief but competent recounting of Kilpatrick's educational career, see Tenenbaum's, *William Heard Kilpatrick: Trail Blazer in Education*.

25. Kilpatrick, *Foundations of Method*, 217–218.

26. In this connection Boyd H. Bode (1873–1953) and George S. Counts (1889–1975) should be mentioned. Bode, *Fundamentals of Education*; idem, *Modern Educational Theories*; idem, *Progressive Education at the Crossroads*; and Counts, *Dare the School Build a New Social Order?*

27. Bode, *Fundamentals of Education*, 241–242.

Chapter 13

1. This federal precedent was followed in legislation affecting veterans of the wars in Korea and Vietnam, although somewhat less generously.

2. *Higher Education for American Democracy: A Report of the President's Commission on Higher Education*, 1:38. This report is excerpted in Hofstadter and Smith, *American Higher Education*, 2:970–1002.

3. Plessy v. Ferguson, 163 U.S. 537.

4. Sweatt v. Painter, 339 U.S. 629.

5. Missouri ex rel. Gaines v. Canada, 305 U.S. 337.

6. Brown v. Board of Education of Topeka, 347 U.S. 483.

7. State courts—Serrano v. Priest (California, 1971)—and the United States Supreme Court—San Antonio Independent School District v. Rodriguez (1973)—have recognized this impediment to equality of opportunity, although the decision of the United States Supreme Court allowed the traditional method of financing local schools to stand.

8. Regents of the University of California v. Bakke, 483 U.S. 265.

9. Section two of the statute allowed that languages other than English "may be taught as languages only after a pupil shall have attained and . . . passed the eighth grade . . . ."

10. Nebraska Dist. of Evangelical Lutheran Synod v. McKelvie, 104 Neb. 93, 175 N.W. 531, 7 A.L.R. 1688.

11. Iowa v. Bartels, 191 Iowa 1060, 181.

12. Meyer v. Nebraska, 262 U.S.

13. Ibid.

14. Children physically unable to attend school, children who had finished the eighth grade, children who lived a distance from a public school and for whom transportation was not provided, and children taught by parents or private teachers provided that parents had, in advance, the written permission of the county superintendent of schools and that such children privately taught be examined by the county superintendent of schools once every three months.

15. Pierce v. Society of Sisters and Hill Military Academy, 268 U.S. 510.

16. Ibid.

17. Ibid.

18. Thomas J. Shelley, "The Oregon School Case and the National Catholic Welfare Conference," *The Catholic Historical Review*, 75:3 (July 1989): 439–457.

19. John L. Childs, "American Democracy and the Common School System," *Jewish Education*, 21 (1949): 32–37.

20. Hollis L. Caswell, "The Great Reappraisal of Public Education," *Teachers College Record*, 54 (1952): 12–22.

21. Quoted in Butts and Cremin, *A History of Education in American Culture*, 527.

22. One amendment, proposed in 1876, read: "No state shall make any law respecting the establishment of religion or prohibiting the free exercise thereof; and no money raised by taxation in any state for the support of public schools or derived from any public fund therefor, nor any public lands devoted thereto, shall ever be under the control of any religious sect or denomination, nor shall any money so raised or lands so devoted be divided between religious sects or denominations. . . ."

23. Doremus v. Board of Education, 342 U.S. 429.

24. School District of Abington Township v. Schempp, 347 U.S. 203.

25. Ibid.

26. Mosier, *Making the American Mind*, 98.

27. Engel v. Vitale, 370 U.S. 421.

28. McCollum v. Board of Education, 333 U.S. 203.

29. Zorach v. Clauson, 343 U.S. 306

30. Ibid.

31. Ibid.

32. 281 U.S. 370.

33. 330 U.S. 1.

34. An interesting, provocative study by Sedlak, Wheeler, Pullin, and Cusick, *Selling Students Short*, illustrates some of the comfortable standards.

35. What is taken for granted may not always represent reality, as Roche shows in *Colonial Colleges*, 76.

36. Chief among these reports are the following: *Action for Excellence* (Education Commission for the States); *A Celebration of Teaching* (National Association of Secondary School Principals and National Association for Independent Schools); *Educating Americans for the 21st Century* (National Science Foundation); *Education and Economic Progress* (Carnegie Corporation); *High School* (Carnegie Foundation for the Advancement of Teaching); *Making the Grade* (Twentieth Century Fund); *A Nation at Risk* (United States Department of Education); *A Place Called School* (Danforth, Ford, and other foundations); *Project EQuality* (College Entrance Examination Board); *The Paideia Proposal* by Mortimer J. Adler; *A Nation Prepared: Teachers for the 21st Century* (Carnegie Forum on Education and the Economy); and *Tomorrow's Teachers* (The Holmes Group).

37. Nineteenth-century colleges are usually perceived as having been liberal, so it might be instructive to consult Kimball, *Orators and Philosophers*.

38. For a spirited criticism of higher education, see Nisbet, *Degradation of the Academic Dogma*.

39. Theodore L. Gross, *Academic Turmoil*, 6–7.

40. President and Fellows of Harvard College, *General Education in a Free Society*.

41. Boyer, *College: The Undergraduate Experience in America* (New York: Harper & Row, Publishers, Inc., 1987).

42. Bloom, *The Closing of the American Mind* (New York: Simon and Schuster, 1987).

Works Cited

Abailard, Pierre. *Sic et Non: A Critical Edition.* Edited by Blanche B. Boyer and Richard McKeon. Chicago: University of Chicago Press, 1976.

Adamson, John W. *Pioneers of Modern Education in the Seventeenth Century.* Cambridge: Cambridge University Press, 1921; New York: Teachers College Press, 1972.

Addams, Jane. *Jane Addams on Education.* Edited by Ellen C. Lagemann. New York: Teachers College Press, 1985.

Adler, Mortimer J. *Philosopher at Large: An Intellectual Autobiography.* New York: Macmillan, 1977.

Aeschines. *The Speeches of Aeschines.* Translated by C. D. Adams. Cambridge: Loeb Classical Library, Harvard University Press, 1919.

Aland, Kurt. *Four Reformers: Luther, Melanchthon, Calvin, Zwingli.* Translated by James L. Schaaf. Minneapolis: Augsburg Publishing House, 1979.

Anderson, James D. *The Education of Blacks in the South, 1860–1935.* Chapel Hill: University of North Carolina Press, 1988.

Aristophanes. *Aristophanes.* 3 vols. Translated by B. B. Rogers. Cambridge: Loeb Classical Library, Harvard University Press, 1924.

Aristotle. *The Complete Works of Aristotle.* 2 vols. Edited by Jonathan Barnes. Princeton: Princeton University Press, 1984.

Ashmore, Harry S. *Unseasonable Truths: The Life of Robert Maynard Hutchins.* Boston: Little, Brown & Co., 1989.

Augustine, Saint. *Confessions.* 2 vols. Translated by W. Watts. Cambridge: Loeb Classical Library, Harvard University Press, 1912.

————. *St. Augustine: On Education.* Edited and translated by George Howie. Chicago: Regnery Co., 1969.

————. *Works.* In *A Select Library of Nicene and Post-Nicene Fathers of the Christian Church.* Second series. 14 vols. Translated and edited by Philip Schaff and Henry Wace. Grand Rapids, Mich.: W. R. Eerdmans, 1952, 1969–1976.

Bacon, Francis. *The Advancement of Learning*. Edited by G. W. Kitchin. London: Dent, 1973.

Baker, Donald N., and Patrick J. Harrigan, eds. *The Making of Frenchmen: Current Directions in the History of Education in France, 1679–1979*. Waterloo, Ont.: Historical Reflections Press, 1980.

Barclay, William. *Educational Ideals in the Ancient World*. London: Collins, 1959; Grand Rapids, Mich: Baker Book, 1974.

Barnard, Henry. *German Educational Reformers*. Hartford: Brown & Gross, 1878.

––––––. *German Teachers and Educators*. Hartford: Brown & Gross, 1878.

––––––. *Henry Barnard, American Educator*. Edited by Vincent P. Lannie. New York: Teachers College Press, 1974.

Barnard, Howard C. *Education and the French Revolution*. London: Cambridge University Press, 1969.

Barnes, Donna R., ed. *For Court, Manor and Church: Education in Medieval Europe*. Minneapolis: Burgess Publishing Co., 1971.

Battersby, W. J. *De La Salle, A Pioneer of Modern Education*. New York: Longmans, Green & Co., 1949.

Becher, Tony, ed. *British Higher Education*. London: Allen & Unwin, 1987.

Beck, Frederick A. G. *Greek Education: 450–350 B.C.* New York: Barnes & Noble, 1964.

Benedict, Saint. *Rule of St. Benedict*. Edited by Timothy Fry. Collegeville, Minn.: Liturgical Press, 1981.

Bestor, Arthur E. *Educational Wastelands: The Retreat from Learning in Our Public Schools*. Urbana: University of Illinois Press, 1953, 1985.

Bluestone, Natalie H. *Women and the Ideal Society: Plato's Republic and Modern Myths of Gender*. Amherst: University of Massachusetts Press, 1987.

Bloom, Allan. *The Closing of the American Mind*. New York: Simon & Schuster, 1987.

Bode, Boyd H. *Fundamentals of Education*. New York: Macmillan, 1921.

––––––. *Modern Educational Theories*. New York: Macmillan, 1927.

––––––. *Progressive Education at the Crossroads*. New York: Newsome & Co., 1938.

Boethius, Anicius Manlius Severinus. *The Consolation of Philosophy*. In the translation of I. T. Edited by William Anderson. Carbondale: Southern Illinois University Press, 1963.

Bolgar, R. R. *The Classical Heritage and Its Beneficiaries.* Cambridge: Cambridge University Press, 1954.

Bonner, Robert J. *Lawyers and Litigants in Ancient Athens: The Genesis of the Legal Profession.* Chicago: University of Chicago Press, 1927.

Bonner, Stanley F. *Education in Ancient Rome: From the Elder Cato to the Younger Pliny.* Berkeley and Los Angeles: University of California Press, 1977.

Boring, Terrence. *Literacy in Ancient Sparta.* Leiden: Brill, 1979.

Borrowman, Merle L., ed. *Teacher Education in America: A Documentary History.* New York: Teachers College Press, 1965.

Boyer, Earnest L. *College: The Undergraduate Experience in America.* New York: Harper & Row, 1987.

Boylan, Anne M. *Sunday School: The Formation of an American Institution, 1790–1880.* New Haven: Yale University Press, 1988.

Boyle, Marjorie O. *Rhetoric and Reform: Erasmus' Civil Dispute with Luther.* Cambridge: Harvard University Press, 1983.

Brecht, Martin. *Martin Luther: His Road to Reformation, 1483–1521.* Translated by James L. Schaaf. Philadelphia: Fortress Press, 1985.

Brehaut, Ernest. *An Encyclopedist of the Dark Ages, Isidore of Seville.* New York: B. Franklin, 1912, 1964.

Brickhouse, Thomas C., and Nicholas D. Smith. *Socrates on Trial.* Princeton: Princeton University Press, 1989.

Brockliss, L. W. B. *French Higher Education in the Seventeenth and Eighteenth Centuries: A Cultural History.* New York: Oxford University Press, 1987.

Broudy, Harry S. *The Uses of Schooling.* New York: Routledge, 1988.

Brown, Elmer E. *The Making of Our Middle Schools: An Account of the Development of Secondary Education in the United States.* 3d ed. New York: Longmans, Green & Co., 1907.

Brubacher, John S., and Willis Rudy. *Higher Education in Transition.* 3d ed. New York: Harper & Row, 1976.

Bruce, Gustav M. *Luther as an Educator.* Minneapolis: Augsburg Publishing House, 1928; Westport, Conn: Greenwood Press, 1979.

Bruce, Robert V. *The Launching of Modern American Science: 1846–1876.* New York: Alfred A. Knopf, 1986.

Bruni, Leonardo. *The Humanism of Leonardo Bruni. Selected Texts.* Translations and introductions by Gordon Griffiths, James Hankins, and David Thompson. Binghamton, N.Y.: Medieval & Renaissance Texts & Studies in conjunction with the Renaissance Society of America, 1987.

Buetow, Harold A. *Of Singular Benefit: The Story of Catholic Education in the United States.* New York: Macmillan, 1970.

Bullock, Alan. *The Humanist Tradition in the West.* New York: Norton, 1985.

Bündesminister fur Bildung und Wissenschaft. *Report of the Federal Government on Education 1970.* Bonn, 1970.

Burke, Colin B. *American Collegiate Populations: A Test of the Traditional View.* New York: New York University Press, 1982.

Bury, J. B. *The Hellenistic Age.* Cambridge: Cambridge University Press, 1923.

————. *A History of Greece to the Death of Alexander.* New York: Random House, 1913; New York: St. Martin's Press, 1978.

Butts, R. Freeman. *The American Tradition in Religion and Education.* Boston: Beacon Press, 1950.

————. *The Civic Mission in Educational Reform: Perspectives for the Public and the Profession.* Stanford, Calif.: Hoover Institution Press, 1989.

————. *The College Charts Its Course.* New York: McGraw-Hill, 1939; New York: Arno Press, 1971.

Butts, R. Freeman, and Lawrence A. Cremin. *A History of Education in American Culture.* New York: Henry Holt & Co., 1953.

Cadiou, René. *Origen: His Life at Alexandria.* Translated by John A. Southwell. St. Louis: B. Herder Book Co., 1944.

Cannon, Mary Agnes. *The Education of Women During the Renaissance.* Washington, D. C.: Catholic University of America Press, 1916.

Carney, James. *Studies in Irish Literature and History.* Dublin: Dublin Institute for Advanced Studies, 1955, 1979.

Carter, James. *Essays upon Popular Education.* Boston, 1826.

Cassiodorus Senator. *An Introduction to Divine and Human Readings.* Translated by Leslie Webber Jones. New York: Columbia University Press, 1946; New York: Octagon Books, 1966.

Castiglioni, Arturo. *A History of Medicine.* Translated and edited by E. B. Krumbhaar. New York: Alfred A. Knopf, 1941.

Chadwick, Owen W. *John Cassian: A Study in Primitive Monasticism.* 2d ed. Cambridge, Eng.: University Press, 1950.

Chambliss, J. J. *Educational Theory as a Theory of Conduct: From Aristotle to Dewey.* Albany: State University of New York Press, 1987.

Chapman, John. *St. Benedict and the Sixth Century.* New York: Longmans, Green & Co., 1929; Westport, Conn.: Greenwood Press, 1971.

Cherniss, Harold F. *The Riddle of the Early Academy.* Berkeley and Los Angeles: University of California Press, 1945.

Cicero. *De Oratore.* 2 vols. Translated by E. W. Sutton and H. Rackham. Cambridge: Loeb Classical Library, Harvard University Press, 1942.

————. *Laws.* Translated by C. W. Keyes. Cambridge: Loeb Classical Library, Harvard University Press, 1928.

————. *On Oratory and Orators;* with *His Letters to Quintus and Brutus.* Translated by J. S. Watson. London: Bell, 1891.

————. *The Orations of Marcus Tullius.* 3 vols. Translated by C. D. Yonge. London: Bell, 1891–1917.

Clark, Donald L. *Rhetoric in Greco-Roman Education.* New York: Columbia University Press, 1957.

Clarke, M. L. *Higher Education in the Ancient World.* London: Routledge & Kegan Paul, 1971.

Clement of Alexandria. *The Writings of Clement of Alexandria.* In *The Ante-Nicene Christian Library.* 24 vols. Translated by Alexander Roberts and James Donaldson. Edinburgh: T. & T. Clark, 1870.

Cobban, Alan B. *Medieval Universities: Their Development and Organization.* London: Methuen & Co., 1975.

Cochrane, Charles N. *Christianity and Classical Culture: A Study of Thought and Action from Augustus to Augustine.* Oxford: Clarendon Press, 1940; New York: Oxford University Press, 1957.

Cohen, Sheldon S. *A History of Colonial Education, 1607–1776.* New York: John Wiley, 1974.

Cole, Percival R. *Later Roman Education in Ausonius, Capella and the Theodosian Code.* New York: Teachers College Press, 1909.

Comenius, John Amos. *The Great Didactic.* Translated and edited by M. W. Keatinge. London: Adam and Charles Black, 1896; New York: Russell & Russell, 1967.

Comte, Auguste. *The Positive Philosophy.* Translated by Harriet Martineau. London: Bell, 1896; New York: AMS Press, 1974.

Cook, T. G., ed. *The History of Education in Europe.* London: Methuen & Co., 1974.

Copleston, Frederick C. *History of Medieval Philosophy.* London: Methuen & Co., 1952.

Counts, George S. *Dare the School Build a New Social Order?* New York: John Day Co., 1932; New York: Arno Press, 1969.

Courtenay, William J. *Schools and Scholars in Fourteenth-Century England.* Princeton: Princeton University Press, 1987.

Cremin, Lawrence A. *The American Common School, An Historical Conception.* New York: Teachers College Press, 1951.

———. *American Education: The Colonial Experience, 1607–1783.* New York: Harper & Row, 1970.

———. *American Education: The Metropolitan Experience, 1876–1980.* New York: Harper & Row, 1988.

———. *American Education: The National Experience, 1783–1876.* New York: Harper & Row, 1980.

———. *The Transformation of the School: Progessivism in American Education, 1876–1957.* New York: Alfred A. Knopf, 1961.

Cressy, David. *Coming Over: Migration and Communication between England and New England in the Seventeenth Century.* New York: Cambridge University Press, 1987.

Culver, Raymond B. *Horace Mann and Religion in the Massachusetts Public Schools.* New Haven: Yale University Press, 1929.

Curti, Merle E. *The Social Ideals of American Educators.* New York: Charles Scribner's Sons, 1935; Totowa, N. J.: Littlefield, Adams, 1974.

Daly, Lowrie J. *The Medieval University.* New York: Sheed and Ward, 1961.

Dearborn, Ned. *The Oswego Movement in American Education.* New York: Teachers College Press, 1925; New York: Arno Press, 1969.

De Faye, Eugene. *Origen and His Work.* Translated by Fred Rothwell. New York: Columbia University Press, 1929.

Demosthenes. *The Public Orations of Demosthenes.* 2 vols. Translated by A. W. Prichard. Oxford: Clarendon Press, 1912.

Dewey, John. *Democracy and Education.* New York: Macmillan, 1916.

———. *Experience and Education.* New York: Macmillan, 1938; 1974.

———. *Logic, The Theory of Inquiry.* New York: Henry Holt & Co., 1938.

Diogenes Laertius. *Lives and Opinions of Eminent Philosophers.* Translated by C. D. Yonge. London: Bell, 1915.

Dionysius. *The Roman Antiquities of Dionysius of Halicarnassus.* 7 vols. Translated by E. Cary. Cambridge: Loeb Classical Library, Harvard University Press, 1937.

Dobinson, Charles H. *Jean-Jacques Rousseau: His Thought and Its Relevance Today.* London: Methuen & Co., 1969.

Dobson, J. F. *Ancient Education and Its Meaning to Us.* New York: Longmans, Green & Co., 1932.

Dodge, Bayard. *Muslim Education in Medieval Times.* Washington, D.C.: Middle East Institute, 1962.

Dorey, T. A., ed. *Erasmus.* Albuquerque: University of New Mexico Press, 1970.

Downs, Robert T. *Henry Barnard.* New York: Twayne Publishers, 1977.

———. *Horace Mann: Champion of Public Schools.* New York: Twayne Publishers, 1974.

Dudden, F. Homes. *Gregory the Great, His Place in History and in Thought.* 2 vols. London, 1905.

Drever, J. *Greek Education: Its Practice and Principles.* Cambridge, Eng.: University Press, 1912.

Dunkel, Harold B. *Herbart and Education.* New York: Random House, 1969.

———. *Herbart and Herbartianism: An Educational Ghost Story.* Chicago: University of Chicago Press, 1970.

Dunston, Arthur J. *Four Centres of Classical Learning in Renaissance Italy.* Sydney: Sydney University Press for Australian Advancement of Humanities, 1972.

Eby, Frederick. *The Development of Modern Education.* 2d ed. Englewood Cliffs, N. J.: Prentice-Hall, 1952.

Eby, Frederick, ed. *Early Protestant Educators: The Educational Writings of Martin Luther, John Calvin, and Other Leaders of Protestant Thought.* New York: McGraw-Hill, 1931; New York: AMS Press, 1971.

Eby, Frederick, and Charles F. Arrowood. *The History and Philosophy of Education: Ancient and Medieval.* Englewood Cliffs, N. J.: Prentice-Hall, 1940.

Eddy, Edward D. *Colleges for Our Land and Time: The Land-Grant Idea in American Education.* New York: Harper & Row, 1957.

Einhard. *Life of Charlemagne.* Translated by E. Scherabon and E. H. Zeydel. Coral Gables, Fla.: University of Miami Press, 1972.

Eliot, Charles W. *Educational Reform: Essays and Addresses.* New York: Century Co., 1898.

Ellspermann, G. L. *The Attitude of the Early Latin Christian Writers Toward Pagan Learning and Literature.* Washington, D. C.: Catholic University of America Press, 1949.

Emerson, Ralph Waldo. *Emerson: Representative Selections.* Edited by Frederick I. Carpenter. New York: American Book Co., 1934.

Ensign, Forest C. *Compulsory School Attendance and Child Labor: A Study of the Historical Development of Regulations Compelling Attendance and Limiting the Labor of Children in a Selected Group of States.* Iowa City: Athens Press, 1921; New York: Arno Press, 1969.

Erasmus, Desiderius. *The Education of a Christian Prince.* Translated with an introduction by Lester K. Born. New York: Columbia University Press, 1936.

————. *On Copia of Words and Ideas.* Translated by Donald B. King and Herbert D. Rix. Milwaukee: Marquette University Press, 1963.

Estes, Glenn E., ed. *American Writers for Children before 1900.* Detroit: Gale Research Co., 1985.

Ernest, Earnest. *Academic Procession: An Informal History of the American College, 1636 to 1953.* Indianapolis: Bobbs-Merrill, 1953.

Euclid. *The Thirteen Books of Euclid's Elements.* 3 vols. 2d ed. Translated by Thomas L. Heath. New York: Dover Publications, 1956.

Euripides. *Euripides.* 4 vols. Translated by A. S. Way. Cambridge: Loeb Classical Library, Harvard University Press, 1912.

Eusebius of Caesarea. *The Ecclesiastical History.* 2 vols. Translated by Kirsopp Lake and J. E. L. Oulton. Cambridge: Loeb Classical Library, Harvard University Press, 1926–1932.

Farrell, Allan P. *The Jesuit Code of Liberal Education.* Milwaukee: Bruce Publishing Co., 1938.

Ferruolo, Stephen C. *The Origins of the University: The Schools of Paris and Their Critics, 1100–1225.* Stanford: Stanford University Press, 1985.

Fitzpatrick, Edward A. *La Salle, Patron of All Teachers.* Milwaukee: Bruce Publishing Co., 1951.

Fleming, Standford. *Children & Puritanism.* New York: Arno Press, 1933, 1969.

Fletcher, Robert S. *A History of Oberlin College from Its Foundation Through the Civil War.* 2 vols. Oberlin, Ohio: Oberlin College Press, 1943; New York: Arno Press, 1971.

Florus. *Epitome of Roman History.* Translated by E. S. Forster. Cambridge: Loeb Classical Library, Harvard University Press, 1929.

Forbes, Charles A. *Greek Physical Education.* New York: Appleton-Century-Crofts, 1929.

Franklin, Benjamin. *Benjamin Franklin on Education.* Edited by John H. Best. New York: Teachers College Press, 1962.

————. *The Papers of Benjamin Franklin.* 24 vols. Edited by L. W. Labaree and Whitfield J. Bell, Jr. New Haven: Yale University Press, 1959–1968.

Freeman, Kenneth J. *Schools of Hellas: An Essay on the Practice and Theory of Ancient Greek Education from 600 to 300 B.C.* 3d ed. London: Macmillan, 1932.

French, Benjamin B. *Witness to the Young Republic: A Yankee Journal, 1828–1870.* Edited by Donald B. Cole and John J. McDonough. Hanover, N. H.: University Press of New England, 1989.

Gardiner, E. Norman. *Athletics in the Ancient World.* New York: Oxford University Press, 1930.

Geiger, Roger L. *To Advance Knowledge: The Growth of American Research Universities, 1900–1940.* New York: Oxford University Press, 1986.

Gerberding, Richard A. *The Rise of the Carolingians and the Liber Historiae Francorum.* New York: Oxford University Press, 1987.

Gibbon, Edward. *The History of the Decline and Fall of the Roman Empire.* 7 vols. Edited by J. B. Bury. London: Methuen & Co., 1896–1900.

Gilman, Daniel Coit. *Launching of a University.* New York: Dodd, Mead & Co., 1906.

Gilson, Etienne. *Heloise and Abelard.* Translated by L. K. Shook. Paris: Vrin, 1948; Ann Arbor: University of Michigan Press, 1960.

Glenn, Charles L., Jr. *The Myth of the Common School.* Amherst: University of Massachusetts Press, 1988.

Graves, Frank P. *Peter Ramus and the Educational Reformation of the Sixteenth Century.* New York: Macmillan, 1912.

Gregory the Great. *Letters.* In *Monumenta Germaniae Historica, Epistulae.* Edited by P. Ewald and M. Hartmann. Berlin, 1890–1891.

Grendler, Paul F. *Schooling in Renaissance Italy: Literacy and Learning, 1300–1600.* Baltimore and London: Johns Hopkins University Press, 1989.

Gross, Theodore L. *Academic Turmoil: The Reality and Promise of Open Education.* Garden City, N.Y.: Anchor/Doubleday, 1980.

Gruen, Erich S. *The Hellenistic World and the Coming of Rome.* 2 vols. Berkeley and Los Angeles: University of California Press, 1984.

Gutek, Gerald L. *Pestalozzi and Education.* New York: Random House, 1968.

Gwynn, Aubrey. *Roman Education from Cicero to Quintilian.* London: Oxford University Press, 1926; New York: Teachers College Press, 1966.

Gwynn, Aubrey, and R. Neville Hadcock. *Medieval Religious Houses: Ireland.* London: Longman Group, 1970.

Haarhoff, T. J. *Schools of Gaul: A Study of Pagan and Christian Education in the Last Century of the Western Empire.* London: Oxford University Press, 1920; Johannesburg: Witwatersrand University Press, 1958.

Hansen, Allen O. *Liberalism and American Education in the Eighteenth Century.* New York: Macmillan, 1926.

Harper, William Rainey. *The Trend in Higher Education.* Chicago: University of Chicago Press, 1905.

Harris, Benjamin. [*The Protestant Tutor.* London, 1679; Boston, 1737.] *The New-England Primer.* Edited by Paul L. Ford. New York: Dodd, Mead & Co., 1897; New York: Teachers College Press, 1962.

Harris, Harold A. *Greek Athletes and Athletics.* Bloomington: Indiana University Press, 1966.

Haskins, Charles H. *The Renaissance of the Twelfth Century.* Cambridge: Harvard University Press, 1927, 1955.

―――. *Studies in Mediaeval Culture.* Oxford: Clarendon Press, 1929; New York: F. Ungar, 1958.

―――. *Studies in the History of Mediaeval Science.* Oxford: Clarendon Press, 1929; New York: F. Ungar, 1960.

Hawke, David F. *Everyday Life in Early America.* New York: Harper & Row, 1988.

Herbart, Johann F. *Outlines of Educational Doctrine.* Translated by A. F. Lange. New York: Macmillan, 1901; Folcroft, Penn.: Folcroft Library Editions, 1977.

―――. *The Science of Education.* Translated by H. M. and E. Felkin. Boston: D. C. Heath & Co., 1908; Washington, D. C.: University Publications of America, 1977.

Herbst, Jurgen. *And Sadly Teach: Teacher Education and Professionalization in American Culture.* Madison: University of Wisconsin Press, 1989.

Herodotus. *The History of Herodotus.* Translated by G. Rawlinson. New York: Appleton, 1893.

Higher Education for American Democracy: A Report of the President's Commission on Higher Education. New York: Harper & Row, 1947.

Highet, Gilbert. *The Art of Teaching.* New York: Alfred A. Knopf, 1950.

Hinsdale, Burke A. *Horace Mann and the Common School Revival in the United States.* New York: Charles Scribner's Sons, 1898.

Hirsch, E. D., Jr. *Cultural Literacy: What Every American Needs to Know.* Boston: Houghton Mifflin Co., 1987.

Hodgson, Geraldine. *Primitive Christian Education.* Edinburgh: T. & T. Clark, 1906.

Hofstadter, Richard, and Wilson Smith. *American Higher Education: A Documentary History.* 2 vols. Chicago: University of Chicago Press, 1961.

Hooker, J. T. *The Ancient Spartans*. London: J. M. Dent, 1980.

Homer. *The Iliad of Homer*. Translated by A. Lang, W. Leaf, and E. Myers. London: Macmillan, 1923.

———. *The Odyssey of Homer*. Translated by S. H. Butcher and A. Lang. London: Macmillan, 1900.

Honeywell, Roy J. *The Educational Work of Thomas Jefferson*. Cambridge: Harvard University Press, 1931.

Horkan, Vincent J. *Educational Theories and Principles of Maffeo Vegio*. Washington, D. C.: Catholic University of America Press, 1953.

Horne, Herman H. *The Democratic Philosophy of Education: A Companion to Dewey's Democracy and Education: Exposition and Comment*. New York: Macmillan, 1932; Westport, Conn.: Greenwood Press, 1978.

Horowitz, Helen L. *Alma Mater: Design and Experience in the Women's Colleges from Their Nineteenth-Century Beginnings to the 1930's*. New York: Alfred A. Knopf, 1984.

Howe, Florence. *Myths of Coeducation: Selected Essays, 1964–1983*. Bloomington: Indiana University Press, 1984.

Howie, George. *Educational Theory and Practice in St. Augustine*. New York: Teachers College Press, 1969.

Hugh of St. Victor. *Didascalicon: A Medieval Guide to the Arts*. Translated with an introduction and notes by Jerome Taylor. New York: Columbia University Press, 1961.

Hunt, Felicity, ed. *Lessons for Life: The Schooling of Girls and Women, 1850–1950*. Oxford, Eng.: Basil Blackwell, 1987.

Hutchins, Robert M. *The Higher Learning in America*. New Haven: Yale University Press, 1937; Westport, Conn.: Greenwood Press, 1979.

Hyde, Douglas. *A Literary History of Ireland*. London: T. Fisher Unwin, 1899; New York: Barnes & Noble, 1967.

Isocrates. *Isocrates*. 3 vols. Translated by G. Norlin and LaRue Van Hook. Cambridge: Loeb Classical Library, Harvard University Press, 1928–1945.

Jackson, Phillip W., ed. *Contributing to Educational Change: Perspectives on Research and Practice*. Berkeley: McCutchan Publishing Co., 1988.

Jaeger, Werner W. *Early Christianity and Greek Paideia*. Cambridge: Belknap Press of Harvard University Press, 1961, 1985.

———. *Paideia: The Ideals of Greek Culture*. 3 vols. Translated by Gilbert Highet. New York: Oxford University Press, 1945.

Jarrett, James L., ed. *The Educational Theories of the Sophists*. New York: Teachers College Press, 1969.

Jefferson, Thomas. *Crusade Against Ignorance: Thomas Jefferson on Education.* Edited by Gordon C. Lee. New York: Teachers College Press, 1961.

―――. *The Papers of Thomas Jefferson.* 22 vols. Edited by Julian P. Boyd, et al. Princeton: Princeton University Press, 1950 et seq.

Jencks, Christopher, et al. *Inequality: A Reassessment of the Effect of Family and Schooling in America.* New York: Basic Books, 1972.

Jernegan, Marcus W. *Laboring and Dependent Classes in Colonial America, 1607–1783.* Chicago: University of Chicago Press, 1931; New York: F. Ungar, 1960.

Jerome, Saint. "Lives of Illustrious Men." In *A Select Library of Nicene and Post-Nicene Fathers of the Christian Church.* Second series. 14 vols. Translated and edited by Philip Schaff and Henry Wace. Grand Rapids, Mich.: W. R. Eerdmans, 1952, 1969–1976.

―――. *Selected Letters of St. Jerome.* 24 vols. Translated by F. A. Wright. Cambridge: Loeb Classical Library, Harvard University Press, 1923.

John of Salisbury. *The Metalogicon of John of Salisbury.* Translated by Daniel D. McGarry. Berkeley and Los Angeles: University of California Press, 1955.

Johnson, Clifton. *Old-Time Schools and School-Books.* New York: Macmillan, 1904.

Johnson, Marietta. *Thirty Years With an Idea.* University: University of Alabama Press, 1974.

Jolowicz, H. F., and Barry Nicholas. *Historical Introduction to the Study of Roman Law.* 3d ed. Cambridge, Eng.: University Press, 1972.

Jones, A. H. M. *The Greek City from Alexander to Justinian.* New York: Oxford University Press, 1940.

Jones, Tom B. *The Silver-Plated Age.* Sandoval, N. M.: Coronado Press, 1962.

―――. *In the Twilight of Antiquity.* Minneapolis: University of Minnesota Press, 1978.

Jorgenson, Lloyd P. *The State and the Non-Public School, 1825–1925.* Columbia: University of Missouri Press, 1987.

Juvenal. *Satires.* Translated by Jerome Mazzaro. Ann Arbor: University of Michigan Press, 1965.

Kaestle, Carl F. *Pillars of the Republic: Common Schools and American Society, 1780–1860.* New York: Hill and Wang, 1983.

Kaestle, Carl F., ed. *Joseph Lancaster and the Monitorial School Movement: A Documentary History.* New York: Teachers College Press, 1973.

Kaestle, Carl F., and Maris Vinovskis. *Education and Social Change in Nineteenth-Century Massachusetts.* New York: Cambridge University Press, 1980.

Kandel, Isaac L. *History of Secondary Education: A Study in the Development of Liberal Education*. Boston: Houghton Mifflin Co., 1930.

———. *The Reform of Secondary Education in France*. New York: Teachers College Press, 1924.

———. *William Chandler Bagley, Stalwart Educator*. New York: Teachers College Press, 1961.

Kannengiesser, Charles, and William L. Petersen. *Origen of Alexandria, His World and His Legacy*. Notre Dame, Ind.: University of Notre Dame Press, 1988.

Karier, Clarence J. *Shaping the American Educational State, 1900 to the Present*. New York: Free Press, 1975.

Kaster, Robert A. *Guardians of Language: The Grammarian and Society in Late Antiquity*. Berkeley and Los Angeles: University of California Press, 1986.

Katz, Michael B. *Class, Bureaucracy, and Schools: The Illusion of Educational Change in America*. New York: Praeger, 1971.

———. *The Irony of Early School Reform*. Cambridge: Harvard University Press, 1968.

———. *Reconstructing American Education*. Cambridge: Harvard University Press, 1986.

Keatinge, M. W. *Comenius*. New York: McGraw-Hill, 1931.

Kelso, Ruth. *Doctrine of the English Gentleman in the Sixteenth Century*. Urbana: University of Illinois Press, 1929.

———. *Doctrine for the Lady of the Renaissance*. Urbana: University of Illinois Press, 1956.

Kennedy, George A. *Classical Rhetoric and Its Christian and Secular Tradition from Ancient to Modern Times*. Chapel Hill: University of North Carolina Press, 1980.

Kibre, Pearl. *The Nations of the Mediaeval Universities*. Cambridge, Mass.: Mediaeval Academy of America, 1948.

———. *Scholarly Privileges in the Middle Ages*. Cambridge, Mass.: Mediaeval Academy of America, 1962.

Kilpatrick, William H. *The Dutch Schools of New Netherland and Colonial New York*. Washington, D. C.: Government Printing Office, 1912.

———. *Foundations of Method: Informal Talks on Teaching*. New York: Macmillan, 1925.

Kimball, Bruce A. *Orators and Philosophers: A History of the Idea of Liberal Education*. New York: Teachers College Press, 1986.

Kimball, Roger. *Tenured Radicals: How Politics Has Corrupted Our Higher Education.* New York: Harper & Row, 1990.

Kittleson, James M., and Pamela Transue, eds. *Rebirth, Reform, and Resilience: Universities in Transition, 1300–1700.* Columbus: Ohio State University Press, 1984.

Knight, Edgar W. *Education in the United States.* 5th ed. Boston: Ginn & Co., 1951.

Knowles, David. *The Evolution of Medieval Thought.* New York: Alfred A. Knopf, 1962; New York: Vintage Books, 1964.

Kramer, D. G. A. H. *Francke's padagogische Schriften.* Langensalza: H. Beyer & Sohne, 1885.

Krug, Edward. *Salient Dates in American Education: 1635–1964.* New York: Harper & Row, 1966.

Kuhn, Thomas. *The Copernican Revolution: Planetary Astronomy in the Development of Western Thought.* Cambridge: Harvard University Press, 1957.

Kuhrt, Amelie, and Susan Sherwin-White, eds. *Hellenism in the East: Interaction of Greek and Non-Greek Civilizations from Syria to Central Asia after Alexander.* Berkeley and Los Angeles: University of California Press, 1987.

Kuklick, Bruce. *Churchmen and Philosophers from Jonathan Edwards to John Dewey.* New Haven: Yale University Press, 1985.

———. *Josiah Royce: An Intellectual Biography.* Indianapolis: Bobbs-Merrill, 1972.

———. *Pragmatism.* Indianapolis: Hackett Publishing Co., 1981.

———. *Rise of American Philosophy, Cambridge, Massachusetts, 1860– 1930.* New Haven: Yale University Press, 1977.

Kunkel, Wolfgang. *An Introduction to Roman Legal and Constitutional History.* Translated by J. M. Kelly. Oxford: Clarendon Press, 1966.

La Fontainerie, François de, ed. and trans. *French Liberalism and Education in the Eighteenth Century: The Writings of La Chalotais, Turgot, Diderot, and Condorcet on National Education.* New York: McGraw-Hill, 1932; New York: B. Franklin, 1971.

Laistner, M. L. W. *Christianity and Pagan Culture in the Later Roman Empire.* Ithaca: Cornell University Press, 1951.

Lang, O.H. *Comenius: His Life and Principles of Education.* New York: E. L. Kellog & Co., 1891.

Lannie, Vincent P. *Public Money and Parochial Education: Bishop Hughes, Governor Seward, and the New York School Controversy.* Cleveland: Press of Case Western Reserve University, 1968.

La Vopa, Anthony J. *Grace, Talent, and Merit: Poor Students, Clerical Careers, and Professional Ideology in Eighteenth-Century Germany.* Cambridge: Cambridge University Press, 1988.

―――. *Prussian Schoolteachers: Profession and Office, 1763–1848.* Chapel Hill: University of North Carolina Press, 1980.

Leach, Arthur F. *Educational Charters and Documents 598 to 1909.* New York: Cambridge University Press, 1911.

―――. *Schools of Medieval England.* London: Methuen & Co., 1915; New York: Barnes & Noble, 1969.

Leff, Gordon. *Paris and Oxford Universities in the Thirteenth and Fourteenth Centuries.* New York: John Wiley, 1968.

Leidecker, Kurt F. *Yankee Teacher: The Life of William Torrey Harris.* New York: Philosophical Library, 1946.

Levy, Daniel C. *Private Education: Studies in Choice and Public Policy.* New York: Oxford University Press, 1986.

Levy, Leonard W. *The Establishment Clause: Religion and the First Amendment.* New York: Macmillan, 1986.

Lindberg, David C., and Ronald L. Numbers, eds. *God and Nature: Historical Essays on the Encounter between Christianity and Science.* Berkeley and Los Angeles: University of California Press, 1986.

Lindsay, Thomas M. *Luther and the German Reformation.* New York: Charles Scribner's Sons, 1900.

Locke, John. *An Essay Concerning Human Understanding,* 28th ed. London: T. Tegg and Son, 1838.

―――. *Some Thoughts Concerning Education.* Edited by Peter Gay. New York: Teachers College Press, 1964.

Lourdaux, W., and D. Verhelst, eds. *Benedictine Culture: 750–1050.* Leuven: Leuven University Press, 1983.

Lowe, Roy. *Education in the Post-War Years: A Social History.* London: Routledge & Kegan Paul, 1988.

Lowry, Martin. *The World of Aldus Manutius: Business and Scholarship in Renaissance Venice.* Ithaca: Cornell University Press, 1979.

Lupton, Joseph H. *Life of John Colet, D. D., Dean of St. Paul's and Founder of St. Paul's School.* 2d ed. Hamden, Conn.: Shoe String Press, 1961.

Lynch, John P. *Aristotle's School: A Study of a Greek Educational Institution.* Berkeley and Los Angeles: University of California Press, 1972.

McCarthy, Joseph M. *Humanistic Emphases in the Educational Thought of Vincent of Beauvais.* Leiden: Brill, 1976.

McClelland, Charles. *State, Society and the University in Germany, 1700–1914.* Cambridge: Cambridge University Press, 1980.

McCormick, Patrick J., and Francis P. Cassidy. *A History of Education.* Washington, D. C.: Catholic Education Press, 1953.

McGrath, Fergal. *Education in Ancient and Medieval Ireland.* Dublin: Studies Special Publications, 1979.

McLaughlin, Raymond. *A History of State Legislation Affecting Private Elementary and Secondary Schools in the United States, 1870–1945.* Washington, D. C.: Catholic University of America Press, 1946.

Maclure, J. Stuart. *Educational Documents: England and Wales, 1816 to the Present Day.* London: Methuen & Co., 1965.

MacMullen, Ramsay. *Christianizing the Roman Empire (A. D. 100–400).* New Haven: Yale University Press, 1984.

Madsen, David. *Early National Education, 1776–1830.* New York: John Wiley, 1974.

Mann, Horace. *The Republic and the School: Horace Mann and the Education of Free Men.* Edited by Lawrence A. Cremin. New York: Teachers College Press, 1957.

Mann, Nicholas. *Petrarch.* New York: Oxford University Press, 1984.

Manschreck, Clyde L. *Melanchthon, the Quiet Reformer.* New York: Abingdon Press, 1958.

Marrou, H. I. *A History of Education in Antiquity.* Translated by George Lamb. New York: Sheed and Ward, 1956; Madison: University of Wisconsin Press, 1982.

———. *Saint Augustin et la Fin de la Culture antique.* Paris: Vrin, 1949; Paris: E. De Boccard, 1958.

Martin, Luther H. *Hellenistic Religions: An Introduction.* New York: Oxford University Press, 1987.

Masi, Michael, ed. *Boethius and the Liberal Arts.* New York: Peter Lang, 1981.

Matthews, Richard K. *The Radical Politics of Thomas Jefferson: A Revisionist View.* Lawrence: University of Kansas Press, 1984.

Mattingly, Paul H. *The Classless Profession: American Schoolmen in the Nineteenth Century.* New York: New York University Press, 1975.

Mattingly, Paul H., and Edward W. Stevens, Jr., eds. *". . . Schools and the Means of Education Shall Forever Be Encouraged": A History of Education in the Old Northwest, 1787–1880.* Athens: Ohio University Libraries, 1987.

Maynes, Mary Jo. *Schooling in Western Europe: A Social History.* Albany: State University of New York Press, 1985.

Melton, James Van Horn. *Absolutism and the Eighteenth-Century Origins of Compulsory Schooling in Prussia and Austria.* New York: Cambridge University Press, 1988.

Mencken, H. L. *The American Language: An Inquiry into the Development of English in the United States.* 4th ed. New York: Alfred A. Knopf, 1936.

Messerli, Jonathan. *Horace Mann: A Biography.* New York: Alfred A. Knopf, 1972.

Miller, Perry. *The New England Mind: The Seventeenth Century.* New York: Macmillan, 1939.

Miller, Perry, ed. *The Transcendentalists.* Cambridge: Harvard University Press, 1950.

Milton, John. *Areopagitica.* Edited by William Haller. New York: Macmillan, 1927.

———. *Milton on Education, The Tractate of Education.* Edited by O. M. Ainsworth. New Haven: Yale University Press, 1928.

Moody, Joseph N. *French Education Since Napoleon.* Syracuse: Syracuse University Press, 1978.

Moore, Paul E. *Hellenistic Philosophies.* Princeton: Princeton University Press, 1923.

Moran, Jo Ann H. *Growth of English Schooling, 1340–1548.* Princeton: Princeton University Press, 1985.

Morgan, Edmund S. *The Puritan Family: Religion and Domestic Relations in Seventeenth-Century New England.* New York: Harper & Row, 1966.

Morgan, John. *Godly Learning: Puritan Attitudes Towards Reason, Learning and Education, 1560–1640.* New York: Cambridge University Press, 1986.

Morison, Samuel Eliot. *Harvard College in the Seventeenth Century.* 2 vols. Cambridge: Harvard University Press, 1936.

———. *The Puritan Pronaos: Studies in the Intellectual Life of New England in the Seventeenth Century.* New York: New York University Press, 1936.

Morrison, J. S., and J. F. Coates. *The Athenian Trireme: The History and Reconstruction of an Ancient Greek Warship.* New York: Cambridge University Press, 1986.

Mosier, Richard D. *Making the American Mind: Social and Moral Ideas in the McGuffey Readers.* New York: King's Crown Press, 1947; New York: Russell & Russell, 1965.

Mullinger, J. Bass. *The Schools of Charles the Great and the Restoration of Learning in the Ninth Century.* London: Longmans, Green & Co., 1877; Folcroft, Penn.: Folcroft Library Editions, 1977.

Murray, A. Victor. *Abelard and St. Bernard: A Study in Twelfth Century "Modernism."* Manchester: Manchester University Press, 1967; New York: Barnes & Noble, 1967.

Nakosteen, Mehdi. *History of Islamic Origins of Western Education.* Boulder: University of Colorado Press, 1964.

National Education Association. *Report of the Committee of Ten on Secondary School Studies.* New York: American Book Company, 1894; New York: Arno Press, 1969.

National Society for the Study of Education. *Philosophies of Education.* Yearbook, vol. 41. Chicago: University of Chicago Press, 1942.

———. *Modern Philosophies and Education.* Yearbook, vol. 54. Chicago: University of Chicago Press, 1955.

———. *Philosophy and Education.* Yearbook, vol. 80. Chicago: University of Chicago Press, 1981.

Nicholas Mary P. *Socrates and the Political Community: An Ancient Debate.* Albany: State University of New York Press, 1987.

Nisbet, Robert A. *The Degradation of the Academic Dogma: The University in America, 1945–1970.* New York: Basic Books, 1971.

Noble, Thomas F. X., and John J. Contreni, eds. *Religion, Culture, and Society in the Early Middle Ages.* Kalamazoo: Medieval Institute Publications, Western Michigan University, 1987.

O'Leary, DeLacy B. *How Greek Science Passed to the Arabs.* London: Routledge & Kegan Paul, 1949.

O'Neill, James M. *Religion and Education under the Constitution.* New York: Harper & Row, 1949.

Orme, Nicholas. *English Schools in the Middle Ages.* London: Methuen & Co., 1973.

Ostwald, Martin. *From Popular Sovereignty to the Sovereignty of Law: Law, Society, and Politics in Fifth-Century Athens.* Berkeley and Los Angeles: University of California Press, 1987.

Padberg, John W. *Colleges in Controversy: The Jesuit Schools in France from Revival to Suppression, 1815–1880.* Cambridge: Harvard University Press, 1969.

Padover, Saul K. *The Mind of Alexander Hamilton.* New York: Harper & Row, 1958.

Paetow, Louis J. *The Arts Course at Mediaeval Universities, with Special Reference to Grammar and Rhetoric.* Urbana: University of Illinois Press, 1910; Dubuque, Iowa: W. C. Brown, 1963.

Painter, F. V. N. *Luther on Education.* St. Louis: Concordia Publishing House, 1928.

Patch, Howard R. *The Tradition of Boethius.* New York: Oxford University Press, 1935; New York: Russell & Russell, 1970.

Paulsen, Friedrich. *German Education, Past and Present.* Translated by T. Lorenz. New York: Charles Scribner's Sons, 1908.

_____. *The German Universities and University Study.* Translated by Frank Thilly and William W. Elwang. New York: Charles Scribner's Sons, 1906.

Pederson, Joyce S. *The Reform of Girls' Secondary and Higher Education in Victorian England: A Study of Elites and Educational Change.* New York: Garland, 1987.

Peirce, Charles Sanders. *Collected Papers of Charles Sanders Peirce.* 8 vols. Edited by Charles Hartshorne and Paul Weiss. Cambridge: Belknap Press of Harvard University Press, 1960.

Peirce, Cyrus. *The First State Normal School in America; the Journals of Cyrus Peirce and Mary Swift.* Cambridge: Harvard University Press, 1926.

Pelikan, Jaroslav J. *The Excellent Empire: The Fall of Rome and the Triumph of the Church.* San Francisco: Harper & Row, 1987.

_____. *Scholarship and Its Survival.* Princeton: Carnegie Foundation for the Advancement of Teaching, 1983.

Perkinson, Henry J. *The Imperfect Panacea: American Faith in Education, 1865–1976.* New York: Random House, 1977.

Pestalozzi, Johann H. *How Gertrude Teaches Her Children.* 5th ed. Translated by Lucy E. Holland and F. C. Turner. Syracuse: C.W. Bardeen, 1915.

Petrarca, Francesco. *Letters on Familiar Matters. Rerum familiarium libri IX–XVI.* Translated by Aldo S. Bernardo. Baltimore and London: Johns Hopkins University Press, 1982.

Pierson, George W. *The Founding of Yale: The Legend of the Forty Folios.* New Haven: Yale University Press, 1988.

Pindar. *The Works of Pindar.* Translated by L. R. Farnell. London: Macmillan, 1930–1932.

Plato. *The Dialogues of Plato.* 5 vols. Translated by Benjamin Jowett. New York: Oxford University Press, 1892.

_____. *Laws.* 2 vols. Translated by R. G. Bury. Cambridge: Loeb Classical Library, Harvard University Press, 1984.

———. *Republic*. 2 vols. Translated by Paul Shorey. Cambridge: Loeb Classical Library, Harvard University Press, 1928.

Pliny. *Letters*. 2 vols. Translated by W. Melmoth; revised by W. M. L. Hutchinson. Cambridge: Loeb Classical Library, Harvard University Press, 1915.

Plutarch. *Moralia*. 14 vols. Translated by F. C. Babbitt, et al. Cambridge: Loeb Classical Library, Harvard University Press, 1927.

———. *Plutarch's Lives*. 11 vols. Translated by B. Perrin. Cambridge: Loeb Classical Library, Harvard University Press, 1914–1926.

Pointer, Richard W. *Protestant Pluralism and the New York Experience: A Study of Eighteenth-Century Religious Diversity*. Bloomington: Indiana University Press, 1988.

Poliakoff, Michael. *Combat Sports in the Ancient World*. New Haven: Yale University Press, 1987.

Poore, Benjamin P., ed. *The Federal and State Constitutions, Colonial Charters, and Other Organic Laws of the United States*. 2 vols. Washington, D. C., 1878.

Popkewitz, Thomas S., ed. *The Formation of School Subjects: The Struggle for Creating an American Institution*. New York: Falmer Press, 1987.

Power, Edward J. *Evolution of Educational Doctrine: Major Educational Theorists of the Western World*. New York: Appleton-Century-Crofts, 1969.

Pratte, Richard. *The Civic Imperative: Examining the Need for Civic Education*. New York: Teachers College Press, 1988.

President and Fellows of Harvard College. *General Education in a Free Society: A Report of the Harvard Committee*. Cambridge: Harvard University Press, 1945.

Proctor, Robert E. *Education's Great Amnesia: Reconsidering the Humanities from Petrarch to Freud, with a Curriculum for Today's Students*. Bloomington: Indiana University Press, 1988.

Quintilian. *On the Early Education of the Citizen-Orator*. Translated by John S. Watson; edited by James J. Murphy. Indianapolis: Bobbs-Merrill, 1965.

———. *The Education of an Orator*. 4 vols. Translated by H. E. Butler. Cambridge: Loeb Classical Library, Harvard University Press, 1921–1926.

———. *Quintilian on Education*. Selected and translated by William M. Smail. Oxford: Clarendon Press, 1938; New York: Teachers College Press, 1966.

Radding, Charles M. *The Origins of Medieval Jurisprudence: Pavia and Bologna, 850–1150*. New Haven: Yale University Press, 1988.

Ramus, Petrus. *Arguments in Rhetoric against Quintilian*. Translated by Carole Newlands. DeKalb: Northern Illinois University Press, 1986.

Rand, Edward K. *Founders of the Middle Ages*. Cambridge: Harvard University Press, 1928: New York: Dover Publications, 1957.

Rashdall, Hastings. *The Universities of Europe in the Middle Ages*. 3 vols. Edited by F. M. Powicke and A. B. Emden. London: Oxford University Press, 1936.

Raven, J. E. *Plato's Thought in the Making*. Cambridge, Eng.: University Press, 1965.

Ravitch, Diane. *The Revisionists Revised: A Critique of the Radical Attack on the Schools*. New York: Basic Books, 1978.

_____. *The Troubled Crusade: American Education, 1945–1980*. New York: Basic Books, 1983.

Rawson, Elizabeth. *Cicero: A Portrait*. Ithaca: Cornell University Press, 1975, 1983.

Reese, William J. *Power and Promise of School Reform: Grassroots Movements During the Progressive Era*. Boston: Routledge & Kegan Paul, 1986.

Riché, Pierre. *Education and Culture in the Barbarian West, Sixth Through Eighth Centuries*. Translated by John J. Contreni. Columbia: University of South Carolina Press, 1976.

Rickover, Hyman. *Education and Freedom*. New York: E. P. Dutton & Co., 1959.

Ringer, Fritz K. *Education and Society in Modern Europe*. Bloomington: Indiana University Press, 1979.

Roach, John P. *A History of Secondary Education in England, 1800–1870*. London: Longman, 1986.

_____. *Public Examinations in England, 1850–1900*. Cambridge: Cambridge University Press, 1971.

Robinson-Hammerstein, Helga, ed. *The Transmission of Ideas in the Lutheran Reformation*. Dublin: Irish Academic Press, 1989.

Roche, John F. *The Colonial Colleges in the War for American Independence*. Milwood, N. Y.: Associated Faculty Press, 1986.

Rolfe, John C. *Cicero and His Influence*. New York: Cooper Square Publishers, 1963.

Rose, Anne C. *Transcendentalism as a Social Movement, 1830–1850*. New Haven: Yale University Press, 1981.

Rosovsky, Henry. *The University: An Owner's Manual*. New York: Norton, 1990.

Ross, Earle D. *Democracy's College: The Land-Grant Movement in the Formative Stage*. Ames: Iowa State College Press, 1942.

Rostovtseff, Mikhail I. *The Social and Economic History of the Hellenistic World.* 3 vols. Oxford: Clarendon Press, 1941.

Rothstein, William G. *American Medical Schools and the Practice of Medicine: A History.* New York: Oxford University Press, 1987.

Rousseau, Jean-Jacques. *Emilé.* Translated by Barbara Foxley. New York: E. P. Dutton & Co., 1911, 1938.

Rudolph, Frederick S. *The American College and University: A History.* New York: Alfred A. Knopf, 1962.

———. *Curriculum: A History of the Undergraduate Course of Study Since 1636.* San Francisco: Jossey-Bass, 1977.

Rudy, Willis. *Universities of Europe: A History.* Rutherford, N. J.: Fairleigh Dickinson University Press; London and Cranbury, N. J.: Associated University Presses, 1984.

Ruggles, Steven. *Prolonged Connections: The Rise of the Extended Family in Nineteenth-Century England and America.* Madison: University of Wisconsin Press, 1987.

Rush, Benjamin. *Letters of Benjamin Rush.* 2 vols. Edited by Lyman H. Butterfield. Princeton: Princeton University Press, 1951.

———. *A Plan for the Establishment of Public Schools and the Diffusion of Knowledge in Pennsylvania.* Philadelphia, 1786.

Russell, James E. *German Higher Schools: The History, Organization and Methods of Secondary Education in Germany.* New York: Longmans, Green & Co., 1899.

Salzman, Louis F. *English Life in the Middle Ages.* Oxford: Clarendon Press, 1926.

Sandys, John E. *A History of Classical Scholarship.* Cambridge: Cambridge University Press, 1921; New York: Hafner Publishing Co., 1958.

Scaglione, Aldo. *The Liberal Arts and the Jesuit College System.* Philadelphia: John Benjamin Publishing Co., 1986.

Schulz, Fritz. *History of Roman Legal Science.* 2d ed. Oxford: Clarendon Press, 1953.

Schwartz, Sally. *"A Mixed Multitude": The Struggle for Toleration in Colonial Pennsylvania.* New York: New York University Press, 1988.

Sedlak, Michael W., Christopher W. Wheeler, Diana C. Pullin, and Philip A. Cusick. *Selling Students Short: Classroom Bargains and Academic Reform in the American High School.* New York: Teachers College Press, 1986.

Seeskin, Kenneth. *Dialogue and Discovery: A Study in Socratic Method.* Albany: State University of New York Press, 1986.

Sheehan, Nancy M., et al., eds. *Schools in the West: Essays in Canadian Educational History.* Calgary: Detselig Enterprises, 1986.

Shrosbree, Colin. *Public Schools and Private Education: The Clarendon Commission, 1861–64, and the Public School Acts.* Manchester: Manchester University Press, 1988; New York: St. Martin's Press, 1988.

Silver, Pamela, and Harold Silver. *The Education of the Poor: The History of a National School, 1824–1974.* London: Routledge & Kegan Paul, 1974.

Simon, Kate. *A Renaissance Tapestry: The Gonzaga of Mantua.* New York: Harper & Row, 1988.

Singer, Bruno. *Fürstenspiegel in Deutschland im Zeilalter des Humanismus und der Reformation.* Munich: W. Fink, 1981.

Sizer, Theodore R. *Secondary Schools at the Turn of the Century.* New Haven: Yale University Press, 1964.

Sizer, Theodore R., ed. *The Age of the Academies.* New York: Teachers College Press, 1964.

Smith, Dennis. *Conflict and Compromise: Class Formation in English Society, 1830–1914.* London: Routledge & Kegan Paul, 1982.

Smith, Mortimer. *And Madly Teach.* Chicago: Regnery Co., 1949.

Smith, Page. *Killing the Spirit: Higher Education in America.* New York: Viking Press, 1990.

Smith, Wesley D. *The Hippocratic Tradition.* Ithaca: Cornell University Press, 1979.

Solomon, Barbara M. *In the Company of Educated Women: A History of Women and Higher Education in America.* New Haven: Yale University Press, 1985.

Soltow, Lee, and Edward Stevens. *The Rise of Literacy and the Common School in the United States.* Chicago: University of Chicago Press, 1981.

Southern, Richard R. *St. Anselm and His Biographer.* Cambridge, Eng.: University Press, 1963.

Southern, R. W. *Medieval Humanism and Others Studies.* Oxford: B. Blackwell, 1970.

Spencer, Herbert. *Education: Intellectual, Moral, Physical.* Boston: Small, 1886; New York: Appleton-Century-Crofts, 1927.

Sperl, Adolf. *Melanchthon Zwischen Humanismus und Reformation.* Munich: Kaiser, 1959.

Spring, Joel. *American Education: An Introduction to Social and Political Aspects.* 4th ed. New York: Longman, 1989.

————. *The American School 1842–1985: Varieties of Historical Interpretation of the Foundations and Development of American Education.* New York: Longman, 1986.

Stahl, William H., and Richard Johnson, with E. L. Burge. *Martianus Capella and the Seven Liberal Arts.* 2 vols. New York: Columbia University Press, 1971, 1977.

Stavley, Keith W. F. *Puritan Legacies: Paradise Lost and the New England Tradition.* Ithaca: Cornell University Press, 1987.

Steinmetz, David C. *Reformers in the Wings.* Philadelphia: Fortress Press, 1971.

Strabo. *The Geography of Strabo.* 8 vols. Translated by H. L. Jones. Cambridge: Loeb Classical Library, Harvard University Press, 1932.

Strauss, Gerald. *Luther's House of Learning: Indoctrination of the Young in the German Reformation.* Baltimore and London: Johns Hopkins University Press, 1978.

Suetonius. *Of Grammarians and Rhetors.* 2 vols. Translated by J. C. Rolfe. Cambridge: Loeb Classical Library, Harvard University Press, 1914.

Sweet, Waldo E. *Sport and Recreation in Ancient Greece: A Sourcebook with Translations.* New York: Oxford University Press, 1987.

Szasz, Margaret C. *Indian Education in the American Colonies, 1607–1783.* Albuquerque: University of New Mexico Press, 1988.

Tacitus. *Annals.* Translated by A. J. Church and W. J. Brodribb. London: Macmillan, 1921.

————. *Diologus.* Translated by W. Petersen. Cambridge: Loeb Classical Library, Harvard University Press, 1925.

Tarn, William W. *Hellenistic Civilization.* London: E. Arnold, 1952.

Tenenbaum, Samuel. *William Heard Kilpatrick: Trail Blazer in Education.* New York: Harper & Row, 1951.

Tester, S. J. *A History of Western Astrology.* Wolfeboro, N. H.: Boydell & Brewster, 1987.

Tewksbury, Donald. *The Founding of American Colleges and Universities before the Civil War.* New York: Teachers College Press, 1932; New York: Arno Press, 1969.

Thierry de Chartres. *The Latin Rhetorical Commentaries.* Edited by Karin M. Fredborg. Toronto: Pontifical Institute of Mediaeval Studies, 1988.

Thorndike, Lynn. *A History of Magic and Experimental Science.* 8 vols. New York: Macmillan, 1923–1928.

————. *University Records and Life in the Middle Ages.* New York: Columbia University Press, 1944.

Thrupp, Sylvia L. *The Merchant Class of Medieval London*. Chicago: University of Chicago Press, 1948; Ann Arbor: University of Michigan Press, 1948.

Tobin, Rosemary Barton. *Vincent of Beauvais' "De Eruditione Filiorum Nobilium" The Education of Women*. New York: Peter Lang, 1984.

Todd, Margo. *Christian Humanism and the Puritan Social Order*. Cambridge: Cambridge University Press, 1987.

Tollington, R. B. *Clement of Alexandria, A Study in Christian Liberalism*. 4 vols. London: Williams and Norgate, 1914.

Tracy, James D. *Erasmus: The Growth of a Mind*. Geneve: Droz, 1972.

Troen, Selwyn K. *The Public and the Schools: Shaping the St. Louis System, 1838–1920*. Columbia: University of Missouri Press, 1975.

Tushnet, Mark V. *The NAACP's Legal Strategy against Segregated Education, 1925–1950*. Chapel Hill: University of North Carolina Press, 1987.

Tyack, David B. *The One Best System: A History of American Urban Education*. Cambridge: Harvard University Press, 1974.

Tyler, Alice Felt. *Freedom's Ferment: Phases of American Social History to 1860*. Minneapolis: University of Minnesota Press, 1944; Freeport, N. Y.: Books for Libraries Press, 1970.

Ullmann, Walter. *Medieval Foundations of Renaissance Humanism*. Ithaca: Cornell University Press, 1977.

United States Office of Education. *Vitalizing Secondary Education: Report of the First Commission on Life Adjustment Education of Youth*. Washington, D. C., 1951.

Untersteiner, Mario. *The Sophists*. Translated by K. Freeman. Oxford: Blackwell, 1954.

Van der Zee, Henri, and Barbara Van der Zee. *A Sweet and Alien Land: The Story of Dutch New York*. New York: Viking Press, 1978.

Veblen, Thorstein. *The Higher Learning in America: A Memorandum on the Conduct of Universities by Businessmen*. New York: Viking Press, 1918; New York: Sagamore Press, 1957; New York: A. M. Kelly, 1965.

Veysey, Laurence R. *The Emergence of the American University*. Chicago: University of Chicago Press, 1965.

Vincent of Beauvais. *De Eruditione Filiorum Nobilium of Vincent of Beauvais*. Edited by Arpad Steiner. Cambridge: Mediaeval Academy of America, 1938.

Vinovskis, Maris A. *The Origins of Public High Schools: A Re-examination of the Beverly High School Controversy*. Madison: University of Wisconsin Press, 1985.

Wade, Wyn C. *The Fiery Cross: The Ku Klux Klan in America.* New York: Simon & Schuster, 1987.

Wagner, David L. *The Seven Liberal Arts in the Middle Ages.* Bloomington: Indiana University Press, 1983.

Wallach, Luitpold. *Alcuin and Charlemagne: Studies in Carolingian History and Literature.*: Ithaca: Cornell University Press, 1959; New York: Johnson Reprint Corp., 1968.

Walsh, Henry H. *The Concordat of 1801: A Study in the Problems of Nationalism in the Relations of Church and State.* New York: Columbia University Press, 1933.

Wardle, David. *English Popular Education, 1780–1975.* Cambridge: Cambridge University Press, 1976.

Washington, George. *Writings of George Washington, 1745–1799.* 39 vols. Edited by John C. Fitzpatrick. Washington, D. C., 1940.

Webster, Noah. *Dissertations on the English Language.* Boston, 1789.

Wertenbaker, Thomas J. *Princeton: 1749–1896.* Princeton: Princeton University Press, 1946.

West, Andrew F. *Alcuin and the Rise of the Christian School.* New York: Charles Scribner's Sons, 1892: Westport, Conn.: Greenwood Press, 1969.

Whitfield, John H. *Petrarch and the Renascence.* London: Oxford University Press, 1943; New York: Haskell House, 1966.

Wickersham, James P. *A History of Education in Pennsylvania.* Lancaster, Penn.: 1886; New York: Arno Press, 1969.

Wiedemann, Thomas. *Adults and Children in the Roman Empire.* New Haven: Yale University Press, 1989.

Wieruszowski, Helene. *Medieval University: Masters, Students, Learning.* Princeton, N. J: Van Nostrand, 1966.

Wilken, Robert L. *John Chrysostom and the Jews: Rhetoric and Reality in the Late Fourth Century.* Berkeley and Los Angeles: University of California Press, 1983.

Williams, Edward I. F. *Horace Mann, Educational Statesman.* New York: Macmillan, 1937.

Winterbottom, Michael. *Problems in Quintilian.* London: University of London, Institute of Classical Studies, 1970.

Winthrop, Hudson S. *Religion in America: An Historical Account of the Development of American Religious Life.* 2d ed. New York: Charles Scribner's Sons, 1973.

Wittgenstein, Ludwig. *Tractatus Logico-Philosophicus.* Translated by D. F. Pears and B. F. McGuinness. New York: Humanities Press, 1961.

Wood, Neal. *Cicero's Social and Political Thought.* Berkeley and Los Angeles: University of California Press, 1988.

Woodward, William H. *Desiderius Erasmus Concerning the Aim and Method of Education.* Cambridge: Cambridge University Press, 1904; New York: Teachers College Press, 1964.

_____. *Studies in Education During the Age of the Renaissance, 1400–1600.* Cambridge: Cambridge University Press, 1906; New York: Teachers College Press, 1967.

_____. *Vittorino da Feltre and Other Humanist Educators.* Cambridge: Cambridge University Press, 1897; New York: Teachers College Press, 1963.

Woody, Thomas. *Life and Education in Early Societies.* New York: Macmillan, 1949.

Wright, Esmond. *Franklin of Philadelphia.* Cambridge: Belknap Press of Harvard University Press, 1986.

Wright, Louis B. *The Cultural Life of the American Colonies, 1607–1763.* New York: Harper & Row, 1957.

Wynne, Edward A. *Traditional Catholic Religious Orders: Living in Community.* New Brunswick, N. J.: Transaction Books, 1988.

Xenophon. *The Works of Xenophon.* 4 vols. Translated by H. G. Dakyns. London: Macmillan, 1890–1897.

Index

A

Abelard, Pierre, 131–132; linguistic analysis of, 134–135; logic of, 134–135; *Sic et Non*, 132, 135
Academy, 8, 13–14, 20, 269, 276
Accursius, 140
Adams, John, 255
Adler, Mortimer J., 301
Advancement of Learning, The, 240–243, 273
Aeneid, 51
Aesop's fables, 13
Affirmative action, 310–311
Against the Sophists, 41
Agricola, Rudolph, 9
Alcuin, 122–124, 125, 127; on the classics, 123; graded readers of, 124; the teacher, 123
Alexander of Hales, 140
Alexander of Villedieu, 136
Alexander the Great, 44, 49–50, 52
Alexandria, 62
Allegorical interpretation, 138–139
Almagestes, 62
Ambrose, St., 101
American Philosophical Society, 249, 258
Americanisms, in language, 248
Analysis, linguistic, 135
Analytic philosophy, 300
Andronicus, Livius, 71

Anglicans, 224; colonial educational activity of, 239
Anselm, St., 132, 140
Anthologies, origin of, 103
Antidosis, 41
Antioch, 62
Antiphon, 23
Arabic notation, 121
Aristippus, 54
Aristophanes, 7–8, 35
Aristotelianism, 65, 228
Aristotle, 10, 15–16, 20, 50, 53, 66, 121, 131, 134, 140, 228; educational theory of, 44–47; influence of, 47–48; political philosophy of, 46; on public education, 46–47; school of, 44–46
Aristoxenus, 54
Arithmetic, teaching of, 75
Ars Versificatoria, 136
Ascham, Roger, 178
Astrology, 62
Astronomy, 62
Attendance, compulsory school, 204, 269, 279
Augustine, St., 73, 99, 102, 117, 126, 174, 198; on anthologies, 103; compromise plan of, 99–104; on program of study, 103; on textbooks, 103
Augustus, 92

391